Community Organization in Action

BASIC LITERATURE AND CRITICAL COMMENTS

Selected
and Edited

by: ERNEST B. HARPER

Professor and Director
School of Social Work
Michigan State University

and: ARTHUR DUNHAM

Professor of Community Organization
School of Social Work
The University of Michigan

Community Organization in Action

BASIC LITERATURE

AND CRITICAL COMMENTS

ASSOCIATION PRESS

NEW YORK

COMMUNITY ORGANIZATION IN ACTION

Foreword

FROM THEIR EXTENSIVE experience in the teaching of community organization, Ernest Harper and Arthur Dunham have seen a need for a collection of "readings" designed primarily for graduate and undergraduate students. In addition to their wide-ranging study of the literature and inherent editorial skills, they have brought to the task the perception of competent and dedicated faculty members, knowledge gained in directing the Association for the Study of Community Organization, and the benefit of numerous educational and social work conferences.

The resulting publication, *Community Organization in Action,* should be welcomed by those responsible for planning courses and institutes in community organization as a tool to make such programs more fruitful. It has other less direct values.

If the overworked practitioner in community organization can find the time, it will be refreshing for him to spend a half-hour from time to time under the guidance of Harper and Dunham, reading a selection and "mulling it over in his mind." He may find his own concepts reinforced; on the other hand, he may want to argue that "that does not jibe with my experience." In either case he may be prompted to discuss the subject with others, or even to produce a comment or document which may appear in later compilations. Both activities will be helpful to the continuing efforts of the teachers and practitioners of community organization for social welfare.

This book will reinforce the conviction of those who founded ASCO and those who continue that work through the community organization activities of the National Association of Social Workers, that more needs to be done to clarify the process of community organization in social work and to develop formal and informal educational patterns to improve social work community organization practice.

PHILIP E. RYAN
Former President, Association for the Study
of Community Organization; First Chairman,
Committee on Community Organization,
National Association of Social Workers

Preface

BECAUSE SOCIAL WORK is a relatively new profession and many social welfare programs are of recent growth, much of the literature is in the form of articles, pamphlets, and various sorts of "ephemeral materials," rather than in textbooks, monographs, or other substantial publications. As this literature has grown and as areas of subject matter have become marked off with increasing clearness, there has been a need, as in other fields of professional practice, for collections of "readings" which would bring together in convenient form some of the best things that have been written on these subjects.

Members of the faculty of the University of Chicago School of Social Service Administration made distinguished contributions as early as the 1920's and 1930's in publishing collections of documents in public welfare administration and other areas.[1] More recently there have been compilations of readings in social casework and social group work as well as on such social welfare subjects as settlements and social security, not to mention numerous symposia and collections of conference papers.[2] There have been collections of readings also in related fields such as adult education, guidance, and administration.

---

[1] Edith Abbott, *Immigration: A Source Book Compiled from Documents and Case Records* (Chicago: University of Chicago Press, 1924); *Some American Pioneers in Social Welfare:* Select Documents with Editorial Notes (Chicago: University of Chicago Press, 1937); and *Public Assistance, American Principles and Policies:* In Five Parts with Select Documents (Chicago: University of Chicago Press, 1940). See, also, Sophonisba P. Breckinridge, *Public Welfare Administration in the United States,* Select Documents (Chicago: University of Chicago Press, 1927); and Grace Abbott, *The Child and the State:* Select Documents with Introductory Notes (Chicago: University of Chicago Press, 1938).

[2] Dora Goldstine, *Readings in the Theory and Practice of Medical Social Work* (Chicago: University of Chicago Press, 1954). William Haber and Wilbur J. Cohen, *Readings in Social Security* (New York: Prentice-Hall Inc., 1948). Charles E. Hendry, ed., *A Decade of Group Work* (New York: Association Press, 1948). Fern Lowry, ed., *Readings in Social Casework, 1920–1938* (New York: Columbia University Press, 1939). Lorene M. Pacey, *Readings in the Development of Settle-*

When the Association for the Study of Community Organization was established in 1946, one of its first proposed projects was the compilation and publication of a Book of Readings on Community Welfare Organization. The first attempt to have this volume produced through the co-operation of a foundation was not successful. However, in 1952, the project was revived by the present editors; ASCO, through its Board of Directors, voted to sponsor the undertaking; and the encouragement and assistance of the Association Press and its director, James Rietmulder, made it practicable to proceed. Before the volume was completed, ASCO merged with six other professional social work associations in 1955 to form the present National Association of Social Workers. Though NASW has not assumed, nor been asked to assume, any sponsorship of this publication, the Foreword to this volume is written by Philip E. Ryan, Executive Director of the National Health Council, who was the last president of ASCO and is the first chairman of the Committee on Community Organization of the NASW.

This book is an attempt to "cream off" the literature—to bring together between two covers a selection of some of the best that has been written on community organization—particularly articles, papers, and other more or less "fugitive materials." With a few exceptions, materials from current texts on community organization have not been included. The main emphasis is upon materials which are now scattered through scores of National Conference Proceedings, copies of periodicals, and separate pamphlets.

To an unusual degree, the compilation of this volume has been a collaborative project, illustrative in itself of the spirit and method of community organization. The editors compiled a preliminary list of over 200 references on community organization. This list was submitted to more than sixty leaders in community organization and social work, and they were invited to offer comments and suggestions as to which of these items, or what other items, would be most useful and valuable for inclusion in the volume. Replies were received from a large majority of these consultants and were of great value to the editors in making their selection. The list of excerpts as tentatively made in the light of these suggestions was then submitted to some twenty teachers of community organization and other persons selected by the Association Press, and their suggestions also were taken into account. For the final choice of selections, however, the editors assume full responsibility.

Conditioning inevitably the editors' ultimate judgment was the conception of community organization as an integral part of the democratic process, expressing itself in fields as varied as social welfare, public health, adult education, labor organization, city planning and urban redevelopment, commercial and civic enterprises, church federation, community development, and general community improvement.

ment Work (New York: Association Press, 1950). Dorothea F. Sullivan, ed., *Readings in Group Work* (New York: Association Press, 1952).

More systematic effort has gone into the conscious development of community organization as a process of social work than in most of the areas that have been mentioned. In this volume the core of the selected materials is drawn from the literature of social work. However, the implications of this collection go far beyond this; and selections will be found on such basic topics as group behavior, group dynamics, and committees; conflict and integration; community structure and relationships; the place of national voluntary organizations in our society; and community development and rural reconstruction.

Moreover, even where the material relates specifically to social work or social welfare, it will be found that experiences, methods, and principles can often be readily applied in or adapted to the use of other fields.

This volume, as it has finally taken shape, contains contributions to community organization made over a period of more than half a century, specifically, from 1900 to 1958. It includes seventy-five major items, representing the work of over fifty individual authors, in addition to certain selections which are agency-sponsored documents, compilations of brief items, or which, for some other reasons, are not listed under the names of individual writers. In general, all materials in this book have already appeared in published form. With one or two brief exceptions, "case materials" as such have been excluded. The effort has been made to preserve the continuity of thought and style of the writer. In a few cases the selection has been reproduced *in toto* or with only minor deletions, but the rest are in the form of carefully edited excerpts, not condensations, abridgments, or abstracts.

The materials have been classified and arranged under six general headings, as follows:

PART	SUBJECT
I.	The Community and Social Welfare
II.	The Process of Community Organization
III.	Community Organization in Practice
IV.	Agencies and Programs
V.	Personnel—Professionals and Laymen
VI.	Community Development in the United States and Elsewhere

Parts II, III, and IV are further subdivided into topical sections. The full scheme of organization will be readily apparent from the Table of Contents. Each "Part" is preceded by an Introduction by one of the editors, with briefer introductions to the subdivisions. Finally, each excerpt is prefaced by a note indicating the significance of the selection and supplying some information concerning the author. It is the editors' hope that this "connective tissue" will serve to provide a logical framework, increase continuity, and afford a certain degree of unity to the presentation.

The process of assembling these materials has revealed both the richness of the existing literature and the gaps that still remain in it. A number of excellent articles were omitted with real reluctance, and only because of limitations of space and the wealth of good material on particular topics. On the other hand, in some cases relatively little was available, and diligent searching was required to discover the kinds of material that seemed appropriate for the purposes of this collection. Where controversial issues are involved, the effort has been made to include selections on both sides of the question.

A selection of literature on a growing subject can, of course, never be definitive or final. A loose-leaf collection would obviously be the only answer to a currently up-to-date compilation of selections. In the opinion of the editors, the NASW Committee on Community Organization, or some other national body, could make a valuable contribution by compiling and publishing annually an annotated list of "outstanding contributions" to the literature of community organization during the preceding year. In any case, other books of readings on this subject, or possibly revisions of this volume, may be needed in the future.

This book records the initial stages in the history of modern community organization and marks a turning point in its development. Having passed the early beginnings, the swing of interest to community organization as a process, the contributions of ASCO, and, most recently, the establishment of the new national committee, community organization is confronted contemporaneously with numerous and intriguing developments in theory and practice. These include growing interest in work with the "whole community," the controversies centering about federated and "independent" financing, the increasing emphasis on "self-help," and the spread of the tremendous movement for community development in technically less-advanced societies. No area of social activity presents sharper challenges or greater opportunities today than community organization.

With respect to its educational possibilities, this volume is designed for use in graduate professional courses in community organization, other graduate and undergraduate courses which are concerned with this subject, and as a source of background information for workshops and institutes relating to various forms of community work. Beyond this, it is hoped that the book may be of practical value to community organization workers in social welfare and other fields, and to all others—citizen participants, interested laymen, and professionals—who are concerned with the great issues of co-operative living and the building of the good society.

ERNEST B. HARPER   ARTHUR DUNHAM

Acknowledgments

To all who have co-operated in bringing this volume to fruition, the editors express their indebtedness.

Particularly, they are grateful to the persons listed below, who aided with advice and consultation, in the early stages of the project; to the members of the Board of Directors of the Association for the Study of Community Organization, and its successor, the Committee on Community Organization of the National Association of Social Workers, for their interest in the project; to the publishers who gave permission to reproduce copyrighted material; and to James Rietmulder of the Association Press, for his interest, encouragement, and co-operation throughout the undertaking.

Those who were consulted and who gave advice and assistance included the following persons:

J. Clyde Baird, Executive Director, Seattle-King County Chapter, American Red Cross.

Mrs. Frank M. Barry, Director, Department of Older Persons and the Chronically Ill, Welfare Federation of Cleveland.

Paul L. Benjamin, Schenectady.

Chester L. Bower, Executive Director, Welfare Planning Council, Los Angeles Region.

Genevieve W. Carter, Director, Program Division, Welfare Federation of Los Angeles Area.

Mrs. Jean T. Cram, Los Angeles.

Richard E. G. Davis, Executive Director, Canadian Welfare Council, Ottawa.

David F. DeMarche, Associate Director, Task Force on Community Resources, Joint Commission on Mental Illness and Health.

Sidney Dillick, Executive Director, Council of Community Services, Providence.

Thomas D. Dublin, M.D., Medical Director, Community Services Programs, National Institutes of Health, Public Health Service, Department of Health, Education, and Welfare.

Myron Falk, Director, United Givers' Fund of Greater Baton Rouge.

Mrs. Virginia S. Ferguson, Executive Secretary, Family and Child Welfare Council, Council of Social Agencies of Columbus and Franklin County, Ohio.

THOMAS W. FETZER, Assistant Executive Director, Health and Welfare Council of the National Capital Area, Washington, D.C.

MRS. KATHARINA FLESCH, Detroit.

WILMER M. FROISTAD, Associate Executive Director, Unitarian Service Committee, New York.

MELVIN A. GLASSER, Assistant to the President, National Foundation for Infantile Paralysis, New York.

MRS. FRANCES GOODALL, Executive Director, Mental Health Society of Greater Chicago.

JENNETTE R. GRUENER, Associate Professor, School of Social Work, University of Illinois, Urbana.

MONNA HEATH, Field Staff, Girl Scouts of the U.S.A., New York.

CHARLES E. HENDRY, Director, School of Social Work, University of Toronto.

ARTHUR HILLMAN, Dean, College of Arts and Sciences, Roosevelt University, Chicago.

JANE M. HOEY, Former Director, Bureau of Public Assistance, Department of Health, Education, and Welfare.

JOE R. HOFFER, Executive Secretary, National Conference on Social Welfare, Columbus.

MARY HOUK, Director, Division of Social Service, University of Indiana, Indianapolis.

DONALD S. HOWARD, Dean, School of Social Welfare, University of California at Los Angeles.

MAURICE O. HUNT, Chief, Bureau of Child Welfare, Maryland State Department of Public Welfare.

NELSON C. JACKSON, Associate Director, National Urban League, New York.

RAY JOHNS, General Executive, Boston Young Men's Christian Association.

ARLIEN JOHNSON, Dean, School of Social Work, University of Southern California, Los Angeles.

ALFRED J. KAHN, Professor of Social Work, New York School of Social Work, Columbia University.

CLARA KAISER, Professor of Social Work, and Acting Dean, New York School of Social Work, Columbia University.

ALFRED KATZ, Executive Director, New York Chapter, Hemophilia Foundation, New York.

CLARENCE KING, Professor Emeritus, New York School of Social Work, Columbia University.

HERTHA KRAUS, Associate Professor, Graduate Department of Social Work and Social Research, Bryn Mawr College, Bryn Mawr.

MICHAEL C. KREIDER, Executive Director, Michigan Association for Retarded Children, Lansing.

HARRY L. LURIE, Former Executive Director, Council of Jewish Federations and Welfare Funds, New York.

ROBERT H. MACRAE, Executive Director, Welfare Council of Metropolitan Chicago.

JOY A. MAINES, Executive Director, Canadian Association of Social Workers, Ottawa.

AUBREY MALLACH, Deputy Director General, Malben (American Joint Distribution Committee), Tel Aviv, Israel.

SYDNEY MASLEN, Regional Relocation Adviser, Housing and Home Finance Agency, Atlanta.

LEONARD W. MAYO, Executive Director, Association for the Aid of Crippled Children, New York.

WAYNE McMILLEN, Professor, School of Social Service Administration, University of Chicago.

C. F. McNEIL, Executive Director, Health and Welfare Council, Philadelphia.

CAMPBELL G. MURPHY, Executive Director, The Health and Welfare Council of Metropolitan St. Louis.

WILBER I. NEWSTETTER, Dean, Graduate School of Social Work, University of Pittsburgh.

WALTER W. PETTIT, Dean Emeritus, New York School of Social Work, Columbia University.

C. WHIT PFEIFFER, Former Executive Director, Welfare Planning Council, Los Angeles Region.

GEORGE W. RABINOFF, Assistant Director, National Social Welfare Assembly, New York.

BERNARD ROSS, Assistant Professor, Graduate Department of Social Work and Social Research, Bryn Mawr College, Bryn Mawr.

PHILIP E. RYAN, Executive Director, National Health Council, New York.

JULIUS SAMUELS, Associate Professor, Graduate School of Social Work, University of Nebraska, Lincoln.

VIOLET M. SIEDER, Professor of Social Work, New York School of Social Work, Columbia University.

* HYMAN SOROKOFF. Former Assistant Director, Bureau of Community Education, Board of Education, New York.

MARIETTA STEVENSON, Director, School of Social Work, University of Illinois, Urbana.

WALTER L. STONE, Professor of Sociology, Hanover College, Hanover, Indiana.

ELWOOD STREET, Professor of Social Service, Institute of Church Social Service, Hartford Seminary Foundation, Hartford.

HERBERT H. STROUP, Professor of Sociology and Anthropology, and Dean of Students, Brooklyn College, Brooklyn.

JACK STUMPF, Consultant, Education-Recreation Division, Health and Welfare Council, Philadelphia.

ARTHUR LESSNER SWIFT, JR., Vice-President and Dean of School of Politics, New School for Social Research, New York.

HARLEIGH B. TRECKER, Dean, School of Social Work, University of Connecticut, Storrs.

ELMER J. TROPMAN, Executive Director, Health and Welfare Federation of Allegheny County.

* JAY A. URICE. Former General Secretary, National Council of the Young Men's Christian Associations of the United States of America.

DONALD VAN VALEN, Director, Office of Program and Community Planning, Pennsylvania Department of Welfare, Harrisburg.

MRS. ELEANOR S. WASHBURN, Boston.

* Deceased.

Contents

State-Wide and National Agencies

Part Five. Personnel—Professionals and Laymen

18 Contents

_____

* At appropriate places throughout the book a number of short, significant quotations relating to various aspects of community organization have been inserted. These are not included in the Contents but are referred to in the Index.

PART ONE

THE COMMUNITY

AND

SOCIAL WELFARE

Introduction

THE TERM "COMMUNITY" is of great significance to social work in general and to social welfare planning in particular. Social workers were interested in the community before the concept had been formally defined by sociologists and anthropologists. Before 1910 there was little social science literature on the community, and no exact sociological definition appeared until 1915 when Galpin developed a technique for delineating rural communities in terms of the trade and service areas surrounding a central village.[1]

Social workers, on the other hand, had been actively concerned with the community since the last quarter of the nineteenth century when the Charity Organization Societies came into being in America. From 1909 on, councils of social agencies, or community welfare councils, began to appear; and in 1913 the first modern community chest was established. "Community organization" has continued to be used as the designation for a major process in social work practice since that time despite the fact that drastic changes have occurred both in the nature of communities themselves and in sociological conceptions of their significance.

Historically these changes began to be manifest between 1920 and 1930. Improved communication, rapid transportation, increased mobility, and expanding urbanization ran counter to the "community movement" of the first decade of the century with its fervent faith in

[1] C. J. Galpin, *The Social Anatomy of an Agricultural Community,* University of Wisconsin, Agricultural Experimental Station, Bulletin No. 34, Madison, Wis., 1915.

the neighborhood and the small community as the foundation of democracy and the medium for the socialization of the individual. Sociologists became more interested in larger areas and began to talk in terms of city, suburban, and regional planning rather than in those of *community organization*. In recent years the traditional autonomous village-type community based on primary group contacts, rural culture patterns, and residential propinquity, has largely disappeared in the modern metropolis in the Western world and is rapidly declining even in non-urban areas.

In a very real sense, however, this change is one in orientation, focus, and degree rather than in basic values and objectives. Interest continues to center in the local area but it is concentrated less on the immediate structural type and more on relational systems, "contact clusters," and occupational and other interest groupings which are city-wide in their scope. Social control, planning, and social organization are now seen as effective only on this broader stage and as related to larger groupings, wider interests, and interlocking associations. Neighborhood improvement, therefore, cannot be attained in isolation since at every point it is inextricably intertwined with city government, regional planning, and state and national resources and controls. Similarly social welfare planning, as such, is closely related to planning, organization, and action in other areas of interest.

This development is completely in line with welfare planning and development in terms of interest groups and functional fields of service which has traditionally been another but related aspect of community organization. A definition that combines the earlier conception of the community in geographical terms with the current emphasis on wider interest groupings—somewhat loosely termed "functional communities" by one writer [2]—is demanded today. "Community welfare organization," for better or for worse, has apparently come to be accepted as the term to designate one of the major processes employed in social work. Interpreted in the broader context indicated above, its limitations are no more serious than those associated with the terms "social casework," or "social group work," or, for that matter, "social work" itself.

A recent and definite revival of interest in the community as thus understood has occurred. This renewed concern results from current sociological and anthropological research, experiments in group dynamics, community adult education and similar movements in America, as well as from the phenomenal expansion of "community development" in the technically less-developed countries in the world. The last definitely involves national planning and organization together with technical assistance, as well as local co-operation and self-help in the

---

[2] Murray G. Ross, *Community Organization—Theory and Principles* (New York: Harper & Brothers, 1955), pp. 23, 40-41, 102.

solution of the problem of how to prevent the destruction of the community spirit in the face of economic aid, industrialization, and increasing urbanization.

The local neighborhood or community is now seen more clearly than ever before as the *locus* or "setting" in which the process of intergroup planning, co-operation, and action operates, and as the front line of community organization in social welfare as in other fields. The first group of selections in the present volume, therefore, are quite naturally devoted to the nature of the community and its significance in social welfare planning and organization. Three excerpts, or series of excerpts, have been chosen. The first is a compilation and analysis of typical definitions of the community which appeared between 1917 and 1955. The second, by Richard Poston, is an example of what might be called the "Back to the Small Community" movement—a plea for social action to restore the traditional community as a device to preserve American democratic society. The last extract stresses the significance for social welfare planning of top leadership and the power structure in the modern metropolis.

These three readings illustrate the nature, objectives, and dynamics of social life and welfare planning in both simple and complex communities. Additional material on rural communities, neighborhood organization, and community development in less-developed countries will be found in Parts IV and VI.

*   *   *   *

. . . AN IDEAL COMMUNITY should furnish to its human constituents:

1. *Order,* or security of life and property through the medium of an efficient government.

2. *Economic well-being,* or security of income through an efficient system of productive industry.

3. *Physical well-being,* or health and sanitation through public health agencies.

4. *Constructive use of leisure time,* or recreation through organized and directed play.

5. *Ethical standards,* or a system of morality supported by the organized community.

6. *Intellectual diffusion,* or education through free and public institutions within the reach of all.

7. *Free avenues of expression,* or means by which all the elements of the community might freely express themselves; free newspapers and public forums.

8. *Democratic forms of organization,* or community-wide organization through which the entire community might express its thought and see that its will is done.

9. *Spiritual motivation,* or religious associations which might diffuse throughout all forms of community organization the religious or spiritual motive. . . .

EDUARD C. LINDEMAN
The Community, 1921, pp. 14-15

1

The Nature of the Community: Selected Definitions

The term "community" is used loosely by many students and practitioners of social work. Such nonscientific definitions include religious, literary, and political conceptions of the community as an ethnic or other common interest group, an Utopian settlement, a political-economic union, or even a state of mind with no territorial base. Examples abound, such as the following: the "Jewish community," or the "social work community" (of any city); New Harmony (Indiana), an atypical ideal settlement that survived for three years; the "Coal-Steel Community" of Western Europe; and Josiah Royce's "Beloved Community." It is also popularly employed in such descriptive phrases as "a sense of community," meaning an attitude of co-operation.

Scientific definitions of the community generally include two main characteristics: (1) physical, geographical, and territorial boundaries which indicate a certain uniqueness or separateness, and (2) social or cultural homogeneity, consensus, self-help, or other forms of communal behavior and interacting relationships. The apparently wide variations among definitions results primarily from a shift in emphasis from one of these aspects to the other. The following statements are arranged in three categories depending upon the relative stress placed upon geographical characteristics, upon both aspects of community life, or upon some phase of the second. Note also the variation in terms of the amount of territory included in the definition.

1. The Community as a Geographical Concept

ROBERT E. PARK and ERNEST W. BURGESS   1921

Community is the term which is applied to societies and social groups where they are considered from the point of view of the geographical distribution of the individuals and institutions of which they are composed. It follows that every community is a society, but not every society is a community.[1]

2. The Community as a "Natural" Local Area Characterized by Equal Stress on Both Aspects

(These definitions may perhaps be said to represent the orthodox sociological conception.)

ROBERT E. HIERONYMUS   1917

A community consists . . . of a group or company of people living fairly close together in a more or less compact, contiguous territory, who are coming to act together in the chief concerns of life.[2]

JESSE F. STEINER   1930

A community may be regarded as made up of groups of people living in a more or less contiguous area so situated with reference to other places that social organization in one form or another arises within it in order to provide for mutual protection and welfare.[3]

KINGSLEY DAVIS   1949

The community is the smallest territorial group that can embrace all aspects of human life. . . . It is a local group broad enough to include all the major institutions, all the statuses and interests, that make a society. It is the smallest local group that can be, and often is, a complete society. . . . The modern community . . . cannot be understood in terms of itself alone. Each segment may be more closely linked with similar segments in other communities than with dissimilar segments in the same community.[4]

---

[1] *Introduction to the Science of Sociology* (Chicago: University of Chicago Press, 1921), p. 161. Note that this definition applies to the community as such; when the authors define "community life" they refer to it as a "constellation of social forces." *Ibid.,* p. 493.

[2] *Balancing Country Life* (New York: Association Press, 1917), p. 60.

[3] *Community Organization* (New York: Century, rev. ed., 1930), p. 20.

[4] *Human Society* (New York: The Macmillan Company, 1949), pp. 312, 315. By permission of The Macmillan Company.

AMOS H. HAWLEY   1950

It is general practice to use the term community to denote an area of local life . . . , the resident population of which is interrelated and integrated with reference to its daily requirements. . . . Participation in a daily rhythm of collective life is the factor which distinguishes and gives unity to the population of a locality.[5]

MABEL A. ELLIOTT and FRANCIS E. MERRILL   1950

The community has two related aspects, the *geographical* and the *psychological*. Geographically, it may be considered as a contiguous distribution of people with their social institutions. . . . Psychologically, we may think of the community in terms of the elements that combine to make it a dynamic and living entity. . . . Since both of these elements are important, we may consider the community to be a complex social unity that has both a physical locus and a psychological consensus.[6]

3. The Community as a Socially Homogeneous Area Characterized by Group Interaction

This conception stresses consensus, identification, a common way of life, shared interests and values, and joint effort. The community is viewed as a self-contained area possessing distinguishing social characteristics which set it off from other areas. These definitions fall into three groups differentiated respectively by, *first,* absence of specific geographical limits to areas defined as communities (MacIver and Stroup); *second,* belief in the small community as the hope of democracy (Morgan and Poston); and, *third,* stress on the dynamics of social interaction. The last type of definition stresses relationships cutting across various social areas as well as interpersonal contacts. This conception is the subject of considerable social psychological research and in reporting investigations writers tend to use the term "social area" rather than "community" or "neighborhood." The last two statements, though not strictly definitions, are included to illustrate some of these newer ideas and methods of community study.

ROBERT M. MAC IVER   1928

By a community I mean any area of common life, village or town, or district, or country, or even wider area. To deserve the name community, the area must be somehow distinguished from further areas, the common life may have some characteristic of its own such that the frontiers of the area have some meaning. . . . Wherever men live

---

[5] *Human Ecology:* A Theory of Community Structure (New York: The Ronald Press, 1950), pp. 257-258.

[6] *Social Disorganization* (New York: Harper & Brothers, 3rd ed., 1950), p. 473.

together they develop in some kind and degree distinctive common characteristics—manners, traditions, modes of speech, and so on. These are the signs and consequences of an effective common life . . . [and] even the [community] poorest in social relationships is a member of a chain of social contacts that stretches to the world's end.[7]

HERBERT HEWITT STROUP   1952

A community may be described generally as composed of a relatively large number of persons having a consciousness of their own interrelatedness, who are dependent upon a common territory, possess limited political autonomy, and seek basic satisfactions in a complex and changing social structure.[8]

ARTHUR E. MORGAN   1942

A community is an association of individuals and families that plan and act in concert as an organized unit in meeting their common needs.[9]

RICHARD WAVERLY POSTON   1953

The term "community" is used here to imply a neighborhood area in which there may be common communal ties and functions, where there may be a variety of interests and mutual services, where people may learn to know each other as individuals, and where they may have some personal measure of control over their own communal destiny. These conditions are possible in a small community. They may be possible in a local neighborhood area of a large city.[10]

HELEN D. GREEN   1954

The dynamics of community are found in group life and associations. In them is the relationship which is "below what we can see." The community may be viewed as a network of interrelated, interdependent groups.[11]

---

[7] *Community: A Sociological Study* (London: Macmillan & Company, Ltd., 1928) pp. 22-23. By permission of the publisher.

[8] *Community Welfare Organization* (New York: Harper & Brothers, 1952), p. 9. (According to the author the term community may include any form of social organization, from hamlet to nation.)

[9] *The Small Community* (Yellow Springs, Ohio: Community Service, 1942, mimeo.), p. 1, Ch. 1. For a later revision see his *The Small Community: Foundation of Democratic Life* (New York: Harper & Brothers, 1942) p. 20.

[10] *Democracy Is You: A Guide to Citizen Action* (New York: Harper & Brothers, 1953), pp. 15-16. By permission of the publisher.

[11] *Social Work Practice in Community Organization* (New York: Whiteside and Morrow Press, 1954), p. 28. Quotation from Autonomous Groups Bulletin, Vol. IV, Nos. 2 and 3.

EDMUND DE S. BRUNNER and WILBUR C. HALLENBECK   **1955**

A community is people inhabiting a given identifiable area, associating and interacting within it. Through interacting they become conscious of their local unity, they set up the means to act in a corporate capacity, they share and make their own slight modifications in the natural culture and their adaptations to it. . . . The dynamics of community life expresses itself in terms of recognized interests and needs and in the machinery set up to meet these needs.[12]

SVEND RIEMER   **1951**

Our observations . . . reveal a phenomenon closely related to neighboring although not identical with it: namely, the phenomeon of contact clusters established either close to the family home or close to any of the more important contact points in the city area. They are not neighborhoods proper because this term cannot be divorced from the circumstance of "near-dwelling" or from "proximity to residential location." . . .

Our thinking about social relations in the city has been dominated by the spatial dimension. A small-town culture trait has thus been superimposed upon the urban environment. In the small town, the coincidence of intense social relations with proximity to the individual residence can be taken for granted. This need not be so in the city. In the city, man has gained the freedom of making social contacts with little regard to geographical distance.[13]

CONRAD M. ARENSBERG   **1954**

Community study is that method in which a problem . . . in the nature, interconnections, or dynamics of behavior and attitudes is explored against or within the surround of other behavior and attitudes of the individuals making up the life of a particular community.[14]

---

[12] *American Society: Urban and Rural Patterns* (New York: Harper & Brothers, 1955), pp. 159, 163. These authors describe four types of community: villages, towns and small cities, suburban communities, and metropolitan areas. By permission of the publisher.

[13] "Villagers in Metropolis," *British Journal of Sociology*, II, No. 1, March, 1951, pp. 31-43. Reproduced in Edgar Schuler *et al.*, *Outside Readings in Sociology* (New York: Thomas Y. Crowell Company, 1952), pp. 653, 655. By permission of the original publisher.

[14] "The Community-Study Method," *American Journal of Sociology* (Chicago: University of Chicago Press), Vol. LX, Sept., 1954, p. 110. In this article the author describes one of the newer approaches, i.e., the study of behavior in a community setting rather than of the community as a structural entity as in the traditional method.

2

Community Action: The Great Need [1]

By RICHARD WAVERLY POSTON

The critical importance of the small community for social welfare and democratic life in general is stressed by Richard Poston in this selection. A strong appeal is made for citizen participation and for the thesis that democracy as a dynamic force in America will function successfully only when self-study, integration of interests, and co-operative effort characterize the individual community. The author's conception of the community, which is included in the list of definitions given in the first reading, is narrowly limited to the neighborhood and the small town and in his concern with the current trend toward overcentralization and specialization he tends to disregard the dynamics, the reality, and the significance of intergroup relations and interaction at various levels.

The excerpt below is the introductory chapter to a guide for community self-study and citizen action. The remainder of Poston's book deals with procedure in organizing community study groups, conducting meetings, and the content to be covered in local surveys of institutions, facilities, and resources. *Democracy Is You* was stimulated by the "Montana Study" and the work of Baker Brownell from 1944 to 1947, which greatly impressed the author. In 1950 Poston published the results of his evaluation of the "Montana Study" under the title, *Small Town Renaissance*. Later he became head of the Bureau of Community Development, at the University of Washington, and after two years' experience in helping citizens to restore the vitality of their small-town communities he produced the current publication. By the time the book was published he had become director of Community Services at Southern Illinois University. His interest and point of view

[1] Excerpted from *Democracy Is You: A Guide to Citizen Action* (New York: Harper & Brothers, 1953), pp. 3-12. By permission of the publisher.

may profitably be compared by the reader with that of the Ogdens, in Virginia.[2]

AMERICAN DEMOCRACY—*The Way of Living That Built a Nation,* gave to men a tradition of freedom, reshaped a world, and conditioned the thinking of generations—today stands on trial. No longer can it remain taken for granted. No longer can it be considered secure, solid, firm. Instead, it struggles for survival.

This, then, is the question: Can the principle of a democratic society with its tradition of freedom succeed in the modern world?

The answer to that question will depend upon the action of people within their communities. For without thought, action, and participation by the people in their own community life no democratic society can long exist. No centralized institution, no organization or association, be it private or public, political or academic, can make the processes of democracy a working method in human society. Democracy as a social force springs only from the people in their communities. It cannot function through actions that are devised or superimposed from above. Yet this has become the method of the age in which we live.

Child of the Industrial Revolution, ours is an age of unrestrained technology, of achievement which has brought material success in a spectacular degree; success which has exceeded even the wildest dreams of our American founders.

This is the age in which we have mastered the principles of mathematics, of physics, of chemistry, and of electricity. We have written these principles into books and we have built schools in which we could teach them to our children so that they could learn what we have been told are the fundamental tools of living. With these tools we have made machines that have brought riches to mankind, made living easier, and housework simpler. And by these means we have released ourselves from the drudgery and the backbreaking labor that chained our grandmothers to the farmhouse.

From it all we have built up a system of business and finance which has produced millions of jobs and added more tools to make life easier. We have developed vast systems of credit which now make it possible to enjoy next year's income this year, while we are still paying for what we enjoyed last year. We have heaped structure upon structure of new laws and government. And we have thus progressed into what is referred to as modern civilization. In the race for advancement our

---

[2] *These Things We Tried.* See Part VI, footnote 1.

schools and universities have been transformed into great mills where graduates are mass produced, where subject matters have been systematized and stored into vast libraries for the scholar. And by this means we have developed the practice of specialization in which the student can devote a lifetime to becoming an expert in the most minute particle of human knowledge.

And so with our newly made tools of knowledge and mass technology we have succeeded spectacularly in remaking the social and cultural fabric of America, and of a good deal of the rest of the world.

But in the process we have made a costly mistake. We have made our technology, our knowledge, and our material goods the ends in life instead of the means by which to create something even more important than the tools. And for this we have paid dearly.

During the great depression of the thirties, the winds swept eastward across the high plains of Mid-America and black clouds of silt moved toward the Atlantic. News writers called it the "Dust Bowl." But the true story of that tragic era was written on the ground. Man, with his technology, had converted the grasslands into a living hell. Homes were abandoned, houses stripped of paint, village church windows boarded over, and streets deserted. Where towns had thrived and thousand-dollar combines had mowed the wheat there was desolation. Man had not been wise enough to use his technology for human values.

Here in graphic form were the human consequences of man's failure to control and adjust the technological creation which he had made. This is a part of the story of what we have lost. The whole story of two world wars is a story of what we have lost. The Korean War is another. And in the threat of a new war which may blast millions from the face of the earth and crush all democratic processes in one last failure, the vast story of human loss from an age of industrialized technological society continues to unfold.

Now we have built the most expensive system of formal education in all history. We are turning out more degrees than at any other time within the memory of man. Our libraries are bulging with recorded knowledge, and we have had to invent the microfilm because we no longer have even space enough to store our records of research. Yet with all our accumulated intelligence and specialized knowledge, human beings grow more frustrated, problems of society multiply, and the mess in the world grows worse.

This is the age in which we live, a bit lopsided perhaps, but it is there gnawing at the sinews of American democracy. It has not come about from democratic processes. It has come from a technology that has shaped and fashioned a new kind of society, a society in which democracy cannot live unless there is developed a modern community setting which will permit it to function.

Perhaps the idea of this community setting can best be gained from a glimpse into our past.

There was a time in America when democracy operated in an atmosphere of town meetings, small communities, and face-to-face relationships. Social science was in the act of living. Co-operation and group discussion, civic responsibility and community pride, did not have to be taught. They were a part of life. It was a simple life—intimately human, warm, personal.

When there was a local problem to be solved the people knew that unless they got busy and solved it for themselves it would not be solved. Instinctively they knew that if the job was to be done they must do it together. Families and groups of families pulled and worked together to provide what they needed. And whatever they needed they created for themselves. The principles of work, thrift, responsibility, initiative, were the natural spiritual products of a rich community life. There was a natural framework for the exchange of ideas and of human spirit, a fertile environment for democratic processes. It was a natural breeding ground for such qualities as leadership, civic integrity, and statesmanship. There were weaknesses, inconsistencies, and undemocratic practices then as now. But it was in this general atmosphere of community life that the American tradition was born, and in which it grew and thrived and made this the land of freedom that it is.

But with the coming of the Industrial Revolution and the development of top-down mass methods community life began to dry up. The small town began to decay. Millions were massed together in urban mobs, and sprawling cities grew up by machine methods with virtually no inner development of true community life. Families lost much of their social significance. Many of the jobs that parents and children once performed in the home were taken over by specialists who had been mass produced from the classroom assembly lines. Human values were lost in a maze of punch cards and number systems which were devoid of flesh and blood. Neighborhood life in any meaningful sense, the environment which had nurtured initiative, civic integrity, and social responsibility, began to grow sterile. The control which men had once exercised over their own lives gradually slipped away into the distant offices of a centralized and impersonal society.

Giant organizations, private and governmental, came into being, far ranging in scope but without roots in the community where men lived. Great pressure groups rose up across the land and cut across community lines, breaking the local neighborhood into segments, each cut off and walled apart from the other. Bigness, commercialism, professionalism, scholarship, efficiency, became the gods of worship and the control over men's lives continued to grow more and more centralized in powers that were far removed from the individual in his community and in which he had little, if any, voice.

Slowly but steadily the new technology with its mass methods gnawed deeper and deeper into the foundations of community life. Like a great parasite it sucked away the strength of neighborhood society until men and women by the millions lost their motivation for community responsibility. An attitude of what's-the-use-anyway spread like a plague across America. Many lost confidence even in their own ability. The majority became bystanders in public affairs, and in all parts of a great nation men and women had assumed an attitude of leaning on someone else.

As community wholeness and integrity continued to decline, America began to lose something of moral and spiritual fiber.

The legislative process became largely a system of specialized pressures all competing for the legislative favor, while the voice of the individual was smothered further and further beneath top-level strategy. Community action of the people had changed largely to a kind of action which was determined from the top down by national organizations, impersonalized institutions, and great trade and professional combinations. And today in an all too realistic sense millions of Americans no longer have a genuine say in the affairs of their own destiny.

Millions are pieces of men living a kind of existence from payday to payday in a great mass of anonymous and socially isolated human fragments. That spirit of neighborhood identity and true participation in community life activities has diminished until millions live side by side without speaking to each other, without caring what happens to the family across the street. Crime, delinquency, frustration, broken homes, a fear of something that men cannot define have grown to tremendous proportions, and it has been estimated that one out of every twenty Americans will spend a portion of his life in a mental institution. These are the symptoms of a society out of adjustment to the technology that created it.

The natural community in which human values flourished and which was conducive to democratic processes is almost gone. It has been crushed by the rising crescendo from a world of knowledge, machinery, and science, to which we have been unable to adjust ourselves in order to preserve the very human values which our technology and knowledge were designed to serve. Man has become the slave to his own mechanical and intellectual creation which now threatens to destroy him in one last mighty blast.

And so the whole mode of American life has been altered. Vast material advantages have been gained. But in towns and cities throughout America democratic living and self-expression have gone.

Vital community life is something creative. It is integrated. It is an organic whole. It is personal, co-operative, and mutually stimulating. People exchange their services, their thoughts, their ideas. They feel responsible for one another. They take part together in many different activities. They work, they play, they visit together. There is a sense of belonging in an atmosphere of neighborliness and understanding, a spirit of unity and of community solidarity.

But the era in which we live has tended to make us a nation of spectators. We have somehow acquired the habit of letting someone else shape our lives for us. Someone else—the expert, the professional—handles our economy, our culture, our politics, tells us how to raise our children, how to do our community planning, and in large measure does our thinking for us. This is all a part of the decline in community vitality. And slowly, but just as surely as the grinding movement of the glacier, it is sapping the life strength from our American heritage. It is destroying the democratic processes. It is leaving our Republic weak and flabby; it is making us a hypocrite before a world in which we are attempting to demonstrate the strength of our American ideals.

The vitality of democracy in America cannot be measured in dollars and cents, shiny automobiles, bathtubs, machines, and libraries full of knowledge. It cannot be measured in terms of efficiency. Democracy is spiritual in nature. It is a basic process, a method of communicating, of exchanging thoughts, ideas, joys, sorrows, and human feelings. It is freedom to live, to choose, to be responsible. It is a process by which free people in a free society are in communication with one another, and together mold and control their own destiny at the neighborhood or community level. It is intangible, yet real and concrete. It cannot be sold to the rest of the world, or even to our own people, unless we can learn to practice it in a more realistic way than we are now practicing it.

Democracy in the American tradition will function only when it functions inside the local communities of which America is made up. It can be a vigorous and dynamic force nationally and internationally only if it is vigorous and dynamic in the home-town community, in the village and rural crossroads, in the city neighborhood and small town, in the places where people live.

A free democratic society at the higher levels—state, regional, national—is but a myth unless the initiative, the controls, the ideals, and the direction come clear and uninterrupted from the people in their home communities. This is where it must be practiced, this is where it must have meaning in the personal everyday lives of men and women if it is to be practiced and have meaning anywhere.

Obviously, we cannot turn back the clock to the early American village, and would not do so if we could. But unless we begin to take more action than we are taking today toward adjusting ourselves to the technological age in such a way as to make our knowledge work *for* human values and community life, instead of allowing it to destroy them, then America will continue to limp along on but a small fraction of the power of which she is capable, and we will continue to lack the moral influence so desperately needed in the world today.

No single factor is more important to the future of America and to the world at large than is the local community. From it come our ideals, our integrity, our moral strength, our leadership; and these qualities will be no stronger in the American people than are the communities in which they live. For it is the community and the environment found in it that will largely make us what we are. If our communities are strong, America will be strong. If they are weak, America will be weak.

This is the critical problem.

Its solution will not be easy. To reverse the spiral of democratic decay we must first recreate a social environment which is conducive to human values and democratic vitality. This means that the community must regain its organic integrity, its wholeness, its self-expression, and to an important degree its self-control. It means, in short, that community life must be redeveloped. For without wholeness and completeness of community life there can be no democratic society.

Democracy is a process in which people are free to exchange ideas in a direct personal manner, to communicate with one another mentally and spiritually, and thereby to work out their own common destiny. If this process is blocked by policies and regulations that are determined from above, by institutions and organizations that are controlled from afar, by the separation of functions, by professional and specialized planners, by religious, social, or economic barriers, or if it is blocked by any other barrier real or imaginary, then democracy cannot function.

A free democratic society requires a certain environment in which to live. This is an environment of wholeness and social completeness, of stability, of self-control, of mutual sympathy and co-operation, of understanding and tolerance among heterogeneous interests. This environment may exist inside the local community, but if it does not exist there it cannot exist anywhere.

In America there are still the resources—human and physical—with which to build such a community environment. They are in the skills, the knowledge, the very creation which has made the technological age. The job now is to make use of the freedom, the intelligence, and the resources that we have for the rebuilding of community life in order to preserve human values.

In the trend toward specialization we have fallen into the habit of breaking up the community into a vast collection of carefully arranged compartments, each walled off and separated from the others. One is labeled business, another is agriculture, another is education, another is health, another is recreation, another is government, another is social service, another is religion, another is the home. The list is almost endless. Each of these compartments has become a special world in which there are further subdivisions. Then there are the organizational, special interest, and occupational groupings.

Operating on or within these compartments are the fixed and formalized disciplines, each seemingly an end in itself. Physical science with its specialized departments functions in its orbit. Biological science with its departments is in another orbit. Social science and another batch of departments occupy still another orbit. Philosophy, religion, the humanities, business administration, public planning, all have their carefully defined orbits.

There is the myriad of specialized agencies, institutions, organizations, associations, which reach down from the top and in some disconnected way operate on one of the so-called areas of the community.

It is the bringing together of all these functions, compartments, areas, and specializations into one integrated whole in a community setting that must be accomplished if American democratic society is to survive in the modern world. This can be done by people of all interests and of all groups working together inside the community itself, and that is the only place where it can be done.

Science—physical, biological, and social—may be utilized to enrich total community life rather than for special purposes without regard to total community values. Each phase and aspect of the community—its business, its agriculture, its educational system, its health services, its governmental facilities, its religious institutions—all may be developed not as specialized functions unto themselves, but as essential parts of the whole which are related in some vital way to all other parts of the community.

By making use of all the resources we have—human and otherwise—to bring together, to integrate, to enrich, and to strengthen all phases of the total life of the community we can create a modern environment in which it will be natural for people of all interests, groups, and beliefs to communicate mentally and spiritually with one another. Only then can our society adjust itself to the technological age in which we live. When this is done in local communities throughout all America the full power of democracy will be released, and America will recapture its human values and moral strength.

Thus, America may again have a natural social framework in which democracy can function. Here the individual may regain his sense of belonging, his sense of personal importance as an integrated and contributing member of society. He may be creative, independent, reliant. Civic responsibility, initiative, and leadership may once more become the natural by-product of life itself. Here there may be a natural motivation for citizen alertness. Through active participation in community life men and women may once more exercise a genuine say in their own destiny. The grass roots may again come to life. To some this may seem like an idealistic dream. It isn't. It has happened already in certain communities. It can happen in others.

The development of community life in modern America will reawaken and revitalize democratic processes. It will also provide the social foundation from which America can rise to new heights as a free society, from which the principles of human rights and representative government may regain their vitality, and from which our Republic may renew her moral influence in the world family of nations. But the critical point in the national fabric is the local community. For unless democracy can survive there it cannot survive anywhere.

This is the broad purpose of the community study outlined in this guide. It is a program in community development through which a group of people may sit down together to study life in their own community in order to find out for themselves how they might enrich and improve it.

Though action projects may be launched by the community study group, the group itself is not intended as a permanent direct-action body for reasons described in Part II of the guide. However, community action that will help to improve the quality of community life is the central objective of this study plan. Exactly what that action will be, just when and how it will come about, is a matter which cannot be prescribed. This is a matter for the people themselves to decide. It is also for them to decide whether they want action, or whether they don't. The program outlined in this guide is no panacea—not a magic formula. It will not work by itself.

Neither can it be predicted what progress the community may expect from the study. Other communities have made much progress, but that was determined by those communities. Who, other than the individual himself, can say when human values have been gained? Community unity and solidarity, a felt need which is self-inspired, the ability and desire to think imaginatively and creatively, an inner urge for community action, the ability to work and pull together—these are the aims of this study. But this achievement will be determined by the people themselves. This is basic. And it is upon this democratic principle that the future of America will rise or fall.

3

Top Leaders and Planning[1]

By FLOYD GIBSON HUNTER

Who makes the social welfare decisions in metropolitan communities? In sharp contrast with Poston's democratic philosophy of citizen action in the small town are the following excerpts from *Community Power Structure*. These support Hunter's conclusion that such decisions are not made by either the rank and file or the professional community organizer but by a handful of top leaders. In "Regional City," the large Southern community which was the subject of the study, these leaders were, in the main, businessmen and industrial employers.

The author was perhaps the first to decribe the nature of top leadership in urban centers, to analyze the process by which social welfare developments are controlled by the "decision makers," and to evaluate the relationship of the community organizer to the power structure. His findings have great significance, therefore, for all social work practitioners, and the planning structure which he proposes as a medium for involving other groups and for democratizing the process is particularly suggestive for the community organization worker.

Floyd Gibson Hunter is a sociologist who is currently an associate professor on the faculty of the School of Social Work, of the University of North Carolina. His study, based largely on personal interviews, is objective, critical, and dispassionate, and was selected to illustrate certain important aspects of the dynamics of the modern community.

[1] Excerpted from *Community Power Structure: A Study of Decision Makers* (Chapel Hill: University of North Carolina Press, 1953), pp. 10-11, 12-13, 65-66, 83-85, 112-113, 172-174, 184-186, 194-195, 233-234, 236-238, 239-240, 241-248. (Proper names are fictitious.) By permission of the publisher.

WITHIN THE PHYSICAL setting of the community, power itself is resident in the men who inhabit it. To locate power in Regional City, it is therefore necessary to identify some of the men who wield power, as well as to describe the physical setting in which they operate. . . .

Of the forty persons studied, the largest number are to be found directing or administering major portions of the activities of large commercial enterprises. There are eleven such men in the list. Since Regional City has been described as a commercial center, this fact is not surprising. Financial direction and supervision of banking and investment operations are represented by the next largest number, namely, seven persons. Again, the occupations of the leaders turned up in the study follow one of the major functions of the community activities concerned with finance. Regional City is a "service" city also, and its service functions are represented on the list by six professional persons, five lawyers and one dentist. Five persons have major industrial responsibilities. Governmental personnel are represented on the list by four persons, which also fits into the functional scheme of the community, since it is both a regional and a state center for many important governmental activities. Two labor leaders are on the list, representing large unions. The five remaining persons in the list of forty leaders may be classified as leisure personnel. They are persons who have social or civic organization leadership capacities and yet do not have business offices or similar places in which they conduct their day-to-day affairs. One of these persons is a woman who actually spends very little time in Regional City, but who contributes approximately $100,000 annually to charitable purposes in the community and is looked upon by many as a leader. . . .

The high consensus regarding the top leaders on the list of forty, plus the lack of any concerted opinion on additional individuals, would indicate that the men being interviewed represented at least a nucleus of a power grouping.

The question was also put to interviewees, "How many men would need to be involved in a major community project in Regional City 'to put it over'?" The answers to this question varied from, "You've got the men right here on this list—maybe ten of them," to "fifty or a hundred." One informant said, "Some of the men on this list would undoubtedly be in on getting the project started. After it got moving, perhaps six hundred men might be involved either directly or indirectly." This was the largest figure any informant gave. The informant elaborated on the answer by saying that a large fund-raising campaign was the thing he had in mind, and he illustrated the point by speaking of a fund drive for a hospital building program that had recently been completed in Regional City. He said that he could count the men on his hands who had "sparked" the drive, but hundreds of volunteers had been used from the civic associations and the general community to "put the drive over the top." He felt that any project for civic improvement would likely involve the same type of organization.

In the above illustration of structured action, the "men of independent decision" are a relatively small group. The "executors of policy" may run into the hundreds. This pattern of a relatively small decision-making group working through a larger understructure is a reality, and if data were available, the total personnel involved in a major community project might possibly form a pyramid of power, but the constituency of the pyramid would change according to the project being acted upon.

In other words, the personnel of the pyramid would change depending upon what needs to be done at a particular time. Ten men might, for example, decide to bring a new industry into the community. Getting the industry physically established and operating might take the disciplined and co-ordinated action of a few more men or several hundred men, depending on the size of the project. Some of the same decision men in another instance might be involved in starting a program for some local governmental change, but another group of men would be involved in carrying out the decisions reached. Both projects are power orientated, but each requires different personnel in the execution. The men in the understructure may have a multiplicity of individual roles within the totality of the community structure which can be set in motion by the men of decision.

As I became familiar with the list of forty names through the interviewing process, it became evident that certain men, even within the relatively narrow range of decision leaders with whom I was dealing, represented a top layer of personnel. Certain men were chosen more frequently than others, not only in relation to who should be chosen to decide on a project, as has already been indicated, but the same men interacted together on committees and were on the whole better known to each other than to those outside this group. Through analyzing the mutual choices made by those interviewed, it will be shown that there is an *esprit de corps* among certain top leaders, and some of them may be said to operate on a very high level of decision in the community; but this will not necessarily mean that one of the top leaders can be considered subordinate to any other in the community as a whole. On specific projects one leader may allow another to carry the ball, as a leader is said to do when he is "out front" on a project which interests him. On the next community-wide project another may carry the ball. Each may subordinate himself to another on a temporary basis, but such a structure of subordination is quite fluid, and it is voluntary. . . .

One cannot, in Regional City at least, look to the organized institutions as policy-determining groupings, nor can one look to the formal associations which are part of these institutions. But let us briefly be specific concerning the role of organizations. There is a multiplicity of organized groups in Regional City. The Chamber of Commerce lists more than 800 organizations from bee-keeping societies to federated industrial groups. The membership lists of some of these organizations often run into the hundreds. In this study organizations were considered as being influential in civic affairs and some ranking of the most important was deemed necessary. Consequently, all persons interviewed were asked to give their opinion on a selected list of supposedly top-ranking organizations in the community. An initial selection of thirty organizations was made by a panel of judges from lists supplied by the Chamber of Commerce and the local Community Council. The persons interviewed in the list of forty leaders narrowed their selections of organizations to seven—organizations to which the majority of these top leaders belonged. They were (in rank order of importance) the Chamber of Commerce, Community Chest, Rotary Club, YMCA, Community Council, Grand Jurors' Association, and Bar Association. There was a scattering of votes for the Christian Council and for one of the larger labor organizations. The Retail Merchants Association was added to our list by two merchants. The understructure professional personnel in civic and social work who were interviewed indicated that they recognized the influence of the same organizations chosen by the top leaders. It may be noted that they generally belonged to only the Community Chest and the Community Council in conjunction with the top leaders.

Some of the top leaders may hold board positions within the associational groupings to lend prestige to the organization, but such members are more noted for their absence than for their attendance at meetings of the respective boards. They can be called upon in an organizational crisis or emergency, and at such times they may function decisively. One leader explained his position in this way: "If I attend meetings too regularly, I am asked to be chairman of this or that committee. I don't have time for that kind of work, but you hate to refuse before a bunch of people. There are usually two or three listening posts, people who can keep me in touch with things, on these boards. I get reports from them from time to time and that way keep a hand in. I also read the minutes of important meetings. Most of the time I know about where any board I belong to stands on various matters. I attend meetings only when I'm really needed."

Occasionally a top leader will take the presidency of one of the associations, but such position is usually unsought and avoided if possible—particularly by the older leaders. The younger leaders may be pushed to take some of the top associational posts as training assignments. They take on such duties, they say, with reluctance and make feeble protests of being terribly busy and pressed for time. The less powerful understructure associational personnel may scramble (in a dignified way, of course) for the top positions in these groupings.

In crisis situations, such as during World War II, many of the older leaders were called to active duty on civic boards. This was particularly true in the large fund-raising organizations where campaign goals were doubled or tripled over previous ones and the prestige of the older leaders was needed to insure the success of particular drives. During the crisis of depression in the 1930's several of the older leaders served on the local welfare board, but as the economic situation improved, they were replaced by "second-rate" and "third-rate" community leaders.

Two of the hypotheses of the study have been discussed in some measure in the preceding analysis. These hypotheses, restated, are as follows:

1. The exercise of power is limited and directed by the formulation and extension of social policy within a framework of socially sanctioned authority.

2. In a given power unit a smaller number of individuals will be found formulating and extending policy than those exercising power.

A corollary of the later hypothesis was also touched upon: All policy makers are men of power, but all men of power are not, per se, policy makers. . . .

It has been pointed out that intracommunity and extracommunity policy matters are handled by essentially the same group of men in this city, but there is a differentiation of functional activity within this policy group. Some men operate on different levels of policy decision, particularly in matters concerning governmental action. Some structural weaknesses in the power structure have been touched upon but at no great length. Finally, it was found that the structure is held together by common interests, mutual obligations, money, habit, delegated responsibilities, and in some cases by coercion and force. . . .

The informal relationships between power personnel described in the chapter on the structure of power and the examples previously related concerning the relation of Harvey Aiken to a particular incident in policy decision, seem to be of primary significance. The description of some of the processes and dynamics of relating the power structure to key problems within the community is a basic task in the present writing. . . .

The situation which will be considered is that of getting an international trade council established in Regional City. The investigator had asked Mr. Treat, president of the Southern Yarn Company, to give an example of how the local power groups operated in getting a major project under way. Mr. Treat did not appear to get the meaning of the question in the way it was put, and the investigator elaborated upon it by saying, "If a major project, such as getting a new hospital, were up for consideration in Regional City, how would the men under discussion act in relation to each other in the matter? Who would contact which others? Would the community associations be drawn in on the project, and so forth?"

Mr. Treat answered the last question first. He said:

"We would not go to the 'associations,' as you call them—that is, not right away. A lot of those associations, if you mean by associations the Chamber of Commerce or the Community Council, sit around and discuss 'goals' and 'ideals.' I don't know what a lot of those things mean. I'll be frank with you. I do not get onto a lot of those committees. A lot of the others in town do, but I don't. In a way, I guess I pretty much follow the lead of one other man in this town—the lead of Charles Homer. Let me give you an example.

"Charles Homer is the biggest man in our crowd. He gets an idea. When he gets an idea, others will get the idea. Don't ask me how he gets the idea or where. He may be in bed. He may think of it at breakfast. He may read a letter on the subject. But recently he got the idea that Regional City should be the national headquarters for an International Trade Council. He called in some of us [the inner crowd], and he talked briefly about his idea. He did not talk much. We do not engage in loose talk about the 'ideals' of the situation and all that other stuff. We get right down to the problem, that is, how to get this Council. We all think it is a good idea right around the circle. There are six of us in the meeting.

"All of us are assigned tasks to carry out. Moster is to draw up the papers of incorporation. He is the lawyer. I have a group of friends that I will carry along. Everyone else has a group of friends he will do the same with. These fellows are what you might call followers. We decide we need to raise $65,000 to put this thing over. We could raise that amount within our own crowd, but eventually this thing is going to be a community proposition, so we decide to bring the other crowds in on the deal. We decide to have a meeting at the Grandview Club with select members of the other crowds.

"When we meet at the Club at dinner with the other crowds, Mr. Homer makes a brief talk; again, he does not need to talk long. He ends his talk by saying he believes in his proposition enough that he is willing to put $10,000 of his own money into it for the first year. He sits down. You can see some of the other crowds getting their heads together, and the Growers Bank crowd, not to be outdone, offers a like amount plus a guarantee that they will go along with the project for three years. Others throw in $5,000 to $10,000, until—I'd say within thirty or forty minutes—we have pledges of the money we need. In three hours the whole thing is settled, including the time for eating!"

Mr. Treat paused for a moment, then continued:

"There is one detail I left out, and it is an important one. We went into that meeting with a board of directors picked. The constitution was all written, and the man who was to head the council as executive was named—a fellow by the name of Lonny Dewberry, a third-string man, a fellow who will take advice."

The investigator asked how the public was apprised of the action. Mr. Treat said:

"The public doesn't know anything about the project until it reaches the stage I've been talking about. After the matter is financially sound, then we go to the newspapers and say there is a proposal for consideration. Of course, it is not news to a lot of people by then, but the Chamber committees and other civic organizations are brought in on the idea. They all think it's a good idea. They help to get the Council located and established. That's about all there is to it. . . ."

The men in Regional City who hold power gather strength in many instances from association with their fellows on an informal and light-hearted level. The luncheon clubs provide a good place in which to exchange ideas, thus helping to keep a kind of like-mindedness. . . .

Big policy is not decided within the framework of the clubs. The carrying out of civic responsibilities on welfare projects and the like fall heavily to the lot of the club leaders, and the structure used is a part of the informal understructure controlled by the policy makers. . . .

In the field study each interviewee was asked to state what the best method might be of getting a project started that would ultimately be community-wide; for example, would he call a committee meeting to initiate the project? Would he get together at a luncheon with key people? Would he make a series of personal calls? Would he merely telephone others to get informal opinions? Or would he use any of these methods in combination? Or would he use other methods than the ones mentioned?

The answers received from the top leaders answering the question indicated that getting together at an informal luncheon was by far the most satisfactory method of soliciting initial interest in a project. Thirteen men indicated that this method was the most highly successful in their experience. Five indicated that they would make a personal call upon their colleagues before going into any kind of committee meeting. Four said they would make their first contact by phone to ascertain interest and then follow up this procedure by a luncheon or dinner meeting on a more formal basis, if initial interest was expressed. Two men said they could not answer the question, since their methods would vary with the type of project. One of these said that he had in mind the problem of housing and slum clearance. There are so many groups involved in this question that he could not see getting all the groups into a single meeting since each group should be approached differently. Four of the men who chose to call upon other men personally said they would prefer not to go alone on their call but would want to go with two or three others and "wait upon" the man they were trying to interest. The latter method is used primarily in getting a top leader to take on the top position in a community venture and pre-supposes that much initial work has already been done.

The understructure professional personnel in civic and social work who were asked the same questions indicated in nine cases out of thir-teen that they would call a committee together with no luncheon in-volved. One would make a personal call by himself, and two preferred the luncheon method. Desirable meeting places for luncheons are not as readily available to the professionals as to the top leaders in Regional City, which may account for the professionals' preference in some measure. The clubs represent places open to the top leaders and are prohibitive in cost and in social sanction to the understructure per-sonnel. Occasionally one of the professionals may be invited to one of the clubs for a meeting on a project, and it is considered an honor which he proudly confesses to his associates. The fact that the under-structure personnel do not frequent the clubs is in itself one of the subtle exclusion devices. The "boys" of the Grandview Club are known to make policy decisions within the confines of the club dining rooms which eventually filter down to the community understructure. . . .

The problem presented by the disparity of the economic conditions of men in Regional City is one that the whole economy has faced for many decades, and no attempt is made here to solve such a problem. However, this factor lies at the bottom of the power struggle and can-not be overlooked. The fears of the leaders are contingent on this very problem. One need not be a social scientist to see the miserable condi-tions which are so apparent in Regional City and to contrast them un-favorably with the conditions of luxury which also exist there. The so-cial scientist, however, need not excuse or leave these conditions un-noticed through fear, and it may be assumed that if the conditions were faced squarely in a structural sense no one need fear them, including the men of power.

The power structure of Regional City has the capacity for attacking the important issue raised, but as it is now constructed it apparently does not have the desire to do so. It now represents a closed system of power or relatively so. The solution to the problem presented by the current structure would seem to be to open the policy-making machinery to more groups than are now represented. Such a simple device as this would enable more individuals to participate in solving the many prob-lems that exist in the community and the fears of the men of power would be allayed in great measure if this step were taken. Social plan-ning is the name that may be given to what is suggested.

Social planning means that groups and individuals who are concerned with issues, projects, and community problems may organize into *effective* bodies to discuss issues, co-ordinate opinion, help lay out policy to cover any specific problem, and suggest alternative ways of action to meet a given social need. . . .

In a city of any appreciable size, the apparent control exercised over all types of information presents a real problem that must be solved by groups devoted to keeping the channels of information and discussion open on both the big and the lesser issues. It has been indicated that the lesser issues may be discussed, but that discussion of the major issues is kept out of the organization and associations by the top leaders. The Community Council in Regional City *might* be a place where such issues could be fully discussed, but as an organization it is so hedged around with protocol maintained by the fears of the policy-making group that there is little likelihood of its being an effective community-wide instrument for community discussion and action. The political organizations are also so completely dominated by the power interests which have been identified that there is little hope of adequate expression being fostered by them at this time.

The personnel most acutely aware of the paralysis of action and the suppression of dissatisfaction with the community structural arrangements are the professional workers. . . . The resistance to the authority of the policy makers in Regional City is expressed by the professionals privately, as has been indicated in earlier discussion, and shows up in the form of pessimism. . . .

The professional workers in Regional City, particularly those employed in the social agencies and in the planning agencies, are quite susceptible to moods of pessimism. They are employed by and subordinate to the upper structure of power whose interests they are supposed to have in mind, and yet in most cases they work with and are dedicated to the improvement of social conditions of the underprivileged. The role of such a professional is thus a marginal one producing conflict within the personality involved and possibly leading to what may be termed professional schizophrenia. The professional is isolated from the upper reaches of power, and he is generally rather effectively isolated from the average citizen. The organization for which he works may call itself community-wide in scope, but the term community should mean a community totality of interests rather than merely a geographical or demographic concept.

Some of the points already made in connection with the community problems of Regional City have grown out of many discussions with the professional personnel of that city and from personal observation. One need not linger in a justification of the "facts" as presented and interpreted, but they lead to another set of facts which from observation also appear to be true. These facts revolve around the notion that no professional person employed in Regional City might be critical of many power decisions and not be overwhelmed with attack damaging to his professional career in the community, whether his facts were right or wrong. The suppression of such facts as have been presented here is often called expediency. . . .

Even though channels of communication may be provided for interaction between the policy makers and subgroups, they are often ineffective through the distortions that are bound to occur in transmission, as well as through the fact that the values of the two groups may be in conflict. The knowledge resident in many of the understructure personnel is not fully utilized in the interaction processes carried on between them and the upper structure. . . .

Planning executives are hired to make plans in the physical and social areas of community life, but they are hedged around so firmly with restrictions by the policy-making groups that many of their ideas are never fully known to the average citizen or even a substantial portion of the more literate citizenry. Outside experts are suspect, if they probe too deeply for solutions to social disorders or become too "nosey" in questioning the dynamics of community processes. The files of the planning agencies in Regional City are crammed with "expert advice" on what should be done to relieve some of the tensions of the city, in spite of the distrust of the policy-making group in braintrusters. But the fact that the bulk of the reports are filed indicates that action on many of the suggested programs has been effectively stopped. The understructure personnel consider it expedient not to press for activity on scores of plans which may already have cost large sums of money and great expenditures of effort in their development. Planning, in Regional City, becomes a ritualistic panorama engaged in by reasonably well-paid understructure personnel whose plans more often than not fail to reach the point of action. Action results when a plan fits the relatively narrow interests of the policy makers, but on many issues there is community paralysis and inaction. . . .

If the professional in one of the social agencies is too zealous in searching out the basic causes of disorganization and social malfunctioning, he is liable to suspicion and censure. If he does engage in fundamental social research which turns up elements pointing to social reform or change in existing community alignments and structure, his materials may be presented to a limited group of persons who profess interest and who dutifully place his report with many like it in the files of the organization. Over the years, to be specific, the Community Council has analyzed the conditions of poor relief in the community and has pointed out repeatedly that public relief recipients have for many years received bare subsistence grants. A recommendation is always appended to these reports that larger grants be given. Sometimes the story of the study is carried in the newspapers. But repeatedly the reports are filed for future reference by subsequent committees.

One of the professionals working in the largest "charity" hospital estimated that more than 50 per cent of the cases coming to the hospital presented illnesses that could be directly traced to malnutrition. Some patients of this type are taken into the hospital for a few days, given proper diets, and released to make the same weary round within a few weeks or months. When asked if the situation had been called to the attention of the Community Council, this worker replied, "I have sat with the committees in the Community Council for the last twenty years—ever since I came to this community—and they are still discussing the adequacy of relief. I sometimes think it is time something were done about it!" Relief costs money. Public relief costs tax money. And the leaders in the community have never been sympathetic to the relatively large budget of the public welfare department. There is little understanding on the part of community leaders of the public welfare program in spite of the persistent effort of the Community Council and its subsidiary agencies to "interpret" the total welfare program to the community.

One of the leaders with whom the welfare program was discussed was a man who had been connected with a private welfare agency as a board member for many years. He expressed some dissatisfaction with the mounting public welfare expenditures and was asked what substitute he would make. He said, "I grew up on the philosophy of 'root hog or die.' My father gave me that bit of wisdom, and it has stuck with me through the years."

The individual and his community, so far as the leaders are concerned, is not a question of "bad" men consciously being cruel to helpless individuals. The leaders of Regional City are individually very pleasant persons to meet, and many of them appear to be good fathers, to attend church, and to have many of the virtues ascribed to "good" men. Few of them would publicly say that the socially helpless should "root hog or die." Some of the problems presented to the top power leaders of the community are too large in scope and too numerous for them to handle. The whole question of adequate relief is a national issue at this writing. "General assistance" to needy families in less wealthy areas such as Old State is considered to be a federal responsibility by many people. The policy on extending aid through this proposed category of social security is unsettled national policy. The men of policy decision in Regional City are overwhelmed with the notion of how much adequate relief grants would cost in taxes. They cannot face the demands that would be entailed at this time. And none feels individually responsible for the situation.

The professional worker, who comes into contact with the human distress occasioned by lack of clear-cut policy on the relief matter, tries to convince an unwilling public to do something about it. The top leaders are individually uncomfortable and try to isolate themselves from discussion of the subject, while the social workers are frustrated and disillusioned, and become pessimistic in their views.

The principle of keeping the taxes low, at the moment, outweighs the principle of raising taxes to meet the real demand for better conditions for welfare recipients. Social workers feel some responsibility to bring the issue to the attention of the community leaders who are on their agency boards of directors. This is done from time to time through studies and committee reports. When these reports are filed—not acted upon—the social workers are inclined to feel that they have done their duty and are not responsible for the chronic conditions which exist among their clientele. The board members, designated as second- and third-rate power leaders, are liable to overlook the matter when they contact those of power above them, for there are usually more pressing matters to be taken up in meetings with the topside leadership. Thus, the top leaders may not be too conscious of the existence of a problem in the area under discussion. In a sense everyone is responsible—and yet no one is. The community structure is not adequate to express effectively the demands that are real enough but which reside with the silent members of the community.

Voiced demands for community services by the underlying population in any community are negligible, as every community organizer knows, except in time of unusual crisis. Needs for community improvement may be apparent enough to any observer, but it is seldom that the general population becomes vocal in its demands for services. The general apathy among the mass of people is a phenomenon which is difficult to explain. The people generally accept the situation in which they find themselves with a remarkable degree of silence. When the people are organized for action, as in the case of labor unions, they may be vocal and powerful, but generally the people are not organized. The masses tolerate living conditions in Regional City that are a constant topic of conversation among the middle-class professionals and intellectuals. The professionals do not identify with the general mass of people in the community, although they are but one step removed from the general mass by birth and family connections in many cases. These professional leaders are acutely aware of the conditions of the working men and women and especially the socially distressed groups. They tend to accommodate themselves to their marginal position by having social interaction within their own professional groupings, and while they speak out for the underprivileged on occasion, they cannot in any sense be classified as the voice of the people. This fact is well-known to the power leaders. The professionals have no strength of support by the people as is the case with labor union representatives, and consequently it is an easy matter to listen politely to the feeble protests of the professional group and not accede to their requests for action.

The professionals are particularly weak and vulnerable as a political group. Many of them attend a semi-monthly luncheon which is called the Liberal Professional Club, but no action is taken by this group. Its program consists mainly of listening to visiting speakers who may have traveled in Europe lately or some remote spot in the world. The connection between the discussions and important policy issues is often nonexistent. During heated political campaigns in the city or state, one or another of the members may be partisan for one or another of the contending candidates, and "literature" will be placed at each luncheon plate favoring the particular candidate. However, there is no open political activity among the members of this group since some are civil servants. The group itself is well known to the power leaders, who watch it for any signs of open movement, and these top leaders are somewhat skeptical of the membership. One of the members, when applying for a change of position, was asked by one of the power leaders about his connection with the Club. Membership in the liberal group did not give the member a black eye with this employer, but the question in itself gave the club members a sense of daring and importance.

Some of the more liberal members of the professional community attend a biracial luncheon group held in one of the associational buildings in the Negro community every two weeks. These meetings are attended by some of the leading citizens of the Negro community, and speakers are drawn from home talent, visiting sociology professors, and the like. No political action is taken by this group, but some of the speeches are definitely political in nature, especially when one of the local citizens is exercised over a political matter.

Since none of the members in the community at large are consulted over political choices for candidates for public office, there is general apathy over political affairs. . . . During an election year, after the candidates are chosen by the respective parties, the interest would be higher, of course. . . .

It is not contended here that policy is determined entirely by behind-the-scenes manipulation, although the policy makers tend to operate as a closed group. To the policy makers their activities are thought to be open and aboveboard in relation to each other. Because of the structural hierarchy of command and decision, policy may appear to be determined in smoke-filled rooms, and behind the scenes. This is the public impression, perhaps and, to the professional workers, who are closer to the policy-making group and yet excluded from it, the appearance of behind-the-scenes manipulations may seem to be a reality. The situation, as observed in this study, is that the policy makers have a fairly definite set of settled policies at their command, which have been historically functional in the community. New problems which may arise are measured by the standards of older policy decisions, and adjustments are made to fit new conditions whenever the situation warrants revision of older policy determination. Often the demands for change in the older alignments are not strong or persistent, and the policy makers do not deem it necessary to go to the people with each minor change. This pattern of manipulation becomes fixed. It is functional, and the ordinary individual in the community is "willing" that the process continue. There is a carry-over from the minor adjustments to the settlement of major issues.

Once policy has been determined, regardless of the way in which it has been reached, there must be obedience to the general framework of policy, or there would be social disorganization which would be intolerable to all in the community. One of our hypotheses was, "Power is exercised as a necessary function in social relationships." Obedience of the people to the decisions of the power command becomes habitual and routinized even in a democracy. Among all segments of the population, including the power leaders, there may be a vaguely formulated recognition that social and economic conditions might be improved, but the scheme of relationships extant at the moment is producing goods and services in sufficient quantities to satisfy the basic needs of the majority in the community. Those who are disadvantaged by the present arrangements are not an articulate group; and, while some of the professionals may speak for a portion of this group, they often do so only with halfhearted conviction. They cannot substitute for the underprivileged, in any event, for they are not actually of this group. It is quite possible, too, that when some of the professional and other understructure personnel speak in behalf of the underprivileged groups they are making an ill-defined bid for "political" support of the latter and are setting forth a veiled demand for inclusion in policy determination among the power leaders. Such disguised and scarcely conscious demands are recognized by the top leaders for what they are—a restiveness in the understructure personnel—and they are handled accordingly.

The method of handling the relatively powerless understructure is through the pressures previously described—warnings, intimidations, threats, and in extreme cases violence. In some cases the method may include isolation from all sources of support for the individual, including his job and therefore his income. The principle of "divide and rule" is as applicable in the community as it is in larger units of political patterning, and it is as effective.

In the realm of policy the top leaders are in substantial agreement most of the time on the big issues related to the basic ideologies of the culture. There is no serious threat to the basic value systems at this time from any of the understructure personnel, and many of the fears of the top leaders on this point appear groundless.

Regardless of ideology, power is a necessity in modern community relations. No utopia will disband all power relations. Some men will rule, others will be ruled. The crucial question perhaps is, "How can policy be determined so that it takes into account the interests of the largest number of people?" As it now stands, policy set within the power relationships of Regional City does not seem to cover all of the social structure, and some modification of existing structure seems necessary if certain problems which arise chronically in this community are to be met.

PART TWO

THE PROCESS
OF COMMUNITY
ORGANIZATION

Introduction

COMMUNITY WELFARE organization is a process of social work, more or less comparable with the processes of social casework and social group work, rather than a division of the "field of social welfare," like family welfare, child welfare, health, or recreation. This is the key to contemporary thinking about community organization for social welfare.

The Lane Report of 1939 (see page 62 of this volume) argued inconclusively that community organization was *both* a process and a field; but McMillen, in 1945, based his volume—the first contemporary textbook on the subject—firmly on the thesis that community organization is a process. Most later thinking has followed this line, although occasional references to community organization as a "field" may still be found in the literature.

The distinction between the two conceptions is vital and practical. A "functional field" is a grouping of social welfare agencies or services that deal with certain *common problems*—problems relating to families or children or health or recreation, or some other grouping.

The term "process," on the other hand, "denotes a course of action developing through a series of related stages." [1] The essence of process is movement; a social work process, like casework, for example, may be applied in many fields, with agencies as different as public assistance, child-placing societies, hospitals, and child guidance clinics. Thus modern writers on community welfare organization usually maintain

---

[1] United Nations, *Social Progress Through Community Development* (E/CN.5/ 303 Rev. 1. ST/ SOA/26, 1955), p. 76.

that the process of community organization is applicable to and is used in *all* "functional fields," or divisions of the field of social welfare.

Some go a step further and maintain that it is community organization as a *social work* process that is most significant, not the social welfare content, as such, and that this process may be employed as a democratic method of effecting group integration and consensus in almost any field of interest. These two approaches, however, are not irreconcilable and indeed may be regarded as complementary rather than contradictory.

The fifteen selections in Part II of this volume all deal with the broad subject of "The Process of Community Organization." The first section is concerned most specifically with the definition and description of the process. The second section brings together a number of attempts to set forth basic concepts and principles of community organization. The next section deals with the historical development of this process, and the final section includes three selections on Community Organization and the Future. In the view of the editors, these fifteen selections as a whole form a logical foundation for the succeeding parts, which deal respectively with Community Organization in Practice, Agencies and Programs, Personnel, and Community Development.

Definitions and Descriptions of the Process
—Introduction

THE SEVEN SELECTIONS in this section all focus on the definition and description of the process of community organization. A collection of typical definitions, from a number of sources, is followed by the "Lane Report," from the *National Conference Proceedings* of 1939, which, more than any other one document, marks the beginning of contemporary thinking about community organization.

Russell H. Kurtz's paper of 1940 carries on this line of thinking and makes it more explicit. Arlien Johnson (1945) presents a discerning discussion of the relation of this general process of community organization to specific methods and skills.

Kenneth L. M. Pray, in his well-known National Conference paper of 1947, deals with the basic problem of when community organization is social work practice. Arthur Hillman (1950) considers the relation of community organization to town, city, and regional planning; and the final selection discusses community organization in relation to adult education.

4

What Is Community Organization? Selected Definitions

Though community organization has been consciously practiced for at least forty or fifty years, even its practitioners and those who have taught the subject have found difficulty in defining it.

Probably fifty to a hundred definitions could be found in American sociological and social welfare literature of the last thirty-five years. The following thirteen definitions, which range in time from 1921 to 1955, are fairly typical, and probably include the definitions that have been most widely used.

In general, four different major ideas are reflected in these definitions. These are: *First,* the idea of co-operation, collaboration, and integration. (Devine, Steiner, McMillen, King, Ross. Devine stresses also the method of education.) *Second,* the idea of meeting needs, and (in most of these definitions) of bringing about a balance between needs and resources. (Pettit, Lane, Mayo, Dunham, McNeil, Ross.) *Third,* the idea that community organization deals with "program relationships" as contrasted with the "direct service" of casework and group work. (Kurtz.) *Fourth,* the broad philosophical concept of community organization as furnishing a working relationship between the *democratic process* and *specialism.* (Lindeman.) Some of these definitions relate to the community only; others see the process as applicable to any geographical area or functional field.

The most recent of these definitions, by Murray G. Ross, combines in an interesting way the two ideas of meeting needs and achieving co-operation. As will be noted, Ross sees community organization as a process by which "a community" identifies needs and takes action, "and in so doing . . . develops co-operative . . . attitudes and practices. . . ."

54

Perhaps no one has yet captured the full essence of this dynamic process, and expressed it in a single paragraph, but these various definitions and descriptive statements which follow, taken together, certainly suggest some of the major conceptions of community organization which prevail today in the field of American social welfare.

EDUARD C. LINDEMAN   1921

The essential problem of community organization is to furnish a working relationship between the *Democratic Process* and *Specialism*. The Democratic Process expresses itself or is personified in the total community membership. The Specialist expresses himself, or is personified in the division of labor which produces highly skilled persons and agencies, organizations, or institutions, equipped to do one thing effectively. . . .

Community Organization is that phase of social organization which constitutes a conscious effort on the part of a community to control its affairs democratically, and to secure the highest services from its specialists, organizations, agencies, and institutions by means of recognized interrelations.[1]

EDWARD T. DEVINE   1922

A third process, which, like casework, is more peculiar to social work, is that which is involved in "educating the public." The educational and preventive social movements of the present century have a common method, consisting of research, publicity, and propaganda, which, while it has taken hints from commercial advertising and other sources, is fairly distinctive. . . . There is finally the kind of work which has for its object the co-ordination and harmonizing of existing agencies, the organization of the resources of the community, as was done, for instance, to provide hospitality and recreation for men in service during the war, or to provide care for the sick during the epidemic of influenza, the kind of planning for future development of a community's social work which is done by the budget committee of some of the financial federations.[2]

---

[1] Eduard C. Lindeman, *The Community* (New York: Association Press, 1921), pp. 139, 173.

[2] Edward T. Devine, *Social Work* (New York: The Macmillan Company, 1922), pp. 67-68.

WALTER W. PETTIT   1925

This use of the term "community organization" is perhaps best defined as assisting a group of people to recognize their common needs
and helping them to meet these needs. In Professor MacIver's terms,
it has to do with the process of like interests becoming common
interests out of which associations develop.[3]

JESSE F. STEINER   1930

. . . [Community organization] may be said to be chiefly concerned
with problems of accommodation and social adjustment. More specifically it is concerned with the interrelationships of groups within
communities, their integration and co-ordination in the interest of
efficiency and unity of action. In a wider sense it may also include the
adjustment of a local community to the larger social unit of which
it is a part. In order to understand the problem with which community organization is dealing, we must think of society as made up of
elements more or less antagonistic to each other, which must through
a process of accommodation develop a working arrangement that
will resolve the conflicts and make consistent progress possible. Community organization is, therefore, not merely an essential process; it
is also a continuous process in which adjustments are being made
and remade to keep pace with changing conditions.[4]

ROBERT P. LANE   1939

We suggest that the general aim of community organization is to
bring about and maintain a progressively more effective adjustment
between social welfare resources and social welfare needs. This implies that community organization is concerned with (a) the discovery and definition of needs; (b) the elimination and prevention
of social needs and disabilities, so far as possible; and (c) the articulation of resources and needs, and the constant readjustment of resources in order better to meet changing needs.[5]

RUSSELL H. KURTZ   1940

. . . community organization is a process dealing primarily with program relationships and is thus to be distinguished in its social work

---

[3] Walter W. Pettit, "Some Prognostications in the Field of Community Work,"
Proceedings, National Conference of Social Work, Denver, 1925 (Chicago: University of Chicago Press, 1925), p. 682.

[4] From *Community Organization,* by Jesse Frederick Steiner. Revised Edition,
copyright, 1930, The Century Co. Reprinted by permission of Appleton-Century-
Crofts, Inc.

[5] Robert P. Lane, "The Field of Community Organization," *Proceedings, National Conference of Social Work,* Buffalo, 1939 (New York: Columbia University Press, 1939), p. 500. Report of discussions within Section III by the chairman of the drafting committee. By permission of National Conference on Social
Welfare.

setting from those other basic processes, casework and group work, which deal with people. Those relationships—of agency to agency, of agency to community, and of community to agency—reach in all directions from any focal point in the social work picture. Community organization may be thought of as the process by which these relationships are initiated, altered, or terminated to meet changing conditions; and it is thus basic to all social work. . . .

It is a function of planning and implementation of services, of correlation of agencies with each other and with respective "communities" (not always compact geographical areas) which finds expression wherever welfare work is engaged in. It is a two-way process, depending largely on democratic procedures for its effectiveness and including both lay and professional persons among its practitioners.[6]

LEONARD W. MAYO   1946

The art of discriminating between noble and ignoble hopes and of capturing, channeling, and giving community expression to the noblest of them is the essence of "the struggle" [for progress]; its focus and method, its changing objectives but constant purpose, constitute the core of community organization. That phase of community organization concerned primarily with the imbalance between welfare needs and welfare resources has been defined as "community organization in social work."[7]

WAYNE MC MILLEN   1947

Community organization in its generic sense is deliberately directed effort to assist groups in attaining unity of purpose and action. It is practiced, though often without recognition of its character, wherever the objective is to achieve or maintain a pooling of the talents and resources of two or more groups in behalf of either general or specific objectives.[8]

---

[6] Russell H. Kurtz, "The Range of Community Organization," *Proceedings, National Conference of Social Work,* Grand Rapids, 1940 (New York: Columbia University Press, 1940), pp. 401 and 412. By permission of National Conference on Social Welfare.

[7] Leonard W. Mayo, "Community Organization Method and Philosophy in 1946," *Proceedings, National Conference of Social Work,* Buffalo, 1946 (New York: Columbia University Press, 1947), p. 129. By permission of National Conference on Social Welfare.

[8] Wayne McMillen, "Community Organization in Social Work," *Social Work Year Book,* 1947 (New York: Russell Sage Foundation, 1947), p. 110. By permission of the publisher. For an earlier definition see McMillen, *Community Organization for Social Welfare* (Chicago: University of Chicago Press, 1945), pp. 22-23.

ARTHUR DUNHAM   1948

By community organization for social welfare I mean the process of
bringing about and maintaining adjustment between social welfare
needs and social welfare resources in a geographical area or a functional field. Resources include, not only agencies and organizations,
but also personnel, physical equipment, finances, laws, leadership,
public understanding, good will, and participation. Community organization is a dynamic, pervasive, far-reaching process.[9]

CLARENCE KING   1948

Thus far we have defined "community organization" as meaning the
process of building and maintaining a "community of interest." Someone has called this "the development of association to meet need."
. . . Some supposed experts on community organization would not
regard this as community organization at all. To many the term
should be confined to the task of co-ordinating the programs of the
various social agencies of a community. That is the technique employed by executives of community chests and councils of social
agencies.[10]

WILBER I. NEWSTETTER   1954

[I assume] that there are three discernible processes in the field of
community organization and planning for social welfare. At least two
of these (the promotional or sales process and the administrative
process on the interagency [or] intergroup level) are not peculiar to
social work practice, but are processes in which every social work
agency from the local to the national and international level is, of
necessity, engaged. The process to which attention is now directed
is, in the judgment of the writer, probably unique as a potential part
of social work practice—social intergroup work. . . .

The adjustmental relations between the groups in terms of some
specific social goal is the over-all objective of the intergroup work
process. . . . two of the crucial aspects of the social intergroup work
process [are]: (1) There must be mutually satisfactory relations between the members of the groups (not merely between one or two of
their representatives in the intergroup) involved in attaining the selected social goal; and (2) what may be termed the "from and to"

---

[9] Arthur Dunham, "What Is the Job of the Community Organization Worker,"
Proceedings, National Conference of Social Work, Atlantic City, 1948 (New
York: Columbia University Press, 1949), p. 162. By permission of National Con-
ference on Social Welfare.
[10] Clarence King, *Organizing for Community Action* (New York: Harper &
Brothers, 1948), pp. 17-18. By permission of the publisher.

relationship between the groups responsibly represented, and their representatives.[11]

C. F. MC NEIL   1954

Community organization for social welfare is the process by which the people of communities, as individual citizens or as representatives of groups, join together to determine social welfare needs, plan ways of meeting them, and mobilize the necessary resources. The focus of effort may be a functional field of social welfare, for example, leisure time and recreation, or a geographical area, such as a neighborhood, city, or county.[12]

MURRAY G. ROSS   1955

Community organization, as the term is to be used in this book, is to mean a process by which a community identifies its needs or objectives, orders (or ranks) these needs or objectives, develops the confidence and will to work at these needs or objectives, finds the resources (internal and/or external) to deal with these needs or objectives, takes action in respect to them, and in so doing extends and develops co-operative and collaborative attitudes and practices in the community.[13]

---

[11] Wilber I. Newstetter, "The Concept of the Community and Other Related Concepts," in: Eleanor E. Cockerill, ed., *Social Work Practice in the Field of Tuberculosis: Proceedings of Symposium,* 1953 (Pittsburgh: University of Pittsburgh, School of Social Work, 1954), pp. 95-97. By permission of the publisher.

[12] C. F. McNeil, "Community Organization for Social Welfare," *Social Work Year Book,* 1954 (New York: American Association of Social Workers, 1954), p. 121. By permission of National Association of Social Workers.

[13] Murray G. Ross, *Community Organization: Theory and Principles* (New York: Harper & Brothers, 1955), p. 39. By permission of the publisher.

5

The Nature and Characteristics of Community
Organization—A Preliminary Inquiry[1]

By ROBERT P. LANE

The "Lane Committee Report" to the National Conference of 1939 is a landmark that may be said almost to mark the beginning of contemporary literature on community welfare organization.

Its importance rests particularly on these foundations: (1) It is a group product—the product of group study, group thinking, and finally group drafting. A considerable number of the national leaders concerned with community organization were involved with this process at one point or another. This report has often been compared with that other group product, *Social Casework, Generic and Specific* (1929), in its nature and historical importance. (2) Aside from a few articles in the *Social Work Year Books* of 1933–1939, the Lane report is practically the first attempt since those of Steiner and McClenahan in the 1920's, to analyze and discuss the "nature and characteristics" of community organization. (3) This report emphasizes community organization as a generic, pervasive process with which *all* social work is concerned—not as something confined to "chests and councils" or other specialized settings. (4) The report states clearly a number of basic concepts, it sets up a frame of reference for the subject, and it suggests areas for further study. (5) In spite of all the lacks of intensive

[1] Excerpted from "The Field of Community Organization," *Proceedings of the National Conference of Social Work* 1939, pp. 495-511. By permission of National Conference on Social Welfare. The title used for this reproduction of the report is suggested by the one given to a preliminary mimeographed edition of it. The title used in the National Conference Proceedings is an unfortunate one, since community organization is now usually regarded as a *process* rather than a "field."

joint study, and divergencies of opinion within the report it yet reveals "considerable agreement on the nature, content, and limitations of the process itself." (6) The report has greatly influenced much subsequent thinking and writing about community organization. (7) Finally, the report, in spite of its production during the pressures of a National Conference week—a "community organization" project of no small stature in itself!—is written with clarity, insight, and a certain literary quality, attributable particularly to the style of the chairman of the Committee. The report, too, even after the lapse of a decade and a half, has a dynamic quality that suggests something of the excitement of the professional quest on which these explorers had embarked.

Robert P. Lane (1891–1953), the chairman of the Committee, was at this time the executive director of the Welfare Council of New York City and one of the keenest and most stimulating participants in the New York Study Committee on community organization and in the cooperative undertaking carried on under the auspices of the National Conference.

A number of local National Conference study committees continued their work during 1939–1940, and a second "Lane Committee Report" was presented to the National Conference of 1940.[2]

WHEN THE CHAIRMAN of Section III of the Conference sent out a call in October, 1938, to the fifteen elected members of the Section, to meet for preliminary work on the 1939 Conference program, a reply was received from one of the members which read in part as follows:

"In reviewing the program suggestions, I am convinced that there is a real need for evaluating the processes and objectives of community organization, much as the caseworkers have done before us and the group workers are now doing. Would we dare, as a Committee, to undertake a study of the concept and its implications to the Conference? It might be possible to form discussion groups in different parts of the country to work on the project simultaneously between now and the 1939 Conference."

This suggestion met with a favorable response and the Section chairman was authorized to name a steering committee to put it into effect. The committee instigated the formation of discussion groups in Boston, Buffalo, Chicago, Detroit, New York City, and Pittsburgh. These

[2] Robert P. Lane, "Report of Groups Studying the Community Organization Process," *Proceedings of the National Conference of Social Work,* 1940, pp. 456-473.

groups held frequent meetings throughout the winter and spring of 1938–1939, coming together finally for a clearance of their findings in an all-day session on the opening day of the Conference (Sunday, June 18, 1939) at Buffalo. At the conclusion of that session, a drafting committee of three—Robert P. Lane, Mary Clarke Burnett and Arthur Dunham—took the six memoranda, together with the minutes of the discussion on them, and prepared the following report, which was presented to the Conference at the concluding session of Section III on June 24, 1939. . . .

1. Initial Agreements

When representatives of the six discussion groups met in Buffalo on June 18, they found themselves in agreement on the following points:

1. That the term community organization is used to refer to a *process,* and, as is often the case in other professions, to refer also to a *field.* This double usage is a familiar phenomenon. Thus we refer to the practice of medicine as a process, and to the field of medicine; to the teaching process, and to the field of teaching; to the practice of law, which is a process, and to the legal field; and so forth.

2. That the process of organizing a community, or some parts of it, goes on outside, as well as inside, the general area of social work. Whatever more careful analysis may disclose this process to consist of, there seems little doubt that it is practiced, for different purposes, by such bodies as chambers of commerce, churches and federations of churches, and political parties—to name only three groups outside of social work to which it may be ascribed. It is the social welfare nature of its objectives when carried on within the area of social work, as well as its general content and setting, that distinguish the community organization work with which we are concerned, from that, for example, at which Mr. James A. Farley is so expert.

3. That within the area of social work the process of community organization is carried on by some organizations as a primary function —that is, by organizations established for the express purpose of carrying it on; and by other organizations as a secondary function—that is, by organizations established for the express purpose of carrying on some other process of social work, which find, however, that *their* primary function is advanced if they engage also in community organization. Obvious examples are a council of social agencies, whose primary function is that of community organization; and a family agency, whose staff and especially whose executive often engage in community organization in order to promote the more effective performance of their primary function of casework, or even to promote the advancement of the total social welfare program in the community.

4. That within the area of social work the process of community

organization is carried on not only in communities or neighborhoods, or on the local level, but also on a state-wide basis and on a nation-wide basis, or on the state and national levels. Examples on the state level are a State Department of Welfare setting and enforcing standards for the operation of child-caring institutions; and, on the national level, the United States Children's Bureau with its field service and its infinitely helpful publications with which we are all familiar.

The process is also carried on between such levels—that is, between the federal and state governments, or between state and local governments; or between national or state voluntary organizations and local voluntary organizations. Examples of this interlevel process are the working agreements between the United States Employment Service and State Employment Services; and the provisions under which State Departments of Welfare reimburse local departments for relief expenditures and set personnel and other standards to which local units of government must conform.

5. That organizations whose primary function is the practice of community organization do not, as a rule, offer help directly to clients. Their work lies rather with functional agencies and interested groups of nonclients; but the aim and justification of the community organization process is improvement in the coverage and quality of service to clients which the community is enabled to provide.

2. What Is Community Organization?

There has been no agreement as yet by the six study groups on a formal definition of community organization. Three of the groups submitted tentative definitions, which are given below; some of the other groups included definitions suggested by individual members.

One group proposed the following definition:

Community organization is the process of dealing with individuals or groups who are or may become concerned with social welfare services or objectives, for the purpose of influencing the volume of such services, improving their quality or distribution, or furthering the attainment of such objectives.

Another group suggested this:

In the social welfare field, community organization may be described as the art and process of discovering social welfare needs and of creating, co-ordinating and systematizing instrumentalities through which group resources and talents may be directed toward the realization of group ideals and the development of the potentialities of group members. Research, interpretation, conference, education, group organization, and social action are the principal tools used in the process.

A third group offered the following:

Community organization is a type of social work concerned with efforts to direct social resources effectively toward the specific or total welfare needs of any geographical area. Its performance may involve such activities as fact finding, co-ordination, improving standards, interpretation, developing welfare programs, changing patterns of social work, and promoting social legislation.

Despite differences in wording, there is an encouraging measure of agreement in these three definitions. The emphasis varies: one stresses the discovery of social welfare needs, and strikes the note of prevention as well as of treatment; one lays stress on the establishment and development of relationships between individuals and groups actually or potentially concerned with "social welfare services or objectives"; one centers around the idea of "directing" social resources to meet welfare needs. But the core idea of each definition is that of mobilizing resources to meet needs; each one expresses or implies the ideas of initiating social services, co-ordinating the efforts of welfare agencies, and building welfare programs.

Clearly, if our limited experience is any indication, the nature of the community organization process, though meagerly treated in professional literature, still enjoys a generous measure of common understanding, and should prove to be susceptible of analysis and statement.

3. Characteristics of Community Organization

Preliminary Considerations

Regarding the characteristics of community organization, the Drafting Committee advances the following suggestions quite tentatively and as a basis for further exploration and discussion. In their present form they have been evolved during the progress of a National Conference week, with all its attendant pressures; obviously, therefore, they require analysis and testing against experience, more carefully and with much more leisure, by groups and social workers representing various sections of the country and various fields of practice.

One clue to the nature of community organization seemed to be suggested in an hypothesis put forward by one member of our group. This hypothesis, which gained a considerable measure of assent, is here stated in a slightly modified form in which we think most members of the group can accept it: namely, that community organization is usually, and perhaps always, concerned with intergroup relationships. It is clear that neighborhood or local community councils, councils of social agencies, community chests, state conferences of social work and national welfare agencies (to take only a few examples) are constantly concerned with intergroup relationships. . . .

General Aim

The general aim of community organization is its basic purpose as a process of social work—its reason for being. We suggest that the general aim of community organization is to bring about and maintain a progressively more effective adjustment between social welfare resources and social welfare needs. This implies that community organization is concerned with (a) the discovery and definition of needs; (b) the elimination and prevention of social needs and disabilities, so far as possible; and (c) the articulation of resources and needs, and the constant readjustment of resources in order better to meet changing needs.

Secondary Objectives

If this is the central and primary aim of community organization, there are also several secondary objectives. These secondary objectives are purposes which community organization seeks to accomplish as a means to the realization of its general aim. We suggest the following six secondary objectives:

1. To secure and maintain an adequate factual basis for sound planning and action.

2. To initiate, develop, and modify welfare programs and services, in the interest of attaining a better adjustment between resources and needs.

3. To improve standards of social work and to increase the effectiveness of individual agencies.

4. To improve and facilitate interrelationships, and to promote coordination, between organizations, groups, and individuals concerned with social welfare programs and services.

5. To develop a better public understanding of welfare problems and needs, and social work objectives, programs and methods.

6. To develop public support of, and public participation in, social welfare activities. Financial support includes income from tax funds, voluntary contributions, and other sources.

We should like to note, parenthetically, that five of these six objectives are substantially the same as the five objectives for a council of social agencies set forth by W. Frank Persons in 1925, in his pamphlet, *The Welfare Council of New York City*. Mr. Persons' analysis has stood the test of time to a remarkable extent and appears to have a high degree of validity as applied to this current analysis of the broad process of community organization.

Methods and Activities

Community organization objectives are attained (or pursued) through specific activities carried on by agencies which engage in community organization. In using the term "activity," we differentiate it from "method," conceiving of an activity as a specific project or service which results when a method is applied in a particular time, place, and situation. An activity is something that is done; a method is the way in which it is done.

We suggest that among the methods of community organization are those listed below. This list is merely illustrative; it is not intended as a complete catalogue of the methods in this field, nor have we been at pains to make the several methods listed mutually exclusive. Where convenient, we have suggested how a general method is transformed into an activity in a concrete situation.

1. Continuous central recording is a method used in the community organization process. Using this method, a given council of social agencies may carry on, as an activity, the collection and publication of financial and service data pertaining to the work of its member agencies.

2. Planning, particularly planning by or in behalf of two or more agencies, is a second method used in community organization. Planning an anti-syphilis campaign by a group of agencies is an activity of those agencies which illustrates the use of the planning method.

3. A third method used is that of making special studies and surveys. The carrying out of a study of recreational needs and resources, in a given city, by a national agency, is an illustrative activity.

4. Joint budgeting—that is, planning applied to finances—is a fourth method used. When a chest and council set up and operate a budgeting program they are carrying on a joint activity by using this method.

5. Methods concerned with education, interpretation, and public relations—including use of newspaper publicity, annual reports, other printed literature, public speaking, radio, exhibits, and so on— are used in the community organization process. When the Welfare Federation of Cleveland publishes an educational book regarding social work for school children, this is an activity arising from the application of one of these methods.

6. Planning and execution of joint financial campaigns as a method of community organization is a common phenomenon.

7. The method of organization is used by a council of social agencies when it creates a child welfare division; or by a state conference of social work when it sets up a committee on welfare legislation; or by a national agency when it establishes a field service; or jointly by a state and county welfare department when the state department's field representative assists the county welfare board in recruiting and training its staff.

8. Interagency consultation, through field service or otherwise, is a common method. This occasionally takes on an authoritarian note, as when one of the activities of a State Welfare Department is the licensing of a private child-caring agency.

9. Development and use of group discussion, the conference process and committees, is a method with which we are all too painfully acquainted to require illustration.

10. Promotion of voluntary agreements through negotiation. Two children's institutions may, but all too frequently do not, avail themselves of this method to carry out the activity of a merger.

11. Operation of joint services. This is a common method, resulting in such a definite activity as operation of a social service exchange.

12. Promotion of legislation, often referred to by the term "social action." So many concrete activities flow from use of this method that illustration is uncalled for except perhaps to say that they include educational and legislative campaigns, promotion of pressure group activities, and the advancing of a cause through personal contacts with officials, political leaders, and other persons and groups.

It may be observed that while social action is usually thought of in reference to legislation, it need not be confined to that area. For example, social action methods may be directed toward a public administrative official, or toward persons not holding public office but able to influence important social policies.

Two comments should be made in regard to this illustrative list of methods of community organization. In the first place, there is an obvious difficulty in deciding how large or how small an area to regard as a single method. For example, shall we speak of social work surveys as a method; or shall we regard as separate methods planning and organizing the survey, carrying on the field work and gathering the data, interpreting the data and writing the report, and so on? Likewise, is "planning and executing a joint financial campaign" a single method; or is it a collection of methods, including planning the campaign, determining quotas, organizing the soliciting force, soliciting the prospects, planning and managing campaign luncheons, and so on?

This problem is raised for further study; we have no answer to it at present. It is obvious that most of the general methods listed above are made up of more specific methods. The careful study and analysis of this hierarchy of methods is urgently needed; but the search must be pursued with some sense of the potential absurdity of relentlessly tracking down methods by successively narrowing the circle until the characteristics of a professional method are lost in a haze of trivialities of individual behavior patterns.

In connection with this further examination of methods, it should be possible to give a somewhat precise meaning to the term "technique" as applied to community organization, and to define the relation of "technique" to "method."

Our second comment is an expression of our recognition that certain common methods are employed in community organization and in the internal administration of social agencies: for example, planning, organization, group discussion. How extensive or how important this common area of methods is, cannot be determined until there are available systematic and fairly comprehensive descriptions of the methods used in both these fields.

The Committee would make clear, however, that while it recognizes the existence of common methods in community organization and administration, it does not regard these two fields as identical. Community organization is a process and a field of social work which we are inclined to regard as comparable with casework and group work; administration is a function of all social agencies, whether they are concerned primarily with casework, group work, or community organization. Administration is, of course, a function of other types of organizations: government departments, armies, churches, schools, business concerns, and so on. It may be correct to say that the job of a particular social agency executive includes activities of both community organization and administration; but this does not mean that the fields of community organization and administration are the same, or that either of these fields is a part of the other. They are separate areas, but certain methods are common to both.

The foregoing analysis of some of the characteristics of community organization is tentative and partial; but we believe it will serve to summarize our present thinking and to provide a starting point for the next stage in exploring the process of community organization. . . .

4. Selection of a Name for Community Organization

It will be noted that so far in this report we have used the expression "community organization" without comment as to whether or not we found it a wholly satisfactory descriptive label for the process and field whose content and limitations we are trying to determine. In the opinion of a number of the groups it is not wholly satisfactory. We are aware that it has gained wide currency and is regarded by many, perhaps by most, social workers as well established and acceptable. We are familiar with the admonition, "Remove not the ancient landmark." In these circumstances it is obviously desirable that the term be continued in general usage unless analysis of the process gradually brings recognition that the term is inadequate, and unless a more accurate and equally convenient term gradually gains acceptance. We definitely are not here proposing adoption of a substitute term. We think it worth while, however, to indicate some of the reasons for the dissatisfaction many of our members felt with the expression community organization, and to mention some of the alternative terms suggested. The reasons for dissatisfaction may be summarized as follows:

The word "community" presented difficulties. To many of us it inevitably suggests only local activities. Further, when coupled with "organization," it seems to suggest that some entire "community" is being "organized." We have indicated our agreement that, first of all, we were seeking to identify a process, and our further agreement that this process is practiced on local, state and federal levels, and between such levels. Many of us were therefore persuaded that we should seek also for a term that would clearly refer to the process alone, without including a word that introduced a confusing and perhaps misleading geographical limitation. This, it was urged, has been done in connection with the casework process and the group work process.

Some of our members thought the absence of the word "social," or any other word identifying the process with the field of social work, was unfortunate, especially as the process is practiced outside the social work field. Here again, we were reminded, the full expressions "social casework" and "social group work" serve as admirable examples.

Substitute terms that were suggested included the following: social planning; social welfare planning; social engineering; social community work; community work; community organization work; community organization for social work; welfare organization work; intergroup work; social organization work; social welfare organization. Most of these terms were examined critically and finally rejected by the very persons who suggested them. . . .

We desire to repeat that selection of a label for the process we are examining did not seem to us a matter of the first importance. For that matter, neither did agreement on a formal definition of the process. Perhaps because so many of us are tainted with scholasticism, we could not forego a measure of hairsplitting and logic chopping in the course of our discussions; but we never deserted our basic conviction that the essential task confronting those concerned with community organization is to know what they are *doing* and trying to do. If agreement is reached on this central point, agreement on lesser points—of which the name of the process is an example—should not prove difficult. . . .

5. Conclusions and Recommendations

The experience of our discussion groups justifies, we believe, two generalizations that are obvious when stated, but that seem to us as important as they are obvious.

First: Despite a scanty amount of close, intensive, *joint* examination of the community organization process, despite a meager literature, despite a dearth of teaching materials, despite the absence of published job analyses, despite a relatively uncriticized nomenclature—despite all these lacks, there is considerable agreement on the nature, content, and limitations of the process itself. Our understanding of some portion of this agreement has been presented above. A continuation of the sort of work we have tried to do, we are satisfied, will reveal still further areas of agreement.

Second: Such a continuation we believe is desirable and important. We favor this not merely that further areas of agreement may be revealed and become widely known, but rather that professional understanding of the entire process of community organization may be sharpened, deepened, and widened. Specifically, we think the following aspects of the process should receive critical examination:

1. What are the objectives of community organization? How should they be formulated? How can they be more widely understood, approved, and supported?

2. What activities are carried on as part of this process? In what kind of communities or geographical areas—or in what circumstances —are such activities most successful?

3. By what methods are these activities carried on? How can these methods be made more effective?

4. What principles underlying the theory and practice of community organization can be—or should be—agreed on?

5. What qualifications are now looked for in persons engaged in community organization? What qualifications should be looked for? What training will best develop these qualifications?

6. How can adequate records of the community organization process be prepared and made available? Can workers in the field be induced to experiment in keeping them? Such records, be it noted, should *reveal methods* rather than merely *report results*.

7. How can we evaluate the objectives, the activities, the methods, and the principles of community organization? Evaluation, of course, should be made in the light of the best professional practice.

As a means of insuring the further examination of these problems, we unite in recommending that the officers of Section III of the National Conference take steps to set up a suitably representative committee for the ensuing year, charged with the duty of carrying on the work on which we have made a modest, but to us a highly pleasurable, beginning.

6

Bench Marks of Community Organization [1]

By RUSSELL H. KURTZ

In the wake of the "Lane Committee Report" of 1939 (see the preceding Selection 5) came a number of significant National Conference papers, pressing further in the exploration of the process of community organization, and seeking to establish its boundaries and to identify its landmarks.

From the perspective of eighteen years later, none of these papers is of more basic importance than Russell H. Kurtz's "The Range of Community Organization."

Mr. Kurtz was at that time editor of the *Social Work Year Book,* published by the Russell Sage Foundation, and he was chairman of the New York Study Committee on Community Organization of 1939–1940, which made so large a contribution to the two "Lane Committee" reports.

One of the fresh insights in Mr. Kurtz's 1940 paper is his observation that "community organization is a process dealing primarily with program relationships. . . ." Even more illuminating and suggestive are his eight "bench marks" that span the range of community organization from its simplest local beginnings to the complexities of the interrelationships of national agencies. Even today one would find little to add to this analysis—the inclusion of joint financing, probably, on both local and state levels and a mention of "international community organization."

[1] Excerpted from "The Range of Community Organization," *Proceedings, National Conference of Social Work,* Grand Rapids (New York: Columbia University Press, 1940), pp. 400-412. By permission of National Conference on Social Welfare.

THIS QUICK SURVEY of the range of community organization starts with the assumption that community organization is a process of human relations having wide application in many fields, of which social work is only one; and proceeds on the thesis, by no means new, that as used in social work or for social welfare objectives the process manifests itself in many diverse geographical areas and functional relationships. It will be my endeavor to develop this thesis by illustrations drawn from observation of agency practice in a number of settings.

I would like first to say a word, however, in support of my initial assumption that community organization is a process widely used outside of, as well as within, the structure of social work. Since no one lives to himself alone in this world, but always as a member of a group, he inevitably finds himself caught up in a network of relationships with his fellows which condition his own life. His "community" is shaped by organizational forces inherent in the group of which he is a part or imposed, in some cases, from without. These forces find expression in the actions of persons who, having selected an objective desirable by their own standards, attempt to attain that objective by persuading other members of the community to go along with them. For example, a political leader seeks to organize his community to vote for the party's ticket; a chamber of commerce tries to organize the businessmen to further the commercial life of the community; a ministerial association attempts to draw all the churches together to make a greater religious impact on the community than is possible where there is disunity or sectarian competition; or a civic group seeks to win community support for a legislative measure calculated to reduce the local tax rate. These efforts to affect the community pattern may all be regarded as illustrations, it seems to me, of the use of the community organization process outside the usually accepted boundaries of the field of social work. They differ in objective, of course, from the activities which social workers include within the meaning of the term, but by broad definition they may be said to be generically related to the latter activities. . . .

May I offer the observation that community organization is a process dealing primarily with program relationships and is thus to be distinguished in its social work setting from those other basic processes, casework and group work, which deal with people? These relationships—of agency to agency, of agency to community, and of community to agency—reach in all directions from any focal point in the social work picture. Community organization may be thought of as the process by which these relationships are initiated, altered, or terminated to meet changing conditions; and it is thus basic to all social work.

To illustrate the use of this process in the simplest possible setting, let us imagine a pioneer community in which, at the outset, no social services exist. Time passes, and as the community grows older and its population increases, troubling social problems begin to appear. At first

72

these are met by voluntary effort, without formal organization of local resources; but eventually the day comes when a small but interested group of citizens decides that something more is necessary, that it would be advantageous to establish a family welfare agency in the community. Promotional activities follow, wider support is secured, and finally an organization is set up, and a social worker employed.

Now here we have seen the community organization process used in its simplest and most direct form. An agency has been created, by laymen, without benefit of professional guidance or participation. I would like to drive my first peg right here and attach to it this tag: *Community organization is effectively practiced in certain circumstances by laymen without the help of professionals.*

Our hypothetical community's first social worker now takes up her duties and finds that she has a job requiring the use of many skills. Not all her responsibilities can be discharged, she discovers, by the use of her carefully acquired casework techniques. She realizes that she is not only a caseworker, concerned with the problems of individual clients, but that she has also become in effect an agency, with all the needs an agency has to relate itself to its environment. She must frequently lay aside her clients' problems for considerable periods and devote herself with her board and others to agency fence building and the winning of community support. In doing this she draws vitality from the community organization spirit of those citizens who established her in this job, and sinks new roots in whatever other soil appears hospitable. Let us set up our second marker here and label it thus: *Community organization is necessarily practiced by every social agency in its struggle for survival and development.*

The years roll by and our community continues to grow both in population and in the complexity of its social pattern. One by one other agencies are established: a hospital, a scout troop, a children's institution, a public welfare department. Some of these agencies are brought into existence on purely local initiative; others are promoted from outside. Our first social worker, now something of a veteran in the local scene, welcomes the new agencies as resources which she can use to advantage in her work. Friendly relationships are established and channels for informal conference and the discussion of joint problems are opened. Without relinquishing any of her own program of community relations, she works with the new agencies to achieve something of a united front for social work. She and her board share with the others a desire to "see the social work of the community whole," and by identifying its gaps and overlappings, to work for a better division of the field and for improved correlation of services. All of this goes on for years without the formal organization among the participants of any sort of instrumentality for regularizing the process. But the process itself is community organization, is it not, used in a promising new relationship? Shall we drive our third peg here and record:

Use of the community organization process is made between agencies in all communities, even where formal councils do not exist.

And now more years pass, further growth occurs, and the family of agencies becomes so large that formation of a council is seen to be necessary to bring order into the social work chaos that is developing. The earlier informality of interagency communication is replaced by a new set of relationships focused about the council. It may be that at first there is little or no surrender of agency autonomy to the council; but as times goes on the council is able to win from its members a series of concessions and compromises which result in greatly improved co-ordination of services in the total community. "Seeing the social work of the community whole" has now become a major objective which the council is charged with responsibility for keeping in view despite the competitive system still existing, in large measure, among the agencies.

The introduction of the council into the social work structure has made it possible for the community organization process to be applied much more methodically in working out relationships between the total group of agencies and the community. By pooling information about problems and services, joint planning, and united action toward a common goal, the agencies make of the council an addition to that total force which they can otherwise muster. The council's primary function is community organization, and it is able to exercise that function with much more telling effect than can the member agencies whose primary functions lie in other fields. It becomes a specialist in the use of the community organization process; and after a while it may have to remind itself that this specialization is not synonymous with monopoly, although at times it may seem to be.

And so we set up our fourth marker: *Intensive use of the community organization process is made by some specialized agencies, such as councils, organized for the purpose.*

At this point it may be well to check up on our pioneer social worker to learn in how many ways she is now engaging in community organization practice. We find her still using the process in keeping her own agency geared to the community. We see her participating with others in its application around the council conference table. And, since her agency is an important member of the council, we find her concerned with the way the council itself uses the process as it goes before the community to speak for all the agencies. This threefold responsibility would seem to be quite enough to load upon any executive trained for the practice of casework, but this worker will tell you that there are still other "communities" with which she must deal and that the community organization process comes into play when she faces them, too.

One of these is the national association of welfare agencies with which her society decided to affiliate some time back. Another is the state department of welfare which licensed her organization for child placing a few years ago and now supervises her work in this field. Still another is the professional association to which she belongs and toward which she feels a sense of responsibility for her social work standards. All these relationships are vital and call for intelligent application of community organization principles. We will drive our fifth peg here and note: *Community organization is practiced vertically, between a local agency and its state and national affiliates, as well as horizontally in the local community.*

In these attempts to relate her agency to the world round about her, our worker seldom finds herself in a commanding position with respect to the forces she is dealing with. She is ever reminded that she is an agent of society rather than its self-appointed "organizer." Through interpretation of her work and participation in the democratic processes attending the social planning of her community, she makes such gains as she can, supplying leadership on some occasions and following it on others. She never forgets that it was lay action which brought her to the community in the first place and that it is lay judgment which determines the extent of her usefulness as long as she remains. She would agree, I think, to our setting up a sixth marker here: *Community organization is generally a joint process in which professionals and nonprofessionals participate, with the nonprofessionals always having the last word.*

And now let us leave this worker and her problems and go farther afield in our search for other examples of the uses of the community organization process in social work. Our first stop will be at the state capital, where we will shift our interest for a time from the private field to the public. Examining the work of the state department of welfare for illustrations of the practice of community organization, we find a repetition of the pattern of relationships just studied on the local level.

The state department as an agency in the "community" of the state exists side by side with other agencies on this level and finds an inevitable necessity to work out harmonious relationships with them. Sometimes this is achieved informally, by conference and interchange of correspondence. In other circumstances it is channeled through a council set up by legislative act or administrative order. Whatever the means used, the department participates in many attempts at correlation of services and finds itself engaging in the practice of community organization when it does so.

Beyond this area of interagency relationships and underlying the department's ability to function at all is, of course, the authorization of the legislature to which the department owes its existence. In a sense the legislature represents the "community" of the state and is the soil in which the agency is planted and from which it must draw its nourishment. The skillful use of community organization methods by the state department is therefore necessary if the legislature, and the electorate which it represents, is to be kept favorably disposed to support of the department's program. The public must be satisfied that the department's work is necessary and its methods sound, or, as is true of any local agency, support will be withdrawn. Thus in its "community" the state-wide public agency has constant need to apply the community organization process in the horizontal relationships that surround it.

But there are vertical relationships as well which must be looked after if the department is to function effectively. These reach both upward and downward.

Among the upward relationships are those which the department has with the federal agencies from whom funds are received and supervision accepted. Functioning independently, in an administrative sense, the department must nevertheless co-operate with such agencies as the Federal Social Security Board in order to continue to receive grants of federal aid for services such as those which it provides through its public assistance program. This co-operation takes the form of adapting state standards to federal requirements on a variety of matters—personnel, determination of client eligibility, methods of administration, and so forth. Frequently the authoritarian note is heard from above so loudly in this relationship that the harmony which community organization seeks to achieve is somewhat impaired; but, despite that fact, the application of community organization principles in this setting remains basic to long-term effectiveness. In using the process here the state department finds ways of adapting it to the exigencies of the situation and is frequently able to show results on the other side of the ledger, in changed federal attitudes and requirements.

On the downward side the department deals with the localities of the state, extending to them aid and supervision in their welfare programs and expecting from them co-operation of the sort it gives to the Federal Government. Now that the tables are reversed, if the department has a dual "Dr. Jekyll and Mr. Hyde" personality it will be quickly apparent. Again, however, the relationship calls for wise use of the community organization process, as any state administrator will tell you. Authoritarian tendencies must be held in check if true co-operation is to be won from the local agencies.

So much for the public department on the state level. What of the private agencies here?

Since most private social work skips the state level and federates into its functional associations on the national level, examples of state-wide voluntary use of the community organization process are few. Exceptions are found, however, in at least three types of association.

First, the state conferences of social work bring together workers, if not agencies, under conditions which vary from simple elbow-to-elbow relationships in a conference audience to joint service on committees engaged in attempting some kind of social action. Granting that a rather diluted application of the community organization process is made under most such conditions, the functional identification of the use of the procedure here with community organization in its broader aspects seems clear enough.

Second, there are occasions on which special conferences are called by the governor, or hearings held by the legislature, or commissions established, to consider problems of state-wide significance in the social welfare field. Such assemblages are likely to be participated in by both lay and professional persons from the private as well as the public field and afford opportunities for the community organization process to be used to advantage.

Third, in at least two states—New York and Pennsylvania—there exist voluntary state-wide agencies whose chief function is that of promoting better welfare organization. The State Charities Aid Association of New York declares its purpose to be "to aid and promote effective public administration . . . in the field of public health, public welfare, and mental hygiene." It is a nonpartisan, nonsectarian, state-wide citizens' organization. The Public Charities Association of Pennsylvania has a similar purpose. . . . It is worth noting that while both of these agencies are voluntary, they use the community organization process largely in relation to the work of governmental agencies and institutions, not only on the state, but also across to the local level. The direction of functional flow in the latter instance might, I suppose, be referred to as diagonal.

Reviewing these illustrations drawn from the organizational work going on in the "community" of the state—and there probably are other examples which could be cited—we would be justified, I think, in establishing here another marker, our seventh: *The community organization process is used on the state level by both public and private agencies, in both horizontal and vertical relationships.*

Next, let us take a look at the national arena. Here we find two large groups of agencies: the public, or federal, and the national voluntary associations. The members of each group all have occasion to use the process of community organization in their individual and collective relationships, applying it again both vertically and horizontally. A few illustrations follow.

First, in the public field. An agency such as the United States Children's Bureau or the Social Security Board finds itself involved in a variety of environmental relationships on at least three fronts: (1) It must win public support for its program and maintain its status in the complicated governmental structure, avoiding curtailment of function through reorganization or the denial of adequate appropriations. This effort involves the use of all those devices—interpretation, negotiation, and perhaps compromise—which local agencies employ in similar situations. (2) Each agency must stand ready to work with co-ordinate governmental departments in attacking, through committees or joint conference bodies, problems of interest to all. And (3) it must work out satisfactory relationships with the states on those matters which require state acceptance of federal standards or regulations. The Social Security Board, for example, must use skills of a high order in winning co-operation from such states as find difficulty in accepting anything, excepting cash, that comes down to them from Washington.

But not only do these federal agencies use the community organization process in their individual relationships, but also, collectively, they apply it in ways which present interesting illustrations. For example, the Interdepartmental Committee to Co-ordinate Health and Welfare Activities functions in specific situations in a manner which in some ways resembles the procedure of a council of social agencies at work on a local problem. . . .

Turning from the governmental to the voluntary agencies on the national level we find the same pattern of relationships in effect. A single national organization such as the Family Welfare Association of America has its problems of maintaining constituency and support horizontally, with individuals and foundations, as well as vertically, with its member agencies; it has opportunities, and often the necessity, to work with other national agencies in a council type of relationship similar to that found on the local level; and it reaches downward into the localities of its member agencies with a variety of activities which certainly fall within the scope of our interest, using techniques of organization and social planning generically of a piece with those employed locally. There are countless variations, of course, in the way national agencies conduct themselves in working out these relationships, but fundamentally they are all practitioners of the process we are talking about.

Here in the national private field also, a certain degree of co-operation and correlation is worked out between agencies through the council device. Three of the most important national councils may be described briefly.

First, there is the National Social Work Council whose membership consists of individuals representing twenty-eight national associations. Its purpose is stated to be: "To provide a means through which those responsible for nationally organized social work, either as volunteers or as professional social workers, may more readily exchange information. . . ." Second is the National Health Council, whose member agencies number thirteen. Its purpose is: "To co-ordinate the activities of its member organizations; to carry on joint projects in the field of public health. . . ." A third is the National Education-Recreation Council consisting of representation from twenty-one national agencies organized into "an informal conference body to exchange information and study common problems in the leisure-time field." . . .

Now let us look at one or two illustrations of the way private and governmental agencies on the national level come together for joint conference and planning. The promotion of the National Health Program in 1938 is a case in point. According to one account of this development,

> a National Health Conference was held . . . delegates representing professional organizations, health and welfare workers, public officials, and representatives of labor, farm organizations, organized women's groups, the press, and the consuming public generally. Before this body was laid detailed findings of the National Health Inventory. . . . The Interdepartmental Committee submitted to the Conference a program of five tentative recommendations. . . . Delegates to the Conference were asked to discuss the recommendations, and to report facts and findings to the organizations they represented.[2]

Another example is the White House Conference on Children in a Democracy. . . . Here again, although the sponsorship was governmental, the participation was both official and nonofficial. Approximately 150 persons shared, as consultants, in the preparation of the reports which were brought before the Conference for action. Many of these were leaders in the private field. This conference represented community organization on a national scale, with boundaries of public and private activity forgotten as the conferees occupied common ground on a common problem.

And here we plant our eighth and final bench mark in this rather sketchy survey of the range of community organization: *Community organization is practiced in the "community" of the nation by public and private agencies individually and collectively, even as on lesser jurisdictional levels. And laymen participate in the process here as elsewhere.*

Summarizing, then, we find the community organization process being used for social welfare purposes on all jurisdictional levels, by single agencies and among groups of agencies; and we also find it employed between levels in a variety of relationships. This interpretation, setting the limits of the full range of community organization in areas far removed from the locality, may not be acceptable to many who would construe the term more narrowly. To some of us, however, the identification of needs for social programs, the formulation and establishment of such programs, and the gearing of them into the social and societal structure, whether on a local, state, or national front, appear as one process despite the fact that its techniques are given a variety of specific applications. It is a function of planning and implementation of services, of correlation of agencies with each other and with their respective "communities" (not always compact geographical areas), which finds expression wherever welfare work is engaged in. It is a two-way process, depending largely on democratic procedures for its effec-

---

[2] Thomas Parran, "Public Health," *Social Work Year Book*, 1939, p. 334.

tiveness and including both lay and professional persons among its practitioners.

If this view of the wide range of community organization is valid, it follows that any study of method which may be undertaken by this conference or by other groups should be equally broad and should include analyses of the social planning experiences of all types of agencies in all settings. From such a study there might be expected to emerge a body of principles and standards to guide future practitioners, wherever they may be at work in the social welfare field.

7

Methods and Skills in Community Organization[1]

By ARLIEN JOHNSON

The series of *Social Work Year Book* articles on community organization constitute an important addition to the literature. Most of them are primarily careful summaries of current facts, developments, and opinions.

However, in the *Year Book* article for 1945, by Arlien Johnson, there is a discussion of methods and skills that has so much freshness, insight, and originality that it seems appropriate to include it here.

Arlien Johnson, Ph.D., dean of the Graduate School of Social Work of the University of Southern California since 1939, has a background of graduate study in New York and Chicago, practical experience, and teaching. She has long been recognized as one of the national leaders in the area of community organization as well as public welfare, and her contributions to professional literature have been unusually thoughtful and provocative.

. . . THE APPLICATION of the sociological concept of process means that community organization in social work is concerned with ongoing, dynamic, changing manifestations of interaction. The fact that this activity is limited to social welfare services relieves the community

[1] Excerpted from article, "Community Organization in Social Work," *Social Work Year Book,* 1945 (New York: Russell Sage Foundation, 1945), pp. 93-95. By permission of the publisher.

organization worker of the sociologist's purpose of complete integration of *all* phases of organized social life within a "community." And finally, the process of community organization, it becomes clear, may be carried on in a variety of settings.

If community organization in social work is a process, as are casework and group work, then we may conclude that its content is the interaction of people in defined situations where a professional service is offered by a social worker. The nature of the professional service and the knowledge, principles, and skills upon which it rests are the subject of this article.

The Common Foundation for the Basic Methods

If we mean by method a special form of procedure which embodies knowledge, principles, and skills, we can discern a common foundation for the methods we call social casework, social group work, and community organization in social work. The foundation rests primarily on psychology, psychiatry, sociology, and related sciences which give an understanding of individual, group, and collective behavior, and of the social institutions that have developed therefrom. From them we learn the principles that govern individual growth and societal growth. Bertha Reynolds has pointed out that the essential characteristics of "scientifically oriented" modern social work include (a) an understanding of the material with which it deals; namely, human beings and the social situations in which the social worker finds them; (b) an acceptance of the objective reality of forces outside social work with which it must co-operate; this enables the social worker to make his services "contribute to and not inhibit what people can do for themselves in their social world"; and (c) the use of the relationship between the personality of the social worker and that of the persons worked with in a professional way, "that is, with mutual confidence and co-operation, with conscious upbuilding of self-respect, with rigorous discipline of the worker's self in order that freed from personal preoccupation, he may give his best skills in service."

Although too little attention has been given consciously to the application of these principles to community organization work, it is evident that certain practices related to them have developed from trial and error experience. Fact finding as a basis for action, and community studies to help in social welfare planning, are examples of aids to understanding people, social situations, and the social institutions surrounding them. Too often, however, these have become ends in themselves rather than devices to further a dynamic process from which "organization" results. Furthermore, the most enduring community organization work has been developed on the second principle above—that collective as well as individual growth is a relative matter, that accomplishment should be gauged by the extent to which the worker has helped a community to utilize its potential capacities for co-operation. Unfortunately, disregard of this principle has led to a somewhat static concept of an ideal of *a* social welfare program for every community, to be attained by manipulation and persuasion if necessary.

But a method is more than a body of knowledge and principles. The essence of it is in the application of knowledge and principles to an activity in such a way that change takes place, in the most effective manner. This is skill, and is described by Virginia Robinson as "the capacity to set in motion and control a process of change in specific material in such a way that the change that takes place in the material is effected with the greatest degree of consideration for and utilization of the quality and capacity of the material." Each profession has its own combination of skills.

When we examine the skills that are common to social casework, social group work, and community organization work, we are led into the whole content of professional education. Perhaps it is sufficient here merely to state that skill cannot be standardized, that it involves the capacity of the worker as well as the subject, and that the aim of training is to help the worker co-ordinate "hand, eye, self, and object." Skill finds expression, however, in ways in which (a) rapport is established; (b) people are helped to release feelings and to overcome resistance; (c) they are helped to grow in personal and social understanding and to be motivated toward desirable social goals; (d) they are enabled to clarify ideas and to express their own goals; ways in which (e) knowledge of social welfare needs, resources, and programs is made known to people for their use; (f) unity and integration of thinking as a basis for action are attained; and (g) movement toward a goal is sustained.

Characteristics Peculiar to Community Organization Method

In addition to other sciences, the community organization worker draws heavily upon sociology for an understanding of forms of human association in groups. He finds illuminating the theories relating to culture, social change, and cultural lag. Social interaction in its various forms, both associative and dissociative, must be understood. A knowledge of forms and means of social control is pertinent. The community organization worker is thus aided in diagnosing a community social welfare situation, and in knowing what he is dealing with and what action is needed to stimulate and supplement the community's own potential activity in the situation.[2]

---

[2] "Community is used as a convenient term to refer to a group of people gathered together in any geographical area, large or small, who have common interests, actually or potentially recognized, in the social welfare field. According to the interpretation proposed above for community organization process and method, the meaning of community is unimportant except for working purposes—

The community organization process is very complex. It involves individual, group, and intergroup relationships. In a given locality the community organization worker always finds a particular set of customs, ideals, and mores, some of which may be in conflict with the locality. The social values of one group may differ widely from those of another, as where different nationality and racial groups live side by side. It may be difficult, therefore, to help the community achieve what Sanderson calls a "common definition of the situation"; or, in other words, to agree upon facts and their significance. Maladjustments in community life, which are usually the starting point for community organization in social work, may be unrecognized and therefore nonexistent as far as the people there are concerned. Until a consciousness of need is aroused, nothing can be accomplished. A variation in degree and extent of awareness of problems among different economic, political, or social groups may make progress very uneven and slow. A first principle, therefore, is to know the community, both structurally and functionally, so that its individuality is clear, and its "growth potential" can be analyzed. A corollary of this principle is that the objectives of the community social welfare program should be determined by it with the help of the professional worker. The latter's function is to facilitate participation, stimulate movement and progress within the group, and bring to bear technical information about social welfare programs. He must leave the people of the community free, however, to make their own decisions.

Some of the skills that might be considered peculiar to community organization work can be only briefly indicated. (1) One of these is the maintenance of many relationships with individuals and groups, simultaneously and often independently of one another, because individuals and groups may be fearful or hostile to one another and yet may all be engaged upon solution of a common problem. (2) Another skill is the use of professional judgment in timing the drawing into contact of these relationships, after the worker has been able to resolve or modify the issues between them by an individual approach. (3) Yet to be more precisely defined is the skill involved in knowing where to take hold and when to let go of a project. Sanderson points out the importance of selecting initially an activity in whose accomplishment people will find satisfaction "not only in the ends attained but in the experience of working together to attain them." Otto Gilmore stresses maintenance of direction and timing as a basic skill and states, "Timing has also to do with the selection of a terminal or slackening-off point, when the job is done or when it is considered that the community has gone as far as it can" until a period is allowed for assimilation. In the

---

it can be defined and redefined as new projects are undertaken. Just as "person" describes a class within which are all types, sizes, ages, and so forth, so "community" is a general term.

present stage of our understanding of method, it is often easier to set
the community organization process in motion than it is to guide and
direct it constructively. (4) Last to be mentioned but permeating the
whole process is skill in group thinking. Just as the interview is the
primary tool in social casework, so the committee is the device in community organization work by which the worker initiates and furthers
the larger area of interaction. Group thinking is not peculiar to community organization but is a basic skill in social group work. The difference in application is that in community organization the group is often
representative of other groups; hence the potential conflict present in
intergroup problem solving may complicate the group thinking process.
Auxiliary tools which can be only mentioned are research or fact finding, and education or interpretation. . . .

8

When Is Community Organization Social Work Practice?[1]

By KENNETH L. M. PRAY

Kenneth L. M. Pray (1882–1948), dean of the Pennsylvania School of Social Work from 1922 until his death, was one of the most creative philosophical thinkers and one of the most eloquent speakers and writers of the social workers of his generation.

The following paper, his last address before the National Conference of Social Work, is one of his ablest contributions, and it has been greatly admired and widely quoted. In it Mr. Pray states his basic philosophical approach and his conceptions of social work and community organization and of their relationships to each other.

He stresses the role of the community organization practitioner as an "enabler," though he does not use that precise term; and he lays down three conditions under which, he believes, community organization may be social work practice. The paper is lucid and closely reasoned, and is expressed in the vigorous and telling phrases that characterized Kenneth Pray's rounded and almost oratorical style.

There is much that is controversial in the content, but whether one agrees or disagrees with all of the writer's conclusions, he must respect the honesty of his thinking and the forcefulness and persuasiveness of his presentation.

[1] Excerpted from paper of the same title, *Proceedings, National Conference of Social Work, San Francisco,* 1947 (New York: Columbia University Press, 1948), pp. 194-204. By permission of National Conference on Social Welfare. Included also in the author's collected papers, *Social Work in a Revolutionary Age and Other Papers* (Philadelphia: University of Pennsylvania Press, 1949), pp. 274-287.

THIS SUBJECT TOUCHES issues far broader and deeper than those concerned only with the technical nature and content of community organization. It throws open to question and to serious re-examination some of the most venerable and universal assumptions underlying the whole development of social work. In the accumulated professional lore and literature of the last twenty-five years, all social work, like all of ancient Gaul, has by general consent been divided into three parts— three basic areas or types of practice—social casework, social group work, and community organization. By the same token, practitioners in all three of these basic areas, it appears, are members of a single inclusive profession of social work. This assumes that this whole profession, like every profession, is united by certain common responsibilities —by a common concern for the treatment of certain defined needs and problems; by a common body of special knowledge applicable to these problems; by certain common specific and defined objectives in relation to them; by a common core of basic processes, methods, and skills appropriate to the attainment of these objectives; and by a common philosophy binding all these professional ingredients together into a single consistent whole.

The question really asks, therefore, not merely when, but whether, at all, community organization practice is integrally related to the common content of problem, philosophy, knowledge, objective, and method which characterizes social work practice as a generic whole—whether, in fact, we are really one profession or, perhaps, two or more related professions. The answer to that question clearly depends upon what we mean by generic social work practice, in the first place, and by community organization practice, in the second. Since there is no generally accepted definition of either social work or community organization— despite all the ardent and able efforts, past and present, that have gone into the search for such definitions—I am under the painful necessity of formulating at the beginning the concepts upon which my own discussion will be based. I am keenly aware that this is a matter of strictly personal choice. But we must start somewhere, and this is where I begin.

What, then, are the essentials of social work practice as a generic whole? What are the kinds of problem with which it deals? What are the specific objectives it seeks? What are its basic methods and skills? What is the philosophy on which it operates?

One of the difficulties we face in defining the area of general social practice, in terms of the kinds of problem with which it deals, is our use of the broad and general term "social" as the only qualifying adjective to designate our specific area of service. The word "social" has none of the precision of such words as "medical" or "legal," for instance, by which other areas of professional practice are defined. It is obviously not enough to say that social work treats "social" problems. For practically every life problem of every individual in this modern world is, in reality, a "social" problem, in one sense or another, and practically every organized undertaking in the world is a "social" enterprise, in the sense that it involves and affects the social life and relationships of people. It is clear that not all these "social" interests and involvements of human beings can lie within the province of a single profession.

Nor does the addition of the word "welfare" to the word "social" do much to clarify or to bound the area of our professional effort. For, in the ordinary and logical use of language, the term "welfare" in this connection denotes only a general purpose of action, which we as a profession share with many other professions and groups in the community, but which we certainly do not monopolize. For, whenever, in the course of daily living, people feel the need and the impulse to apply some sort of deliberate direction to otherwise intuitive social developments, with the conscious purpose of making them serve more fully or more directly the needs of human beings in their social relationships, "social welfare" enterprises come into being. They may take any form, they may be concerned with any aspect of social experience, they may seek to deal with any one or many of the social problems people face. By this reasonable test, the church, the school, the court, the hospital, the labor union, and even industry itself—when motivated and managed with a view to the fuller satisfaction of human social interests—are "social welfare" enterprises. But they are not in themselves "social work" enterprises.

Social work can and does appear, however, in any of these institutions or in any other part of the social setting—and this is the crux of the definition I propose—whenever, in pursuit of a "social welfare" purpose, effort is applied specifically and directly to facilitating the actual process by which people are enabled and assisted to use these instrumentalities or any of the other social relations open to them, for the more effectual fulfillment of their own social well-being, within the framework of a stable society. The problems, then, with which social work deals are not problems of social structure, as such, nor of individual personality, as such. They are not definable in terms of particular sets of circumstances or of particular forces or qualities, either in the social environment or in people themselves, that may obstruct or frustrate satisfying and fruitful social living. They are the problems which people find in the actual process of adjustment to each other or to any part or aspect of their social environment. That is to say, they are problems of relationships.

The common, specific objectives of social work practice must, of course, be related to these focal problems. Its central objective, then, is to facilitate the actual process of social adjustment of individual people, through the development and constructive use of social relationships within which these human beings can find their own fulfillment and can discharge adequately their social responsibilities. This objective may be sought through helping individuals and groups of individuals to find satisfying and fruitful relations to and within the social realities in which they are at the time involved. On the other hand, it may be sought through facilitating the adaptation and modification of the larger environmental arrangements and relationships upon which satisfying social adjustment of all human beings depends. Commonly, both these avenues to the ultimate objective may be used at one and the same time. In any case, the objective always remains the same—not in any particular product or form of adjustment, but in the process of adjustment itself. The objective is not to make over either the environment or the people involved in it, but rather to introduce and sustain a process of dealing with the problems of social relationship and social adjustment, which will enable and assist those involved in the problems to find solutions satisfying to themselves and acceptable to the society of which they are a part.

The philosophy of social work shines forth in these objectives. It rests upon a profound faith in human beings, in their inherent and inviolable right to choose and to achieve their own destiny, through social relations of their own making, within the essential framework of a stable and progressive society. It rests upon a deep appreciation of the validity and the value to society as a whole, of these individual differences in human beings. It conceives of social unity and progress as the outcome of the integration, not the suppression or conquest, of these differences. Accordingly, it tests all social arrangements and institutions by their impact upon individual lives, by their capacity to utilize for the common good the unique potentialities of individual human beings, through relationships that enlist their active and productive participation. It is, in short, a genuinely and consistently democratic philosophy.

Social work methods and skills exemplify this philosophy in action. Social work, always and everywhere, is, in the first place, a helping, not a controlling, function. It applies always the methods of co-operation, not of manipulation. It offers a service, to be used by others if they need and want to use it; it does not use others, or treat others, for the attainment of its own ends. Because its objectives are always focused in the creation and maintenance of constructive relationships, its own methods and skills are focused in its own capacity for, and use of, a co-operative and helping relationship. Because its service is focused in facilitating a process of adjustment, rather than in the attainment of a specific product or end, its own methods and skills and disciplines are focused in the management of its own process, in the maintenance of a sensitive awareness of what is happening to everybody in that process and of how the worker's own participation is affecting the feeling and interest of all the rest and their expression in participative action. Because of the democratic philosophy on which the whole operation rests —because of the worker's awareness that responsibility for the outcome rests with others, not with himself—his method and skill are consistently addressed to freeing and enlisting the honest, voluntary, responsible contribution of feeling, understanding, experience, and purpose of each and every person involved in the relationship, and the honest, objective, appreciative use of these contributions in a process of integration. Always mindful of the decisive responsibility of others for ultimate choice and decision, the social worker, nevertheless, contributes his own professional difference—in the clarification of alternatives and their potential consequences, in the analysis of the factors that enter into the choice, and in the evaluation of those elements, in relation to the ultimate objective, in terms of available resources, and in the light of a broader specialized experience in dealing with similar problems.

The core of these processes, methods, and skills of generic social work practice is obviously in the disciplined use of one's self in direct relations with people, both individually and in groups. All else is secondary and incidental and assumes significance only as it eventuates in the more effectual performance of the worker in that direct relationship.

There is, however, one unique and decisive factor in the setting within which the social worker operates, which profoundly affects his use of himself in the helping relationship. That is the fact that he is the representative of a social agency, which determines, by its own choice of purpose and service and policy, the limits within which the worker serves. The agency, in relation to our present subject, has two vital effects upon method and process. In the first place, it introduces into the development of individual and group relationships and purposes the stake of the larger community in the outcome, the basic social structure within which these lesser relationships must find their place. The agency represents that stable social whole with which individuals and groups must find their own adjustment, with which they must come to terms, if they are to avail themselves of its help. In the second place, it sustains and protects the worker in the helpful, noncontrolling use of himself in relation with others, exacting from him disciplined restraint upon the undue exercise of his own will and power, either in understanding or feeling, and upon the undue expression of his own interest, judgment, and purpose, in the choice of ends or means. Thus, the agency conserves the basic democratic quality of the helping relationship, while at the same time sustaining the essential framework of a stable democratic society.

This, then, at long last, is generic social work practice as I conceive it. In summary: It deals with *problems* not of the social environment, as such, nor of human personalities, as such, but with the problems of relationship between them. Its objective is not in changes of social structure or of personality but in improvement and facilitation of the actual process by which people are enabled to find, sustain, and use constructive social relationships. Its methods and skills are encompassed in a disciplined capacity to initiate, sustain, and use a direct helping relationship with people, based upon a sensitive, alert awareness of the meaning and effect of one's own feeling, thought, and action, and that of other persons, in the development of the co-operative process that is going on between them, and based, also, upon a clear acceptance of the limits of his own role and responsibility, as determined by the function of the agency he represents. Finally, social work is guided and enlivened by a democratic philosophy which recognizes the right and the responsibility of individuals to manage their own lives, but always within the framework of a democratically organized and democratically controlled social whole.

Now, what is the relation of community organization practice to this generic social work as we have defined it? Do the problems, the objectives, the methods and skills, the dominating philosophy, of community organization fall within these general boundaries?

If we define community organization in its broadest sense, as a recent writer has done, as "deliberately directed effort to assist groups in attaining unity of purpose and action . . . in behalf of either general or special objectives," [2] it is clear that a substantial part of community organization falls even outside the broader field of "social welfare," of which the whole of social work is an integral part. But it is also clear that another substantial part, whose function has been described in a recent report as that of creating and maintaining "a progressively more effective adjustment between social welfare resources and social welfare needs," [3] certainly belongs within the "social welfare" field. But does this practice of community organization for a "social welfare" purpose conform to our criteria of generic social work practice?

So far as its scope has been defined in terms of the focal problems with which its practice is concerned, it seems to me clear that there is a steadily advancing agreement among its practitioners and leaders that those problems, like the basic subject matter of social work as a whole, center definitely in social relationships as such, as distinct from any particular set of circumstances or any particular forces or sources of difficulty, either in the social environment or in the human personality. One cannot conceive of "social needs" without thinking of people in social relationships; one cannot conceive of "adjusting social resources to social needs" without recognizing that the basic problem with which one is dealing is that of relationships between people. If one chooses to accept Wilber Newstetter's original conception of community organiza-

[2] Wayne McMillen, "Community Organization in Social Work," *Social Work Year Book,* 1947, Russell H. Kurtz, ed. (New York: Russell Sage Foundation, 1947), p. 110.

[3] Arthur Dunham, "The Literature of Community Organization," *Proceedings, National Conference of Social Work* (New York: Columbia University Press, 1940), p. 413.

tion as "intergroup work," the case for identifying its basic problems with those of generic social work is even more convincing.

But what are its specific objectives in dealing with these problems? Is community organization practice concerned specifically with facilitating the process of social adjustment, or is it directed to the attainment of more tangible and specific ends? It is clear, I think, that we approach more debatable ground when we face this question. Despite the growth of articulated theory which identifies the objective of community organization with the characteristic objectives we have ascribed to generic social work, there remain two obstacles to the realization of this theory in actual practice. In the first place, community organization is often dissociated from actual service of specific individuals or groups; that is, the needs to which it is addressed are frequently outside the immediate experience or sphere of responsibility of those who are involved in the community organizing process and relationship. It is easy, therefore, for both promoters and participants in the process to find their satisfaction and sense of achievement in the creation of a well-articulated, symmetrical, deftly organized structure and mechanism rather than in the process of helping individual people fulfill their own social needs, to which that structure and mechanism are ostensibly and truly dedicated. There is nothing discreditable in this kind of satisfaction. We all share it in some measure. But it does dissociate the activity which it dominates from what we have called the province of social work. For social work, if we are right about it, is expressly and exclusively concerned with helping people find satisfying social adjustment to and through their social institutions and relationships. Its true objective is in facilitating this process of adjustment. Its only concern with social organization, as such, is to introduce and sustain through that organization the relationships and processes which actually do facilitate that adjustment.

The second source of possible doubt about the identification of the specific objectives of community organization with those of generic social work is in the fact that the process of organization often follows rather than precedes the choice of goals. In the planning stage, before organization itself really begins, not only is the problem likely to be identified and defined, but a diagram of the specific outcome to be achieved is likely to emerge, and the achievement of this outcome, then, can easily become the criterion of the success of the whole undertaking. From this point forward, organization can center in the objective of obtaining acceptance and realization of the particular plan—that is, the attainment of a preconceived product of organization—rather than in the process of helping the community to identify and appreciate the need, to choose a suitable means of filling the need, and to muster its strength to achieve this self-determined goal.

In this respect, community organization faces precisely the same hazards that have beset social casework and social group work from the beginning, and which they have only recently and only partially mastered. The old formula, for instance, of "investigation, diagnosis, and treatment," so long revered in social casework, as the basis of a presumably scientific and systematic professional process, carries with it the same threat to make a preconceived plan or end—chosen, it is true, prayerfully and sincerely out of superior professional vision and understanding—the decisive objective and ultimate criterion of achievement in the life of the client rather than the freeing and helping of the client to choose and achieve his own end. The same threat pursues the social group worker, whose effort can easily be diverted from facilitating the process of group development and growth, to the operation of a particular program of group activity which seems to the professional leader the most suitable and satisfying for a particular group in a particular setting. Community organizers, if they are to achieve the fruits of their service within the framework of social work, have to guard themselves against this same insidious temptation to choose for the community a plan which the organizer then proceeds to carry through.

It is obvious, I think, that here, as elsewhere in social work, the choice of objectives reflects the acceptance of a basic philosophy, which in turn comes to expression in process, method, and skill. The philosophy underlying social work practice, we have declared, is definitely and wholly a democratic philosophy. On that principle it cannot compromise. It may grope and fumble in its quest for insight and strength to realize all its implications. And it faces, always, the basic problem of democratic life—the integration of the knowledge and skill of the expert with the broad and varied experience of the mass of men, in the process of democratic decision and action—but it holds firmly to the fundamental concept that in the making of such decisions the "expert must always be on tap, never—almost never—on top." The community organizer, whose primary client, it may be said, is the whole community, faces this problem in more acute and potent form than any of the rest of us, for he is dealing with powerful, discordant forces that take even a longer time to become integrated, than do those in individuals and face-to-face groups. He has to believe and to remember, constantly, that the community is the master of its own destiny; that it has the right to make its own mistakes; that it also has within itself a reservoir of infinitely varied insights and strengths of all its members, which must find outlet in the formulation and achievement of its own purpose, if the genius of democracy and its special values are to be conserved and fulfilled.

It is when we turn to the methods and processes of community organization, and the skills it requires, that the haze of uncertainty and ambiguity as to its relationship with generic social work becomes most difficult to dispel. This is not surprising, in view of the relatively brief time within which these problems have been subjected to systematic study. There is, however, undoubtedly developing an ever-widening acceptance of a basic concept of method and skill in this area of practice which identifies it positively with that which dominates other areas of social work, namely, the worker's capacity to initiate and sustain a direct helping relationship with individual people and groups of people. The use of such method and skill is obviously modified and complicated by the fact that the individuals and groups with which the community organizer works are often representatives of other groups whom he may not directly or regularly meet, but of whose interests and feelings and purposes he must be alertly aware. But his relationship to those groups is, nevertheless, from this point of view, ultimately dependent most directly upon the way in which he uses himself in his relations with their individual representatives.

There is, however, at least one historical and contemporary manifestation of a contrary concept of what constitutes the basic process, method, and skill in community organization, which tends to separate and distinguish it from what we have described as generic social work practice. That is the concept which places heavy emphasis upon the methods and skills necessarily involved in research, administration, planning, and interpretation, as factors in the professional equipment of the community organizer. There is little doubt in my own mind that all these processes, in their best estate, involve not a little of the same self-awareness and sensitivity to others in a relationship which we have described as the dominant attributes of sound method and skill in all social work. There is nothing inherently incompatible between these skills and the basic skill of social work. But the danger signal, in relation to the question under discussion, must be hoisted, because of the way in which, in the literature as well as in practice, they are apparently separated and dissociated one from another. Research, planning, administration, and interpretation are frequently assumed to be concerned only with things, with facts, with ideas, rather than with people; they are made to appear as products of some sort of occult, private operation, apart from any process that goes on in relationship with others. Then they are made to assume such importance in the total equipment and activity of the community organizer as to overshadow the primary social work process, method, and skill of using one's self in direct personal and group relations. They are thought to require an utterly different kind of person, subject to a different kind of discipline.

Indeed, one writer has recently suggested that the primary skill of developing and using constructive individual and group relationships is so imperfectly understood and is so largely dependent upon inherent personal quality rather than professional discipline, that what we have called the secondary skills and responsibilities of research, administration, planning, and interpretation must continue, apparently, to determine the major equipment of the community organizer. Yet the same writer remarks that the development of the professional process of community organization in social work has placed increasing emphasis, "not upon the attainment of immediate objectives, but upon methods of strengthening the intergroup process."[4] How is that "intergroup process" going to be strengthened, through professional intervention, except by the disciplined command of one's professional self in direct relationships with individuals and groups?

In summary, then, I conclude that community organization practice is social work practice, that its practitioners can share in the development of a single profession of social work, on three conditions: (1) if and when their focal concerns and their primary objectives relate always to the development and guidance of the process by which people find satisfying and fruitful social relationships, and not to the attainment of specific, preconceived products or forms of relationship; (2) if and when these objectives are sought consistently through the realization of a democratic philosophy and faith which respects the right and the responsibility of communities, as of individuals, to create their own satisfying relationships, and to use those relationships to their own chosen ends; and (3) if and when the basic processes, methods, and skills that are demanded and employed in actual practice are those that inhere in the worker's capacity to initiate and sustain a helping, not a controlling, relationship with individuals and groups.

All of this demands extraordinary faith—faith in people, in their capacity, individually and in the mass, to discover and to fulfill their own needs, and, above all, faith in a helping process itself, as a medium through which people individually, in groups, in intergroup relationships, and in the mass, can, if they will, discover their own purposes and powers, face their actual alternatives, appraise their potential consequences, and muster their resources to choose and achieve their own appropriate ends. It requires, also, the kind of faith and the kind of feeling that finds its highest satisfaction in facilitating the achievement of others rather than in the exercise of personal power. It demands faith, also, that progress in a democratic society must have democratic roots as well as democratic trunk and branches.

This is the faith on which social work as an integral whole is founded, and which it has justified by works of unquestioned validity and significance in our society. If community organization actually demands and expresses that same faith in its daily operations, it is, indeed, a part—a vital, constructive part—of social work practice.

---

[4] McMillen, *loc. cit.*

9

Community Organization and Planning [1]

By ARTHUR HILLMAN

"The methods by which communities deliberately change their structure and way of life" is the theme of Arthur Hillman's volume on *Community Organization and Planning*. He has approached the subject from a broad sociological point of view, and, more than any other one writer, he has emphasized the interplay and integration of "community planning" and "community organization."

The present passage indicates his approach to the subject, and suggests the nature of planning in a democratic society.

Arthur Hillman was chairman of the Department of Sociology at Roosevelt College, Chicago, from 1946 to 1955 when he became dean of the College of Arts and Sciences while continuing also as professor of sociology. He has had many contacts with social work, including staff service with the federal Office of Community War Services during World War II and later with the Council of Social Agencies of Chicago.

COMMUNITY ORGANIZATION is found wherever people have learned to live together. In simple societies it rests upon customs or traditional ways of regulating social relationships. . . . The inertia of habit and custom is a conservative force in modern society, which must be taken into account in any analysis of social changes. However, in

[1] Excerpted from *Community Organization and Planning* (New York: The Macmillan Company, 1950), pp. vii-ix; 35-36. By permission of The Macmillan Company.

industrial, urban society, which is characteristic of contemporary life, many evidences of conscious social reconstruction are found. Such methods of effecting change are deviations from the traditional organization of community life. The methods by which communities deliberately change their structure and way of life is the theme of this book.

Community organization is a necessary condition of conscious co-operation for local planning and for other forms of common action. This concept of community organization is used inclusively to indicate not only social structures within which co-operative activities take place but also the various processes of social interaction which indicate that the forms have functional meaning for the people involved. This aspect of life in contemporary communities can be better understood if placed in relation to other changes that have taken place, and by contrast with the organization of simple local societies, as the first two chapters will indicate.

The concepts of community organization and planning are interlocked. Planning may be broader in scope than the community, but its essentials can be illustrated by organized local action. Planning in its local aspects is an activity of organized and representative community bodies that can act on behalf of the whole community or major segments of it. It is essentially a matter of deliberately selecting goals and systematically implementing them. Since we are concerned here with American communities, we proceed on the assumption that the efforts at community organization and planning are to be directed toward democratic ends and are to be accomplished by democratic means. Democracy as a value means that community organization and planning are carried on in the interests of the people of the community and are based upon the participation of the people generally in the making of the decisions.

The enlarging interest in community organization and planning, which is demonstrated by the marked attention it is getting in many quarters, stems basically from certain broad developments in national life. Among these is the experience gained in the last war which can be applied to peacetime problems of community co-operation. During the war many American communities met emergency problems with boldness and vigor. There was then a special concern about the internal health of democratic society, and more specifically a need to plan community services to meet wartime demands. Some community leaders now seem to recognize that what was defensive community action can become an offensive against the unresolved problems of democracy in peace.

The centralization of government activities has increased during the last few decades at the expense of traditionally local functions. Much as conservatives may wish to reverse the trend toward enlarged federal control, this does not seem likely to occur in the face of the complex and large-scale organization of our economic life. The tremendous potentials of electrical power and atomic energy developments also point to unmistakable trends toward national and regional political and economic organization. However, the role of local communities can be re-evaluated in relation to the common interests and the meeting of needs that arise locally. Even with assistance from federal and state governments or other agencies, there are many urgent problems that require understanding and action within the community.

The diversity and specialization of organized groups and community agencies, especially in large cities, often create in their leaders and professional workers a sense of fragmentation of efforts. This is frequently the immediate impetus to undertaking programs of community organization and joint planning in order that the specialized activities may become integrated in a co-ordinated program. School officials, recreation workers, public administrators generally, ministers and other professional people have tended to become more conscious of the community setting of their programs and the need for public interpretation and support. In the social work field, where the term community organization has a somewhat specialized meaning, interest has also developed in broader citizen participation and in more comprehensive social planning.

Planning as a Process

Planning is a new name for an old activity. Men have taken thought of tomorrow wherever individuals or groups have exercised prudence or common sense. They have done so largely as a matter of course. Such looking ahead can also be done systematically. It is the new needs and opportunities for planning which justify the special attention which is being given to it. . . .

Planning is not something apart from other community activities. It is related to and inherent in the operation of various agencies and the actions of voluntary associations. Much but not all of community planning is under governmental auspices. Community planning may cover areas of varying size, and one of the problems noted in connection with planning in rural areas as well as in metropolitan regions is that no single governmental unit usually corresponds to the range of economic and social interdependence of the area.

This suggests some obvious limits in planning. Financial resources may be lacking, or governmental powers may not be adequate to cope with the problems. Even more basic is the citizen support and understanding which is essential in defining goals and in implementing planning decisions. Special emphasis is therefore given to citizen participation especially in policy formation.

Planning is a progressive, step-by-step process, not a visionary master blueprint of Utopia. Planning is never completed. It can be and, in democratic societies, it must be a democratic process where the technician and the layman each have distinctive and necessary roles to play.

10

Community Education in Action [1]

By COMMITTEE ON COMMUNITY ORGANIZATION, ADULT EDUCATION ASSOCIATION

"Community organization always serves as a highway; it is never a destination." This is one of the insights of the report on "Community Education in Action," prepared by the Committee on Community Organization of the American Association for Adult Education and published in 1948. Robert A. Luke, executive secretary of the Adult Education Council of Metropolitan Cincinnati, was chairman of the Committee.

Using the familiar concept of community organization as "something people do when they try to balance their community needs with their community resources," the report gives illustrations from specific communities, and emphasizes the contribution of adult education to community organization.

The whole report makes clear the large amount of common ground held by social work and adult education in their respective approaches to community organization.

As a co-operative way of getting things done, community organization has been used whenever people want to pool their resources and work toward an improvement in their way of living.

[1] Excerpted from *Community Education in Action: A Report on Community Organization and Adult Education* (New York: Association for Adult Education, 1948), pp. 5-9; also summaries from pp. 38-39 and 43-48; and excerpt, pp. 53-54. By permission of the publisher.

On the frontier, the pioneers organized to assist each other in clearing the land, in house raising, in protecting squatters' rights and in the sharing of life's necessities. The organization required to maintain essential services and provide opportunities for democratic participation varied in proportion to the requirements of each new situation.

On the contemporary scene, communities have organized for participation in total war, to insure the success of a Community Chest campaign, to carry out the purpose of agricultural extension, to elect new candidates to public office, to pressure for a veterans' hospital, improve the schools, and develop community recreation facilities.

The organization required to maintain present-day community life is far from simple. Often the forces which operate in the community receive their direction from some remote source. There is a limit to what a community or a state can do by itself to combat inflation, provide unemployment relief, adjust freight rates or wipe out slum housing. With the vast majority of American citizens placing hope in the United Nations as a way of avoiding war, the gap between the community and the forces which influence it becomes even wider.

In terms of definition, the community is any group of persons sharing a common geographical area and holding common interests. . . .

Obviously, no community is without some sort of organization. The community exists to support the school, church, store, and essential services such as police protection and public road maintenance. It provides an administrative framework within which organized groups can communicate with each other and establish identifiable boundaries for their activities.

Community groups sometimes pull in separate directions rather than in mutually agreed-upon directions. At other times only a small fraction of the individuals living in the community participate in any of the established community groups. Worth-while projects can fail—or never be thought of—if opportunities are denied individuals to talk their problems over together and do their planning together. The teen-age canteen cannot be successfully planned by adults for young people. The Youth Council cannot function effectively without the sympathetic help of responsible adults. A program of family life education needs the co-operation of the casework agencies, the group work programs, the educators and every other organized aspect of community life. An intelligent decision as to the site for a new library, the need for a county health department, the desirability of a local labor-management committee or a series of neighborhood forums on the UN, requires thoughtful participation on the part of all people who have a stake in the community.

In each community there are many areas of essential community interest—government, commerce, health, recreation, education, welfare. Sometimes the enthusiasm brought to any one of these special areas of community interest overshadows the interrelationships that exist among them all; the planning done for specialized areas is not always done as a part of a total community-wide effort. For effective community growth, the already organized areas of interest must see the total needs of a community as well as their own needs. It is toward this kind of community-wide organization that we have directed greatest attention in this report.

Community-wide organization provides one sure way in which people can come together to think, plan, and act together. It provides a total community approach to community-wide problems. It involves the individual members of the community in surveying community needs and in creating community support as a prelude to community action. In this role, it is one of democracy's surest safeguards. It operates against the small, well-organized group that, convinced of the righteousness of its own cause, presumes to speak for all citizens. It provides opportunities for the most humble citizen to be a participant in making things happen in accordance with his own needs and wishes. Viewed in this light community organization always serves as a highway; it is never a destination. . . .

Community organization can be defined as something people do when they try to balance their community needs with their community resources. The people who come together for this purpose are those who live in a given area—block, neighborhood, farm community, or metropolitan area—and have some sense of "belonging" to that area.

In return for the effort organization requires, the individuals concerned hope to reward themselves and their neighbors with a better community in which to earn a living and raise a family.

On the basis of the community reports we have studied, the organization of a community seems to involve two things: (a) correlation or "interorganization" of the activities of many community agencies and groups; (b) active participation on the part of people in the solution of problems of common community concern.

Sometimes community organization is chiefly an interorganizational matter. Schools, churches, departments of local government, social services, clubs, and civic organizations get together to pool their resources. They plan and act collectively to meet urgent community needs that none can meet independently. Membership in such a group is often limited to the officers or official representatives of already organized groups.

In some instances community organization is predominantly an organization of people. This is often the case in sparsely populated rural areas where there are few already organized agencies and groups. To a limited extent this has also happened in sections of some large cities where an organization of residents in a block or neighborhood has been formed to help meet local needs.

Communities that have, on the surface at least, common problems and common goals may develop substantially different programs and structures. In the work of the agricultural extension service, where use has been made of occupational motives and program building in terms of everyday experience, a number of patterns for securing community co-operation have been developed. Extension personnel often assisted local citizens in setting up community planning groups. Representative of both agricultural and non-agricultural interests, these organizations survey community needs, co-ordinate existing resources, and marshal the forces of a united community for co-operative action.

Sometimes, community organization means a centralization of related community efforts. This is well illustrated by community planning for social welfare. Today, councils of social agencies, representative of all local social work agencies, carry on a continuous program of planning and research for the community's entire social work program.

In many instances, a good deal of the stimulus for, and aid to, community organization has come from sources outside of the immediate community. The Committee for Kentucky, for example, is taking the initiative in stimulating community organization in the blue grass state; the New York State Citizens Council, and the Georgia Citizens Council are similarly serving local communities in their respective states. In the Tennessee Valley the remarkable development of natural resources has been paralleled by an equally striking growth in community consciousness fostered by the Tennessee Valley Authority. . . .

From the twenty-six instances of community development noted in this report, five characteristics of community organization emerge. These are: (1) an increasing emphasis upon "wholeness"; (2) the effort to involve all members in making the decisions in which they have a stake; (3) the emphasis upon informed participation; (4) the range and variety of persons holding leader positions; and (5) the growing emphasis upon education. . . .

Adult education can help community organization—

improve the ability of the local citizens to identify their community needs.

improve the ability to identify resources.

improve techniques for group action.

improve the ways in which personal needs are met through community activities.

improve techniques for intergroup relations.

improve the ways in which basic information is made available to all citizens.

improve the techniques for continuous evaluation.

increase the general level of understanding in the community.

by supplying a reservoir of active participants in community organization. . . .

We see the large common ground of community organization and adult education. We also see there is some difference in emphasis—a difference of amount rather than of kind.

Community organization emphasizes the action process and gives chief attention to organized groups.

Adult education emphasizes the learning process and gives most attention to individuals and to informal groups.

Community organization is concerned with learning and with individuals but to a lesser degree than adult education. It must concentrate upon the strategy and tactics of achieving results directly related to community-wide projects.

Adult education wants its learnings to contribute to community action and it deals continuously with groups, but its focus is on the growth in learning by the individual.

Principles of Community Organization
—Introduction

AT LEAST TWO of the early writers on community organization, Bessie A. McClenahan and Jesse F. Steiner, attempted formulations of "principles" of community organization.[1]

In connection with one of the National Conference community organization study committee reports of 1940, Florence G. Cassidy, then of the staff of the Detroit Council of Social Agencies, formulated an exceedingly thoughtful statement of principles, which has served as an important point of reference for several subsequent writers.

A "principle," as we are using the term, refers to a "rule of 'right' action," or a value-judgment as to what is "sound" or "good" community organization. In this sense, "principle" is closely related to "standard." Obviously the "principles of community organization" formulated by citizens of a democracy will be likely to be in accordance with the general democratic ideology or value-system.

A "concept," as distinguished from a principle, is essentially a generalized idea: it may be a statement of fact or a descriptive hypothesis rather than a value-judgment. Two of the four following excerpts include both concepts and principles.

Three of the selections are taken from C. F. McNeil's article on community organization in the *Social Work Year Book,* 1954; from Ray Johns and David F. DeMarche's textbook on *Community Organization and Agency Responsibility,* and from Florence Cassidy's 1940 statement on *Principles of Community Organization.* The final excerpt from *Community Organization, Theory and Principles,* by Murray G. Ross, is one of the most recent formulations of principles that has appeared, as well as one of the most systematic.

---

[1] Bessie A. McClenahan, *Organizing the Community* (New York: Century Company, 1922), Chs. V and VIII. Jesse F. Steiner, *Community Organization* (New York: Century Company, 1925), Ch. XXIII. This chapter is not included in the revised edition of 1930.

104

11

Some Principles and Concepts of Community Organization

C. F. McNeil is the executive director of the Health and Welfare Council of Philadelphia, Delaware, and Montgomery Counties, Pennsylvania. He was formerly director of the School of Social Administration of Ohio State University.

Ray Johns is general secretary of the Boston YMCA as well as a lecturer on community organization in several institutions. He was formerly national director of Field Operations of the United Service Organizations. He is the author of two books, *The Co-operative Process Among National Agencies* and *Executive Responsibility,* as well as monographs, papers, and articles on various aspects of social welfare.

David F. DeMarche's experience includes work in a small community, a metropolitan district, and a five-state area. He has also done considerable community research including a study of youth work in postwar Germany, as well as some teaching. Formerly director of Community Organization and Research, United Service Organizations, New York City, he is currently associate director, Task Force on Community Resources, of the Joint Commission on Mental Illness and Health.

Florence G. Cassidy is director of the Nationality Department of United Community Services of Metropolitan Detroit. One of the chief functions of this Department, according to Miss Cassidy, is that of "drawing nationality communities into fuller partnership and participation in the organized civic, social work, and educational activities of the Detroit Metropolitan Area as a whole."

Murray G. Ross is a vice-president of the University of Toronto and professor of social work. In the chapters from which his excerpts are taken the principles stated here are discussed in detail.

Principles in Community Organization for Social Welfare [1]

By C. F. MCNEIL

FROM THE EXPERIENCE of many agencies have emerged certain accepted principles which seem universally applicable.

1. Community organization for social welfare is concerned with people and their needs. Its objective is to enrich human life by bringing about and maintaining a progressively more effective adjustment between social welfare resources and social welfare needs.

2. The community is the primary client in community organization for social welfare. The community may be a neighborhood, city, county, state or nation. Rapidly, too, there has emerged the international community. The factor of interdependence of people and groups living and working together becomes the source of problems with which community organization concerns itself and the force from which it derives the motivation and power necessary to bring about solutions to the problems.

3. It is an axiom in community organization that the community is to be understood and accepted as it is and where it is. Understanding the climate in which community organization process is taking place is essential if seeds of that process are to bear fruit. The professional worker in community organization for social welfare is no more concerned with changing the community's "personality" than is the social caseworker in altering the individual's basic personality structure. The focus in both areas is toward recognizing the inherent values in the personality and in enabling development to the fullest capacity. The full and constructive use of existing resources is indicated.

4. All of the people of the community are concerned in its health and welfare services. Representation of all interests and elements in the population and their full and meaningful participation are essential objectives in community organization.

5. The fact of ever-changing human needs and the reality of relationships between and among people and groups are the dynamics in the community organization process. Acceptance of the concept of purposeful change and John Dewey's philosophy of the "ever-enduring process of perfecting, maturing, refining" as goals in community organization is basic.

6. Interdependence of all threads in the social welfare fabric of or-

[1] Excerpted from "Community Organization for Social Welfare," *Social Work Year Book*, 1954 (New York: American Association of Social Workers, 1954), p. 123. By permission of National Association of Social Workers.

ganization is a fundamental truth. No single agency can usefully "live unto itself alone," but is constantly performing its functions in relation to others.

7. Community organization for social welfare as a process is a part of generic social work. Knowledge of its methods and skill in their application will enhance the potentialities for growth and development of any community effort to meet human needs. Professional education for the practice of community organization for social welfare can best be provided through schools of social work.

General Principles of Community Organization [2]

By RAY JOHNS and DAVID F. DEMARCHE

---

1. COMMUNITY ORGANIZATION *is a means and not an end.* As in casework or group work, community organization seeks to enrich the life of the individual. The individual is the *raison d'être* for community organization. Organizations, personnel, program, knowledge, and skills are only means to an end—the welfare and growth of people is the end.

2. *Communities, like individuals and groups, are different.* Each has its own peculiarities, its own problems and needs. To deal with communities effectively, they must be individualized.

3. *Communities, like individuals, have a right to self-determination.* In community organization the worker enables the community to develop its own policies, plans, and programs. They are not superimposed.

4. *Social need is the basis for organization.* The determining factor in initiating, continuing, modifying, or terminating an organization, is social need. An organization should come into existence to meet a felt need, and should be continued only if it adjusts to changing needs.

5. *Community welfare rather than agency self-interest should be the first consideration in determining program.* The program of an organization should be defined in relation to the content of the programs of other agencies, and in relation to the needs of the community. No

---

[2] Excerpted from *Community Organization and Agency Responsibility*, Johns and DeMarche (New York: Association Press, 1951), pp. 235-239. By permission of the publisher.

agency should pre-empt so large a portion of the community problems or so large a geographical area as to inhibit the development of other organizations when the total problem is apparently beyond its own resources.

6. *Co-ordination is a process of growth.* Co-ordination through authoritarian pressure and repression is not compatible with democratic principles. Co-ordination should be the result of intelligent recognition of common interests and objectives. Effective social planning is the result of "learning through doing." Thus, the interagency body is a laboratory within which this practice takes place.

7. *Community organization structure should be kept as simple as possible.* Too much machinery may well bog down and get in the way of process, which relates groups to each other so as to meet the welfare needs of the community more effectively.

8. *Services should be distributed equitably.* The social services of a community should be made available equally and without discrimination to all who need them.

9. *Diversity in program approach should be respected.* The determining factors in program approach should be community needs. A community plan which utilizes diverse contributions, rather than forcing agency regimentation should be the rule.

10. *There should be broad representation in interagency bodies.* Every group whose interests are represented by the interagency body should be given the opportunity for an explicit voicing of its interests in the council, where the common problems of the several groups are under consideration.

11. *There must be balance between centralization and decentralization.* Agencies, though united in a community chest for financial security, or in a council for common interests, may maintain at the same time their own special interests and their own individual programs. This permits common organization for common interests and special organizations for special interests.

12. *Barriers to communication must be broken down.* Community organization should result in freer contacts among the various social groups within a community. Attitudes of concern for the welfare of the total community must be developed through the exposure of individuals and groups to new and ever-widening interests and to new associations, and through opportunities to work together on common projects. The greater the differentiation in community life, the greater the need to develop an understanding of the needs and contributions of other social groups.

13. *Communities need professional help.* The role of the professional worker is that of helping the community to discover, identify, and plan to meet its social welfare needs. The success of community organization depends in large part upon the ability of the worker to bring about voluntary participation in achieving a common goal.

Principles with Regard to Neighborhood Councils

Though the general principles above are applicable to the community organization process whether it takes place on the community-wide level or on the neighborhood level, the principles with regard to neighborhood councils have been singled out for special attention because of the growing interest in the neighborhood council movement. The following are principles of organization and operation.[3]

1. *The function of the neighborhood council should be community organization rather than the direct operation of services.* Quite often a neighborhood council becomes so enthusiastic about some project that it wants to get immediately to work and do the job itself. By confusing the co-ordinating and planning functions with that of a direct-service agency, many councils have died prematurely.

2. *The neighborhood council should be composed primarily of delegates of the organizations of the neighborhood.* There should be broad representation of local civic, social, religious, professional, consumer, and business groups. The make-up of councils is tending to shift from membership of individuals to membership of organizations.

3. *The organizational pattern of neighborhood councils should be kept simple and flexible.* There should be only enough structure to permit the council to function adequately. It has been suggested that project committees that end with the solution of a problem seem more effective than functional divisions usual to a city-wide council.

4. *Neighborhood councils should be autonomous bodies.* They should be free to determine their own program and to take action.

5. *Neighborhood councils within a given community should be related to each other.* This relationship may be accomplished through a city-wide association of neighborhood councils or through a council division or committee composed of representatives of local councils who meet regularly to exchange ideas and to plan for joint action.

6. *Neighborhood councils should be related to city-wide councils.* Community welfare councils have long been concerned with bringing people and services together. This has been primarily a one-way process, from the agencies to the people. Through neighborhood councils, closely related to over-all welfare councils, the neighborhood can make the larger community aware of gaps and inequalities of service. By representation of neighborhood councils on the city-wide council, it becomes possible for the over-all council to keep sensitive to the needs of the people and to enlist the participation of neighborhoods in getting needs met.

---

[3] Some of these principles are adapted from the report on Community Coordination of the National Conference on Prevention and Control of Juvenile Delinquency (Washington, D.C.: Government Printing Office, November, 1946), pp. 15-17.

7. *The program of a neighborhood council should not be confined to one interest.* They should be concerned with the total field of welfare. Many councils become concerned with a single interest or project, such as organizing a recreation center. When one such aim is accomplished, the council members lose interest and the council dies for lack of a continuing program.

8. *Professional staff should be related to neighborhood councils.* Staff service on a continuing basis by trained and experienced community organization workers is recognized as necessary if the neighborhood councils are to function effectively. Staff service made available by the city-wide council should be selected jointly with the neighborhood groups.

Principles of Community Organization [4]

By FLORENCE G. CASSIDY

Social Need as a Basis for Organization

SOCIAL NEED SHOULD BE the determining factor in initiating, continuing, modifying, or terminating an organization. This general proposition covers three related principles:

1. No agency or federation should be organized save on the basis of felt need. This statement is understood to mean that the need should be felt by a considerable nucleus group in the community, and that need should include present actual need and anticipated need. In other words, no organization should be superimposed upon the community.

2. No organization should be perpetuated after need for it has passed.

3. An agency's objectives should be sufficiently broad and its program sufficiently flexible to allow for constant adjustments to changing needs. . . .

---

[4] Excerpted from "Principles of Community Organization," a statement prepared for and appended to the Report of the Michigan Committee on the Study of Community Organization (Detroit, 1940, mimeographed). By permission of the author.

Adequacy of Community Services

The social services available in a community should be sufficient in volume and quality to meet the welfare needs of the community. . . .

Citizen Control an Essential Part of Agency Operation

A social agency should be sponsored and controlled by responsible citizens. This sponsorship in a private agency should take the form of a duly constituted governing board; in a public agency, responsibility to a duly constituted executive or governing board, and through them ultimately to the electorate. In a private agency the board should be elected by the membership, and self-perpetuating boards should be replaced as rapidly as possible by a more democratic control. As in the public agency, the board is ultimately responsible to the community. . . .

The Establishment of Free Contacts and the Breaking Down of Barriers

One of the tasks of community organization should be the conscious breaking down of barriers which deny wider experiences to any social group within the community. . . .

The Role of the Leader in Developing Participation

The success of a specific project or of a continuing association depends in a large part upon the ability of its leadership to bring about voluntary participation. This is partly implied in the general principle that social agencies should work *with* people and not *for* them. The role of the leader in developing participation is stated thus by Ordway Tead: "Leaders guide and develop individuals so that they may the better share in realizing group ends in the shaping of which they will also share." . . .

Some Principles Relating to Community Organization [5]

By MURRAY G. ROSS

DISCONTENT WITH EXISTING conditions in the community must initiate and/or nourish the development of the association (organization)....

Discontent must be focused and channeled into organization, planning, and action in respect to specific problems....

The discontent which initiates or sustains community organization must be widely shared in the community....

The association must involve leaders (both formal and informal) identified with, and accepted by, major subgroups in the community....

The association must have goals and methods of procedure of high acceptability....

The program of the association should include some activities with emotional content....

The association should seek to utilize the manifest and latent good will which exists in the community....

The association must develop active and effective lines of communication both within the association and between the association and the community....

The association should seek to support and strengthen the groups which it brings together in co-operative work....

The association should be flexible in its organizational procedures without disrupting its regular decision-making routines....

The association should develop a pace for its work relative to existing conditions in the community....

The association should seek to develop effective leaders....

The association must develop strength, stability, and prestige in the community....

---

[5] Excerpted from *Community Organization: Theory and Principles* (New York: Harper & Brothers, 1955), Chs. 6 and 7, pp. 155-199. By permission of the publisher.

The Historical Development of
Community Organization
—Introduction

LITTLE HAS BEEN WRITTEN about the history of community organization. The history of social work and social welfare as a whole has been largely a neglected subject, and community organization has been even less explored than some other areas. Even in the textbooks, community organization history has usually been dealt with only sketchily. The chief exceptions are Campbell G. Murphy's historical chapters, which relate community organization to a broad social and economic background, and Wayne McMillen's historical presentations under specific topics.[1]

The history of community organization since 1870 may be thought of as falling into three broad periods: the first, centered about the charity organization movement, from the 1870's to about 1917; the second, characterized by the rise of federation—chests and councils—and extending from World War I to the end of the depression of the 1930's; the third, the period since 1939, marked by the broadened recognition of the process of community organization, greater leadership by public welfare agencies, and an increased emphasis upon the professional aspects of community organization practice.[2]

The following section on historical developments contains four quite varied selections.

The first identifies a series of landmarks or key dates in the development of community organization. This is followed by Steiner's account of the Cincinnati Social Unit Experiment of 1917–1919, one of the most original and significant early ventures in community organization. The article by Leonard Mayo is an attempt to interpret historical trends and developments, as seen in 1952; and the last selection, from Violet M. Sieder, presents an interpretation of "the developing concept of community organization."

---

[1] Campbell G. Murphy, *Community Organization Practice* (Boston: Houghton Mifflin Company, 1954); Wayne McMillen, *Community Organization for Social Welfare* (Chicago: University of Chicago Press, 1945).

[2] See Arthur Dunham, *Community Welfare Organization: Principles and Practice* (New York: Thomas Y. Crowell Company, 1958) pp. 69-89.

12

Landmarks in the Development of Community Welfare Organization [1]

By ARTHUR DUNHAM

(WHERE A SPECIFIC AGENCY is listed, this is usually the first agency of its kind to be established in the United States. Some international events are included in this list.)

1872   State Charities Aid Association, New York

1873   National Conference of Charities and Correction (since 1917, National Conference of Social Work)

1876   Boston Registration Bureau—precursor of the social service exchange.

1877   Buffalo Charity Organization Society

1881   Wisconsin Conference of Social Work

1886   Neighborhood Guild, New York—first settlement in the United States. Later named University Settlement.

1905–1906   Survey of the city of Washington, D.C., by staff of magazine, *Charities and Commons* (later, *The Survey*). Beginning of the "social survey movement."

About 1906   Beginnings of modern type of social service exchange (central index)

1908   Pittsburgh "central council" of Associated Charities (first council of social agencies)

1909   First White House Conference on child welfare called by President Theodore Roosevelt (later conferences, 1919, 1930, 1940, 1950)

1911   Margaret F. Byington—*What Social Workers Should Know About Their Own Communities.* National Associa-

---

[1] Excerpted from *Community Welfare Organization—Principles and Practice* (New York: Thomas Y. Crowell Company, 1958), Appendix A.

tion of Societies for Organizing Charity (now Family Service Association of America)

1912   United States Children's Bureau

1913   Cleveland Federation of Charities and Philanthropies— first modern community chest

1917   Illinois Department of Public Welfare—first modern state welfare department

1917–1918   PARTICIPATION BY U.S. IN WORLD WAR I
Rise of war chests
Cincinnati Social Unit experiment

1918   American Association for Community (Now United Community Funds and Councils of America)

1920–1930   Widespread organization of community chests and councils of social agencies
Many social service exchanges organized under or transferred to auspices of councils and chests

1920–1946   LEAGUE OF NATIONS

1921   National Health Council
American Association of Social Workers

1922   National Social Work Council (1922–1945)

1925   Jesse F. Steiner—*Community Organization*

1926   International Conference of Social Work organized (first conference held at Paris, 1928)

1928   Walter W. Pettit—*Case Studies in Community Organization*

1929–1939   DEPRESSION—WIDESPREAD UNEMPLOYMENT

1930   *Social Work Year Book, 1929*. Articles on various aspects of community organization included in this and subsequent volumes.

1933   Federal Emergency Relief Administration (1933–1936)

1935   Social Security Act

1939   "The Field of Community Organization." Report of committee under chairmanship of Robert P. Lane, *National Conference of Social Work, Proceedings, 1939*. Followed activities of a number of local committees for study of community organization, 1939.

1939   Federal Security Agency

1941–1945   UNITED STATES PARTICIPATED IN WORLD WAR II
State war chests

1942   National War Fund (1942–1947)

1943   United Nations Relief and Rehabilitation Administration (UNRRA, 1943–1948)

1945   UNITED NATIONS
UN Economic and Social Council (ECOSOC)
National Social Welfare Assembly (succeeded National Social Work Council, 1922–1945)

Wayne McMillen—*Community Organization for Social Welfare* (first modern textbook on community welfare organization)

1946   Association for the Study of Community Organization (1946–1955)

UN Secretariat—Department of Social Affairs

1948   UNIVERSAL DECLARATION OF HUMAN RIGHTS ADOPTED BY UNITED NATIONS ASSEMBLY

1949   United Foundation, Detroit (united fund) organized as a response to the problem of "multiple appeals"

1950–1953   UNITED STATES PARTICIPATED IN WAR IN KOREA

1950   United Community Defense Services (1950–1956)

United Defense Fund (1950–1955)

1952   UN unit on Community Organization and Development established in Secretariat. (Succeeded in 1954 by Section on Community Development)

Bradley Buell and associates—*Community Planning for Human Services*

1953   U.S. Department of Health, Education, and Welfare (Cabinet department, succeeding Federal Security Agency, 1939–1953)

1955   National Association of Social Workers organized as the result of a merger of the American Association of Social Workers and six other professional associations.

13

The Cincinnati Social Unit Experiment [1]

By JESSE FREDERICK STEINER

Jesse F. Steiner's *Community Organization,* published originally in 1925, and revised and expanded in 1930, was the first "textbook" on community organization, in the sense of an attempt at systematic description and analysis of related developments in a number of different fields. As a sociologist, starting from a sociological analysis of the community, Steiner took as his focus what he called the "community movement," and he ranged over a territory that included organized recreation, chests and councils, public health, public welfare, industrial welfare, interchurch co-operation, rural life, and relationships between national and local agencies.

This breadth of coverage was especially valuable in social work's formative years, during the 1920's; and Jesse Steiner, along with Bessie A. McClenahan, Eduard C. Lindeman, Walter W. Pettit, and some other pioneers, helped to develop and preserve the idea of community organization as something broadly focused and not merely a property of the rapidly multiplying "community chests and councils."

Thirty years after its publication, Steiner's book still stands as one of the main historical references on community organization, and as the best picture we have of it in the years immediately following the charity organization period.

One of the incidental but invaluable services which Steiner performed was to preserve a fresh and objective account of the Cincinnati Social Unit of 1917–1919—one of the most imaginative and significant social

---

[1] Excerpted from *Community Organization: A Study of Its Theory and Current Practice,* by Jesse Frederick Steiner. Copyright, 1925, The Century Co. Reprinted by permission of Appleton-Century-Crofts, Inc., from Revised Edition, 1930, pp. 348-359.

117

experiments in the history of American community organization. The following excerpt presents this "case study" of the Social Unit.[2]

Professor Steiner was a member of the Sociology Department of the University of Washington from 1931 to his retirement in 1948; he was head of the Department from 1933 to 1945. He had some early experience in family welfare and in the American Red Cross, and he taught at several institutions, among them the University of North Carolina and Tulane University.

Initiation of the Cincinnati Experiment

WHILE THE SOCIAL UNIT PLAN was fostered and largely financed by the national Social Unit organization, Cincinnati waged a vigorous campaign to secure the demonstration and pledged one-third of the three-year budget. In a series of meetings of leading social, health, and civic organizations the whole plan was presented in detail to five or six hundred people, so that prior to the initiation of the experiment a considerable group of influential leaders was interested and ready to give it hearty support. The widespread interest in the new movement is seen in the fact that the first organization meeting was attended by more than six hundred persons representing practically every trade and profession, as well as a large number of groups of various kinds. At this meeting the Cincinnati Social Unit Organization was formed with the Mayor as the honorary executive. In order that the people might participate directly in the establishment of the organization, the various neighborhoods and groups in the city were given the privilege of nominating the membership of the citizens' and occupational councils. A great deal of time and energy was spent in the building up of this city-wide organization, although it was purely advisory in nature, and was not in direct charge of the demonstration which was limited to a single district in the city.

The selection of the location of the experiment was made a matter of competition among the districts in the city that desired to secure it. The Mohawk-Brighton district, which was chosen after three months' deliberation, demonstrated its interest in the social unit plan by organizing a campaign committee under whose auspices public meetings were held, endorsements of local organizations secured, and petitions signed by large numbers of residents. The final choice of the district was made

---

[2] For a much more detailed account of the Social Unit, by one of the two promoters and professional leaders in the enterprise, see Wilbur C. Phillips, *Adventuring for Democracy* (New York: Social Unit Press, 1940).

at a public hearing attended by 500 people, many of whom were Mohawk-Brighton residents who set forth the advantages of their community as a location for the demonstration. These facts are particularly worthy of note, for they indicate the effort that was made by the national organization to develop local initiative and avoid the danger of imposing a preconceived plan upon the people in an arbitrary manner.

Organization of the Mohawk-Brighton District

The Mohawk-Brighton district, which had a population of about 15,000, was located on the upper edge of Cincinnati's "basin" area, and was a typical residential section inhabited by middle-class people, many of whom were of German extraction. On the whole, it was a fairly well-defined locality, with its own business and other organizations, and possessing a considerable degree of community spirit as was demonstrated in the campaign to secure the social unit experiment.

The work in the district was initiated by the campaign committee which met and constituted itself a temporary organizing committee. Subcommittees on districting, nominations, and constitution were appointed and during a period of about six months these committees, aided by the executives in charge of the experiment, carried out the details of the organization of the social unit. The district was divided into thirty-one blocks, each having a population of approximately five hundred. In each block, as far as possible, public meetings were held for the election of a block council which in turn appointed a citizen of the block to serve as its executive or block worker. The citizens' council whose membership was made up of these thirty-one block workers, was entrusted with the responsibility of keeping in close touch with the needs of the district and formed a convenient means through which the people could participate in determining the policies of the social unit organization.

Along with this organization of the citizens' council on a geographical basis, there was developed an occupational council composed of representatives of the skilled and professional groups of the district. The physicians, ministers, social workers, business men's club, central labor council, and other occupational interests were requested to designate one delegate from each group to serve as a planning body of specialists whose skilled services were available to meet the needs discovered in the district. This group together with the citizens' council comprised the general council, which was the controlling authority in the social unit demonstration. The citizens' council and the occupational council chose their own executives to administer their affairs, and both councils acting together elected a general executive to serve as head of the entire organization.

Development of the Child Health Program

Immediately upon completion of the local organization the question arose as to the nature of the work that should first be undertaken. The bulletins that had been issued by the national social unit suggested an infant welfare service as the most suitable means of testing the value of the new type of organization. In accord with the policy which was consistently followed throughout the entire demonstration, this question was submitted to the general council for decision. After full discussion not only in public meetings, but by the physicians' council and by the block workers in their own neighborhoods, an agreement was reached to begin work in the field of child health.

The postnatal service, the first organized work undertaken by the social unit, included nursing supervision in the home and medical examination at the health station located in the social unit headquarters in the district. Following the general plan of organization, the physicians' council assumed responsibility for the medical work, and appointed from among the physicians resident in the district a rotating staff to supervise the medical examination of the children. The physicians serving in this capacity were paid by the social unit for the time given to the health station. The nurses who assisted in the examinations and did the follow-up work in the homes were full-time employees of the social unit.

The block workers were assigned the task of locating all the homes with babies under one year of age, and persuading the mothers to bring their children to the station for examination. It was soon found that these neighborhood workers possessed intimate knowledge of their own constituency and were remarkably successful in getting the people to take an interest in the health work. Through their efforts a complete census of the babies was quickly secured, and within a year 90 per cent had been brought to the station for examination. Without a doubt a large part of the good will and understanding of the people with reference to the child health work was due to the fact that the whole plan was constantly being explained and interpreted by the block workers the people had chosen from among their own number. In order that this task of interpretation might be done efficiently, the block workers were given detailed instruction by the doctors and nurses concerning the whole health program. In recognition, also, of the demands this work would make upon their time, these workers, who were usually women in charge of their own homes, were paid a small sum to compensate them for the loss of time from their household duties. This plan of paying for the type of service ordinarily rendered in other organizations by volunteers recruited largely from the leisure class, was a distinct innovation designed to make possible the active participation of the common people in the work of the organization.

The success of the infant welfare service led gradually to an enlargement of the health program until it included prenatal supervision of mothers, general bedside nursing service, nursing supervision in the home and medical examination in the health station for preschool children, nursing supervision in the home of tuberculous and pretuberculous patients and medical examination of adults. In all this medical service the emphasis was upon prevention rather than cure. Only in emergency cases was treatment given at the health station. When disease or physical defects were discovered the family physician was notified, and, if necessary, hospital or dispensary care was arranged for. Since this health work was primarily preventive in nature, the usual public indifference was encountered which gradually lessened as the demonstration proceeded. The statistics of the health services seem to offer conclusive evidence as to the effectiveness of the social unit plan in arousing public interest in health measures.[3] Dr. Haven Emerson who was requested by the Medical Council of the National Social Unit Organization to evaluate the health work of the Mohawk-Brighton social unit, stated his conclusions in the following words:

"It must appear to anyone who will take the trouble to inquire as to the facts from the people of the Mohawk-Brighton district, that they have had a determining voice in selecting and controlling all the health education, preventive medicine, and sickness service features of the community organization. . . . Inquiry develops practical unanimity in the opinion of physicians of the district that the medical needs of the district have been better met than before, that medical practice has been benefited, and that if all taint of donation of services were removed by the assumption of costs by those who were served, there would be no further reservation in the willingness to appraise and approve of the organization and its results." [4]

An Experiment in Democracy

The purpose of the social unit as stated by its founders was "to promote a type of democratic community organization through which the citizenship as a whole can participate directly in the control of community affairs while at the same time making constant use of the highest technical skill available." Throughout the entire history of the Cincinnati experiment this democratic ideal was kept prominently in the foreground. The administrative machinery that was set up, the time and effort expended to acquaint the people with the plan, and the willingness of the promoters to accept the decisions of the general

---

[3] See Courtenay Dinwiddie, *Community Responsibility: A Review of the Cincinnati Social Unit Experiment* (New York: New York School of Social Work, 1921), pp. 161-169.

[4] Haven Emerson, "The Social Unit and Public Health," *Proceedings of the National Social Unit Conference,* 1919.

council upon matters of policy, all give evidence of a consistent effort to develop a democratic type of community organization.

Without doubt the plan of organization of the social unit is admirably adapted not merely to participation of the people in the determination of policies, but also to an effective alliance between the general public and the skilled groups so that both can work together more efficiently. The social unit's claim to uniqueness lies, indeed, in this division of function between the citizens' and occupational councils which makes it possible for the various elements in the community to make the contribution they are best fitted to perform. Democracy from the point of view of the social unit involves more than an opportunity on the part of the people to control their own affairs. To be efficient it must go a step farther and provide means whereby the technical specialists can discuss the problems within their special province and accept responsibility for working out their solution.

While the social unit possessed the advantage of this close integration of occupational groups and local neighborhood councils with full control of its own affairs, its plan of organization as carried out in Cincinnati might easily lay itself open to the charge of clever manipulation if not arbitrary control by outside leadership. The very nature of the experiment made it necessary for its promoters to be chosen as its executives. From the start the social unit was provided with unusually capable leaders whose preconceived ideas as to the program to be followed may have more or less unwittingly been the controlling force in the decisions of the general council. Of course such was not the intention and those in charge of the demonstration apparently made every effort to bring about popular control; nevertheless the type of organization adopted would lend itself to use as a political machine if its leaders were interested in using it for that purpose. Especially might this be true in view of the fact that the demonstration was financed entirely outside the district where it was located. Its outside leaders had been responsible for the raising of the funds, and a tentative budget had been prepared before the local experiment was begun. The question may well be asked whether the lack of financial responsibility does not destroy the value of the experiment from the point of view of democracy. It seems necessary to admit that the circumstances surrounding this particular demonstration made inevitable a certain amount of arbitrary procedure at least in the initiation and financial support of the Mohawk-Brighton organization. Nevertheless these factors to which exception may be taken are not inherent in the plan itself and would not appear if the social unit were generally adopted.

The important fact to be kept in mind is not the way in which the demonstration originated, but the essential philosophy of the plan itself. Social work of the traditional sort ordinarily grows out of the humanitarian ideas of people of means who impose their plan of organization and policies upon their beneficiaries in a more or less arbitrary manner.

Whether it is a social settlement, a charity society, or a recreation center, the initiative usually comes from those in a [the] higher social stratum, whose position and wealth give them a large degree of power. In sharp contrast to this method of operation, the social unit is organized only in response to the desire of the people, and its councils are so devised that they can never fall into the control of a limited group of people representing only one phase of community life. Here is the distinctive achievement of the social unit which makes it worthy of serious study. Dr. Devine's conclusions concerning this aspect of its work are well worth quoting:

"The evidence seems convincing that the principle of democracy in the thoroughgoing sense attached to that term by the organizers of the Social Unit has been consistently adhered to and that the whole tendency of the movement has been to make its activities more completely democratic, more completely under the intelligent control of committees selected by the community, and that the extension of the Unit idea has been through a slow and patient process of education and demonstration. It is not claimed that a complete democracy exists in the Mohawk-Brighton District. The avowed and principal purpose of the Social Unit is to create one and to perform such services as an intelligent and well-equipped democracy may conceive to be desirable through such instrumentalities as may be devised by the expert specialists who are working in the community and accept social direction." [5]

Political Implications

From one point of view the social unit was an intensive demonstration in the field of public health. Since its practical achievements, which could most readily be tabulated and measured, were chiefly in this field, the public became much more interested in its health program than in its political philosophy. Nevertheless the fundamental purpose of the demonstration was to test the value of a new type of organization and the health activities were simply a means to this end. The demonstration for very obvious reasons was made first in the field of voluntary community work, but if successful here, its application to governmental activities would apparently be the logical next step. Beginning with a small phase of community life, its expanding organization might very well absorb new functions until it would finally take the place of existing political machinery as well as voluntary social and health agencies. The relation of the social unit to political organization necessarily remained in the background as long as the experiment was limited to a single district of a city. Perhaps these more remote implications of the movement would have attracted little or no attention during this preliminary period of experimentation if it had not been for the tenseness

[5] E. T. Devine, "The Social Unit in Cincinnati," *Survey*, 43:120.

of the war situation which made the public unduly fearful of anything that might appear to be critical of the existing government. The attack on the social unit by the Mayor of Cincinnati on the ground that it was "a government within a government, a step away from Bolshevism, with dangerous radical tendencies," was entirely unwarranted, but served to direct attention to its political theories. This untimely discussion of its more wide-reaching implications at a time when its demonstration in a single district was not completed, was very unfortunate, for it alienated public support and hampered the progress of the work during the most important stage of the experiment.

Since the social unit demonstration was limited to a single section of a large city and was not carried through to completion even on this small scale, an evaluation of its role in political organization must be largely speculative in nature. Its citizens' councils beginning with the small blocks and extending to larger municipal areas seem to afford unusually full opportunity for the people to participate in governmental control. On the other hand, even this praiseworthy attempt to give greater importance to the small neighborhood unit brings in its train administrative problems that merit careful consideration. Likewise, the new role assigned the professional groups in working out the problems of government may or may not lead to greater efficiency in the guidance of community affairs. Further experiments of this kind are necessary before conclusions can be reached. In this connection the keen criticism of the social unit by Professor Lowrie from the point of view of the political scientist is worthy of quotation:

"As a substitute for our form of government, the Social Unit has offered little that is tangible. There are too many questions concerning its operation as yet unanswered. It is not apparent that the citizens' councils as they are formed successively from the blocks to the largest areas, will avoid the evils of indirect representation which have been so inimical to 'genuine democracy' as it has worked out in our own governmental systems; why the instructed vote will be satisfactory here when it has not been elsewhere; or how the difficulties of the large council elected by wards we have been trying to escape in our cities will become virtues under the Social Unit system. On the administrative side, the system seems to be weak in providing no method of selecting expert administrators and still more weak in avoiding any administrative cohesion or centralized authority. The staff of the Social Unit, it is true, is·of such unusual ability, as to seem to answer one of these criticisms. But these efficient members were selected first by the executives and later elected to executiveships. This suggests the tendency for a strong extragovernmental organization here, such as grew up in our own political system in the party, which became strong by absorbing features of government when the regularly instituted agencies were weak. Imagine motives of a sordid and selfish character in place of those of altruism and public service, which have always dominated those who have had charge of the experiment, and one is driven to the conclusion that a governmental type more easily corrupted could hardly be erected upon a democratic basis.

"It would be difficult to predict how the occupational councils would operate. There is less in our political experience to guide us. The desirability of having the professional groups mindful of the governmental problems lying within their respective fields and ready to advance the helpful suggestions which the most recent discoveries of science afford, is evident. It is hard to tell how far we should give power to these specialists—how far we should go toward allowing the schools to be controlled by the school teachers; the dental regulations written by the dentists; the health regulations by the doctors and nurses; the building code by the carpenters and architects; or the plumbing code by the plumbers. Possibly the interaction of one group upon another and the necessity of having these decisions approved by the citizens' councils would maintain a sufficient balance. So far, we have hardly been successful in getting our professional groups to concern themselves about the public aspects of their professions except as this might be necessitated by their private practices. And many have been slow to learn that public problems frequently differ from private ones. This may be just what is needed to stimulate that interest but, on the other hand, it might be dangerous to repose control before that interest is aroused." [6]

In a recent evaluation of the Social Unit, Professor Eldridge comes to a similar point of view. In his opinion it is doubtful whether the Unit plan could be applied, in the form in which it was developed, to fundamental political problems. Its dual form of citizenship raises questions which have been much debated but which require more experimentation before its value could be demonstrated. Furthermore its application to larger areas and to different kinds of situations must remain in doubt until determined by experiments in various places.[7]

Contribution to Community Organization

Whatever conclusions may be reached as to political implications, it is obvious that the social unit plan of organization is a direct challenge to the traditional methods of administration of community work. The experiments in community organization which have had wide vogue in this country have to a large degree been supported and directed by a

---

[6] S. G. Lowrie, "The Social Unit—An Experiment in Politics," *National Municipal Review,* 9:565-66.

[7] Seba Eldridge, "Community Organization and Citizenship," *Social Forces,* 7:140 (1928).

small number of public-spirited people, and consequently fail to be truly representative of all the interests of the community. This is even true of such experiments as the community center movement which has consistently emphasized democratic ideals and has endeavored to secure participation of all the people. The social unit in striking contrast with other democratic types of community organization has not relied upon such familiar devices as the mass meeting to give the people a voice in community affairs, nor has it contented itself by merely facilitating the coming together of the various agencies and groups in the community. On the contrary, it has sought to secure popular representation through the organization of small neighborhood units and then has added to the effectiveness of this democratic control by throwing upon the skilled groups of the community the responsibility of devising means whereby the policies agreed upon may be carried to successful completion. Unlike the federation movement, which would bring order out of the multiplicity of agencies by building up machinery for joint action, the social unit was sufficiently inclusive to cover the various problems of community welfare, thus making unnecessary the establishment and support of additional agencies. The experiment in the Mohawk-Brighton district did not extend far enough to demonstrate the full possibilities of the movement. Those who were called in to evaluate the social unit near the end of the three-year period were impressed with what had been accomplished, but felt that further demonstration was necessary before final conclusions could be reached. The war situation, as already mentioned, hampered the development of the program of work and was largely responsible for the criticism that the social unit was revolutionary in nature. Under more normal conditions the plan would hardly have met with this official opposition which played a large part in the failure to provide local funds to continue the experiment. The social unit plan, although incompletely demonstrated, stands out as an unusually significant experiment which seems to point the way to a more logical and effective means of community organization.

14

Community Welfare Planning: Accomplishments and Obstacles [1]

By LEONARD W. MAYO

No contemporary social worker has surpassed Leonard W. Mayo in the ability to summarize and assess current trends and tendencies in social welfare and to suggest desirable directions for growth and movement. More than once he has rendered signal service of this sort to those who are especially interested in community organization. His 1946 National Conference paper on "Community Organization in 1946" summarized the situation a year after the end of World War II.

The 1952 paper which is excerpted below deals more specifically but no less cogently with community planning for health and welfare—current developments, shortcomings and blocks, and bases for orderly progress.

Leonard Mayo has had a distinguished career in social work, including institutional service for children, teaching at the New York School of Social Work, service with a community welfare council, dean of the School of Applied Social Sciences, Western Reserve University, vice-president of that University, and his present position as director of the Association for the Aid of Crippled Children, New York. He has held many positions of national social welfare and civic leadership, and he was president of the National Conference of Social Work on the occasion of its 75th annual meeting in 1948.

[1] Excerpted from "Community Planning for Health and Welfare," *The Social Welfare Forum,* Proceedings, National Conference of Social Work, Chicago, 1952 (New York: Columbia University Press, 1952), pp. 220-231. By permission of National Conference on Social Welfare.

COMMUNITY PLANNING for health and welfare is the process by which individuals and groups in a community consciously seek to determine, establish, and sustain those conditions, programs, and facilities which in their judgment will help to prevent the breakdown of individual and communal life, and make possible a high level of well-being for all people. Underlying this concept are the philosophy and the methods which guide the wisest leaders in obtaining full expression from the community as to its needs and their priorities, and in organizing a plan of action in relation thereto. An example would be a study of the nature and incidence of chronic illness, full discussion and interpretation of the resulting data, and a decision as to the best program suggested by the entire procedure.

Also included in any broad definition of community planning are the mobilization of public support, the dissemination of pertinent information, the appointment of appropriate committees, the hearing and weighing of arguments presented by the opposition, and the development of a plan of action designed to reconcile differences. The basic methods used in community planning for health and welfare should be essentially those of community organization as public health and social work understand and employ them.

Sound planning for health and welfare involves the recognition and use of basic community facts and forces, both positive and negative, and the full use of all appropriate community facilities. The facts include basic population data and indices of human need, some of which can be determined and measured by tested methods. The positive forces include the health and welfare services which may be mobilized to meet current or anticipated needs, the agencies which conduct such services, and the boards of directors, civic groups, and individuals who may be counted upon to aid in the planning process. Those individuals and groups temperamentally or otherwise opposed to planning and to the adequate support of present programs, reactionary city and county governments, and the cultural lag and lethargy to be found to some degree in every community are among the negative forces which confront even the most skillful planning efforts.

Community planning as here defined takes place in small local areas, on a city, county, and regional basis, and on a national scale. The examples of national planning that come to mind most readily are segmental in character, involving a single program or objective, such as food conservation, cancer control, and the like. An example of more inclusive planning in the health and welfare fields are, respectively, the President's appointed committee on the nation's health, the National Health Council, and the National Social Welfare Assembly.

A review of current and contemplated activities in the casework, health, and social group work and recreation divisions of some fifteen of the leading community welfare councils in the country in 1951 shows that these groups have developments of fundamental importance under way. They include the following:

1. Direct action of various kinds to meet the gaps in services as revealed by studies and surveys.

2. The consummation of agency mergers, the extension of existing programs and agencies, and the establishment of new programs and devices and, in a few instances, new agencies.

3. Studies of children, the aged, the chronically ill, and the handicapped as a basis for making long-range plans and establishing programs and facilities to meet their needs.

4. An awareness of new needs and an appreciation of the causes of old and more familiar problems; for example, while a new interest was shown in the challenge of the aging and no specific mention was made of juvenile delinquency as such, active concern was noted for many of the community conditions which contribute to behavior problems of children and youth.

5. Those who replied to the questionnaires expressed interest in evaluating social work services and programs, in establishing criteria, and in building wider community support.

In summary, the present status of community planning for health and welfare might be expressed as follows:

1. We have made reasonable progress in the last two decades in identifying certain common human needs at the community level, in collecting and analyzing population and other basic data, in developing new services and in modifying old ones, in improving the administration and the flexibility of agencies, and in enlisting broader community support.

2. We have broadened and deepened our knowledge concerning individual, group, and community behavior.

3. We are beginning to see the differences and the relation between needs, services, programs, and agencies. An increasing number of professional workers as well as board members now embrace the concept that the greatest of these is needs.

4. We have developed the techniques of community organization and to some extent we have broadened the base of community planning with the inclusion of individuals and groups outside of our own professions.

5. We have made some contribution to the methods and the philosophy of planning in other groups; our enabling and permissive philosophy, our techniques in the use of committees and in informal education, are winning merited attention. We have learned more than most professions about how to encourage and relate expressions of community opinion and how to organize for purposeful, democratic action.

Along with these solid gains we must record some of our shortcomings and problems:

1. Our planning goals are limited, and our sights are too low. While we recognize the importance of the aid and backing of key individuals and groups and the co-operation of other planning bodies in the community, we underestimate our ability to enlist these potential partners in what is in reality a common cause.

Whenever public health and social work have made significant contributions to community planning in their own or related fields, it has been in co-operation with other groups, professional and lay, governmental and voluntary. Cases in point are slum clearance and public housing, the handling of day care problems during the Second World War, and the reduction of infant and maternal mortality rates during the last twenty years. In these instances, there have been conscious teamwork efforts among several groups in fact finding and analyses, in the search for the factors standing in the way of solutions, in interpretation, in formulating plans of action, and in evaluating results.

We are just beginning to give something more than lip service to the multidisciplinary approach in medical care and social work treatment; the same approach and philosophy should now be carried into long-range community planning for health and welfare.

2. Our planning objectives and methods are not defined clearly enough. In child welfare, for example, we are usually not clear as to whether our main and immediate objective is more foster homes, more and better personnel, or an all-out effort to prevent the kind of family disintegration that makes it necessary for a child to be placed in the first instance. Granted the need to move forward on all three of these fronts, we do not as a rule give them proper weighting or present them in their proper relationship.

3. We tend to place ourselves and our agencies at the center and confine our planning to the narrow sphere thus circumscribed.

4. The research, upon which all sound community planning depends, is still in its beginning stages. Frequently, when we do produce a creditable study we lack the skill and the objectivity to let the facts speak for themselves and to be guided by them.

5. By and large, community planning for health and welfare has not been given a place of vital importance in most communities. Planning is all too frequently regarded as something to be undertaken if and when the time and money can be found, and by some as a slightly socialistic enterprise to be avoided by all respectable citizens. Apparently, we have not yet succeeded in expressing succinctly and eloquently enough the code of values and the sense of obligation and responsibility which should motivate and guide communities in their health and welfare planning.

There are major blocks to successful planning, some of them admittedly outside the immediate control of the social work and public health professions. They include the following:

1. The presence of power structures. Every community harbors some groups and individuals whose backing, or at least tacit approval, appears to be a must for the success of any major undertaking. Not all power of this character, however, is vested in business, industry, labor, or government. There are, unfortunately, power structures made up of health and welfare agencies exclusively which control, or attempt to control, welfare policy in some communities. This observer feels about these groups as Heywood Broun once said he felt about fascism: "I do not like fascism," he said, "not even when it works."

2. A considerable proportion of the planning which is affecting the future of many thousands of people in the nation is presently vested in groups whose motivations are frequently good, but whose interests are primarily commercial. Among the most dynamic "planners" of this era are the large life insurance companies and real estate concerns whose programs are in some instances rapidly changing the faces of entire communities through extensive housing projects and other developments. If, as Lewis Mumford has stated, housing is the key to urban redevelopment, the future of many urban areas is subject to the control of groups which may or may not be proceeding on a long-range basis in terms of what people need and desire and the community should have.

3. The immediate pressures of economic depressions, defense programs, and industrial and military mobilization constitute further hazards to effective planning. Emergencies tend to emphasize rather than improve our present technical inadequacies and to postpone our slow progress toward fundamental health and welfare goals; granted that we must meet such emergencies as they arise, the long-range purpose of broad social planning must be to prevent rather than to tolerate them.

Unless, and until, planning for health and welfare is given a new status, until it is consciously developed as an objective, a method, and a philosophy, until it is placed not merely on a par with the practice of health and social work but as fundamental to it, we shall continue to sail uncharted community seas without a compass. Without planning we have no reliable means of identifying and measuring needs, no way of determining how needs can best be met in the present and the future, that is, through what service program, agency, or combination thereof; without planning we have no really effective way of learning how to allocate funds for the alleviation and prevention of basic social problems.

Health and welfare must join hands with other groups in finding the answers to such far-reaching problems as the rebuilding of impoverished areas of our country, the restoration and reclaiming of unproductive land, reforestation and flood control, the resettlement of large numbers of people, and in making adequate provision for migrant workers in this country and for the dispossessed of other lands. There is also the pertinent and basic problem of the recruitment, training, and placement of professional personnel. Acute shortages now exist in professions and occupations essential to military and industrial mobilization and in basic community services. The sum total of the present requirements represented in these fields and the competition for qualified staff are such that it is highly inefficient to continue without some orderly plan for the staffing of at least the most crucial services in strategic areas.

These are problems of deep and widespread concern affecting all of health and welfare, and they are problems which cannot be effectively tackled in a partial or segmental manner. They require concerted action by many groups over a long period of time. Co-operative planning is at least one key to their control and ultimate solution, in so far as such problems can be solved.

We have reached the point in our planning experience that calls for an objective effort to weigh and analyze present methods and machinery. We shall be defeated at the start, however, if our objective is to preserve and protect our present planning structure and methods. Nothing less than thorough and objective analysis will suffice to determine whether present methods are the best means of accomplishing what communities need to achieve well-being for all their people.

We have seen that in most large communities there are at present two almost separate areas of concern: city planning, as that function is usually understood; and planning for health and welfare services. There is an important and largely neglected middle ground or overlapping area, however, where both groups might well meet to share responsibility and to plan jointly. This area has to do with the finding and defining of both physical and social needs, the selection of planning priorities, decisions as to logical divisions of labor, and joint participation in the development of services, facilities, and programs.

It is conceivable that in large cities or regions a committee or commission with an over-all supervisory mandate, but without staff or operating responsibility, may be required to view the problems of the community as a whole and maintain some semblance of balance and co-ordination between "physical" and "social" planning. Reluctant as we may be to add another unit to the present planning structure, some new device, or at least some new provisions or point of departure, may well be necessary to insure a more inclusive approach.

As noted earlier there are a large number of governmental and private, local, and national groups devoted to one or more aspects of community planning. The National Social Welfare Assembly and the National Health Council have national responsibility for welfare and health planning. The regional offices of the Federal Security Agency are active in planning the programs for which they are responsible, local school boards plan their programs and facilities, and chambers of com-

merce and labor organizations plan in behalf of their interests. Not all
these groups and their objectives are in harmony at all times in any
community. Their very existence and the strong and sometimes conflicting stakes each of them has in the community, emphasize the importance of some machinery or device, or one group with an over-all
mandate to view the community as a whole with no other axe to grind.

We have reached the age as a nation when entire towns, cities, and
regions have gone to seed economically and physically, and when
imaginative, long-range physical planning and social engineering are
required. Organized health and welfare groups should be a dynamic
and integral part of such movements, but they should not and cannot
handle them alone. Over thirty years ago Patrick Geddes, the social
scientist, coined the phrase "geotechnics," which was his term for "the
science of making the earth more habitable." It is something as broad
and comprehensive as that which must concern us in health and welfare
planning.

Basically, what we need are philosophical, scientific, and practical
answers, in that order, to the hard question of how we can mobilize voluntarily and use wisely our human resources and the natural resources
of soil, sun, water, and forests to benefit all the people. That question
is not only much larger and deeper than the professions of health and
welfare, it will always be too large for any one profession or group,
and it is too comprehensive at present for any combination of groups
in our country, including government. Government at any level is
neither impressive nor desirable in the role of solo planner, and there
are substantial reasons why the people of a community and of the
nation should be represented through private as well as public bodies
in all aspects of planning.

For the present we must proceed as best we can in our planning
to comprehend the whole in so far as we are capable of doing so, to
plan effectively within our part of the whole, and to the best of our ability relate our activities to those of other responsible planning bodies.
Thus health and welfare may gradually improve their relations with
other professions and planning groups and help to develop the kind
of joint agreements and action that should lead to far better planning
coverage.

In the final analysis, however, there can be no significant planning
unless and until people are free to plan: until men and women are relatively free from biases and prejudices, from confinement to single issues
and limited views, from entanglement in the webs of their own individual objectives. It is upon these things that power structures are
built; these are the ingredients from which the blocks to effective planning for health and welfare are fashioned.

Social work and public health will not solve the problems that stand
in the way of planning simply by organizing their own power structures.
Granted we could in due course develop power that would be feared,

in the end we would do no more than meet hostility with hostility, force with force, power with power. A program of that kind and objectives of that nature are repugnant to the inner spirit and professional purpose of health and welfare.

The path to health and welfare planning which we must carve out of the undergrowth of indifference, ignorance, and reaction lies in a far different direction. Our responsibility, and our obligation, is to the entire community, as it is to the whole person and to the whole group in casework and social group work practice. That responsibility must be expressed in community planning by creating the climate and helping to set the stage wherein and whereon individuals and groups may be free and encouraged to determine community needs, establish priorities, select their own solutions, and jointly decide upon and then pursue a common plan of action.

To many of us this is "old hat." Nevertheless, we give evidence all too frequently of abiding by this general philosophy in casework and social group work practice and departing from it in community planning. We are patient, long-suffering, and professional, for example, in allowing an individual to unfold his story of frustration and conflict. We cannot, therefore, upon discovering that a portion of his problem is due to community factors become didactic and authoritative in trying to root them out. If we are willing to enhance and to co-operate with the normal processes of catharsis and the ensuing period of growth in the first instance, we can do no less in the second.

Toynbee, the British historian, wrote of the necessity for providing "equal access to all of the primary goods of life for all members of the community." If the author would allow us to change the plural word "goods" to the singular, we might then adopt the quotation to express our philosophy of community planning for health and welfare. The basic question for all of us is how we can proceed together to direct and channel the inventive genius, the organizing ability, and the vast reservoir of good will of the American people to help achieve this end in some measure both for our own nation and for other lands.

15

Developing Goals and Methods of Community Organization [1]

By VIOLET M. SIEDER

Although various texts include sketches of the history of community organization as a movement and a division of social work, little or nothing has been published on the development of conceptions concerning its essential nature. At the National Conference of Social Welfare, in St. Louis, 1956, however, Violet M. Sieder attempted to remedy this deficiency. Her paper, another section of which is included in Part V (Selection No. 67), constitutes a distinctly significant contribution not only toward social work practice in community organization, but also to its emerging theory and definition.

In the original version of her paper (see footnote 1 below) she presents a systematic and interesting analysis of the historical development of the conceptual base of community organization. She sees our understanding of the nature and purpose of community organization as having evolved through five stages, each incorporating and enlarging upon the ideas previously held.

Briefly these successive periods may be summarized in terms of shifting emphases as follows: (1) concentration on the development of appropriate structures for co-ordinating welfare services from 1909 to 1939; (2) from 1939 to 1947 the emphasis was placed on the process of problem solving and on skills and methods employed in adjusting welfare resources to welfare needs; (3) a change of emphasis which

---

[1] Excerpted from "What Is Community Organization Practice?", *The Social Welfare Forum*, Proceedings, National Conference of Social Work, St. Louis, 1956 (New York: Columbia University Press, 1956), pp. 160-166. Also published in original form in *Community Organization in Social Work: Its Practice in Old and New Settings* (New York: Council on Social Work Education, 1956), pp. 1-13. Pages 1-7 of the original paper are omitted in the NCSW version. By permission of National Conference on Social Welfare.

occurred at the NCSW in 1947, when the focus of attention was placed on community organization as a process concerned primarily with promoting satisfying social relationships and community integration, rather than with welfare needs; (4) various post-1947 contributions stressing the equal importance of social goals; and (5) the emerging conception of community organization as a social service to both local and nonlocal groupings which incorporates also a special knowledge of the contributions of the social sciences, and is oriented to the community as the client rather than to its agencies as such. Many of the references cited by the author in support of this analysis of concepts are included in this volume.

In contrast with many well-known but less vocal practitioners of community organization who have been too occupied with problem solving to record their experience and knowledge, Violet Sieder has not been too busy to write. Though her professional career has included some four years' experience in casework, three or more in child labor, and thirteen in community organization practice and consultation work, she has written numerous articles, reports, and papers, two of which are included in the present collection.

Born in Buenos Aires of American parentage, Violet Sieder received her master's degree from the University of Chicago's School of Social Service Administration in 1936. Following a number of years' experience as a child labor investigator, case supervisor, research worker, and consultant in the U.S. Children's Bureau, she became the executive secretary of the Bronx (New York) Council for Social Welfare. In February, 1944, she joined the staff of Community Chests and Councils of America and eventually became associate director of the Health and Welfare Planning Department. In 1951, as a consultant on community organization under a State Department European program, she worked with councils of social agencies in Berlin and other cities. Finally, in September, 1954, she entered the academic field as a professor of social work in the New York School of Social Work, of Columbia University, and is currently teaching courses in community organization and administration.

WE ARE EVOLVING FOR community organization practice a working philosophy, principles, and methods. We shall attempt to show that community organization practice is identified with the generic concepts of social work, that it draws heavily on the processes of casework and social group work, but that it also depends on specialized areas of knowledge and skill necessary for working with a community.

The various stages of the evolution of community organization objectives and goals have affected the development of methods and processes used by the community organization practitioner in social work:

1. First, we witnessed an effort to prevent client abuse of services offered by a multiplicity of independent voluntary agencies. This was reflected in the early settlement movement and more particularly in the community organization societies in the latter half of the nineteenth century. Methods developed to achieve this goal included the social service exchange, interagency agreements and referral procedures, and a beginning attention to standards, along with a concern for promoting social reform.

2. Second, we saw a need to avoid waste and duplication of money and effort in serving clients through an integration of services. This grew out of the Community Organization Society movement and characterized the early Jewish federations and chests and councils of 1909–15.

Agencies came together to develop methods for joint financing which, in the days when services were predominantly voluntary, were considered "two sides of the same coin." This approach necessitated use of fact finding, agency and community studies, and budgeting and promotional procedures.

3. Next evolved attempts to adjust and relate the resources of agencies, both public and voluntary, to the needs of people. This was sharpened by the Lane report at the 1939 Conference of Social Work on "The Field of Community Organization." [2]

So far as methods were concerned, we had the development of the social statistics project, first operated by the United States Children's Bureau and later by Community Chests and Councils; and the "social breakdown index" which attempted to measure need by statistical evidence of the incidence of social problems. A pioneer effort of bringing to bear on identified problems the full artillery of social services on an integrated basis was the Tremont Area Project in Cleveland followed by other community demonstrations, of which Bradley Buell is the current chief exponent.

4. Community organization was next seen as a method not only for meeting but for preventing social problems—getting at "causative factors" in the community. This meant looking to a broader participation of organizations and groups in the planning and action program extending the scope of program concern, as well as to refinements in the process used by the professional worker.

In regard to process, we had the contributions, to the 1947 Na-

[2] Robert P. Lane, "The Field of Community Organization," in *Proceedings of the National Conference of Social Work,* 1939 (New York: Columbia University Press, 1939), pp. 495-511.

tional Conference, of Kenneth Pray [3] who identified the community organization practitioner as the "enabler" who works with, and not "on," the community; and Wilber Newstetter [4] who identified the "intergroup" process as the "to-and-from" interaction involving representative and delegate roles in community organization. Important to the development of social work practice were the contributions of such organizations as United Community Funds and Councils of America, Inc. (formerly Community Chests and Councils) in policy statements and guides to various community organization methodologies; the Association for the Study of Community Organization which under Arthur Dunham's leadership from 1946 to 1955 stimulated discussion and interest in professional practice; and the National Social Welfare Assembly activities on the national level.

5. Most recently, community organization is seen as a direct service to communities through which individuals and groups representing a cross section of diversified special interests are helped to work together to identify and meet their own needs by participating as effective parts of a democratic society. The goal here is to achieve an integrated community through the broad involvement on a meaningful basis at every level of participation of the many appropriate groups and subgroups in the community concerned with a common problem.

Evidence of this may be found in the neighborhood approach to community planning and the recognition given it in the 1950 policy statement of Community Chests and Councils which identified a role of councils as providing staff consultation service:

> "To assist organizations and individuals to improve social conditions in the districts or neighborhoods in which they work; to relate local planning efforts through appropriate channels and resources to community-wide planning; to keep community-wide services sensitive to local needs, and to stimulate maximum use and support of community services and resources to meet and prevent health and welfare problems."

Other evidences of this approach are found in the programs of United Community Defense Services to new and unserved areas in the United States; and community development programs at the international level. It is in this direct service approach that the social sciences and social work begin to work together more consciously; and that city planning and social work planning are seen as interdependent. In a recent book by Murray Ross this concept is sharpened.[5]

[3] Kenneth L. M. Pray, "When Is Community Organization Social Work Practice?" in *Proceedings of the National Conference of Social Work*, 1947 (New York: Columbia University Press, 1948), pp. 194-204.

[4] Wilber I. Newstetter, "The Social Intergroup Work Process," *ibid.*, pp. 205-17.

[5] Murray G. Ross, *Community Organization: Theory and Principles* (New York: Harper & Brothers, 1955).

These five approaches are not mutually exclusive; rather, as a continuum, they are all still necessary and in effect in most community planning organizations. The evolution is expressed through a broadening and deepening of goals and by placing different degrees of weight or emphasis on their various aspects.

It should be noted further that throughout this history, but with increasing intensity as both centralized public and federated voluntary financing of services has reached substantial proportions, we have been faced with the major dilemma of a democracy. The question still to be resolved is how to achieve the advantages of centralization of planning, financing, and social policy and action, while at the same time preserving autonomy and the growth of diversity in the integral parts of the community structure.

If, indeed, there has been as much movement, fermentation, documentation, and practical experience as this paper would thus far indicate, why, you ask, is there a tendency for community organization to be questioned as legitimate social work practice? In my judgment, its acceptance has been handicapped by:

1. Its historical roots in organizational structure which made it adjunct to, but not recognized as part of, social work practice since it was visualized as an indirect service to clients through agencies and reckoned as an administrative charge as a percentage of total welfare expenditures.

2. The emphasis on medical and psychiatric concepts in casework and identification with these older and established professions diverting social work from its earlier identification with the need to correct social injustice through social reform as a legitimate social work process.

3. Disappointment with a seeming inability of community organization agencies to fulfill ambitious community goals such as finding panaceas for resolving difficult problems, or for providing sufficient services and financial support.

4. The tendency to place full responsibility for failure on the community organization worker and organization while permitting them to take no credit for success.

5. Failure to recognize that every social worker carries some responsibility for community organization practice, regardless of his area of specialization—and hence needs an exposure to knowledge of community organization process.

6. The complexities of community structure, sociologically and organizationally, and the indirect role of the community organization worker, making it difficult for him to grasp his basic social work function and methodology.

7. A traditional tendency to distrust centralization fortified by observed abuses of good professional practice in the use of manipulation of

power to bring about change without appropriate and sufficient participation of autonomous groups and individuals directly involved.

8. A tendency for some community organization practitioners to identify with volunteer leaders who represent at one and the same time his employers, constituents, and clients; and to dissociate himself from professional social workers as having a lower status.

Community organization as social work practice has its roots in a philosophy common to all areas of social work specialization. Social work is a working expression of a democratic way of life; and democracy itself finds its aegis in a Judaic-Christian philosophy. Social work is characterized as a process which helps people solve their own problems. It recognizes and respects the rights of people to determine and to meet their individual needs to the extent of their ability, and their right to personal fulfillment. It further recognizes the interdependence of people and that the welfare of each affects the welfare of all. It knows that people find it natural and necessary to come together through association in the family, small groups, and special interest organizations. Social work, further, is based on the knowledge that the individual needs to be a part of the larger life of the community. This is most generally achieved as he becomes a member of a group which works with other groups to achieve common social objectives.

Social work is also based on a concept of growth and change; a recognition of the need for individuals, families, groups, and communities to adapt to new conditions and standards of human well-being through a continuous readjustment of personal and family life and social institutions.

The full expression of our democratic ideal demands that the right to self-determination and the autonomy of individuals and organizations must be neatly balanced against the common good of the majority. Social work, then, becomes a necessary service to those individuals, groups, or segments of a community which unassisted may fall into difficulty or fail to reach their full potential development in this process of change and adjustment. The recipients of this service we refer to as our clients; thus the client becomes the individual or family, the group or the community. It follows that the client is always a person or people—human beings; and that no matter in which of these three settings they come to the attention of the professional social worker, inevitably they must be seen and helped in the other two aspects of their relationships. For example, fully to help the individual, the social caseworker must know about his relationships to his family, his social and economic groups, and his role in the community. The group must be seen by the group worker as an entity, but also as a collection of individuals and in its relationship to other groups in the community. The community, in turn, must be worked with by the community organization worker in terms of its over-all characteristics, personality, and problems as expressed in the interaction of groups and individuals, but to do so involves understanding organizational patterns of group life and working both with organized groups and with individuals.

Thus we see casework, group work, and community organization all identified as related parts of social work practice. The common core is found in a disciplined use of self in working with people; a common working philosophy; in an emphasis on working with (not for) clients; a problem-centered approach; in the use of social diagnosis based on analysis of the articulation of the problem and the facts; in formulation of a plan toward solution or action; continuous evaluation; and in the fact that each area of specialization is involved in varying degrees with interpersonal, group, and intergroup process.

* * * *

Americans and Voluntary Associations

Americans of all ages, all conditions, and all dispositions, constantly form associations. They have not only commercial and manufacturing companies, in which all take part, but associations of a thousand other kinds—religious moral, serious, futile, extensive or restricted, enormous or diminutive. The Americans make associations to give entertainments, to found establishments for education, to build inns, to construct churches, to diffuse books, to send missionaries to the antipodes; and in this manner they found hospitals, prisons, and schools. If it be proposed to advance some truth, or to foster some feeling by the encouragement of a great example, they form a society.

> Alexis de Tocqueville: *Democracy in America* (London: Saunders and Otley 1840), extract from Chapter V, "Of the Use Which Americans Make of Public Associations in Civil Life," pp. 220-221

Community Organization and the Future
—Introduction

THE FOLLOWING SELECTIONS, from three leaders in the profession of social work, are notable for their imaginative and "prophetic" qualities. Hertha Kraus discusses social work and the "social generalist," while Donald S. Howard stresses the need for "social statesmanship." Both of these conceptions have vital implications for community organization. In the last selection, "New Wine and Old Bottles," Robert H. MacRae considers more specifically the need for adapting community organization to current trends.

16

Community Organization and Social Statesmanship [1]

By DONALD S. HOWARD

"We must press with all possible vigor the development of the skills required for 'social organization' and 'social statesmanship' and press as rapidly as possible toward inclusion of the teaching of these skills in our programs of social work education. . . ."

This is the challenge with which Donald S. Howard confronts social work and social workers in this article. The author conceives of "social organization" as bringing "to the solution of broad social questions a combination of skills much as 'community organization' brings a defined group of skills to the solution of community problems. . . ." Many community organization workers would say that this "social organization" *is* community organization in its farthest reaches, on national and international levels.

The form of words is not important—the concept and the challenge are. They concern the degree of future usefulness of social work, and the role that it will play in the coming years. Can social work—at certain times and in certain places, at least—attain to the stature of social statesmanship?

Donald Stevenson Howard is peculiarly well qualified to formulate and convey this challenge. He has had a rich and varied experience in this country and abroad: in community organization, public welfare, research, teaching, and in positions of leadership in UNRRA and the International Conference of Social Work. At the time this article was published, Mr. Howard was director of the Department of Social Work Administration of the Russell Sage Foundation; since 1948 he has

[1] Excerpted from "New Horizons for Social Work," *The Compass,* Vol. XXVIII, Nov., 1947, pp. 3-13; 28. By permission of National Association of Social Workers.

been dean of the School of Social Welfare, University of California, Los Angeles. He is the author of *The WPA and Federal Relief Policy* (Russell Sage Foundation, 1943) and other publications.

ANYONE INTERESTED in new horizons for social work might profitably project into the future a number of trends. However, there are two in particular which deserve special consideration to see where they might lead us, say, in 1972.

The first of these is the gradual enlargement of our technical fields of competence and the growing realization that there are still further fields in which we—or if not we then some other profession—must develop a competence. The second is the movement of social work away from a patching-up operation to more constructive kinds of activity.

Looking at the first trend, it is trite to remind ourselves that the most highly developed competence of social work is in the field of case-work. It is also trite to say that group work and community organization, though evidencing new interest in shifting from amateur and "semi-pro" to professional status, still stand in urgent need of further analysis and development. There will probably be much less agreement, however, as to whether or not the further extension of social work skills which I think I see on the horizon will or will not qualify as social work. . . .

The important new role for social work which I envisage involves the ability to analyze broad economic, social, physical, educational, and cultural aspects of world, national, and community life; to appraise their effect upon the welfare of the men and women and children concerned; to ascertain ways in which these broad areas of life may better promote the well-being of individuals and communities; and to bring together the professions and resources needed to improve them. The whole, which would add up to a sort of social statesmanship, might be termed "social organization" in that it would bring to the solution of broad social questions a combination of skills much as "community organization" brings a defined group of skills to the solution of community problems. . . .

It goes without saying that social work does not now possess all the skills required for the future here envisaged. However, social work, even today, comes closer than does any other profession or group to the possession of the requisite skills. What are these, do you ask?

In my opinion social work's first claim to competence in this area is that it cares, and cares deeply, about the well-being of people as people. An important aspect of the social worker's ability to care is that he has sufficient human and social insight to be alert to need even if it is relatively subtle and even though it affects relatively few persons. Anyone can see that those wrecks of human beings uncovered in concentration camps needed something. Similarly, anyone would know that a famishing province of India or China should be given some kind of aid. It takes a certain discipline, however, to get "steamed up" over the malfunctioning of broad economic, health, educational, and cultural programs which, though serving the masses relatively well, fail to meet small needs or the needs of a small minority.

The second aspect of social work's competence in the broader field which I have mentioned is its ability to know not only that people are in need, but to know, further, what they need. Through knowledge of minimum and optimum requirements for constructive living, we are in a position to know—and to help our fellow citizens to understand what happens to people who lack these essentials. Or, if we do not know, we have experience in social research through which we can soon find out what it is that people need.

A third aspect of social work's competence is its knowledge of resources—knowing where to turn to find the particular types of professional help required to meet ascertained needs. Just as social workers have learned to bring together under the roof of the casework agency the doctor, psychiatrist, psychometrist, nurse, bookkeeper, and auditor, so also, I believe they have the ability to determine when the services of the economist, the industrial engineer, the lawyer, and public administrator are required to work for some redirection of our economic, health, educational or other programs or institutions in order to serve people better.

A final aspect of social work competence—one gained largely through our knowledge of community organization—is the bringing together of these various professions in the interest of a common social objective. . . .

Perhaps the best illustration of the kind of job for which I am saying social workers should have special competence is the position of social welfare advisor in the British West Indies as recommended by the West India Royal Commission of 1938–39. The social welfare advisor, in the Commission's conception, was not to be a department head but was to have direct access to the Governor.

Specific responsibilities of the advisor, as outlined by the Commission (which declared—whimsically, I hope—that these were not intended to be a "comprehensive list"), included: community and leisure-time services; land settlement and other rural services; social security services; care and protection of children and young persons; delinquency services; housing; industrial welfare services; investigation of social problems; responsibility for formulating a social welfare program; coordination and interlocking of public and voluntary services; stimulation of voluntary services and of voluntary assistance to public bodies; training of social workers, public and voluntary.

This is a far cry from casework or group work and, though related to community organization, goes considerably farther, approaching the social statesmanship which, in my opinion, offers social work unprecedentedly challenging opportunities.

"And how," do you ask, "will social workers be drawn into posts such as those described here?" By proving that we really have something to offer. Before we can expect much increase in demand for our "social organizers" or "social statesmen" we must give evidence through voluntary action that we can see needs that others overlook and that we know what to do about those needs. As time proves the validity of our insights, diagnoses, recommendations, and actions job opportunities are likely to expand far more rapidly than our capacity to fill them.

In his role as "social organizer" in planning, policy making, and administration at all levels the social worker might work very much like his colleague the caseworker who operates at the level of the individual. The latter does not himself assume the responsibilities of a nurse or a dentist or a schoolteacher or a policeman or a court officer. Rather, the social worker is the catalytic agent through which the services of these professions contribute to the total welfare of the whole individual. Similarly, the social statesman will not arrogate to himself the responsibilities of other professions, but, like the caseworker, will serve as catalyzer of those forces which must work together not only to serve individuals but to serve larger social wholes including entire peoples.

Caseworkers, says Kenneth Pray, help individuals to face the alternatives open to them, to appraise these alternatives, to struggle with their conflicting interests and feelings, to choose—and to pursue—a course of action.[2] Similarly the social organizer or social statesman could help administrators, officers, leaders, and the public concerned with governmental or voluntary, local, state, national, or international programs affecting the welfare of people to face the alternatives open to them and to choose and pursue those actions best calculated to assure the highest level of well-being for the largest possible number of persons.

By my standards it is not too much to hope that we may soon have in the social field the counterpart of the President's Council of Economic Advisors to plan the nation's grand strategy in social affairs and to lay down principles to guide not only federal and state departments concerned with social well-being but to guide, also, voluntary organizations dealing with these issues. If this should come it would require social statesmanship of the highest order. . . .

---

[2] Kenneth L. M. Pray, "Social Work in a Revolutionary Age," *Proceedings, National Conference of Social Work,* Buffalo, 1946 (New York: Columbia University Press, 1946), pp. 3-17.

Certainly, the competence which social work already possesses for these broader responsibilities must be much further developed if the challenge of the future is to be successfully met. Training for the future must give new emphasis to social research, to economics, to social psychology, to advanced community organization and administration if workers are to be equipped for social organization and social statesmanship. . . .

The second trend I want to discuss—one which has the utmost significance for the future—is the gradual development of social work from a salvage operation picking up broken bits of humanity to a far more constructive role.

It was inevitable, perhaps, that social work should first have become concerned with remedial measures. When resources, competence, and personnel are inadequate to the total need, it is not unreasonable to direct attention first to those who are most in need. But it is also clear why social work turned as soon as it could to prevention. This, it will be recalled, began timidly. Attention was focused not upon society as a whole, not upon entire communities, but rather upon those individuals in the community who appeared most likely to require remedial services unless preventive services could somehow obviate that need. The focus was upon such individuals as "predelinquents," upon persons "predisposed" to tuberculosis. The emphasis was still largely upon the individual with only a shift in timing as to when aid would be made available to him.

It was at a somewhat later stage that the focus was shifted from individuals to groups. But here again, preventive services were thought of in relation to "vulnerable" or "disadvantaged" groups and to "blighted areas" rather than to the community at large. At the turn of the century we were concerned primarily with what General William Booth, in England, termed the "submerged tenth." Under the inspiring leadership of President Roosevelt we developed concern for one-third of a nation—an absolute gain of some 23.33 per cent in thirty-five years!

Even today social work still accepts as its basic role the job of helping to make life as constructive as possible for those who are "disadvantaged" whether their disadvantage is attributable to economic need, to physical or mental disability, to lack of parental support, or any of the other social disabilities one suffers in our modern socioeconomic order, or, shall we say, disorder?

All, or at least most, of the while that social work has been preoccupied with services to disadvantaged groups, we talked as though we were equally concerned with the well-being of all groups. But, this was mostly talk which unfortunately was not validated by our actions. For example, we had a lot to say about families as the best possible environment for children and even for socially handicapped persons, unless they particularly needed some special type of institutional care. But we did not really mean this.

What we really meant and supported by our action was that families were the best places for poor children. We went to great lengths to make it possible for poor fathers and poor mothers to meet their responsibilities toward their children. However, we were peculiarly silent when wealthy families failed or were on the verge of failing to meet their responsibilities to their youngsters. . . .

Or, take the question of standards of living. Social work has gone to great lengths to assure economically needy families the material base necessary for family life, even though we know that assistance standards frequently exceed the standard of living which economically "independent" wage earners are able to secure for themselves. . . .

In the face of criticism . . . social work has two alternatives. . . . One choice would be to reduce assistance standards. . . .

The other choice, however, if one wanted not to retreat but to press forward, would be to attack the disparity between assistance standards and the still lower standard of living of many "economically independent" families by raising the latter. Further extension of the principle of the annual wage, raising of legally enforceable minimum wage levels, and adoption of the principle of family allowances are only some of the devices which might be employed to assure a more nearly adequate level of life for families of the nation's wage earners.

The dilemma which we now face in this field is not different from that which faced this country during the 1820's with respect to public education. Poor children, or, as we called them then, "pauper children," who were privileged to go to "charity schools" because their parents were poor, enjoyed educational benefits denied to the majority of children of the "working classes." This anomaly in its day aroused almost exactly the same kind of resentment which is raised today by assistance standards in excess of those which wage-earners can maintain.

To avoid the criticism that poor children were being better educated than were children of workers' families, the free education of pauper children might have been abandoned. Fortunately, however, the leaders of the 1820's did not retreat. They counterattacked and utimately succeeded in making free education available not only to poor children but to all children including those who were rich.

Today, we, in our turn, are confronted by a similar challenge to make available not only to poor children and to poor families, but to all children and all families including those who are rich, social education and social services required to strengthen family life, to improve levels of nutrition, and to assure adequate standards of living—to name but a few of the social objectives before us. The primary concern of social work in the future, in my opinion, should be the conscious effort, both constructive and preventive, to aid people to achieve for themselves the highest level of individual and collective well-being attainable and to assure provision for the economic, physical, and social require-ments of particular regions, groups, or individuals whose needs are not otherwise met. . . .

That American social workers—or at least some of them—recog-nize the need for positive action in broader fields of service, is clearly evidenced by such declarations as the various platform statements of the American Association of Social Workers.

But, you will ask, even if it is conceded that these high new social goals are the proper concern of the social worker, what specifically is he responsible for doing about them?

Certainly we will do about them in the future not less than we have done in the past. Some of us will continue to render in conjunction with these broad programs the professional services which we are already rendering. We will also develop our present equipment, particularly our skills in community organization and in administration, so that we may better use these tools in the interest of broader objectives. We will continue to participate in social action. Finally, we must—in my opin-ion—develop the skills embodied in what I have already described as "social organization" and "social statesmanship": namely, the capacity to care what happens to people when their well-being is threatened and their social development thwarted; the ability to measure and to help the public to understand the effects of conditions which harm or limit social well-being; and finally, the administrative and organizational "know-how" and "do-how" required for the advancement of the general welfare.

Again, we may ask ourselves, if social work does not prepare itself for this future role, who will? And, if this role is not filled, will we be content to leave these important functions to pure chance?

If increased attention were given to broad-scale preventive and, better still, constructive social measures, we would find unlimited opportu-nities before us. In the health field, for example, we would no longer be satisfied merely to give money to a handful of needy people so that they may purchase for themselves such care as they can buy on the open market. Neither would we be content to organize small clinics or free hospital services through which doctors imbued with more than an ordinary sense of social responsibility might give free or cheap medi-cal care to comparatively small numbers of patients. Neither would emphasis be placed upon developing some kind of low-grade or sub-standard care that could be made available to limited numbers of medi-cally needy persons. What would be indicated, rather, would be em-phasis upon the importance of helping to mobilize all of the nation's health resources so as to assure all people the highest attainable level of physical well-being.

In the economic field we would concentrate less exclusively upon assistance to those who are in need, less upon insurance to tide over periods when earnings are not available, less upon work relief programs to provide substitute employment for persons squeezed out of normal work opportunities. Emphasis rather would be placed upon the significance of real employment, upon the consequent importance of maintaining high-level employment, upon raising minimum wage standards, upon annual wage plans, family allowance schemes, and methods of relating wage levels to price levels so as to assure a continuity of income, and income adjusted to family needs.

In the field of personal and social relations we would make clear that we are interested not only in the integrity and mutual relations among members of poor families but also in the preservation and strengthening of all families. In the educational and cultural fields, we would urge adult education, playgrounds, and recreational and cultural opportunities not only in poor neighborhoods and in "settlement districts" but in all communities.

Obviously, "social organization" cannot be initiated in too many new areas simultaneously, and social work cannot aspire to fill a role for which it is not yet prepared. Nevertheless, it is important that at least a beginning should be made. We must pick those areas in which broad social action is most needed. We must then get the facts about what is now happening to people because of our failure to realize the highest possible level of social well-being in these areas. We must use to the fullest our own skills, including our ability to ascertain what other skills are required to meet the needs disclosed. And finally, we must press with all possible vigor the development of skills required for "social organization" and "social statesmanship" and press as rapidly as possible toward inclusion of the teaching of these skills in our programs of social work education. . . .

However, social work may have to make some new plans for itself if it wants to help build . . . a bulwark to give the greatest possible support to the largest possible number of people in the world-wide fight for a better life for all mankind.

17

Social Work and the "Social Generalist" [1]

By HERTHA KRAUS

Approaching the subject of the future of social work from a somewhat different angle from Mr. Howard in Selection 16, Hertha Kraus throws down before social work an equally significant challenge.

Can social workers serve as "social generalists"? Can we "offer a specific professional competence in helping to shape a changing society so that it may produce a better order for all"? Are social workers prepared to function in such a role?

Dr. Kraus came to this country in 1933, after serving as director of Public Welfare of the City of Cologne. In this country and abroad she has made a great variety of contributions in the areas of community organization, public welfare, international social welfare, research, and teaching. She has always had a broad philosophical approach to problems of social program and policy, united with a firm grounding in economics and political science.

Here she has a vision of something that social work—and particularly community organization—should seek to attain. "Professional social service," she says, "should become a channel for applied insight, knowledge, and skill, directing them effectively toward more adequate community planning and service production."

[1] Excerpted from "The Future of Social Work: Some Comments on Social Work Function," *Social Work Journal,* Vol. XXIX, Jan., 1948, pp. 3-9. By permission of National Association of Social Workers.

I

. . . OUR CONCERN IS . . . [with] millions of men, women, and children, on every age level. We see them handicapped in meeting common human needs, in their individual strife for living up to their highest potential. We have developed valuable and important techniques to assist a few of them within very definite limitations of our own and the community's capacity for such personalized help, frequently improvising resources around each individual's need.

Can we face the reality of masses of people in need of help, distributed throughout a gigantic country, living in hamlets, small towns, cities and crowded metropolitan areas—and still rely, in the main, on the ideal of a professional service dependent on social techniques of reaching one by one? . . .

We claim [2] that social work's contribution to the community of today and of tomorrow is in the field of social relationships "specifically related to the strains and tensions of inevitable growth and change. . . . Social work comes into play when familiar satisfying social relationships are threatened, weakened, or broken and when new ones fail to materialize or are shrouded in uncertainty or involved in conflict. It develops when people, individually or collectively, need help in clarifying their responsibilities and opportunities within their own circle of relationships." Social work "is identified with the individual but only in his effort to derive satisfaction and benefit from the social relationships which are or can be opened to him." If identified with the community, it is "always in the process of helping—helping individuals, groups or communities to realize for themselves the potential values which are embedded in their essential relationships . . . , for the heart of the social worker's service is in his own relationship with those whom he endeavors to serve. . . ."

This concept of social work, widely accepted today, has most important implications. It influences profoundly public attitudes, the community's use of social work in the areas of social planning, design, construction, social management. It restricts professional practice and professional education. It influences strongly the self-selection and the schools' selection of candidates for professional training, welcoming into the fold those predominantly interested in the art and science of social relations. It makes it rather difficult for those visualizing another social work potential to find substantial and suitable preparation—or even to survive the discipline as now offered. It determines the basic selection of areas of knowledge and skills transmitted to the student. It determines the relative weight of classroom and field instruction, of theoretical studies and clinical experience. It affects the selection of agen-

---

[2] Kenneth L. M. Pray, "Social Work in a Revolutionary Age," *Proceedings of the National Conference of Social Work,* 1946, pp. 3 ff.

we do not follow through in its logical consequences. They believe in cies for fieldwork and the student's exposure to community experience, emphasizing the value of certain experiences under sheltered conditions, eliminating the possibility of other socially significant experiences from his ken. . . .

We do know, however, that the outstanding proponents of the social work concept as stated are perfectly aware of another aspect—which social work's "ancient, simple, all-inclusive objective of helping human beings to find the opportunity and incentive to make the most of them-selves and so to make the largest possible contribution to the progress and well-being of the whole society." [3]

Commonly two consequences of our concern for such "opportunities" are indicated, a professional and a civic one. The professional challenge leads to work with groups and communities as if they were individuals, helping them "to develop relationships. . . ."

The other alternative is offered in more civic participation in all creative endeavors of social significance. It should be noted that in this interpretation the social worker today is strongly encouraged to live up to the highest ideals of co-operative citizenship in a democracy. He is expected to make a civic contribution to the development of the Good Community. His contribution is seen, however, as nonprofessional and extracurricular. He is not expected, as part of his professional expert-ness, to contribute knowledge and skills toward this development, ex-cept that at times he may give "valid, uniquely valuable testimony" based on competence and experience in dealing professionally with the people's social relationships. . . .

II

It seems timely to outline the case for a broader concept of the social work function for community service, and some of its implications.

In line with a distinguished tradition, firmly established by the great pioneers of social work everywhere, we may well offer a specific pro-fessional competence in helping to shape a changing society so that it may produce a better order for all. After due preparation we should re-establish our claim for professional, not only civic, participation in this important work. I submit that we have, as the very core of our professional contribution, not as a specialization, a professional function related to those "opportunities"—both organized and intangible com-munity resources—on which emotional and economic security, mental and physical health, quality of family and community life, and optimum productivity of our society depend so widely.

Our basic efforts have always dealt and will always deal with the un-ending task of helping human beings to live more satisfying and more

---

[3] See among others, Pray, *op. cit.,* p. 6.

productive lives within a given society. In a democracy, however, our concern is every human being in need of help, not just the hand-picked few, admitted by highly selective agencies. To free the highest potential of the many, the masses, we must develop and apply that professional knowledge and skill which will strengthen the social design and the total service production of our society. . . .

We have helped to finance, staff, and operate these instrumentalities with increasing finesse. We have always assisted in finding societal solutions to meet segmental problems. They were rarely, however, integrated, comprehensive solutions. We have accepted hit-or-miss developments, often based on outdated precedent, superficially modernized. . . .

Yes, we have made considerable progress in coverage of a few needs. But not in a fundamentally new approach, not in devising new and effective patterns of service, not in basic integration, not in dealing systematically with causes of needs instead of painful, wasteful results.

We are quite aware of this problem; we discuss it widely. But we do not turn toward our own ranks for a steady contribution of expertness to overcome slowly a thoroughly bad situation. In this vast area of improving traditional community resources, creating new ones, socializing all of them—in reviewing our total equipment for the good life—we should surely not depend alone on hunches and hearsay, on occasional gleanings of foreign experience, on the composite thought and skill of the butcher, the baker, and the candlestick maker contributed to social design and service production.

Community resources in education, in health, in religion, in recreation, in housing and home substitution, in employment and income protection, are clearly different from each other in many respects. They require for their detailed planning and operation a team including technical experts. But they hold one thing in common: they are organized responses of society to common, repetitive human needs. Health and happiness, the productivity and dignity of innumerable individuals, are strongly affected by their policies, organization, and structure, by their distribution, accessibility, standards and scope. So they require also—as an essential member of the planning and producing teams—the socially conscious generalist who is professionally concerned with the whole person, of any age, with the whole family, and their interaction with the whole community.

Is there any other professional group available to assume the role of the social generalist? Are social workers ready to function in this role?

Social workers know a great deal of the results of deficient community resources tragically inadequate for the prevention of breakdown and deterioration, equally inadequate often for the treatment of such conditions. Such knowledge carries with it compelling responsibilities. It must be deepened and supplemented by a planned search for more knowledge. It must be disciplined, blended, and sharply focused. It must be applied to comprehensive and basic measures. Professional social service should become a channel for applied insight, knowledge and skill, directing them effectively toward more adequate community planning and service production. This planning and production, furthermore, should be more adequately focused on the welfare of the individual in a more co-operative and more socially oriented economy. . . .

Perhaps we can manage to produce, out of vision and knowledge and skill, spurred by sincerest motivation, the kind of social and economic order in which all people will find the essential provisions for greater security of home and family life, of sound bodies and minds, of educational and spiritual goals, of satisfying work and of reasonable income: prerequisites to high productivity and a decent standard of living.

We are just beginning to arrange our society so as to offer some of these opportunities to each individual. We have hardly started work in dead seriousness on the institutional implementation of the slightly more limited "American dream." Such implementation will call for a valid design of the good community by good craftsmen. Qualified "statesmen and craftsmen" (Kenneth Pray) should be available to help transfer such a design from blueprints into community action. To see it through—all over the land—from conception and birth and the hazards of early infancy to vigorous maturity.

The validity of the design will surely depend on a clear and continuous recognition of its central function: building a community fit for man.

This community will provide him with the common tools and the group equipment, the organized resources and opportunities for developing, realizing, and utilizing his highest potential.

The designer must aim at a master plan of the good community on every level—local, regional, national, international—and for many functional aspects. He must plan in terms of millions, irrespective of residence, of economic status, or minority or majority affiliation. He must aim at vastly more than splinter projects or specialized fractional programs dealing with symptoms. He must go far beyond providing trim units in slum settings, bright spots of dramatic service for a few, while millions continue to waste their dignity and their power in the deep shadows of neighborhood blight and community neglect. He must rethink solutions, recognize community needs more than agency traditions. . . . He may have to discard many a time-honored division of service functions and specialties as costly, competitive, and meaningless; he may have to discard a good deal of the ancient crazy quilt. . . .

The master plan must relate to man as a whole, not to any of his abstractions. All his needs are interdependent. So should be our specialized efforts to educate, to treat, to train, to counsel him, to provide a floor under his income, to strengthen his capacity to manage, to release or redirect his energies toward socially acceptable goals. We need joint and interlocking operations, vastly more effective and economical than now. We need their blending into new streamlined service units worthy of an advanced technology: sound community investments.

Is there any professional group, outside social work, who would have a stronger mandate to participate, continuously and professionally, in this task? Is there any other group equally qualified by tradition, experience, social exposure, professional objectives, insight?

I suggest that we should stand ready to claim and assume our rightful role as social generalists—among many specialists—willing and able to help transform a competitive into a social economy. . . .

III

It may be well to outline some of the implications of this concept. How would it affect the professional worker's areas of practice?

Quite generally speaking, social workers should be found or at least should be in demand wherever community services are in the process of socialization: where they are directed or redirected toward helping people to live more adequately. Thus the social worker's place would be in every field of community planning and in the development of good social design for the smallest or largest service units. He would belong among the legislative drafters, but also among the mobilizers of citizen groups toward stronger efforts for social welfare. His place would be in all educational programs, especially in education for family and neighborhood life, for productive work and for enlightened citizenship.

The social worker—as a generalist—should also be trusted with the management of many public and private service units. He should be found in key positions of such operation so that their product would become increasingly well related to human needs and essential human values. He would attempt to close the gap between our proposed goals in service and many of our traditional methods, for instance in much of our institutional service production. It would be a major part of his professional function to analyze and to develop policies and procedures, to remove blocks within "channels," to expedite the production of service and to improve both quality and quantity. . . .

In other types of agencies well-trained social workers may well be found on the operating level, functioning somewhat along the lines of the best private agency practice of today, engaged in the direct production of a variety of individualized services. Perhaps these agencies will actually represent experimental and research projects. If we want to improve our methods of production, if we want to develop new and more effective approaches, we must stand ready to test our working hypotheses in such tentative, small-scale operations. We must also be willing to demonstrate the value of desirable changes—for instance, reintegration of many traditionally specialized programs—before we can expect acceptance by a skeptical public within and outside our profession. Such testing and demonstration—never an end in itself—requires a maximum of professional skill, knowledge, and integrity; it requires the full professional investment. This investment may cease to be suitaable when the testing period is over. . . .

Finally, an important area of practice must be seen in the social orientation of allied professions, in classrooms and field, and in the professional education of our own groups.

This sketchy listing already points out certain implications regarding personnel policy: It involves a major redistribution of our professional power. It implies the absorption of many qualified workers in administrative and educational key positions not necessarily in recognized "social" agencies. It implies that the majority of positions on the operating level will be filled with social technicians, of the best possible general education oriented to our time. Their skills, their technical orientation and information, and their point of view will largely depend on in-service training: on the quality of professional leadership and staff development offered to them.

Within such redistribution, there is also the exciting possibility of a changed alliance between public and voluntary efforts in social welfare. Perhaps voluntary agencies will be willing to abandon a tradition of isolated service units—with necessarily most limited output—for the sake of a richer and more far-reaching social product based on a new partnership. Instead of maintaining independent establishments, and absorbing within them a very considerable percentage of the best professional workers, federated voluntary agencies may be willing to contribute units of professional staff and volunteers to an expanding public service which may then become more effectively socialized and alive.

Such contributions could be made in the form of consultant units, teaching units, clinical units, experimental and research units, or units of voluntary aids, each under the most qualified professional direction and, with the exception of the last, professionally staffed. Such voluntary contribution would be concentrated on staff service, free of overhead, but at the price of lessened agency identification and a less artificial division of functions. It would facilitate staff development in the public services, permit more quality, intensity, and some desirable specializations.

The introduction and guidance of units of voluntary workers would aid in making the public service more personal and human, more frequent in contacts, more project-minded. It would also add significantly to the social education of the taxpayer and voter. As participant observer—in general and mental hospitals, county homes and county welfare departments, in health centers and play centers—the citizen will discover some "facts of life" for which he often holds major responsibility.

Undoubtedly some voluntary agencies will be needed, independent of the public service, preserving full identity and concentrating on some carefully selected functions. They will probably be in the area which we have always recognized as being particularly suited to voluntary enterprise: service production which goes beyond publicly accepted social objectives or which enters into highly controversial fields. Other service units will experiment with and/or demonstrate a new type of service, ready to proceed to further experimentation whenever they have proved and interpreted the validity of their original approach.

Finally, within our culture some voluntary service units may be focused on service limited by sectarian considerations, wishing to express a specific religious attitude as an integral part of the service to be rendered. . . .

Without going into detail, it will be readily understood that the broader concept of social work profoundly affects the plan of professional education. We are agreed that the present one is not yet perfect. We are deeply interested in improving it, and in adapting it to changed needs. Our effective adaptation, however, must largely depend on our own definition of needs. If we continue to base our definition on a study of current professional practice, on the current interest of our students influenced by actual practice, and on the current demand of the more articulate agencies traditionally interested in employing professional workers, we will obtain a picture of "need" for professional workers rather different from the requirements of the field as based on a study of history and a more conceptual analysis. We must break the vicious circle of a one-sided concept of social work, practice related to this concept, education related to both. Jointly they have brought us to a social service production and to a social service function of a strangely one-sided, limited character. They are not truly indicative of our real potential, of our continuing responsibility in a democratic, dynamic, challenging community.

18

New Wine and Old Bottles [1]

By ROBERT H. MAC RAE

Rarely has the spirit of progressive community organization been more aptly expressed than in this article by Robert MacRae. With insight and breadth of vision, he surveys health and welfare planning in terms of the "new wines" in our social situation, the "old bottles" that limit our effectiveness, and what can be done "to make the 'old bottle' of community organization adequate to handle the 'new wine' of emerging problems."

Robert MacRae has had long experience in leadership in community welfare planning—formerly as executive of the Detroit Chest and Council and more recently in his present position as executive director of the Welfare Council of Metropolitan Chicago.

NEW WINE IN OLD BOTTLES, as was pointed out in St. Matthew, is a hazardous combination. Remarkable things are taking place in these United States. These are the "new wines" about to be poured into old community organization "bottles." Let's list some of them.

---

[1] Excerpted from article of the same title, *Community* (New York: Community Chests and Councils of America, Inc., Vol. 30, May, 1955), pp. 163-164; 175. From a speech delivered at the Spring Meeting of the National Social Welfare Assembly, April, 1955. By permission of United Community Funds and Councils of America, Inc.

The New Wines

1. The most explosive thing in America is our population growth. Forecasters believe there will be a population increase of 20 per cent by 1965; 40 per cent by 1975. Translated into numbers this means 190,-000,000 Americans by 1965 and 220,000,000 by 1975.

Even more interesting than the numbers will be the composition of this soaring population in 1965. With an increase of about 30 million there will be approximately six million more people over 65 and about sixteen million more under 20 than there are today. The increase in the labor force during this period has caused Peter Drucker to characterize the next decade as the period of the coming labor shortage.

2. The second trend in our "new wine" group is increasing urbanism, with the staggering growth of suburban living. The trend toward making the parent city simply a workshop and the flight of leadership and business to suburbs is too well-known to require documentation. Most certainly it does require thoughtful attention.

3. The growth of automation in industry is the third trend requiring our consideration. Accompanying it, clearly, will be an increase in leisure time and a demand for more technically skilled manpower for industry.

4. The continuing mobility of the American people to meet the needs of modern industry is a fact that community organizers cannot ignore. Currently, it is reported that 30 million Americans change their residences each year—a fact full of significance for social welfare.

5. Desegregation and lessening of racial discrimination are encouraging factors of our times. But on the discouraging side is the continuance of world tension and the necessity for the U. S. to live as a form of garrison state. Every social worker dealing with young people can testify to the impact of military service. If universal military training comes, the impact will be even sharper.

6. Finally, barring war it is reasonable to asume a continuing improvement in the standard of living measured in economic terms. In the campaign against poverty, America is winning some of the battle.

The Old Bottles

So much for some of the new wine. Now a look at some of the old bottles.

1. Negative community attitudes about the wisdom and validity of planning. Social planning is regarded as near-subversive in some influential quarters.

2. A traditional Council of Social Agencies structure which is agency-centered rather than problem-centered. Such a structure is more competent to deal with adjustments of present agency programs than it is to face new issues.

3. Community welfare planning councils tend to lack status and are generally understaffed and underfinanced.

4. Skills in community planning are still inadequate for the magnitude of the task.

5. There is only limited development of regional, state, and national level planning operations.

6. Apparently, we are unable to communicate the objectives of community planning with any marked success.

What Can Be Done?

What should we do to make the "old bottle" of community organization adequate to handle the "new wine" of emerging problems? The answers will be found in structure, policies, techniques, and leadership personnel.

The first step should be an enlargement of the concept of community welfare planning. The traditional Council of Social Agencies with its agency-centered program is no longer adequate. The larger concept of community welfare planning which is problem-centered can attract a wider range of community leadership and can attack more fundamental problems. A mere change of name is not adequate. What is required is a change of attitude and a new willingness to become a vehicle for citizen action on basic problems of health and welfare.

Here, a word of warning is in order. We cannot and must not ignore the agency structure. It is the channel through which we will work and the source of much leadership and knowledge. Nevertheless, the new Community Welfare Council must draw on a much wider representation than the existing agencies can offer. The inclusion of labor participation in recent years is an illustration of the community forces outside of the agency structure eager to have a part in community welfare planning.

Accompanying the change in structure of the parent council must come the further development of the neighborhood council approach in large cities. The planning process must be decentralized. There must be a mechanism to provide citizens an opportunity to voice their needs and have a part in the process of the filling of those needs. One of the most critical problems of urban living lies in the fact that the average citizen feels that he does not count, that he has no way of participating in community affairs. The neighborhood council can fill that need in part. Our very limited investment in this approach suggests a potential of tremendous significance.

The growth of suburban areas requires further adaptations on the part of parent city welfare planning councils. Suburban communities, facing a welter of social and health problems, want help in dealing with those problems. At the same time it is imperative that the suburban community planning be related to the parent city and the region surrounding it. A narrow provincialism will defeat economical, efficient, and humane community planning.

At this point, let me also observe the importance of further strengthening of national community planning through the National Social Welfare Assembly. The near-anarchy of the national scene seriously complicates local welfare planning.

Accompanying the structural changes in local councils outlined above must come the opening of lines of communication with the physical and economic planners operating in the same area. The opportunities for mutual help and strengthening of community services are great in such a partnership.

Wanted: Policy Statements

A basic instrument for planning in the day of the "new wine" is a set of policy statements to guide the division of responsibility between governmental and voluntary auspices. The majority of communities now operate largely on a catch-as-catch-can hodgepodge of policies lacking consistent design. This was probably inevitable as we felt our way and even characteristic of a pluralistic society. Yet the time has come for a conscious design of such a set of policies. They will differ from community to community, reflecting community tradition and mores. They will always be guides, not absolute dictates for action. Yet they are essential. Problems of financing and our growing insight into human needs require that we have such a set of policies to guide our planning. I grow increasingly concerned at the efforts of voluntary agencies in the casework and group work fields attempting to offer coverage service with resources which grow increasingly inadequate as the services are more widely accepted. The effort can end only in unsatisfactory and unsatisfying work. We must have an honest facing up to the real limitations of voluntary agencies and the need to use the broader base of government. There is and always will be in a democratic society a place for the voluntary agency. Its role, however, is not that of attempting to do coverage jobs on pin money budgets.

Community Welfare Councils should be the vehicle for tough-minded thinking on the appropriate division of responsibility between the voluntary dollar and the tax dollar. Today we act most frequently on sentiment and emotion, not logical thought.

Evaluative Research

An essential tool for planning for "new wine" is evaluative research. Too often we waste money on services which are of limited value and may even be harmful. The Assembly and the CCC might well join some of the large Councils in designing evaluative research studies, and in seeking foundation support. The evaluative research tools will be enormously difficult to design but our consciences and our contributors will insist on them.

The next essential for the days ahead is the development of more adequately prepared professional leadership for Welfare Planning Councils. Chest and Council leaders exercise tremendous influence for good or ill on the development of community health and welfare programs. I am appalled at how ill-prepared some of us are to exercise the leadership we must give. Equally appalling with lack of professional skill is the number of community organizers who have no spiritual identification with the social work movement. How can a man guide or represent a movement in which he does not believe?

The community organization movement should now be sufficiently mature to recruit more carefully and to weed out the disbelievers and incompetents. Furthermore, there is need for strengthening the professional curriculum for community organization in our schools of social work. The Assembly and CCC need to provide more aggressive leadership in this area in the days immediately ahead.

The Process Itself

As we prepare for the problems ahead I am hopeful we will give critical examination to the community organization process itself. Community organizers as a professional group have been pragmatists, far more interested in results than they have been in applying critical judgment to process. It is high time we did so. Furthermore the process has such great influence on American social work that it seems strange that foundations have not attempted research on the community organization process. Have we done all we could on designing research and enlisting foundation interest? Obviously not.

The Problem of Communication

Finally, among the greatest of our problems remains the problem of communication. We have learned to design good campaign posters. We have learned to stir some people's emotions either of sympathy or fear. What we have largely failed to do is to interpret to the mass of citizens their personal stake in strong social welfare programs. Understanding continues to rest all too widely on a base of patronizing charity. It is imperative that we deepen that understanding. Social welfare will gain status when we discipline its sentimentalism and communicate its significance to a good society.

These items I have mentioned and others as well, are problems before us in preparing the "old bottles" for the "new wine." I hope we have the collective wisdom and the commitment to deal with them successfully so that social welfare services play their full part in building a wholesome society.

I have mentioned the necessity of improved professional competence. In the process I hope we may not lose two qualities essential to vital social work which capture public imagination. These qualities are moral indignation and idealism. Without them we will not succeed.

Let me close with a quotation from Albert Schweitzer which seems central to our purpose:

"What shall be my attitude toward other life? It can only be of a piece with my attitude toward my own life. If I am a thinking being, I must regard other life than my own with equal reverence. For I shall know that it longs for fullness and development as deeply as I do myself. Therefore, I see that evil is what annihilates, hampers or hinders life. . . . Goodness, by the same token, is saving or helping of life, the enabling of whatever life I can influence to attain its highest development."

Introduction

PART II DEALT WITH THE THEORY and principles of community organization, its history, and the outlook for its future. Part III deals with "Community Organization in Practice"—the dynamics of community organization, and how the process is applied through specific methods. The twenty-five selections in Part III are grouped under eight headings. The first deals with Steps and General Methods in the Community Organization Process. There is certainly not complete agreement on what are to be regarded as the methods of community organization, yet the editors believe that there would be rather general agreement on most of the seven methods represented in this Part. These seven methods are fact finding; planning; conference and committees—achieving integration; education, interpretation, and public relations; fund raising; social action; and recording.

Some writers regard social action as a separate process, parallel with community organization, rather than as an aspect of community organization. However, a section on social action is included here for two reasons: first, there is a considerable body of opinion (which, incidentally, the editors share) that social action in respect to social welfare objectives is properly regarded as an aspect of community organization; and second, because the same practitioners frequently engage in social action and other forms of community organization, it seems best to include social action methods along with the other methods presented, as part of the normal practice of community organization workers.

Though the literature on community organization methods is somewhat inadequate and "spotty" as a whole, a number of the most authoritative and most useful contributions that have been made are included among the selections which follow. The crucial subject of citizen leadership and participation is not included, as it might have been, as a separate topic under this general heading; but its importance is implicit in many of the selections throughout this volume: for example, those by MacRae (33), Sieder (46), United Community Funds and Councils (52), Blanchard (56), Glasser (69), and all the selections on community development (70–75).

Steps and General Methods
—Introduction

IN SOCIAL CASEWORK, the idea of typical successive "steps"—for example, psychosocial study, diagnosis, planning, and treatment—has long been accepted in professional thinking and practice. So, too, in community organization several attempts have been made to analyze the "typical steps" in the development of community organization projects. Two such analyses are represented in the selections that follow. Probably the earliest and best-known analysis is that by Eduard C. Lindeman, in his book on *The Community* (1921). This is followed by a thoughtful and stimulating discussion of "choices and steps" in community organization, by Hertha Kraus (1948).

Suggested summaries of "methods of community organization" are found in the Lane Report of 1939, in *Social Work Year Book* articles on community organization, and in some of the textbooks on the subject. All these inventories differ from each other, except in one or two instances, where one author has followed the analysis of an earlier writer. The summary in the Lane Report is reproduced elsewhere in this volume (Selection 5). In this section two broad considerations of method are introduced—Clarence King's discussion of "leadership in community integration," and Wilber I. Newstetter's presentation of "social intergroup work" as the unique central aspect of community organization.

19

Ten Steps in Community Action [1]

By EDUARD C. LINDEMAN

Lindeman's "ten steps" are probably the most widely known passage from his book on *The Community,* as well as being doubtless the earliest attempt to analyze the typical "steps" in community organization.

Lindeman's approach to this task was inductive rather than deductive. He introduces his formulation with a casual and tantalizing remark, which suggests nothing so much as the "unrecorded cases" of Sherlock Holmes! He says: "In making the study which forms the basis of this chapter, community projects were considered. . . . Slightly more than seven hundred such projects [!] have been studied with the aim of determining whether, or not, any psychological and sociological facts might be induced." After a few other remarks, he proceeds to the cautious introductory paragraph and the statement of the ten steps below.

Steps in Community Action

It appears that there are certain definite steps which community groups pass through in arriving at points of action. The division of these steps, here attempted, is quite arbitrary, and should not be considered in a

[1] Excerpted from *The Community—An Introduction to the Study of Community Leadership and Organization* (New York: Association Press, 1921), pp. 120-123. The "ten steps" are reproduced in Dwight Sanderson and Robert A. Polson, *Rural Community Organization* (New York: John Wiley & Sons, Inc., 1939), pp. 223-224.

strictly scientific manner. Persons who have studied these summaries do not agree on the classification here used. Further study and analysis of a larger number of projects may change the classification materially.

A portion of these steps in community action are sociological, and some are psychological. There is no apparent means by which the sciences of sociology and of social psychology can be separated in this analysis.

Step Number One

Consciousness of need: some person, either within or without the community, expresses the need which is later represented by the definite project.

Step Number Two

Spreading the consciousness of need: a leader, within some institution or group within the community, convinces his or her group, or a portion of the group, of the reality of the need.

Step Number Three

Projection of consciousness of need: the group interested attempts to project the consciousness of need upon the leadership of the community; the consciousness of need becomes more general.

Step Number Four

Emotional impulse to meet the need quickly: some influential assistance is enlisted, in the attempt to arrive at a quick means of meeting the need.

Step Number Five

Presentation of other solutions: other means of meeting the need are presented.

Step Number Six

Conflict of solutions: various groups lend their support to one or the other of the various solutions presented.

Step Number Seven

Investigation: it appears to be increasingly customary to pause at this point, and to investigate the project with expert assistance. (This step, however, is usually omitted and the following one takes its place.)

Step Number Eight

Open discussion of issue: a public mass meeting or gathering of some sort is held, at which the project is presented, and the groups with most influence attempt to secure adoption of their plans.

Step Number Nine

Integration of solutions: the various solutions presented are tested, with an effort to retain something out of each, in the practicable solution which is now emerging.

Step Number Ten

Compromise on basis of tentative progress: certain groups relinquish certain elements of their plans in order to save themselves from complete defeat, and the solution which results is a compromise with certain reservations. The means selected for meeting the need are not satisfactory to all groups, but are regarded as tentatively progressive.

Many projects end at Step Number Four, on the emotional plane. Other projects are closed, either favorably or unfavorably, at some one of the following six steps. (It must be remembered that all projects do not originate in the manner here indicated, nor do all of them pass through all of these steps. This Outline merely represents the procedure that emerges from a study of those projects which are more or less typical of the processes that make up the present stage of community action.) . . .

The underlying forces which have produced the Community Movement have also made it necessary to devise some sort of social machinery which will give functional reality to the movement. The Community Movement as a social force and community organization as a phase of social process should not be confused. The essential problem of community organization is to furnish a working relationship between the *Democratic Process and Specialism.* The Democratic Process expresses itself, or is personified in the total community membership. The Specialist expresses himself, or is personified, in the division of labor which produces highly skilled persons and agencies, organizations, or institutions, equipped to do one thing effectively.

The specialist, as an individual or as a representative of an institution, can achieve more rapidly in an autocratic environment in which specialism is recognized scientifically. When scientific education becomes more or less universal, the specialist's progress will be more direct and more rapid. But, in societies where scientific education is not universal, the specialist comes into what appears to be a direct conflict with Democracy. The democratic method is slow, cumbersome, halting and beset with many back-eddies which seem to be antiprogressive. The specialist becomes impatient with all of this and desires to go straight toward his goal. He *knows.* The constituents of Democracy do not know, and must be shown the way. The way may be long and devious but it cannot be avoided; there is no short-cut toward Democracy. If there were, it would be "too light a thing" as an ideal, and the children of earth would not suffer for its achievement.

Community organization exists wherever Democracy and Specialism are approximating working relationships. It may not be possible to diagram this relationship—for it may be nothing more than an element of good will—but it is nevertheless a phase of community organization which presages some later form of mechanics of organization. There is a tendency among many community organization enthusiasts to perfect a mechanical structure in advance of a social and spiritual foundation. Charts and diagrams of schemes for community organization have their value, if it is clearly understood that they are mere pictures and that they, like all pictures, depict but poorly the image of a reality. Such pictorial schemes of community organization contain dangers for students, inasmuch as they portray something which is almost wholly imaginary and which does not exist in fact. Social engineering, as it evolves toward the stage of art, will be more closely akin to the art of the poet than to that of the draughtsman or the painter. It will be an expression of spirit and of function, rather than of structure. . . .

20

Choices and Steps in Community Organization[1]

BY HERTHA KRAUS

What are some of the major choices or alternatives in the use of the process of community welfare organization? In presenting a thought-provoking answer to this question, Hertha Kraus formulates some basic concepts and principles, and she analyzes also the probable phases or steps "in attempting a better adjustment of organized resources to needs." Dr. Kraus has had an international experience. She was director of public welfare in Cologne, Germany, before coming to the United States in 1933; she has since worked in several different countries and on various aspects of problems of international social welfare. Since 1936 she has been a member of the faculty of the Carola Woerishoffer Graduate Department of Social Economy and Social Research, Bryn Mawr College. She has made a number of basic philosophical contributions to the literature of community organization: excerpts from one of these—"The Future of Social Work: Some Comments on Social Work Function"—appears in these Selections (No. 17). Another challenging paper is entitled *Common Services in a Free Society: Attempt at a Frame of Reference.*[2]

[1] Excerpted from "Community Organization in Social Work—A Note on Choices and Steps," *Social Forces,* Vol. 27 (Oct., 1948), pp. 54-57. By permission of *Social Forces,* University of North Carolina Press.

[2] (New York: Association for the Study of Community Organization, 1954), mimeographed, 26 pp.

Phases in Community Organization

IN THE PROCESS OF attempting a better adjustment of organized resources to needs, we are likely to pass through several consecutive phases, an observation which should be tested by recording and by repeated analysis of actual proceedings. Some phases are much better understood than others. Some absorb an extraordinary share of attention and energy, such as fact finding, with meager leavings for the other phases.

Records and analysis of the community organization process in action, applied to project units, may benefit by some frame of reference in which each step can be usefully related to a characteristic phase.

We always need to understand and to define our production goal in service. We also need to trace our flow of work toward this goal. The goal must provide over-all direction for the movement, but there are important stages in production which have to be reached and passed, one by one, for the sake of the quality and stability of the final product. It may well be part of the knowledge and skill of the professional worker in community organization to be able to visualize clearly all necessary steps and their sequence in such a manner that a tentative "production schedule" may be planned for each unit of project operation, allowing adequate talent, time, and funds for each.

1. A definite statement of the objective of the service (or of the project) may not seem important wherever there is a good deal of unity of purpose and a tacitly accepted common basis for goals to be achieved. Its formulation may not attract interested attention and may not seem thought provoking. It will, however, offer the welcome chance to articulate within the working group an area of common understanding. It will also provide the all-important direction for the activities to follow and a yardstick by which methods and procedures, also partial achievements, should be measured.

In other cases, however, our goal may imply quite controversial subjects, such as raising the standards of living of dependent groups, or helping our enemies, or extending organized services beyond age-old frontiers. If so, the development of some common ground of understanding, of unity in objective, may become a major task in need of wise and deliberate efforts.

2. In the course of implementing a defined goal—the first phase—community organization must pass, in the next phase, through a number of efforts for the provision of a factual basis. As professional workers we are perfectly aware of the importance of such fact finding and of its contribution to the co-operative process. We know about the wide range of techniques which can be applied to this stage. Data may be sought about the characteristics of people in trouble; about available resources and the scope and quality of their service production; about unused service potentials within the community; about the community

proper and its individual characteristics as they affect both needs and services, actual and potential.

3. In the light of sifted, summarized, and analyzed information covering these major items, the processes of the third phase will take place. They center about the outline of a pattern of service considered effective in terms of the desired adjustment between needs and services. At the same time intermediate objectives will be defined. An effective plan for action-strategy, which will lead gradually from partial to full achievement, as visualized in establishing the goal, must be developed.

4. The fourth stage will test the validity of the tentative plan and selected service pattern by exposing it to public scrutiny. It will interpret the plan, including its background of facts and motivation, to various publics, seeking their approval and ultimately their support. The professed objectives and the proposed ways and means of reaching them will thus be checked against public opinion in general and against that of selected groups particularly interested in the area of planned adjustment: representatives of existent service resources, professional groups related to the field in question, potential beneficiaries. . . .

Although *testing by experiment,* or limited application, should be considered in addition, the working hypothesis may become the center of a promotional effort only. The publics will be approached with an interpretation of needs as seen by the planning group. They will learn of goals and objectives to be achieved through some form of service, tentatively narrowed down to a pre-selected pattern assumed to be most effective. The publics will be invited to contribute comment, encouragement, moral and financial support to this defined undertaking.

It is in this fourth phase that the tentative plan tends to develop from a working hypothesis toward a rigid set of formulas and prescriptions. The very fact that a working hypothesis has been publicly presented and has not been specifically rejected in the course of its promotion may seem to make it a pledge to the supporting publics. We hesitate to amend it during the following phases.

5. As a matter of fact, we are only now getting ready to develop, as the important fifth phase, a master plan which may well be different from the tentative plan of the third phase, because public discussions and exposure to experimentation should have brought to light comments and criticism of various kinds. These new factors should allow the planning group to modify the original plan in the light of the tests and experiences of the preceding stage. The working hypothesis may also have revealed weaknesses and mistakes. Perhaps the factual basis of information was not entirely adequate and has now been strengthened. Goals may need to be restated, the content of the desired service redefined.

Even at this phase, the development of a rigid and detailed formula for operation should be prevented. Instead, as part of our social strategy, we should anticipate a variety of problems, many of which may never actually occur. We should allow freedom for the adaptation of operational details and technical methods to conditions in the field. Such freedom, however, presupposes the leadership of qualified personnel throughout the final stage.

6. This phase should apply, with suitable strategy, the master plan to a change in service production. Such change may involve extension, reconditioning or raising of standards of existent services. It may call for joint operations, or for the building of connecting links. It may lead to the development of entirely new sets of services, new voluntary or public programs. In some cases this stage may call for additional years of comprehensive effort. We may have to go back through the entire circle of phases already passed in the first round. All growth is spiral, as we know.

21

Leadership in Community Integration [1]

By CLARENCE KING

There is no warmer and more "human" book in the literature of community organization than Clarence King's *Organizing for Community Action*. It is primarily a collection of well-chosen case materials, vividly set forth, and held together by wise but informal comments, all lighted up by a delightful sense of humor.

The following selected passages illustrate King's approach, in these commentaries, although they do not reproduce any of the case materials.

Clarence King has had varied experience in community organization, public welfare, and international social welfare, and he was a member of the faculty of the New York School of Social Work from 1930 until his retirement in 1949. He is the author of a pioneer book (now unfortunately out of print) on *Social Agency Boards and How to Make Them Effective* (1938) and *Your Committee in Community Action* (1952), a kind of companion-volume to *Organizing for Community Action*.

What Is a Community? In What Sense May We Organize It?

OBVIOUSLY MISS PARKER [a community organization worker] did not "organize" the city of Woodhurst, physically speaking. Webster, to whom we turn to define the indefinable, speaks of two kinds of com-

---

[1] Excerpted from *Organizing for Community Action* (New York: Harper & Brothers, 1948), pp. 9-10, 18, 127-130. By permission of the publisher.

munities. The first is "a body of people living in the same place under the same laws." The second is "a body of people having common interests." The first is geographical; the second is psychological or spiritual. No one is satisfied with the name "community organization," but none better has been invented. As related to the geographical community it is a misnomer, though as related to a "community of interest" it has a certain validity. Miss Parker organized a "common-interest group" which grew in size and strength until it compelled effective action in the geographical community.

What Are the Advantages of Indirect Leadership and Interpretation by Participation?

The real test of successful community organization is what happens *after* the leader has departed. Much that passes for effective community organization is in fact "strong-arm promotion" which will probably collapse when the personality of the promoter has been withdrawn. Sometimes there is an adverse reaction to such a "shot-in-the-arm" which leaves the community poorer than before.

Miss Parker was consciously practicing indirect leadership when she urged her executive to present the cause to the Board and when they both urged a board member to present the case to the Council. Miss Parker could doubtless have presented the matter better, but then it would still have been *her* cause. The moment her executive undertook to present the case he made the cause his own, and it thus had two protagonists instead of one. The same thing happened with the board member.

We never become thoroughly identified with a movement until we participate in it. The "indirect leader" who is content to let someone else take the "visible" leadership and get the credit will probably do far more for his cause than the leader who is so possessive that the movement remains his alone, doomed to die if he should leave. . . .

How to Build the Initial Nucleus of Common Interest?

If we can mentally recapture a skill which most of us possessed at the age of twelve it will help us to master the initial steps in building a community of interest. Imagine that it is a winter morning after a fresh fall of snow. You step out of your door determined to roll the largest snowball that ever was built. What do you do first? Do you take a shovel and mound the snow together and round it off? Of course you do not. You begin by rolling a *small* snowball. All depends on that central, cohesive core. If the snow will not "pack" you may have to go back in the house and await a better day. At least it may be necessary to remove your gloves and apply warmth and human pressure. There is a counterpart for this also in community organization.

But once that small snowball begins to attract other particles to it-self the trick is half done. Given a sufficient expanse of snow and a steep enough slope, you could give the ball a push and it would go on without you, enlarging itself indefinitely. So it is in community organization. . . .

We can push the analogy of the snowball one step further. Have you seen your snowball in March, standing unmelted with green grass about it, when all the surrounding snow is gone? It lasts because of that hard cohesive center which you built so well. Many an aggregation of human beings melts away at the first discouragement because it was built hastily of a large number having all an equally tepid enthusiasm without any firm central cohesive core.

Yes, this central nucleus is the thing! Its size is not important. What counts is the intensity of the enthusiasm which unites the individual elements and their joint ability to attract others to the group. The Plymouth Colony after the first winter of famine was but fifty in number, and yet it had the vitality to endure, renew itself, and lay the foundation of our New England culture. Every great movement which has endured, from Christianity to mental hygiene, has lived because it had at its center a cohesive group of individuals, united by a common enthusiasm, so strong that it outlived the original leader. The most suc-cessful example of community organization in all history is that of the Twelve Disciples. Their success need not be interpreted mystically; twelve men carefully selected from various walks of life, knit together and inspired by their Leader until after his death, his indirect influence has continued on for more than nineteen centuries and is still over-turning thrones and inspiring the best we know in our modern civiliza-tion. . . .

Who Has the Greatest Need for Skill in Community Organization?

We are not thinking of community organization as a skill to be prac-ticed primarily by full-time specialists in that art. In the field of social work, for example, it is a necessary part of the equipment of each case-worker and group worker and of each board member. Its practice can-not be left to a specialist in public relations or to the agency executive. Each staff member and each board member personifies the work of the agency before the public, whether he realizes it or not. Each is poten-tially an effective ambassador for the agency. He should be prepared to interpret the work in informal, personal contacts, which may prove more effective than more formal methods of interpretation.

22

Social Intergroup Work [1]

By WILBER I. NEWSTETTER

Wilber I. Newstetter has made a unique contribution to the literature of community organization in stressing the importance of "social intergroup work" as an aspect of community organization. Mr. Newstetter regards intergroup work as "probably unique as a potential part of social work practice." Perhaps the most definitive statement of his approach is found in this well-known National Conference paper, presented in 1947. Other related discussions are found in "Teaching Community Organization in Schools of Social Work," a 1941 paper reprinted in McMillen's *Community Organization for Social Welfare,* pp. 59-67, and two contributions to a symposium on *Social Work Practice in the Field of Tuberculosis,* edited by Eleanor E. Cockerill, and published by the University of Pittsburgh, School of Social Work, 1954.

Mr. Newstetter, who was originally a group worker, has long been a leader in the field of social work education. Since 1938 he has been dean of the School of Social Work of the University of Pittsburgh; he has served also as president of the American Association of Schools of Social Work.

[1] Excerpted from "The Social Intergroup Work Process," *Proceedings of the National Conference of Social Work,* San Francisco, 1947 (New York: Columbia University Press, 1948), pp. 205-217. By permission of National Conference on Social Welfare.

IN A DISCUSSION of the social intergroup work process certain assumptions may be made:

1. Social process is essentially the psychic interaction that takes place between people in connection with adjustive efforts of group and communal living. These adjustive efforts include man's attempt to satisfy his basic biological and personal needs in conformity with the cultural atmosphere of social life. These adjustive efforts include man's attempt as an individual to rise above the biological level and to live harmoniously in relation to the culture of which he is a dynamic part. These adjustive efforts also include man's attempt to modify this culture from time to time as a more suitable climate in which he may live a personally satisfying life.

These adjustive efforts likewise include collective man's attempt, that is, the community's and society's attempt, to meet community needs, such as a reliable system of law, order, protection, health, housing, division of labor, education, transportation, recreation, welfare, and religious expression. The democratic community also needs provision for the learning of co-operation, participation, delegation of responsibility and authority, accountability. These are all needs which have to be satisfied, or the community and society will collapse, leaving a condition in which individual man would find it difficult if not impossible to satisfy his personal needs.

Just as an individual cannot exist apart from the reasonable satisfaction of certain biological and personal needs, so also a community and a society cannot exist unless the collective and corporate needs are adequately satisfied. These two aspects of social adjustive effort provide the two foci about which the mutual seeking and mutual becoming of the social process revolve.

2. The nature and quality of any specific instance of social process are affected by the objectives, knowledge, methods, techniques, and philosophies of those who are parties to that process. In a sense, the process may be viewed as the result of the application of methods and techniques as well as of the other factors, such as the component parts of the immediate situation and, particularly, the existing relationships of the parties to the process.

3. There is a core of indispensable and communicable knowledge which, when directed toward the specifically defined purposes of social work, and when disciplined by the use of consistent social work methods and techniques applied in a defined role, constitute the professional practice of social work.

4. A social process, such as some specific effort in community organization and planning, becomes a social work process in the technical sense when (1) the objectives are social work objectives; (2) the process is being consciously effected by a person selected or accepted by the groups involved, whose professional capacity is primarily

180

that of bringing the disciplines of social work knowledge and methods to bear on the problem.

5. It follows that many community organization and planning efforts do not qualify as social work processes with respect to one or both of these delineating factors.

6. We can agree to such broad definitions of community organization as have been so ably stated by Walter Pettit, Wayne McMillen, Arthur Dunham, Leonard Mayo, Arlien Johnson, and others. For our purposes we shall assume that there are three discernible processes in the field of community organization, at least two of which—the educational and promotional process and administrative process on the interagency level—are not peculiar to social work, but in which every agency from the local to the international level is, of necessity, engaged. The process to which my attention is directed is, in my judgment, probably unique as a potential part of social work practice, but it is only one of the three processes which we may identify as a part of community organization and planning.

7. Only a person with professional qualifications for social work practice would be able to use methods which would permit us to identify the resulting process as a social work process.

In the social group work process, there are two purposes to which the adjustive efforts are primarily directed: (1) the meeting of personal needs of particular individuals through voluntary group association; and (2) the meeting of community or societal needs. The emphasis is directed toward mutually satisfactory interpersonal relations between the members of the given group through which the individuals may satisfy their need for social adjustment, development, and growth, on the one hand; and through which at the same time certain basic community needs may be met, such as the need for people to co-operate, to learn the accepted values represented by that community, and to learn to participate in the process of modifying and creating social value in the indispensable community processes of co-operating, adjusting to division of labor, learning social responsibility, accountability, delegation of authority, and the like.

It is intended that individuals should use group life to satisfy individual, personal needs; but it is also intended that there should be a dividend to society in this process, and that individuals should learn to articulate themselves in an effective relationship to other groups which compose the community. It is also intended that this group shall learn to participate responsibly in the community process of relating themselves to other groups while furthering the social action which seems to them important in the process of fulfilling, modifying, and creating community values.

The social worker's role is one of employing social work knowledge, methods, and techniques in meeting personal and community needs through the group. This results in what we term the "social group work process." It is important to note that there are forms of work with groups which center primarily on only one of these two basic objectives. For example, there are significant efforts in which the process revolves primarily around meeting the personal needs of particular individuals. Some of these efforts are termed "group therapy"; others may be more properly called "work with individuals in groups." These put the great preponderance of effort on bringing about personality change, or concentrate on helping to meet personal need. The emphasis is on only one of the two foci, although it may be assumed that in a general way this in itself represents fulfillment of the community need.

There are other notable and fruitful efforts in working with groups without equal focus on particular individuals. The educational campaigns and meetings connected with the abolition of child labor, the promotion of fair employment practices and concepts, the open forum and group discussion centering on various social issues are among the more important. These efforts we do not understand, important as they are, as typical instances of social group work process, any more than we understand the former to be. Here again the overwhelming emphasis is rightly on only one focus.

Both types of process are examples of social process. In both of them the worker employs some methods that are also employed in the other. Both represent work with groups. However, it is only when we find the combined and consistent and balanced pursuit of both of these objectives—meeting personal needs of particular individuals and specific community needs—that we have what I call social group work.

There are certainly other valid definitions, but they do not depart too far from this basic conception; and the role of social worker in this process is clearly that of a disciplined enabler. As much as possible of the responsibility for the process, the activities of the group, and the results, is carried by the members of the group. The professional practitioner shares an appropriate responsibility. The community and society insist upon this.

It is well to point out that one of the methods by which the members of the group and society are enabled to benefit directly through the process of group interaction so that individual growth and social results are simultaneously accomplished, is by helping the group to relate itself to other community groups in such a way that the individuals benefit and the community benefits. It is because of community benefit that the community and the society commission and sanction this kind of effort, and that persons who may become proficient in the art of performing this definite service may be classified as professional in the learned and responsible sense.

It is also to be noted that while each one of these group members may be representative of some other group or groups, he is not there primarily in such capacity. It is not the adjustmental relations between these groups of which our group members are representative that constitute one of the two foci in this process of social group work, but rather the adjustmental relations between the individuals themselves. This is an important distinction, as we shall see when we examine the concept of social intergroup work.

The first focus in the social intergroup work process deals with the adjustmental relations between groups and not the personal needs of the members of the intergroup who are primarily representatives of some group or groups. The need, therefore, is not primarily that of particular individuals for adjusting themselves to other individuals; it is the need of groups in a given community to maintain mutually satisfying relations with other groups. In the social group work process one main focus is in terms of the interpersonal relations of group members. Here, this is important only as a means to an end, the end being the relations between the groups.

The second focus is again related to meeting community and societal needs, but it may be defined as specific social goals selected and accepted by the groups involved, such as, for example, child welfare service, family welfare service, recreation, housing, fair employment practices, and the like. In other words, this process is directed toward the adjustmental relations between the groups in terms of some specific social goal. There is no real accomplishment in this process, no matter how well adjusted and related the individuals may become with respect to each other, unless and until the adjustmental relations between groups are furthered in terms of the selected goal. No matter how well adjusted to each other the individuals become through the social process in the intergroup, such results, although important, are to be judged unfruitful from the intergroup work point of view unless the adjustmental relations between the members of the groups in their routine contacts are actually improved in terms of the specific selected and accepted goals.

For example, representatives from groups such as unions, management, racial and religious groups, participating in an intergroup work process in which the selected social goal is fair employment practices, are not effective in achieving this goal unless, on the one hand, they are instrumental in bringing about employment of members of the racial and religious groups involved by members of the management group; and, on the other hand, they bring about active union membership of these employees. This points to two crucial aspects of the social intergroup work process: (1) there must be mutually satisfactory relations between all members of the groups in their contacts involving the selected social goal; and (2) what we call the "from and to" between the groups responsibly represented, and their representatives. At the latter point a great proportion of these efforts break down. A responsible relationship is one in which there is response. Irresponsible participation of individuals too often results in adjustment between the individuals in terms of social goals, but it does not accomplish the real purposes which are to be expected from such a process. Where the "from and to" of the groups and their representatives in the intergroup become weak, we have a situation of representative irresponsibility, the result of which usually eventuates in a condition more nearly described by the social group work situation than by the social intergroup work one. We have seen this happen time and time again when social group workers have attempted to deal with "house councils" and where over a period of time the responsible relations to the groups represented are not maintained and effectively developed; finally, the intergroup is used by the individual members primarily to meet individual and personal needs.

The role of the worker in the intergroup work process is to bring social work methods to bear on the attainment of the goals selected by the groups. The worker is primarily in the role of an enabler and not a "doer," as are so many people operating in the field of community organization. We are agreed that there are aspects of community organization where the worker rightfully assumes primarily the role of a "doer." This is necessary under many conditions of social welfare administration. Such a role, however, would be as out of place in social intergroup work, as it is in social casework practice, and in social group work practice.

Someone is going to say that processes are not aimed at goals. I think it can be demonstrated that they are. There is no point to them if they are not. One kind of process is developed because it is presumed to be more effective than some other kind of process in attaining certain ends. I should like to challenge the idea that the worker's responsibility is only on the side of process, and that the clientele takes all the responsibility for outcome. In my judgment, since every social process involves mutual seeking and mutual becoming, the responsibility must be shared. The client, or the group members, or the intergroup and groups involved must co-operate in, and share responsibility for, the appropriate social work process; while the worker, by virtue of the fact that he employs one rather than another kind of method, cannot avoid sharing some of the responsibility for the results.

The specific functions of the social worker practicing social intergroup work may be divided into seven categories:

A. Broad general functions:
  1. To understand: the individual representatives, the groups represented, the adjustmental relations between representatives, the adjustmental relations between groups, the intergroup, and the wide geographical and/or otherwise pertinent communities and groups.
  2. To assist in the selection, creation, modification, and discard of specific social goals.

3. To further the development of mutually satisfactory relations between groups represented in the intergroup, in terms of the selected social goals.
4. To enable the intergroup to form, to function, and, if need be, to disband.
5. To develop and maintain suitable adjustmental relations as a professional person with the intergroup, the groups represented, with the group representatives, and with such other groups or individuals as are pertinent to social intergroup work process objectives.
6. To enable the "from and to," which is the lifeline of the social intergroup work process.
7. To act as resource person for the intergroup and the groups and the individual representatives.
8. To interpret the worker's functions.
9. To help intergroup members, within the limits of the worker's competence, to face personal problems, only in so far as they relate to serious blocking of the intergroup work process.

B. Dealing with the groups to be represented in the intergroup:
1. To enable the group to participate in identifying the social problem and in selecting the social goal or goals.
2. To enable the group to select suitable representatives or delegates.
3. To enable the group to identify and examine their own interest in relation to the social problem or goals visualized and that of the wider community or society as well; this may include suggesting other groups to be involved.
4. To discuss and interpret the role of the actual or proposed intergroup to the group.
5. To interpret other groups to be represented in the intergroup.
6. To interpret the function of the agency that is making the worker's services available, if that is not the intergroup.
7. To interpret the functions of the worker.

C. Dealing with each representative in regard to his functioning in the intergroup:
1. As group representative
   a. To enable the intergroup member to establish and maintain a responsible relation with the group or groups he is presumably representative of (type 3), or is officially representing (types 1 and 2) as delegate or representative.
   b. To help each intergroup member to function responsibly, that is, to understand, accept, delimit, and perform his role as group representative.
   c. To help him understand the other intergroup members, the groups they represent, and the nature of the process in which he is engaged.

    d. To help him establish and maintain mutually satisfactory relations with the other representatives and the worker.

    e. To help the representative to gain or lose status in the intergroup.

    f. To enable him to present and represent his group viewpoint adequately.

2. As intergroup member

    a. In general, to enable him to understand, accept, and perform his role as intergroup member, consistent with his role as group representative.

    b. To share in the responsibility of the intergroup to develop its functions, structure, and operating practices.

    c. To enable him to carry his specific responsibility as officer of the intergroup, chairman or member of a committee, or representative of the intergroup in some other group.

    d. To help him to identify any purely personal opinion as such, or as the viewpoint of some group other than the one he is presumed to represent.

D. Dealing with each representative in relation to his functioning in his group or groups:

1. To help him understand his group or groups.

2. To enable him to help his group identify and examine their own interest in the social problem or goals visualized, but at the same time, that of other groups as well as of the community in general and of society; and to act and react responsibly.

3. To enable him to interpret other groups represented in the intergroup.

4. To enable the group through the representatives to interact with the other groups represented in the intergroup, in terms of the social goals.

5. In emergencies to substitute for and supplement the representative, or to enable the representative to make adequate provision for any unavoidable absence.

6. To enable the representative to be informed of action taken in his absence and to act accordingly.

E. Dealing with the intergroup as a whole, or its constituted parts, such as committees:

1. To help it relate to other groups or individuals in the geographical or wide community.

2. To enable it to discover, modify, and discard specific social goals.

3. To help it develop suitable structure and operating practices to implement its goals, and to evaluate its accomplishment from time to time.

4. To help it determine and modify its membership basis, the number and the scope of groups involved.

5. To enable it to develop and to contain a group bond of strength sufficient only to maintain its operations adequately.
6. To interpret the worker's function and that of the agency making services available, if that is not the intergroup itself.
7. To interpret constantly the intergroup's function.
8. To serve as resource person, and to enable certain administrative functions to be performed, such as minutes, agenda, arrangements, notifications, etc.

F. Dealing with groups not represented in the intergroup, but related to its activities and purpose:
1. To help a designated person represent, or in certain circumstances actually to represent, the intergroup.
2. To interpret the intergroup, its purposes, its activities, and its proposals to other groups.

G. Dealing with the agency that makes his services available, if that is not the intergroup itself:
1. To interpret the intergroup and its program.
2. To help the agency see the limitations of its relation to the intergroup.

Generally speaking, the role of the worker is specifically: (1) to enable the intergroup to develop suitable structure and operating practices to attain the achievement of the social goals selected; (2) to enable individuals in the intergroup to function adequately both with respect to the activities of the intergroup and with respect to the groups they are representing or are representative of; and (3) to enable the groups represented to participate appropriately in the process.

We may visualize at least three types of intergroup. In type 1 the members are the official delegates of their group, are instructed, and voting action is thus restricted. In type 2 the members are official representatives of their groups but are more or less free to take responsible action within limitations which the representatives themselves impose. In type 3 the members are merely representative of certain groups. Often described as "influential people," or as people with a "contribution" to make, they are usually not designated or selected by the groups which they represent but are selected by some person or some group for a given purpose related to the intergroup or its functioning. Sometimes these persons are selected by workers of the agency which is seeking to organize the intergroup.

These types vary with respect to potentialities for maintaining the lifeline of the intergroup work process, namely, for the "from and to" between the intergroups and the groups involved. Type 1 is an intergroup with a partially insured "from and to"; type 2 is a group with a nominal "from and to"; while type 3 is a group with only a potential "from and to." No one of these types appears to be inherently "better" than the others. Many intergroups are combinations of types. No intergroup can be made up of just individuals. This would be a group rather than an intergroup.

In type 3 it is sometimes hard to develop the "response" in responsibility. In fact, many workers fail to realize that this is even essential. The result frequently is that the intergroup does not function as such, but primarily as a group. This is disastrous time and again.

Nothing that is allowed to go under the name of social work practice should permit or encourage "individuals" to remain as mere individuals in the intergroup situation. It seems to me that the individual has no social significance apart from responsible group functioning; and that, except to its own members, the group has no social significance apart from responsible community functioning.

It is important to note that I am not using the work "group" as synonymous with the word "agency." A council of social agencies, in my opinion, needs to be balanced by wider representation of groups other than social agencies. And these groups need to be responsibly represented.

Let us look more closely at the functions of the social worker in intergroup work, and let us examine briefly the so-called "how" of things. Here are two examples from student records of some simple ways in which the "from and to" was consciously developed:

> "At a meeting of one of the clubs which I was attending as an observer and resource person, one of the members made a suggestion which involved modifying the social goal of the intergroup. The president of the club, who was also the club's representative in the intergroup, asked me to deal with the suggestion. There had been little 'from and to' between the intergroup and the group, so I used this as an opportunity to suggest that the whole club discuss the member's proposal, and instruct their representative regarding the presentation of their conclusions at the next meeting of the intergroup."

And again:

> "In a meeting of the intergroup, there was discussion regarding a name for the newspaper, the production of which was then the social goal. This reached an impasse, and I did not encourage the achievement of a solution by the intergroup in order that the issue might be a tool in encouraging the development of 'from and to.' I suggested that this question be referred back to the clubs for discussion and that their recommendations be brought to the intergroup at its next meeting."

Now let us take a look at the activities of the social worker in intergroup work in another one of the functions mentioned above: "working with representative in regard to his functioning in the intergroup, as an intergroup member." In this case, the student's record says:

" 'I'm on so many committees, I don't know whether I'm coming or going,' was the complaint of the new chairman of the Recreation Committee of the Kingsbury Community Council in his first conference with the worker. The worker asked if there were some way she could help him so he would not be so rushed, and he said he felt that she could. He said he did not know why he had been appointed, except that he did know a lot of people since he had lived in the Kingsbury district all his life.

"The worker was faced with the job of helping to build a lay committee since the previous committee had consisted largely of professionals, and was not able to do a successful grass roots job. The chairman expressed some insecurity at the outset as to his ability to function as chairman. Yet he had real ability, was a dentist who had worked hard for his education. Moreover, he had been active in politics and had attempted fifteen years ago to buck the machine and get elected on an independent ticket. A Negro, he had many patients from various racial and religious groups. In campaigning he had called on almost every family in the neighborhood. During the war he was one of three on the ward's draft board.

"The first two meeting dates—first of the subcommittee and then of the committee itself—were set by the worker after conferring with the chairman. The worker then went to see him to report on the contacts she had made and to discuss with him the actual plan for the subcommittee meeting. She said it was his job to preside at the meeting, until such time as there was a chairman for the group. 'Oh, I'm not so good at presiding at meetings,' he said with hesitancy; after a pause he added, 'but I guess I've got to learn to do that sometime.' The worker said she thought this would be a good opportunity, and he knew most of the people personally.

"Two days later, however, in a conference about the approaching meeting, he said, 'Oh, I thought the meeting was next week.' The worker reminded him that he was referring to the committee itself, skipping the subcommittee meeting which was to be held first. He said he had another meeting that night at his club and was disturbed that there were so many meetings. He said his doctor was telling him to do less. Then he said he would try to get to the subcommittee meeting.

"The worker reviewed what the meeting would hope to accomplish and discussed the problem of the leadership of this subcommittee. The specific problem was one of how a chairman could be obtained so that the group could immediately assume more responsibility for its own self-direction. The chairman conceded he could get there at 8:30 and leave at 9:30, the meeting having been set for 8:00 on the one night he had no office hours.

"On Monday the worker reported to the chairman, as prearranged, on contacts she had made. She gave the chairman a list of people whom she had contacted, and their addresses, and checked those persons who had agreed to come. 'Most of the folks already know what the meeting is about, then?' the chairman asked the worker. The worker replied, 'Yes,' and that she had told each one what her function was, what the committee was attempting to do, and the nature of the contribution that each one could make. Moreover, she had asked what each one thought about the problem.

"The worker asked the chairman whether he thought it would be necessary for him to state the purpose of the meeting, even though the worker had stated it to each one individually, since there would be a few new ones present, and it would be good to have the group hear the purpose all together. 'Oh, yes, you have to do that every chance you get,' the chairman said. Then the worker suggested that the chairman lead the discussion so that the group would have an opportunity to state the specific purpose and to agree on what they want to work for. Then they could consider what the jobs are, and what they need to do to reach their goal. The worker reported to the chairman the several approaches that had been suggested by the persons whom she had contacted. The chairman picked up the most popular one—that a petition be circulated—and said this was the way he thought we needed to work. The worker suggested that these ideas as to method be brought out again from the people present that night. She said she would speak only if some of the relevant ideas of people who were interested but unable to be present, were not otherwise brought out. Then she would submit these. The group would actually decide on the methods to be used.

"The worker and chairman tentatively outlined the four jobs which needed to be done. The chairman said he thought a committee of three would be good to work on each of these jobs. The worker said that was a fine idea, it would give almost everyone something to do. The chairman said, yes, and then they would be more interested. The worker then suggested combining the two ideas they had had about selecting leadership: have people volunteer for the jobs they wanted to help with, and have the chairman appoint a chairman for each of the jobs. Then the four or more chairmen could constitute a steering committee to whom the worker would be responsible until such time as the group knew itself well enough to elect officers. This would eliminate the fears of the worker and the chairman that the one person whom he might appoint as chairman would not be acceptable to everyone and would alienate some; or that the person might not be adequate for the whole task. The chairman seemed pleased with this suggestion and relieved that the outlook for the progress of the committee was brighter. He seemed to have found a better sense of direction, which the worker felt too. He turned to her and, smiling, said, 'I do believe I'll have to clean your teeth for you some day, this is working out so well.' "

From the preceding enumerations of functions, as well as from simple illustrations of "how," it appears that the "what" and the "how"—ends and means—are really inseparable in professional practice; that they are really combined in what could be described as professional methods. It seems to me that here we have something that is basically akin to the methods of social casework, or social group work; something that meets the criteria of social work practice and entitles the process which is the result in part of the use of these methods to be classified as social work practice.

When the essential task in response to specific invitation, or accepted offer of service, is to enable groups through their own representatives to determine specific social goals, to enable groups to plan co-operatively for the achievement of these goals, and to obtain unity of responsible action and interaction in their achievement; when the quality of the relations between groups is just as important a consideration as the specific social goals pursued; when the role of the social worker is primarily a disciplined enabling job in the area of intergroup relations; when the worker feels that his role, while doing all of this, is at the same time to give equal emphasis to community need by helping groups to identify the wider community interest in the social goal, and to enable the intergroup to include representatives from all groups who have a stake in the specific social goal, then I suggest that we need the application of social work methods which will produce the social intergroup work process.

Fact Finding
—Introduction

RESEARCH IN THE SENSE of fact finding is a primary method in community organization practice and constitutes the necessary foundation for planning and action. As such it should be distinguished from routine statistical reporting, on the one hand, and from theoretical, or "pure" research in the social sciences, on the other, as well as from *research* as a "specialization" in social work. This dual role of research within the field of social work is somewhat confusing but is analogous to that of administration. Certain administrative methods are employed in the practice of casework, group work, and community organization, while administration as a process may also be considered as a specialization.

As a specialization or independent social work process, research cuts across all types of practice, fields of social welfare, and areas of social science knowledge. Though perhaps still an "applied" type of scientific study, it is, nevertheless, concerned with fundamental problems such as the evaluation of methods, interdisciplinary relationships, professional education, and job requirements, and with the establishment of principles, concepts, and generalizations in these and other areas. It is objective in its approach, long-range rather than immediate in its perspective, and concerned more with knowing than with doing.

Fact finding, as seen typically in the survey, on the other hand, is immediate in its concern, specific in its interest, and perhaps more elemental and ephemeral in its nature. It is operational, instrumental to good practice, and helpful, rather than detached in its purpose. In the hands of the community organization practitioner it is a basic tool in defining problems, evaluating services, determining needs, establishing priorities, setting standards, and determining policies. There are various kinds of fact finding. Among the more common types are the collection and statistical interpretation of data, social surveys, financial

192

studies, opinion polls, resource inventories, canvasses of interagency relations, periodic evaluations of welfare programs, and over-all community studies.[1]

All community organization workers must use fact finding to some extent. The process may be simple and informal, or elaborate, and systematic as carried on in research bureaus attached to the larger community welfare councils. In some cases it becomes broadly scientific, and shades into research as a specialization. When this point is reached the distinction becomes largely one of terminology and semantics. Finally, it might be noted that with the absorption of the professional organization, the Social Work Research Group, into the new National Association of Social Workers, the distinction may become purely relative and merely a matter of degree or depth.

The following two selections enunciate some of the principles of "action research" in general and describe the social survey as a common type of such research.

---

[1] See Roland L. Warren, *Studying Your Community* (New York: Russell Sage Foundation, 1955), 385 pp.

23

Action Research [1]

By GENEVIEVE W. CARTER

What are the characteristics of fact finding, or research, in community organization where the primary objective is planning and social action? Eight principles of "action research" are stated and discussed in the following article which differentiate it from basic research in social work as well as from more theoretical and abstract scientific studies. Despite the modifications implicit in the principles laid down, "action research," the author insists, must still conform to the scientific method.

Dr. Carter is director now of the Program Division, Welfare Federation of Los Angeles Area, and has written extensively on social work research.

THIS ARTICLE IS DIRECTED to social workers who have an interest as participants in the type of research which underlies social action or who have professional responsibility for the conduct of such studies. This sort of community planning research carried on under social work auspices, we will call action research. We are not primarily concerned at this point with defining the term "action research" nor in differentiating it from other research activities which have social change as one of the objectives. Rather it will be the purpose of this presenta-

[1] Excerpted from "Action Research in Community Planning," *Social Work Journal*, XXXIII (Jan., 1952), pp. 23-28. By permission of National Association of Social Workers.

tion to formulate certain guiding principles which have been generated by many experiences in social planning studies. Later, as proposed principles are tested and new ones formulated, it will be possible to describe the common elements in all social work research as well as the unique characteristics of action research.

The principles which follow can be utilized in two ways: (1) they provide a check-list of characteristics of a type of research practiced in a social work agency whose primary function is the planning of community health and welfare services; (2) they set forth operating practices which should be tested by further experience or by research method.

Principle No. 1. The problem for research should stem from a recognized community need rather than [an] hypothesis generated from the personal interest of the research specialist.

A research practitioner in a welfare council or in any social planning body should not select problems for research on the basis of their theoretical value or because the results will add to basic knowledge about community life or human relationships. This kind of research should be concerned with problems dictated by community need. However, this does not rule out the necessity of other types of research. The researcher may initiate a study in methodology because the proper tools and techniques are lacking to pursue practical problems. Or, in a basic research problem where he cannot grapple with the immediate question until there is more foundation on which to build, he may do research which is not inspired directly by community needs. Occasionally he organizes secondary data in readily available form, anticipating needs of the community.

For instance, let us assume a community group is studying adoptions. The researcher should not recommend that the group test the effectiveness of independent adoption versus agency adoption solely because the hypothesis presents opportunities to test methodology, or because the findings will add to general understanding of growth and change in child behavior. Rather, he should derive the problems for research from specific questions raised by the study committee as it examines the social situation to be remedied. Almost any community problem has many facets which can be investigated; the selection of the most appropriate hypotheses becomes very important in directing the investigation and producing usable study findings. The original hypothesis, based on questions raised in the initial examination of the social problem, may later be restated in terms of new knowledge developed during the investigation. . . .

Principle No. 2. For maximum effectiveness, those who are expected to implement the recommendations should participate in the study process.

Frequently those who are the most competent professionally or who are most familiar with the social problem are least qualified to implement recommended legislative changes, to promote a necessary bond issue, or to present the case before public officials. The persons to whom these assignments are to be entrusted should be involved in the study from the beginning.

One measure of the effectiveness of a study of a community problem is: "Did anything happen as a result of the study?" Frequently there is no provision for a continuing structure to carry out the recommendations of a costly study. This is particularly true of studies conducted by research experts brought in from outside the community or studies sponsored by a group composed of professionals only. Some out-of-town research teams provide for one member to remain, or return at agreed intervals as a community consultant. This reinforces the implementation of study recommendations.

In formulating recommendations, it is valuable to have a sounding-out period prior to the final presentation. . . . After findings have been obtained, a maturation period is sometimes required before a study is released. . . .

Principle No. 3. Before launching a study, the planning group should examine community readiness.

This general principle calls for the application of such criteria as these: Is research the most appropriate method for answering the questions raised? Has community readiness for change been considered? Is there enough money and competent technical staff to carry through a study of the type proposed? Is there a broad base of community interest in the problem so that the conclusions and recommendations will be followed?

Too often a small community segment has launched into a survey or study without considering preparation and timing. What is "best" for a community or what constitutes truth, or what results from the findings of the most exact scientific process does not necessarily move or influence people toward desirable social change.

It should also be kept in mind that the verbalized willingness from sponsoring agencies or individuals may not constitute real readiness to enter into a study and to follow through on its findings. Tradition, pride, vested interests and other psychological and socio-economic needs of community leaders as well as professionals may seriously impair a study undertaken injudiciously in terms of sponsorship or timing.

Community readiness criteria will vary according to the social problem for study. For example, a community may be ready to develop better group work and recreation service and at the same time not be ready to modify its institutional care program for children. Such variations may occur because of past experiences with surveys or studies, or because of changes in legal structure or agency board composition, or because of the individual attitudes of community leaders.

Principle No. 4. Action research requires technical assistance and direction to insure the objectivity and accuracy of the data collected.

One important principle for social workers and lay groups to recognize is that research is a technical job with its own skills and techniques. However, the layman, too, has a distinct and valuable contribution to make, and it is important that the relative contribution of each be clarified early in their relationship. The researcher has much to learn about the community problem and what it might want to do about the findings of the study. From other professionals he learns about such details as the nature of health data, of the effect of recreation policy on playground attendance, the importance of agency function on case recording, and so on. Each participant has his area of competence, and it is a wise team that can define its member function early in the game. . . .

Groups often go off on a fact-gathering rampage only to end up in embarrassment when their figures or facts are repudiated. Lay groups have an affinity for dashing off "simple little questionnaires" drawn from committee discussion without regard for any of the most basic principles of schedule construction, sampling, or pilot study. They don't want any fancy study—just a little quickie with a few open-end questions to tap general feeling and opinion for any of those who care to answer! Then they call for help: "Let us have some technical assistance; we are having difficulty in analyzing our data."

Technical assistance for a study group should include, in addition to research technicians, administrative personnel, which can budget money, staff, and time, and provide the co-ordination that is needed to keep the flow of work moving. Such a provision precludes the mistakes that occur because no *one* person was responsible for technical direction of the study.

In a living research laboratory such as a community, all aspects of an organization must be considered in planning research. Changes in the project are frequently necessary because the original research plan may be too disruptive to ongoing programs. When it is necessary to make deviations or concessions in the research plan, it is advisable to call upon technical assistance to evaluate the effects of those adjustments.

Principle No. 5. Social problems must be reformulated into a researchable problem.

Restating the social problem into a research problem is the most crucial phase of the study process. A community group may be concerned about the problem of transient men during the winter months. It is not possible or feasible to study all the aspects of the problem of transient men. Community groups need time and real discussion leadership to draw forth all the questions which bother them. Some of these questions may have no relation to ameliorative social action. Other questions may not be researchable, since they are value-questions, such as: why should our city pay for the care of out-of-state indigents? . . .

As a study progresses, changes in direction may be indicated because of the implications emerging from the new data collected. However, it is still necessary at the outset to make a clean-cut definition of the purpose of the study and a list of questions which the group hopes the study can answer. It is important to make sure that all concerned agree to the questions which are finally formulated. Otherwise, an important community segment might say, "This study missed the boat because it does not tell us about the quality of the agency program," or "The case material analysis was extremely interesting, but it does not tell us the extent of community need for this service."

Principle No. 6. Action research in community planning implies teamwork among researchers, other professionals, technicians, and lay citizenry.

Frequently the nature of the problem is such that collaboration among several professions is required. This is particularly true of certain community self-studies which involve social work, education, medicine, the basic social sciences, city planning, and other professional groups.

Research technicians often overlook the possibilities of lay help in conducting studies. Interviewing, one of our principal techniques in collecting data, can be done by the trained layman. Census interviewers, opinion poll interviewers, or market research interviewers are usually lay citizens who have developed the necessary skills in a short period of training.

Lay participation in action research has been successful not only in interviewing but also in collection of block data and in routine transfer of data from other sources to a schedule, that is, transferring name, age, address, sex, race, and so forth, from agency rosters to a schedule. The laymen who become thus involved in the study can be instrumental in the group decision for social change. One of the identifying characteristics of action research in social work lies in the opportunities for citizen participation throughout the conduct of the study. However, this teamwork among individuals of different disciplines and of different levels of understandings about social welfare services does not occur without conscious effort. Here, principles of good group functioning apply. . . .

Principle No. 7. The motivations for action research affect the nature of the research as well as its utilization.

In the reconnaissance period preceding the actual study process, the researcher as well as the study sponsors should critically consider the events leading up to the study request. The reasons *why* a group wants a study have a direct effect on study procedures as well as study results. Motivations do not always fall into clean-cut categories, but the three which are described below are fairly common.

a. *Persuasive research.* Community groups or individuals who request research on a given problem may be seeking objective data to substantiate a decision already made regarding a course of action. For example, a board is ready to fire an executive but hesitates before a study can be made of the present administration of the agency. . . .

b. *Escape research.* Here the individuals requesting research are motivated by a need to delay or avoid action. In such a case, action research is not intended to lead to action but to preclude it. In these studies one is likely to find a large sponsoring committee of the "right people," but with very little citizen involvement except in a superficial way. Or one may find the study conducted by a small group led by out-of-town experts; the only result is the familiar question: "Whatever happened to that study that was supposed to expose the laxity in our Juvenile Detention Home?" Sometimes when a board is in disagreement about expansion plans for agency program, it initiates a study which is supposed to take "the heat off" until certain board members retire or die. When a researcher finds himself in this situation, with his months of hard work buried in the manuscript copy, he may need to seek professional help to repair the damage to his own frustrated personality!

c. *Action research* leading to intelligent social action. Not all motivation for action research is as devious as the foregoing might indicate. Community groups or individuals who see the need for action may find they do not have the information necessary for intelligent social planning. To cite a few examples: a planning group has money for a neighborhood settlement center and wants to work with disadvantaged children in an unserved area. Their question is: "Where should our program be located?" A community has completed a mass X-ray tuberculosis survey and wants information on alternative plans for meeting the tremendous need which has been uncovered. . . .

Principle No. 8. An action research project should result in recommendations for action or social change.

Researchers in an applied research setting are aware that not all of the recommendations which follow a study are based directly on the findings. Advice in matters of social policy may be based on anything from crude empiricism to systematic applied research. When the researcher has around him competent social work professionals as well as community leaders who are aware of local feeling, it is questionable if he should go further than to develop the research findings and the implications. What the community does about the findings is hardly within the province of the researcher, unless he also sees himself as a "social engineer" or a "social crusader." There is disagreement among researchers upon this point. Some feel competent to make specific recommendations. Some have such responsibility thrust on them. In our experience, we may maintain technical responsibility for the study through the presentation of findings and formulation of conclusions. We feel that the recommendations which follow need a wider base of participation and responsibility. The amount of money to be spent for needed changes, the tempo with which change can be brought about, priorities, or the need for strategy may modify recommendations. But the scientific integrity of a study as such is not affected by what the community decides to do about the findings.

. . . In summary, it should be emphasized that respectable action research employs the same theory, methodology, and scientific principles found in pure research. Too often the terms "self-study" or "action research" mean that a group of interested lay citizens undertake a survey without technical assistance. Groups of social workers, too, who are usually very keen about specializations and levels of competence frequently get into a study far too complicated for their limited experience with research. Whether you call it action research, a community self-study, social planning research or any other name, the research activity must observe the principles of scientific method.

There has been much written lately about the nature of social work research, of its confused status in administration or community organization. Research in any science is usually identified by criteria of scientific method rather than where it takes place or which subject it treats.

24

Social Surveys [1]

By COUNCIL OF JEWISH WELFARE FEDERATIONS AND WELFARE FUNDS

The most characteristic form of "action research," perhaps, is the social survey. What are the major types of surveys and what are the characteristic methods employed? Though not a technical survey manual, the following report, prepared by the Council of Jewish Federations and Welfare Funds, is an excellent guide to the selection and use of various survey methods. It is a working document designed for the use of local committees and describes the results that may be expected to follow from a community survey. Consultation, as an alternative procedure, is also evaluated.

What Is a Survey?

THE TERM "SOCIAL SURVEY" is applied to a variety of situations and is used in differing manners by various fields of study. An early definition is advanced in the Bibliography of Social Surveys as,

"social investigation within a given area of related current problems and the analysis and interpretation of its findings in ways to make them educational forces in the community." Another definition might

[1] Excerpted from *Social Surveys: A Guide for Use in Local Planning* (New York: Council of Jewish Federations and Welfare Funds, 1949; processed), pp. 2-23. By permission of the publisher.

be "a study designed to examine the need for social services in a community, to determine the degree to which these needs are being met, the effectiveness of existing agencies in meeting the needs, and to develop a plan for co-ordinated social action."

However defined, all or most of the following elements are necessary to a social survey:

   a. A clear definition of scope and purpose of the study.
   b. Gathering of factual data.
   c. Limitation to field of social, health, and welfare services and needs.
   d. Exercise of judgment in evaluating statistical and case data.
   e. The participation of community representatives as well as professional personnel.
   f. The framing of conclusions and recommendations pointed toward action to improve services.

The social survey differs from other forms of social investigation. For example, the survey is distinguished from basic research studies which are concerned with the analysis of problems and the collection of data without reference to immediate utility. Similarly, surveys are distinguished from regular statistical reporting and fact gathering utilized by agencies, councils of agencies, and national organizations as a part of their normal administrative and budgeting process.

Basically the survey should be viewed as one means of community organization and social planning—a process which uses many techniques of research and, in addition, adds a large measure of judgment by professional and lay leadership.

A. *Major Types of Surveys—by Scope*

   1. *Program Analysis*—A survey concerned with the operation of a given agency or a group of agencies. The study may include all or any part of the following: program of services extended, staff activities, quality of service, volume of service, internal administration, financing, board and staff and administrative relationships, reporting, institutional management. This is usually *an evaluative type of study* which calls for case reading, possibly institutional analysis, and study of organization and structure as well as activities.

     In this type of survey certain preliminary or basic standards are usually available from national standard setting organizations such as Family Service Association of America, Child Welfare League of America, Jewish Welfare Board, American Medical Association, etc., depending on the functional area to be studied. A substantial amount of professional judgment is involved, however, in applying and interpreting these standards as they relate to a local situation.

2. *Needs and Resources*—A study of community needs in a given field (for example, child care or health) and the available resources for meeting these needs. This type of survey may call for examination of the quality of service to meet existing needs or more often may be concerned only with the volume of available service. This method calls for case finding and analysis among Jewish, nonsectarian, and governmental agencies, close examination of resources serving these needs, and comment on the extent to which unmet needs exist.

3. *General Community Survey*—A study of needs and resources touching several fields and the central planning body (federation, welfare fund, or council). This usually covers all Jewish health, social, and other services, *with special reference to planning for community needs,* as against individual agency or specific program needs. It emphasizes relationship between agencies and central organization.

   Co-operation with various national organizations (group work, Jewish education, community relations, vocational service) is especially important. Consultant services from these fields and a carefully planned team approach are usually involved. Frequently studies of population characteristics must be undertaken as a first step.

4. *Study of Interagency Relationships*—A survey of the way in which various operating agencies are working together in meeting community needs. Usually, this is a part of one of the preceding types but occasionally interagency co-operation or the relationship between functional agencies and central financing and planning bodies are of specific concern.

B. *Types of Surveys—by Method*

1. *Inventory or Library Method*—Compilation of facts from already collected sources. Evaluation of a local problem is based upon such data. Regularly collected information is available from councils of social agencies, reporting services of various national agencies and local, state, and national tax-supported agencies. However, such statistical data are seldom comparable, are usually incomplete, and are not capable of giving an adequate picture of local services. They are, therefore, seldom used except for highly specialized and selected projects.

2. *Survey by Experts*—Employment of a qualified surveyor by the local community to collect data, evaluate it and to report the facts. Usually the surveyor makes recommendations for action. The scope of the survey is usually established by the local community through its appropriate surveying committee. In some cases, this may be left to the surveyor in co-operation with the local committee. This method calls for the least local participa-

tion. Once the survey starts there is no local sharing until a report is made.

This method may include any or all of the following steps: collection of source data, evaluation of published data, case studies, interviews and conference with agencies, professional and board leadership, physical inspection of agencies.

3. *The Process Survey*—A survey characterized by the widest participation of local lay and professional leadership with survey staff at all stages—setting objectives and scope, evaluation of collected material, the framing of conclusions, recommendations and follow-up action. The survey staff may frame preliminary recommendations which are subsequently modified in discussion with survey committees, or factual findings may be presented prior to a joint framing of recommendations between survey committee and staff.

This method is most effective when community policy and understanding are at stake.

4. *Self-Study*—An extension and modification of the process survey. The amount of responsibility in the actual study, including fact gathering as well as evaluation is predominantly in the hands of local committees and local professional personnel. The functions of survey personnel are undertaken by local professional staff.

Survey consultation is often required from outside the resources of the local community. This consultation may be about the organization of the survey, or help in evaluating findings and results.

This method usually avoids responsibility for evaluating technical competence in performance, unless qualified professional personnel are available or selected to undertake this aspect of a study. More frequently the self-survey is concerned with matters of community organization and agency administration, volume of service and need for various kinds of service, and their support.

A major result, if not the primary purpose of this method, is a much wider and more informed lay leadership. The self-study makes exceptional demands upon lay and professional personnel for time and vision as well as competence in fact finding and analysis.

5. *Continuous Self-Study*—In recent years communities have begun to plan their social services as well as they plan their fund-raising campaigns. This has resulted in a continuous process of self-examination by central agencies. It calls for a steady flow of information on social services, regularly analyzed and discussed by lay and professional committees, and connected with the communities' program for raising money and supporting agencies. . . .

After consideration of the preceding questions several practical matters still remain. Does the purpose for which a survey is sought involve a matter of fact finding and analysis, or does it involve a matter of policy determination? . . .

The remaining questions concern themselves with the local "climate" as it might affect the survey. Are the community groups involved prepared to take part freely in a program of self-evaluation and self-examination in order to lay the foundation for considered action? For example, will the agencies participate? It is frequently assumed that a central decision to survey automatically carries with it free access to agency data. Nothing is farther from the truth and it must be determined early whether the agencies involved will, by board and executive action, officially agree to participate in the survey, freely to provide access to their records and to share in the community thinking. This must be distinguished from any commitment to accept in advance the recommendations of the survey (which is not at all necessary).

Involved in the co-operation of the local agencies is the matter of suitability and acceptability of the survey staff. Will the agencies have adequate respect for the competence of any other professional concerning their activities? Is the community situation such that they will accept the professional judgment of any outside professional expert who may be retained? . . .

Is community interest sufficiently broad to assure that some action may reasonably be expected? It is important to determine whether the extent of interest includes not only numbers of individuals but all significant segments of the community concerned with the problem under study. . . .

Finally, certain specific questions should be examined as a matter of routine. . . . Practical steps to consider include: (1) Costs and who will pay them. (2) Length of time required. (3) Consent of the agencies to be included. (4) Selection of a surveyor. . . .

What to Expect from a Survey (The Follow-Up)

The action following a survey report is the most important phase of a study. It is frequently expected that a survey will be a completed project within a given span of time. As a matter of practice, those which result in literal completion within a given time period are likely to be failures and are pigeonholed. An effective survey calls for change in the relationship of forces concerned with community services. A survey does not provide ready-made answers or blueprints for all of the problems which a community is facing. In order to avoid disappointment, it is important to clarify that a survey will be helpful only to the extent that a community is willing to undertake the necessary continuing work.

If a survey has been a process study then the recommendations are the community's own recommendations for itself and not an outside expert's recommendation for the community. Where a survey calls for significant changes in an agency program or organization, strong leadership is called for with conviction and vision about services a community can achieve.

In almost every instance, the strength of leadership required must exist in the local central planning body and its professional executives. . . .

The surveyors have borne basic responsibility during the conduct of a survey. Once the final report is made, their role becomes secondary. Their duties now are to clarify those aspects of the survey which were not clear at the time of the final report. . . .

With the foregoing qualifications about survey effectiveness, the following summarizes what may be achieved positively by a survey:

1. A survey can measure what is needed and what is being done in a local community by applying generally accepted standards of performance. There are few workable standards available; however, professional associations offer general guides and in rare instances data from other communities may be reliably adapted.

2. A survey can contribute the experience of other communities in facing similar problems. The experience of other communities proves valuable only when organically merged with local experience and needs.

3. A survey may inject some measure of objectivity into community planning. This will be achieved through the objective collection of data and its evaluation. The objective collection of data is likely to prove effective only if intimately merged with local understanding of local problems.

4. A survey will prove most successful when its continuing activities provide an opportunity for partnership between technical skill and interested lay community forces. . . .

Consultation

Consultation with specially qualified personnel is the most frequent alternative to a survey. It is especially helpful where a situation is in a state of flux or where the issues have not been clearly defined. Consultation has the advantage of providing an opportunity for the local community to think aloud with a relatively objective individual about local problems without commitment. Consultation will not prove fruitful, however, unless the local community has given at least preliminary thought to its problems and clarified in preliminary form the issues which it wishes to examine. Frequently utilized are discussions by boards or planning committees of federations, boards of local functional agencies, joint planning committees of functional agencies and federations.

While consultation is usually requested in order to clarify thinking it occasionally happens that a community has arrived at its own conclusions and wishes to test out its plans with an outside expert. Consultation can be a very effective means for a local community to determine whether its plans have real conviction, and whether they are in conformity with such basic standards as may exist. Consultation of this type to a large extent calls for the judgment of the consultant involved. Professional judgment may vary. The confidence the community has in the individual consultant selected or the organization he represents is a decisive factor.

Consultation seldom is completed in the course of one meeting. It is most effective if the professional personnel or the lay committee or board desiring the consultation are prepared for continued examination of the problem confronting them as new aspects are uncovered. The consultant should have opportunity for orientation to the problem through the reading of minutes in advance, through conference with field staff of the Council and through conferences with individual lay and professional leadership in the community prior to any committee meeting.

A natural tendency is to expect a specialist to give the solutions to difficult problems on the basis of very limited examination of the situation. Some consultants with wide experience are able to evaluate a situation more quickly than others. However, it is too frequently true that the rapid opinions given to a community are likely to be theoretical concepts about desirable programs and are not based on the realities of the local situation, resources, and local agency interrelationships.

Assistance from several consultants on *one problem* is difficult to manage especially since the conflicting and differing points of view of varying specialists are likely to be confusing. If at all possible the local community should decide the type of help it wants, secure an individual consultant in whom they have sufficiently broad confidence and then rely upon the assistance from that individual. Where this method does not meet the community's needs it will usually be preferable to utilize the consultative services of the Council or other national agency.

Where *several different problems* exist, the services of various specialists can be utilized but one consultant must be in charge. He serves to integrate and unify the work of various specialists and to assure that attention is given to all problems. He also acts to clear up professional differences of opinion and thus avoids confusion.

Whenever a community has determined on a specific course of action it may be successful in utilizing the services of a consultant who is adept at presenting and urging certain already tested out courses of action. However, where the community has not made such determination the consultant should be an individual capable of grasping local community differences and adapting programs to these differences.

While local communities frequently have resident professional personnel capable of giving consultation it is often found that such individuals are too close to local problems and local rivalries to make their work most effective even though on the basis of professional skill alone they might be the most competent. Wherever possible the local community should be assisted to consider local personnel available before going beyond its own borders.

To sum up, consultation may be most effective in the following situations:

1. To help a local organization or committee or individual clarify a set of relationships or to clarify the role of certain organizations or to clarify the meaning of certain facts.

2. To secure a competent professional opinion against which to test community thinking.

3. To assist the local community in grappling with difficult problems of personnel relationship.

Planning
—Introduction

PLANNING is so important an aspect of community organization that the term "health and welfare planning" has been widely used to describe the "over-all community organization" practiced by community welfare councils and community chests.

The method of planning, as a specific method of community organization, is here presented in two selections—a National Conference paper of 1936, which Harleigh B. Trecker has rightly called a "classic" on this subject—and Trecker's own discussion of the topic in his *Group Process in Administration*—a volume which makes important contributions to community organization as well as to administration.

* * * *

The Long View

We have learned to take the long view, to realize that the very stars in their courses, not our small army alone, are overcoming the weaknesses and misery of the world.

Mary E. Richmond; *The Long View*

25

Social Welfare Planning [1]

By NEVA R. DEARDORFF

In this article, Neva R. Deardorff gave, it is probable, the most illuminating commentary on "social welfare planning" to be found in the literature of community welfare organization. Dr. Deardorff made distinguished contributions to social work and social research; these have included service as director of the Research Bureau of the Welfare Council of New York City, 1927–1938 and 1941–1946, and as assistant executive director of the Council, 1940–1946. From 1946 until her death in 1958 she had been the director of Statistics and Research, Health Insurance Plan of Greater New York.

WHAT IS SOCIAL WELFARE PLANNING? Essentially, planning is the formulation of coherent ideas calling for and describing action in the future. It has to do with rounded recommendations, proposals, and suggestions of courses of action to be followed. Since these are a thrust into the future, they always introduce elements of risk and uncertainty. Such proposals and suggestions seem more acceptable when each phase of them has been examined and weighed by people who have had experience with the subject of the planning operation and who have given

---

[1] Excerpted from "Areas of Responsibility of Voluntary Social Work During Periods of Changing Local and National Governmental Programs," *Proceedings, National Conference of Social Work,* 1936 (Chicago: The University of Chicago Press, 1936), pp. 315-323. By permission of National Conference on Social Welfare.

thought and study to it and when knowledge and experience are synthe-sized. But knowledge and even experience are not the whole story. Planning implies capacity to invent new ways of accomplishing pur-poses and deliberately to adapt old ways to new circumstances.

In a recent publication on city planning Abram Garfield, chairman of the Cleveland City Planning Commission, describes with real honesty our plight with regard to planning. He says:

"Now finally, so that we may know what we want when we go to the [City] Council and ask for an appropriation, let us at least re-alize that our wish is not answered by employing ten or a dozen draftsmen and setting them to work. That suggestion has actually been made, but, the fact is, no one would know what to tell them to do. The thing that we want, I believe, is the employment of some one person, qualified as nearly as possible in every essential respect, to make this subject his sole interest for a period of several years and to give him whatever assistance, paid and otherwise, that he needs." [2]

I suppose it was these creative, synthesizing elements that Mr. Gar-field had especially in his mind when he suggested, not a dictator—for he would give his man no final power—but an artist, a designer.

There is still another angle on this matter of social welfare planning that we are sure to run into, once it gets past the disaster relief stage. Sooner or later the question of what for arises. What are we really driving at? What are we trying to get the community to purchase? And when the definition of underlying purpose is formulated, it somehow leads around to the principles that people think should govern in hu-man relationships. And that is something again to think about in con-nection with our people, lay and professional, in voluntary social work —or in public, for that matter.

But whatever the ends of public welfare programs, their planning for concrete action must concern itself with the organization of the means, that is, with the several factors of activity or function, with the size of operation or coverage, with the quality of service to be rendered, and with public understanding and support, and may I say that public un-derstanding is vitally necessary not only to secure support; public under-standing is quite as necessary to prevent perversion of services, as well.

Planning implies that these ideas of quality and quantity must not be played off one against another as they often have been in the past, but that they will be harmonized and integrated. In short, planning implies that there must be growing clarity as to what social welfare programs will undertake to do in terms of definite activities; how much of each given activity is to be carried on at a given time; how it is to be done, that is, the method to be applied; how well it is to be done, that is, quality and expertness in the application of method; and how it is to be supported, and that these must all be thought of together. . . .

[2] *The Contribution of the Citizens to a City Plan* (Cleveland, Ohio, 1936).

. . . planning endeavors in the social welfare field are emerging here and there and . . . these strongly point to the conviction that if we conceive of planning as consisting, on the one hand, of study that takes concentrated thought to define and describe problems and possibilities of attack, and, on the other hand, laborious processes of concerting opinion and of arriving at understandings among people that will stand up under subsequent pressures of all sorts, then we must see that it takes time to participate in that process. . . .

Areas of Responsibility for Participation in a Planned Community Welfare Program

With regard to activities and their aims, has not voluntary social work the obligations: to describe each kind of social work activity accurately; to tell what it is intended to accomplish; to tell how the need for it might have been prevented; when aims shift, to report that change; to report scientifically whether or not, or to what extent, these activities achieved their aims? With regard to quantity of effort expended, has voluntary social work any duty to take an interest in total volume of social welfare services performed in each field for the whole community; to organize means and methods for measuring at regular intervals the volume of effort expended; to measure regularly the volume of effort against demonstrated need for services of a definite character?

With regard to methods, that is, social work practice, does voluntary social work have any duty closely to scrutinize the methods that it uses in order to develop a more truly scientific foundation; to increase the chance of success in outcome; to lower unit costs without sacrifice of quality and chance of successful results? With regard to the development of expertness and skill in the application of method, does voluntary social work have any duty to analyze the elements of skill and expertness in workers; to classify social work processes in terms of their demands for skill of the various degrees; to develop ways and means to enhance the skill of the personnel in social work?

With regard to support of the community's welfare program, do voluntary agencies have any duty to employ such accounting methods as will make possible analysis of expenditure from the community point of view, to find out and advise the community accurately as to its own economic basis? Are the people in voluntary social work prepared to face the possibilities: that definite opportunities for revising beneficially the total program of voluntary social work itself will appear in many places; that control of growth will probably require at least the provisional establishment of some priorities among the several parts to a welfare program to encourage the exploration and development of certain types of work, to expand or contract volume here or there, to accent teaching or research in connection with some organization?

There can, however, be no effective consideration and planning of the elements together until there are genuinely acceptable instruments by which consideration of action, in the interest of the whole, can take place. This consideration and action will be achieved only at the price of some forfeit of the right of complete self-determination. Whatever Mr. Garfield may think of the one-man system of devising plans for the physical reorganization of Cleveland, the reorganization of the welfare service program of most American communities will have to employ collective and co-operative consideration.

These ideas are recited not because they are new but because most of them still await application and trial. Our purpose here is to see if it is still around these that we should orient our thinking or whether the world has entered a new phase in which they are no longer pertinent or real leads to the future. Should we try to get our bearings by means of some new compass for voluntary social work?

I still should like to say a final word about community welfare planning. If it is anything, it is a high form of social art based on knowledge of community conditions and of what constitutes a workmanlike, efficient job, but it transcends knowledge. As in the case with other arts, there is always need for its practice by great artists, and room in its galleries for minor ones and for amateurs. Our country needs a substantial body of people with capacity to think and to lead in affairs of social work as it never has before. Not fault finding, not nostalgia for an old order, not a clinging to some prerogative by either Brahmin or Bolshevik, not panaceas, but hard, honest work to push through to new solutions, new adaptations, new ways of applying broadly the soundest knowledge that we have.

*   *   *   *

Planning

Make no little plans; they have no magic to stir men's blood and probably themselves will not be realized. Make big plans. Aim high in hope and work remembering that a noble, logical diagram once recorded will be a living thing asserting itself with ever growing insistency.

Daniel Burnham: quoted in *The Social Welfare Forum,* Proceedings, National Conference of Social Work, Atlantic City, 1951 (New York: Columbia University Press, 1951), p. 310

26

Planning [1]

By HARLEIGH B. TRECKER

Planning is one of the methods which is common to community organization and administration. The following discussion is from Harleigh B. Trecker's book on *Group Process in Administration,* but most of it can be adapted rather readily to community organization.

Harleigh Trecker, dean of the School of Social Work of the University of Connecticut, has a varied background of teaching and experience. He has made notable contributions to the literature of social group work, group process, and social welfare administration.

THE NATURE OF PLANNING is frequently obscured by our feelings about it. It is strange but true that many people have a fear of planning because they envision someone else making the plan for them to obey or execute. The fear is not of planning per se but rather a fear of *how* the planning is done. In the last analysis it is fear of control rather than of planning.[2]

Obviously, we cannot live our lives a single day without planning, for planning is an established fact. A collective and interdependent

---

[1] Excerpted from *Group Process in Administration* (New York: Woman's Press, rev. ed., 1950), Ch. 12, "The Planning Process," pp. 232-245. By permission of Association Press, copyright owner.

[2] See "Individualism in a Planned Society" by Mary Parker Follett in *Dynamic Administration—The Collected Papers of Mary Parker Follett,* Metcalf and Urwick, eds. (New York: Harper & Brothers, 1942).

society is absolutely and finally dependent upon its planning processes to secure for all its people an increasingly better world.

We may be helped to understand the nature of planning if we think of its opposite. Unplanned administration is haphazard, scattered, disorderly, and confusing. Planning is simply the introduction of orderly thinking into areas of life which have heretofore been ruled by unconsidered judgment. Planning is the conscious and deliberate guidance of thinking so as to create logical means for achieving agreed-upon goals. Planning always and inevitably sets priorities and calls for value-judgments. Planning is a basic and fundamental approach or way of dealing with the human problems which beset us. Planning is a point of view, an attitude, an assumption that says it is possible for us to anticipate, predict, guide, and control our own destiny.

The alternative to a plan is no plan. When we accept the approach of planning we give expression to our philosophy, or the sum of our beliefs about people and their capacity for controlling the future. It is perhaps pertinent to point out that planning implies a pragmatic realism as contrasted with a mystical fatalism. It means that we believe there are rational forces in sufficient degree to enable man to have a place in deciding his future and the future of his institutions. It denies the *laissez faire* doctrine of "Let nature take its course," "Everything works out for the best," and "What is going to happen will happen." Facts supplant magic; deliberation replaces inertia. Design, rhythm, and relationship emerge to remove the blockings of the mind and the barriers to progress.

If we are to have planning we must have planners. They are the persons who give special attention to the making of plans. They are equipped with highly developed skills of a professional nature. But in a democratic society they do not make the plans; rather they help people to make their own plans by giving aid to the process of planning. The professional worker must know the *questions* rather than the answers. A few of the questions are these: What are the needs? What is our function in relation to these needs? What are the most serious gaps, the most acute problems? What are the resources? What co-ordination of effort is needed? These questions—in terms of professional skill—result in five closely related aspects of planning:

1. Professional skill is needed in setting up a continuous process by which problems are identified.

2. Professional skill is required in setting up a process of fact gathering in order that there will be a free flow of information with reference to the problems.

3. Professional skill must be utilized in creating a working method of analyzing the facts as a prerequisite to the formulation of the plan.

4. The formulation of the actual plan becomes just a moment in

the larger process. What goes on before and after is of much larger importance.

5. Professional skill is needed in the laying out of procedures for the implementation of the plan.

The essence of administrative skill in planning thus resides in the leadership of a continuous, well-integrated, step-by-step process.

This conception of planning carries with it several prominent implications of administration and administrators:

1. We should see time devoted to planning as a thoroughly legitimate part of administration and not an "ivory tower" luxury which we can do without.

2. We should be clear as to the purposes of our planning to avoid the twin hazards of time wastage and unreal conclusions.

3. We should be aware that *everyone*—rather than just a few of the "elite"—has a part to play in the planning process.

4. We thus see our part in planning as leadership designed to set in motion and sustain a process.

5. To be effective in providing this leadership we must understand the psychological requirements of planning.

6. The principles of administration are basic to planning as well.

7. The essence of good planning is participation.

In a discussion of social planning the need to consider objectives and the difficulties of so doing are pointed out: "The hardest part of planning is the statement of objectives. We want them to be at once both realistically obtainable and general enough or high enough to command the loyalties and kindle the aspiration of the multitude. The scientist states his objective in terms of an hypothesis, the statesman in terms of human and social needs, the religious leader in terms which challenge or comfort our searching spirits." [3]

Planning, theoretically, cannot be done in a vacuum. There must be objectives. The plan must intend to result in some achievement. But, "It is quite extraordinary how many undertakings and parts of undertakings are discovered which are just going along by their own momentum, with only the very vaguest and most hazy idea of where they're trying to go or why." [4] This may be a result of our tendency to separate the formulation of objectives from planning. This schism is probably unconscious for many of us because we have accepted a concept of purpose instead of *creating* purposes to match the times. The

---

[3] Quoted from "Social Planning in the Postwar World" by Charles W. Eliot in *Graduate Studies in a World Reborn* (Los Angeles: University of Southern California, 25th Anniversary of the Graduate School and School of Research, 1945), p. 193.

[4] L. Urwick, *The Elements of Administration* (New York: Harper & Brothers, 1943), p. 26.

formulation of aims and objectives is truly an early step in planning, as is suggested in *Administration in the YWCA: Planning:* "The definition of function, statement of aims or objectives, or some concrete indication of general agreement about what the specific Association sees as its task, becomes an early step in the planning process." [5]

Objectives are like a map. They show us where we want to go and point out some of the roads we may take to get there. Objectives make concrete and real the things for which we strive. Objectives make it possible for us to evaluate the extent to which we have approached a realization of our fundamental aspirations. Good objectives arise and function within activity. Good objectives guide or control the present— they are useful right now! The formulation of objectives is primarily a job for people who think clearly, who possess a deep appreciation of the enduring heritage of truth but who are gripped with a desire to chart the bold outlines of a better future. We must understand the nature of our broad social situation and the underlying motivations for change.

We must have a familiarity with the community in which we wish to serve because the offerings of our agencies must spring from the desires of the people. This suggests the need to base our objectives firmly upon the evolving conception of the dignity and worth of persons plus knowledge of how all may be helped to larger self-fulfillment. The *function of social work,* the *role of the agency in the community,* the *specific needs of the group,* and the *specific needs of the individual* in the group constitute four areas of thought which attract our attention both separately and in the composite as we set our goals.

When objectives are clear and meaningful the gathering of facts, the articulation of plans, the presentation of a program, and the evaluation of results are greatly influenced. Without objectives these steps can become but mechanistic repetitions of sterile techniques devoid of vital and sustaining substance. The form is present. We go through the motions; but the missing element somehow negates even the most scientific operations. If we are to plan realistically we must take the first step and restate our purposes.

The administrator, the staff, the board, the constituency, and the community are all involved in planning. Together they must mature their understanding of the nature of planning and its place in administration. Together they must experience the reality of planning with its difficulties, complexities, and satisfactions. Together they must carry their plans into programs of action. Together they must evaluate. However, togetherness does not spring from the innate tendencies of people; rather it must be cultivated and nurtured to the fullest degree. Here the administrative personnel occupy a prominent role. Psychologically

[5] Belle Ingels, *Administration in the YWCA: Planning* (New York: Woman's Press, 1944), p. 7.

they stand as symbols and stimulators for the many with whom they work. They have a responsibility for helping to create a psychological readiness and a positive willingness to plan. In order that they may assume a leadership role it is advisable for them to be clear in their minds. We must understand planning before we can help others to understand it.

First, we must see planning as a positive rather than a negative process. To many of us, planning implies that something is wrong, hence we must plan to right it. It is still true that we too frequently lock the barn after the horse is stolen. But planning which proceeds from a positive orientation that builds upon *what is right* about a situation and how it can be made more satisfactory is far superior to hunting for the wrongs.

Second, we must free ourselves from the fear that planning inevitably results in someone's telling someone else what to do. Because the planning process carries with it the very stuff out of which "collective self-control" evolves, the fear of supercontrol is groundless. In fact, there is greater danger of submission to outside control when there is an absence of thoughtful planning within.

Third, we have the impatient minds among us who loudly call out that what we need is "action" not "more paper plans." In our culture the "doer" seems to command a larger measure of confidence than does the "planner." Perhaps the public relations staffs have some influence here because they stress the doing rather than the planning. It is true beyond any doubt that the doer is also a planner or that he has someone or some group which does the planning for him. It is true that planning takes time. It is true that "the best of plans sometimes go awry." Plans even "die a-borning." But it is incorrect to allow ourselves to presume that there can be purposeful action without purposeful plans. Nor can we speed up the realization of plans without planning to do so!

Fourth, we are making a mistake when we compromise at the point of partial planning. For example, many of our plans emphasize the mere changing of the form or structure of society or a unit therein without realizing that the habits and attitudes of the people must be changed if real progress is to result. Planning must include the setting in motion of educational programs that will strike deeply at the attitudes, habits, and social skills of the people who must ultimately help to formulate, accept, carry out, and evaluate the entire process.

Fifth, we have problems of unit size in relation to timing. We want so much for so little! It is prevalent weakness among us to show great regard for the affairs of those far removed and astonishingly little regard for problems which are right in our own backyards. We seem to have a dual time sense when it comes to expressing a wish for speed on the part of the other fellow while simultaneously we remonstrate, "Don't rush us!" As to the unit size of good planning it can be said that it should bear a relationship to the ability, skill, and experience of the persons engaged. It is clear that the same considerations enter into expectations in regard to time.

It is helpful to identify some of the basic problems, but it is not enough. We must have an appreciation of the underlying principles which support the planning process. In a large sense these are similar to the principles of administration as outlined earlier. Yet there is a difference in degree if not in kind.

Out of the experiences of the past we are able to formulate or restate principles of planning which have meaning for the present. Though in no sense exhaustive, this list is an attempt to single out the most important of these principles:

1. To be effective, *planning should grow out of the expressed interests and needs of the persons who compose the agency.* The agenda for planning should include the ideas of all rather than the imposition of one.

2. To be effective, *those who will be directly affected by the results of planning should have a share in the making of the plan.* This is a long-standing principle of democracy. It is axiomatic that persons are more important than plans and that the meaning of planning in terms of its direct implications for people must be a first consideration.

3. To be effective, *planning must have an adequate factual basis.* It calls for the use of a scientific approach in which the ultimate truths are tenaciously sought after. The extent to which plans are based on facts reflects the reality-orientation of the planners.

4. *The most effective plans have come out of a process which combines face-to-face methods with the more formal methods of committee work.* Here we have an opportunity to set in motion a network of influences that will make for acceptance and implementation of the plan with a minimum of objection and resistance.

5. *The planning process must be individualized or particularized because of the differences in situations.* Though zealous advocates of specific approaches sometimes give the impression that their way is superior to all other ways, good planning calls for variety and a combination of approaches indigenous to the situation in which we are.

6. *Planning requires professional leadership.* The professional must define his role and help others to understand it.

7. *Planning requires the efforts of volunteer, nonprofessional, community leadership, as well as professionals.* The division of responsibility between these groups is a prerequisite to a satisfactory prosecution of a program. It is necessary to allocate and co-ordinate these responsibilities as well as to divide and integrate them.

8. *Planning calls for documentation and full recording so that re-*

sults of discussions and deliberations will be preserved to provide continuity and direction. It is important to ultilize records for purposes of summary and for purposes of evaluation.

9. *Planning should make use of existing plans and resources rather than starting from scratch with every new problem.* It is fundamental to build upon that which we already have, provided it is sound and furnishes a firm foundation.

10. *Planning is dependent upon thinking prior to action.* "Planning is fundamentally an intellectual process, a mental predisposition to do things in an orderly way, to think before action, and to act in the light of facts rather than guesses." [6]

There can be no denial of the importance of participation in planning. Nor can we refute the fact that the administrator must endeavor to increase substantially his skill in developing the participation powers of people. A forthright examination of the evidence is dismal and discouraging because at the very time when we should be "stepping up" the amount and quality of participation there is a notable and serious falling off. For a long period of time the trend has been toward increasing centralization and specialization. This is probably inevitable in a complex technological society. It cannot be desirable if we are to deepen and make vivid in the lives of people the democratic ideals in which we believe.

As centralization and specialization have increased, the individual has found it more difficult to participate. Centers of control seem remote. It is hard to get at them. There are no handles which we can grasp and thus pull ourselves into the orbit of influence. So much special knowledge is required that the novice feels inadequate. "Our ideas won't count for anything," we say. All this despite the vast improvements in communication from a scientific standpoint. We have the instruments for communication but we are confused about what we shall communicate and to what end.

If we are to break the bottleneck of nonparticipation it will require an all-out attack on a large scale. The central focus of such an attack must be aimed at the reversal of the trend toward passivity and the cultivation of a new attitude toward the role and significance of all persons and groups. We must begin with a searching analysis of our agencies to acertain whether or not we are doing everything within our power to facilitate the intermingling of minds. Here are some of the questions which may well be asked:

> *To what extent do our members understand the nature of the agency and their obligation to participate?* Perhaps we have a job of interpretation to do.

---

[6] L. Urwick, *The Elements of Administration* (New York: Harper & Brothers, 1943), p. 33.

To what extent have we established channels of communication so that there is a two-way flow of ideas, opinions, experiences, and contributions? It may be that we have yet to set up such avenues of exchange.

To what extent do our members, our boards, and our staffs possess ability to participate with ease and effectiveness? It could be that we must do considerably more training in the arts of group thinking, of fact finding, and of planning.

To what extent do we organize our work so that units demanding attention are sufficiently clear for participants to see where they may take hold? It sometimes happens that we expect people to take on jobs which are too large for them to handle.

To what extent does participation with us result in personal satisfaction as well as agency accomplishment? There may be need for a careful study of the basic human satisfactions received or not received in working together.

To what extent are we able to direct a process of participation so that results can be seen without too much delay? In the future we might make more use of progress reports, of recognizing step-by-step gains, even though the ultimate has yet to be achieved.

Participation is a response we make to the compelling demands of our situation. Mary Parker Follett in one of her final papers, "Individualism in a Planned Society," called it "the socially constructive passion in every man." She went on to conclude: "We have talked of our rights. We have guarded our freedom. Our highest virtues have been service and sacrifice. Are we not now thinking of these virtues somewhat differently? The spirit of a new age is fast gripping every one of us. The appeal which life makes to us today is to the socially constructive passion in every man. This is something to which the whole of me can respond. This is the great affirmative. Sacrifice sometimes seems too negative, dwells on what I give up. Service sometimes seems to emphasize the fact of service rather than the value of the service. Yet service and sacrifice are noble ideals. We cannot do without them. Let them, however, be the handmaids of the great purpose of our life, namely, our contribution to that new world we wish to see rise out of our present chaos, that age which shall bring us individual freedom through collective control." [7]

[7] Quoted from Henry C. Metcalf and L. Urwick, eds., *Dynamic Administration —The Collected Papers of Mary Parker Follett* (New York: Harper & Brothers, 1942), p. 314.

Conferences and Committees:
Achieving Integration
—Introduction

THE METHOD of conference, the bringing about of a "meeting of minds," and the achievement of integration of thinking is one of the most genuinely creative aspects of community organization. The committee, as the most important medium of conference, is a central instrument or tool by which community organization is accomplished.

There is an extensive literature on conference and "group discussion" and on the results of research in group behavior or "group dynamics," and a less adequate literature on committees. Most of this material is not written with special reference to community organization, but much of it is nevertheless readily adaptable to the uses of community organization practitioners.

The first of the five selections in this section is the classic description of "group thinking" by Mary P. Follett, in 1918. This is followed by two selections on committees—Edward F. Sheffield's analysis of the nature and functions of committees, and a discussion of committee operation by Mildred C. Barry.

A discussion of "What Groups Live By" by Gordon L. Lippitt and Warren H. Schmidt suggests some general guides to effective group operation, based on some of the explorations of researchers in group dynamics. "Principles of Effective Committee Work" are concisely summarized by Audrey R. and Harleigh B. Trecker.[1]

---

[1] For a detailed illustration and analysis of the committee process the reader is referred also to Selection 68 by Donald Van Valen, entitled "Community Organization, Manipulation or Group Process?"

*   *   *   *

Committees

A long table and a square table, or seats about the walls, seem things of form, but are things of substance; for at a long table, a few at the upper end, in effect, sway all the business; but in the other form there is more use of the counsellors' opinions that sit lower.

A King, when he presides in a council, let him beware how he opens his own inclination too much in that which he propoundeth. For else counsellors will but take the mind of him, and instead of giving free counsel, will sing him a song of placebo.

Francis Bacon's Essays, "Of Counsel"

27

Democracy and Group Thinking[1]

By MARY P. FOLLETT

Some twenty years before the beginnings of contemporary research in "group dynamics," Mary Parker Follett of Boston (1868–
1933) wrote a classic description of "group thinking." The passage
which follows is excerpted from the first and second chapters of *The
New State: Group Organization the Solution of Popular Government,*
one of the most refreshing volumes on social and political problems
published during the "reconstruction" period following World War I.

Miss Follett was not a professional social worker, although she gave
valuable volunteer leadership in settlement activities and in developing
the Boston School Centers. She was a kind of political and social scientist without portfolio—a free-lance thinker and proponent of creative
democracy. Miss Follett was the author of a later book, *Creative Experience* (1924), and two volumes of her papers were published after
her death: *Dynamic Administration,* edited by Henry C. Metcalf and
L. Urwick (1940), and *Freedom and Co-ordination: Lectures in Administration,* edited by L. Urwick (1949).

Group process is basic to community organization. In the passage
that follows are some of the keenest insights into group process that
anyone has yet recorded—and these are presented in the vivid, flash-
ing, and vibrant style that was characteristic of Mary P. Follett.

[1] Excerpted from *The New State—Group Organization the Solution of Popular
Government* (New York: Longmans, Green & Co., Inc., 1918) pp. 22-32. By
permission of the publisher.

. . . To be a democrat is not to decide on a certain form of human association, it is to learn how to live with other men. . . .

I have used group in this book with the meaning of men associating under the law of interpenetration as opposed to the law of the crowd—suggestion and imitation. . . . Social psychology may include both group psychology and crowd psychology, but of these two group psychology is much the more important. . . . While I recognize that men are more often at present under the laws of the crowd than of the group, I believe that progress depends on the group, and, therefore, that the group should be the basis of a progressive social psychology. The group process contains the secret of collective life, it is the key to democracy, it is the master lesson for every individual to learn, it is our chief hope for the political, the social, the international life of the future. . . .

The Group Process: The Collective Idea

Let us begin at once to consider the group process. Perhaps the most familiar example of the evolving of a group idea is a committee meeting. The object of a committee meeting is first of all to create a common idea. I do not go to a committee meeting merely to give my own ideas. If that were all, I might write my fellow members a letter. But neither do I go to learn other people's ideas. If that were all, I might ask each to write me a letter. I go to a committee meeting in order that all together we may create a group idea, an idea which will be better than any one of our ideas alone, moreover which will be better than all of our ideas added together. For this group idea will not be produced by any process of addition, but by the interpenetration of us all. This subtle psychic process by which the resulting idea shapes itself is the process we want to study.

Let us imagine that you, I, A, B, and C are in conference. Now what from our observation of groups will take place? Will you say something, and then I add a little something, and then A, and B, and C, until we have together built up, brickwise, an idea, constructed some plan of action? Never. A has one idea, B another, C's idea is something different from either, and so on, but we cannot add all these ideas to find the group idea. They will not add any more than apples and chairs will add. But we gradually find that our problem can be solved, not indeed by mechanical aggregation, but by the subtle process of the intermingling of all the different ideas of the group. A says something. Thereupon a thought arises in B's mind. Is it B's idea or A's? Neither. It is a mingling of the two. We find that A's idea, after having been presented to B and returned to A, has become slightly, or largely, different from what it was originally. In like manner it is affected by C and so on. But in the same way B's idea has been affected by all the others, and not only does A's idea feel the modifying influence of each of the others, but A's ideas are affected by B's relation to all the others, and A's plus B's are affected by all the others individually and collectively, and so on and on until the common idea springs into being.

We find in the end that it is not a question of my idea being supplemented by yours, but that there has been evolved a composite idea. But by the time we have reached this point we have become tremendously civilized people, for we have learned one of the most important lessons of life: we have learned to do that most wonderful thing, to say "I" representing a whole instead of "I" representing one of our separate selves. The course of action desired upon is what we all together want, and I see that it is better than what I had wanted alone. It is what *I* now want. We have all experienced this at committee meetings or conferences.

We see therefore that we cannot view the content of the collective mind as a holiday procession, one part after another passing before our mental eyes; every part is bound up with every other part, every tendency is conditioned by every other tendency. It is like a game of tennis. A serves the ball to B. B returns the serve but his play is influenced as largely by the way the ball has been served to him as it is by his own method of return. A sends the ball back to B, but his return is made up of his own play plus the way in which the ball has been played to him by B plus his own original serve. Thus in the end do action and reaction become inextricably bound up together.

I have described briefly the group process. Let us consider what is required of the individual in order that the group idea shall be produced. First and foremost each is to do his part. But just here we have to get rid of some rather antiquated notions. The individual is not to facilitate agreement by courteously (!) waiving his own point of view. That is just a way of shirking. Nor may I say, "Others are able to plan this better than I." Such an attitude is the result either of laziness or of a misconception. There are probably many present at the conference who could make wiser plans than I alone, but that is not the point; we have come together each to give something. I must not subordinate myself, I must affirm myself and give my full positive value to that meeting.

And as the psychic coherence of the group can be obtained only by the full contribution of every member, so we see that a readiness to compromise must be no part of the individual's attitude. Just so far as people think that the basis of working together is compromise or concession, just so far they do not understand the first principles of working together. Such people think that when they have reached an appreciation of the necessity of compromise they have reached a high plane of social development; they conceive themselves as nobly willing to sacrifice part of their desire, part of their idea, part of their will, in order to secure the undoubted benefit of concerted action. But compromise is still on the same plane as fighting. War will continue—between capital and labor, between nation and nation—until we relinquish the ideas of compromise and concession.[2]

But at the same time that we offer fully what we have to give, we must be eager for what all others have to give. If I ought not to go to my group feeling that I must give up my own ideas in order to accept the opinions of others, neither ought I to go to force my ideas upon others. The "harmony" that comes from the domination of one man is not the kind we want. At a board of directors' meeting once Mr. E. H. Harriman said, "Gentlemen, we must have co-operation. I insist upon it." They "co-operated," and all his motions were put through. At the end of the meeting someone asked Mr. Harriman to define co-operation. "Oh, that's simple," he said, "do as I say and do it damned quick."

There are many people who conscientiously go to their group thinking it their duty to impose their ideas upon others, but the time is coming soon when we are going to see that we have no more right to get our own way by persuading people than by bullying or bribing them. To take our full share in the synthesis is all that is legitimate.[3]

Thus the majority idea is not the group idea. Suppose I belong to a committee composed of five: of A, B, C, D, and myself. According to the old theory of my duties as a committee member I might say, "A agrees with me; if I can get B to agree with me that will make a majority and I can carry my point." That is, we five can then present this idea to the world as our group idea. But this is not a group idea, although it may be the best substitute we can get for the moment. To a genuine group idea every man must contribute what is in him to contribute. Thus even the passing of a unanimous vote by a group of five does not prove the existence of a group idea if two or three (or even one) out of indifference or laziness or prejudice, or shut-upness, or a misconception of their function, have not added their individual thought to the creation of the group thought. No member of a group which is to create can be passive. All must be active and constructively active.

It is not, however, to be constructively active merely to add a share: it must be a share which is related to and bound up with every other share. And it must be given in such a way that it fits in with what others are giving. Someone said to me the other day, "Don't you think Mr. X

---

[2] This is the heart of the latest ethical teaching based on the most progressive psychology: between two apparently conflicting courses of action, *a* and *b*, *a* is not to be followed and *b* suppressed, nor *b* followed and *a* suppressed, nor must a compromise between the two be sought, but the process must always be one of integration. Our progress is measured by our ability to proceed from integration to integration.

[3] This statement may be misunderstood unless there is borne in mind at the same time: (1) the necessity for the keenest individual thinking as the basis of group thinking, and (2) that every man should maintain his point of view until it has found its place in the group thought, that is, until he has been neither overruled nor absorbed but integrated.

talks better than anyone else in Boston?" Well, the fact is that Mr. X talks so well that I can never talk with him. Everything he says has such a ring of finality, is such a rounding up of the whole question, that it leaves nothing more to be said on the subject. This is particularly the kind of thing to be avoided in a committee meeting or conference.

There are many people, moreover, who want to score, to be brilliant, rather than to find agreement. Others come prepared with what they are going to say and either this has often been said long before they get a chance to speak, or, in any case, it allows no give-and-take, so they contribute nothing; when we really learn the process our ideas will be struck out by the interplay. To compare notes on what we have thought separately is not to think together.

I asked a man once to join a committee I was organizing and he replied that he would be very glad to come and give his advice. I didn't want him—and didn't have him. I asked another man and he said he would like very much to come and learn but that he couldn't contribute anything. I didn't have him either—I hadn't a school. Probably the last man thought he was being modest and, therefore, estimable. But what I wanted was to get a group of people who would deliberately work out a thing together. I should have liked very much to have the man who felt that he had advice to give if he had had also what we are now learning to call the social attitude, that is, that of a man willing to take his place in the group, no less and no more. This definition of social attitude is very different from our old one—the willingness to give; my friend who wanted to come and give advice had that, but that is a crude position compared with the one we are now advocating.

It is clear then that we do not go to our group—trade union, city council, college faculty—to be passive and learn, and we do not go to push through something we have already decided we want. Each must discover and contribute that which distinguishes him from others, his difference. The only use for my difference is to join it with other differences. The unifying of opposites is the eternal process.[4] We must have an imagination which will leap from the particular to the universal. Our joy, our satisfaction, must always be in the more inclusive aspect of our problem.

We can test our group in this way: do we come together to register the results of individual thought, to compare the results of individual thought in order to make selections therefrom, or do we come together to create a common idea? Whenever we have a real group something new *is* actually created. We can now see therefore that the object of group life is not to find the best individual thought, but the collective thought. A committee meeting isn't like a prize show aimed at calling out the best each can possibly produce and then the prize (the vote)

---

[4] We must not of course confuse the type of unifying spoken of here (an integration), which is a psychological process, with the "reconciliation of opposites," which is a logical process.

awarded to the best of all these individual opinions. The object of a conference is not to get at a lot of different ideas, as is often thought, but just the opposite—to get at one idea. There is nothing rigid or fixed about thoughts, they are entirely plastic, and ready to yield themselves completely to their master—the group spirit.[5]

I have given some of the conditions necessary for collective thinking. In every governing board—city councils, hospital and library trustees, the boards of colleges and churches, in business and industry, in directors' meetings—no device should be neglected which will help to produce joint rather than individual thinking. But no one has yet given us a scientific analysis of the conditions necessary or how to fulfill them. We do not yet know, for instance, the best number to bring out the group idea, the number, that is, which will bring out as many differences as possible and yet form a whole or group. We cannot guess at it but only get it through scientific experiments. Much laboratory work has to be done. The numbers on Boards of Education, on Governors' Commissions, should be determined by psychological as well as by political reasons.

Again it is said that private sessions are undemocratic. If they contribute to true collective thinking (instead of efforts to dazzle the gallery), then, in so far, they are democratic, for there is nothing in the world so democratic as the production of a genuine group will. . . .

The members of a group are reciprocally conditioning forces none of which acts as it would act if any one member were different or absent. You can often see this in a board of directors: if one director leaves the room, every man becomes slightly different.

When the conditions for collective thinking are more or less fulfilled, then the expansion of life will begin. Through my group I learn the secret of wholeness.[6] The inspiration of the group is proportionate to the degree in which we do actually identify ourselves with the whole and think that *we* are doing this, not Mr. A and Mr. B and I, but we, the united we, the singular not the plural pronoun we. (We shall have to write a new grammar to meet the needs of the times, as non-Euclidean geometries are now being published.) Then we shall no longer have a feeling of individual triumph, but feel only elation that the group has accomplished something. Much of the evil of our political and social life comes from the fact that we crave personal recognition and personal satisfaction; as soon as our greatest satisfaction is group satisfaction, many of our present problems will disappear. When one thinks of one's self as part of a group, it means keener moral perceptions,

---

[5] I am sometimes told that mine is a counsel of perfection only to be realized in the millennium, but we cannot take even the first step until we have chosen our path.

[6] The break in the English Cabinet in 1915, which led to the coalition Cabinet came when both Kitchener and Churchill tried to substitute individual for group action.

greater strength of will, more enthusiasm and zest in life. We shall enjoy living the social life when we understand it; the things which we do and achieve together will give us much greater happiness than the things we do and achieve by ourselves. It has been asked what, in peace, is going to take the place of those songs men sing as they march to battle which at the same time thrill and unite them. The songs which the hearts of men will sing as they go forward in life with one desire—the song of the common will, the social will of man.

Men descend to meet? This is not my experience. The *laissez-aller* which people allow themselves when alone disappears when they meet. Then they pull themselves together and give one another of their best. We see this again and again. Sometimes the ideal of the group stands quite visibly before us as one which none of us is quite living up to by himself. We feel it there, an impalpable, substantial thing in our midst. It raises us to the nth power of action, it fires our minds and glows in our hearts and fulfills and actuates itself no less, but rather on this very account, because it has been generated only by our being together.

28

The Nature and Function of Committees[1]

By EDWARD F. SHEFFIELD

Edward F. Sheffield, registrar of Carleton College, Ottawa, has written a compact and highly practical handbook on *Making Committees Effective*.

He plunges at once into his subject with the listing of the "characteristics of an effective committee"—the passage with which the following excerpt begins. He discusses also the immense importance of defining the committee's task through a clear and complete assignment, charge, or—more formally—"terms of reference."

Characteristics of an Effective Committee

1. AN EFFECTIVE COMMITTEE has or develops a task which is important and well-defined, a task which can be performed better by a committee than by any available individual or existing organization.

2. It is a small group of people who are interested in the job the committee has to do, and who are carefully selected for their proven or potential ability to contribute to its purpose.

3. Its procedure is informal and democratic. It is led by a skillful and co-operative chairman who does not attempt to dominate the group.

[1] Excerpted from *Making Committees Effective* (Toronto: Ryerson Press, 1951), pp. 1; 5-6. By permission of the publisher.

Its discussions involve all members of the committee and result in clear-cut decisions acceptable to, or at least accepted by, every member.

4. The arrangements for its meetings are carefully attended to so that time and place are suitable, and members know when and where to go and what is to be done. Appropriate records are kept of the results of the committee's work.

5. The committee looks at itself from time to time to see how it is getting on with its job and whether it is using effective committee procedure.

Functions of Committees

When committees are at their best they are valuable aids to administration, they contribute to the active kind of democracy which is our goal, and they enrich the lives of the people who belong to them.

Unless a committee can justify itself as an aid to administration it will have none of the other values named, for a committee cannot be effective if it does not make administration easier or better than some other device would, and if it is not effective it makes no contribution to either democracy or the lives of the people who work on it. . . .

There is no formula by which one can discover easily whether a committee should be appointed. Before the step is taken, however, it should be possible to answer "Definitely, yes" to each of these questions:

1. Is there a definite and important job to be done or a real problem to be solved?

2. Can it be handled better by a committee than by any available individual or organization?

3. Are appropriate people available to serve on the proposed committee?

Getting Organized

Once it is determined that a committee is required, the next steps are to define in precise terms its function and scope, and arrange for the selection, invitation, and appointment of its members and officers.

Too often the reason a committee fails is that it has no real and important job to do or its purpose is not clearly and specifically understood. The time to define a committee's task is before it is formed. If the assignment cannot be stated in unmistakable terms then, the committee probably is not needed at all, and should not be appointed.

The outline of a committee's responsibilities is usually referred to as its *terms of reference,* sometimes called orders of reference. In large organizations it is desirable that terms of reference be written, although in small informal groups a clear oral understanding may be satisfactory. In either case these things should be made clear:

1. The purpose of the committee and the name by which it is to be known. (The name should reflect the purpose.)

2. Exactly what tasks or problems it is to tackle—described in sufficient detail to allow no doubt about the scope of the committee's concern. (The tasks should be possible to accomplish.)

3. The source and extent of the committee's authority and responsibility. Is the committee to act on its conclusions? Is it to submit reports and make recommendations? If so, to whom, and when? (A deadline helps a committee to plan its work, and serves to spur it on.)

4. For what period the committee is to function. (Standing committees usually function on a more or less permanent basis, being reappointed, if needed, on each occasion when officers of the organization are elected. Special committees should be discharged as soon as their specific job is done, although they may be reappointed for another task at that time.)

Because the tasks of special committees can be so much more specific than those of standing committees, there is much to be said for using special committees whenever feasible. When a standing committee is likely to be faced with a succession of real tasks, though, there is an advantage in having it and its specialized members standing by, available for whatever problems arise.

Some committees, and their terms of reference, are provided for by an organization's constitution. Many are created by action taken at a general meeting of the organization. When formation of a committee is decided upon at a general meeting it is customary for the appointment to be made the subject of a motion. Sometimes the terms of reference of the proposed committees are included in the motion for appointment; sometimes they are contained in a subsequent motion.

If, as happens frequently, a committee is appointed without its task being carefully outlined, the committee itself should decide at its first meeting just what it plans to accomplish and within what limits it will work. If there is an opportunity to get approval of its own task-outline from the body to which it is responsible, such approval should be sought before the committee gets too far along with its job.

A committee cannot be effective unless it knows where it is going. . . .

29

A Committee at Work[1]

By MILDRED C. BARRY

The paper upon which these excerpts are based was first presented at a meeting in connection with the National Conference of Social Work, in 1950, and it aroused immediate interest because of the originality and vivacity of its approach. In the article, which later appeared in the *Social Work Journal,* attention focuses particularly on the community organization process as seen in a committee meeting. It includes a discerning and stimulating discussion of the personalities and the complex factors involved, the "hidden agendas," and the role of the professional community organization worker.

Mrs. Barry was formerly a member of the faculty of the School of Applied Social Sciences, Western Reserve University; she is now secretary to the Planning Committee on Older Persons, of the Welfare Federation of Cleveland.

COMMUNITY ORGANIZATION in social work is the process of creating and maintaining a progressively more effective adjustment between community resources and community welfare needs. This adjustment is achieved through the help of the professional worker and through the participation of individuals and groups in the community.

[1] Excerpted from Mildred C. Barry, "Community Organization Process—An Approach to Better Understanding," *Social Work Journal,* XXXI (Oct., 1950), pp. 157-163. By permission of National Association of Social Workers.
234

It involves the articulation of problems and needs, the determination of solutions, and the formulation and conduct of a plan of action.

The intent of this paper is to elaborate on this proposed definition of community organization in social work. It is important to recognize that the emphasis here is upon process and that this process is generic, that is, it is applicable in whatever structural setting the community organization worker operates.

Process, according to one definition in Webster's Dictionary, is a "series of actions, motions, or operations, definitely conducing to an end, whether voluntary or involuntary. . . . It denotes a progressive action or series of acts or steps." In community organization we start with a community problem or need and are concerned with the process of reaching a solution to that problem, or, specifically, with the steps from problem to solution. This process of community organization is affected by the interplay of many personal and social factors and also by the participation of the professional worker.

It would seem, therefore, that the meaning of process can be clarified by looking at (1) steps and procedures in the problem-to-solution cycle, (2) factors that affect the participation of individuals and groups and therefore the process itself, and (3) the role of the professional worker and the knowledge and skill that he needs in order to do his job effectively. It would also seem that case material may prove helpful to illustrate these concepts.

In the following pages we shall present a community organization case, following which we shall briefly discuss the three points mentioned above.

Mrs. Alonzo Smith was driving Mrs. Worthington Brown home from the Vassar Club tea. The speaker had talked on the subject "Our Population Is Growing Older." The audience had been responsive, and Mrs. Smith and Mrs. Brown were particularly impressed. They were discussing the problems of elderly people as they drove through the wooded, winding roads to their spacious homes. They were friends, confidantes too, and it was natural that Mrs. Worthington Brown should talk about the latest difficulties with her mother-in-law, a wealthy invalid who insisted she needed the care that only her son's home could provide. Mrs. Alonzo Smith put on the brakes, exclaimed: "You and the speaker have given me an idea. There must be many fine elderly women who are sick and difficult, yes, decidedly difficult. There should be a home for them, a beautiful place with gardens and good silver and a nurse."

This was the beginning. There was a dinner party, then a meeting of a carefully selected group from the Vassar Club, talks with husbands and friends of husbands. Finally, one evening, there was a meeting of those selected persons who had become interested. Most of those present were known socially by Mrs. Smith and Mrs. Brown. In concluding the meeting, Mrs. Alonzo Smith said: "We have now constituted ourselves the Board of Directors of the Alonzo Home. We have a house, the former home of my husband's mother, donated to this cause by my husband, Alonzo Smith. The contributions which you have so generously given (special thanks to Mrs. Worthington Brown for her gift of $5,000) will enable us to equip this residence so that about thirty elderly women can be comfortably accommodated. We have agreed, after, shall I say 'warm discussion' (laughter), to follow the suggestion of our treasurer, Alexander Green, to approach the Community Chest for operating funds for this residence, not as charity, you understand, but because this is a community service. Mr. Green knows the director, and he and I shall go down tomorrow to see him. We should be able to open our Alonzo Home within a short time. The committee on furnishings will report at the next meeting."

The meeting with the Community Chest executive was held the next day. The Chest executive explained that allocation of chest money was done by the Council of Social Agencies. At Mrs. Smith's urgent request, the Chest executive arranged an appointment immediately with the Council executive.

The Council executive listened, and explained. Mrs. Alonzo Smith and Mr. Alexander Green learned that funds were allocated once a year, that prior to such allocation, a thorough review of the need for the service as well as the proposed service itself was necessary, and that this was handled, not by him, but by divisions of the Council composed of lay and professional representatives from the agencies. Mrs. Smith and Mr. Green were surprised and disappointed, but were not daunted. The Council executive asked some questions which he suggested they explore and said he would have the secretary of the Health Division get in touch with them soon.

While Mrs. Smith and Mr. Green were explaining the red tape to a not overly appreciative group, the Council executive was conferring with the secretary of his Health Division and the staff worker who was responsible for a Committee on the Aged, a committee of the Council that had recently conducted a study and prepared a report on inadequacies of services for elderly people, with particular reference to lack of facilities for the care of the chronically ill. It was agreed that the representatives of the Alonzo Home Board would present their request to the Committee on Need of the Health Division, a committee previously authorized by the Council to handle requests of this nature. Representatives of the Committee on the Aged were to be invited to the meeting also. A conference between the Health Division secretary and representatives of Alonzo Home was to be arranged prior to this meeting for the purpose of clarifying procedures, interpreting the program of the Health Division, getting more information and encouraging the Alonzo Home group to consider all angles of the situation.

Some mention of the activities of the Health Division and the Committee on the Aged is necessary at this point. The Health Division had received only a slight increase in its Chest allocation after the last campaign, and the several Chest-supported agencies had received only token increases, not sufficient to cover increased costs, much less some new services which they considered vital. The public agencies were resisting the increased demands made upon them by the inadequacies of voluntary financing. The Committee on Need of the Division had strongly recommended two new services which the Division had been unable to accept because they could not be financed by either public or voluntary funds. Neither the Division or its Committee on Need, therefore, was likely to be receptive to a new request.

The Committee on the Aged had completed a comprehensive survey of the needs of the aged and was preparing a series of recommendations to the Planning Committee of the Council, among which were recommendations that the community should provide a hospital for the chronically ill and additional nursing homes for elderly people and should undertake to improve standards in the existing homes for the aged.

The Committee on Need of the Health Division met on the scheduled date. Mrs. Alonzo Smith and Mr. Alexander Green attended, accompanied this time by Mrs. Worthington Brown, who the others felt would lend not only the strength of her name, but the appeal of personal concern. (It is she, you recall, who had the mother-in-law.) Present also at the meeting, were three representatives from the Committee on the Aged, a prominent, well-informed lay woman, known socially by the Smiths, Browns, and Greens; a Negro minister, respected in the community by Negroes and whites alike; and a professor of social work, known for her liberalism and forthrightness. The Committee on Need had fourteen members, twelve of whom were present. Two staff workers—the Division Secretary and the secretary to the Committee on the Aged—were present also, the former serving as secretary and professional worker to this committee.

The committee first heard the report of the three representatives from Alonzo Home. It was evident that the Board had done considerable work following the initial conference with the Council executive and prior to this meeting. Their report contained detailed information about the need for a respectable, comfortable nursing home where elderly people could have adequate medical and nursing care, where patients would contribute financially according to ability to pay. Here was a proposal made by persons of affluence and influence, a request for partial operating expenses only, since the building and equipment would be furnished and part of the operating costs would be covered by fees.

Following this presentation, the representatives of the Committee on the Aged presented a summary of their study, not for action, but to provide background information for the Alonzo Home proposal. They expressed general approval of the Alonzo Home request although they pointed up certain inadequacies in the plan, particularly with reference to standards and admission policies, and they indicated that it would meet only a small part of the need. The Negro minister asked if it would serve all racial groups.

At the point where the meeting was open for discussion, the chairman said: "The major issue does not appear to be a question of need for this type of service, for we have evidence of need not only from the Alonzo Home Board, but from the Committee on the Aged. The problem before us is the adequacy of this particular proposal to meet the need and the problem of financing. In other words, if we recognize that a need exists, what are the various possibilities for providing service, is the establishment of the Alonzo Home a partial way of meeting this need, how can it be financed, what modifications or additions should be made to the proposed plan?"

Here let us pause. . . . Let us imagine, for a moment, that we are omniscient eavesdroppers reading the thoughts and emotions of the members. That is what we learn.

Mr. A, champion of minority rights, accepts the accuracy of the report of the Committee on the Aged because of the remarks of the Negro minister, and on the same account is prejudiced against Alonzo Home because the representatives have not stated it was to be interracial.

Mr. B, on the other hand, has heard a lot of rumors recently about Negroes, such as "shoving days," and "All Negroes are Communists," and he resents the interracial question of the Negro minister to the extent that the committee report is somewhat invalidated.

Mr. C is employed by a concern that is currently trying to do business with the firm headed by Mr. Alexander Green, so Mr. C, previously outspoken against any new requests, remains silent and implies approval of the idea.

Mr. D, labor leader, distrusts the upper class and industrialists and decides that a request proposed by such people is not in the interests of society. He feels his constituency, the local Council, CIO, would oppose use of Community Chest funds for such a home.

Mrs. E is striving for social position, remembers with pride meeting Mrs. Worthington Brown on a former occasion, is moved by Mrs. Brown's pleas, and is eloquent in her support.

Mr. F had heard a preliminary report of the Committee on the Aged and was outspoken in his objection to it because it seemed to be an evidence of pampering people. He was sure it had something to do with the "Welfare State." He likes the Alonzo Home Proposal, however, for he respects the opinion of Alexander Green, whom he sees at the Union Club. He suggests that the proposal be approved, feeling that this will take care of the problem presented by the Committee on the Aged and thus appease them, but will keep care of the aged out of the hands of the bureaucrats.

Mr. G, executive of an agency that has been trying to get a budget increase, feels strongly against supporting any new services, much less a project of the wealthy who ought to finance it themselves. He has been told by a member of his board that a depression is imminent and so is afraid the Chest will not make its goal next year and his agency will be cut.

Mrs. H, also a private agency executive, has somewhat the same feeling but she wants to interest Mrs. Alonzo Smith in her board and decides she had better praise the plan but deplore the financial situation facing all agencies.

Mr. I is a sociologist who is well-informed about problems of the aged both locally and nationally. He quotes pertinently from several national publications.

Miss J has spent years caring for an invalid parent and has a strong emotional urge to support the request for Alonzo Home and the report of the Committee on the Aged. She is in awe of Mrs. Alonzo Smith, however, and this, plus guilty feelings about her own parent, keep her from saying anything, although she fidgets and looks distressed.

Mr. K is impatient with the discussion. He thinks the Health Division and the Committee on the Aged should support President Truman's proposals, that care of the aged and the chronically ill should be provided by the state and that if the "four hundred" wish to have their mothers-in-law cared for, they should pay for it.

Mrs. Alonzo Smith, usually eloquent and forceful, is acutely conscious of the social work professor. The presence of this woman, well-known in the community for her professional position and scholarship, makes Mrs. Smith feel intellectually inadequate. Mrs. Smith feels cordial toward the Negro minister, for she has always prided herself on being without prejudice. She is not worried about his question on the interracial character of Alonzo Home, for that is what she expects any Negro to ask.

The lay representative from the Committee on the Aged is intently interested in the questions being discussed. She knows Mrs. Smith, Mrs. Brown, and Mr. Green, feels perfectly comfortable with them and is free to ask them questions. Her experience in various agency and council activities has made her familiar with procedures and with much of the material under consideration. She feels at ease with the people in the room, most of whom she knows. She makes pertinent contributions to the committee discussion. . . .

The community organization worker did not have our omniscience so could not know all these thoughts that were hovering in the atmosphere of the committee chamber. He knew a considerable amount about most of those present, however, from observing and hearing about them, and he was sensitive to the implications of facial expressions, banter, and the various ways people have of showing their reactions. . . .

The community organization worker saw his role as twofold: the first relating to the material being discussed and the facts pertaining thereto; and the second relating to the individuals and the group itself.

With respect to the first, he saw his role as helping to clarify the issues and seeing that information necessary to the intelligent discussion of the problem was available. . . .

With respect to the individuals and the group, the community organization worker· saw his role as creating an atmosphere that would free the individuals as much as possible from their stereotyped reactions and enable them to look at the situation on its own merits. In this instance he did a number of things.

Prior to the meeting he had urged Mr. I, the sociologist, to attend, even though Mr. I had indicated that he had another engagement. The worker recognized that any real integration of ideas would be largely dependent upon the stabilizing, objective approach of Mr. I and the chairman, both of whom were liked and respected by the committee members.

In his conference with the Alonzo Home representatives prior to this meeting, he had realized the frustration they must feel at the seemingly involved procedures, particularly in view of their social position, which usually enabled them to command quick action. He had interpreted the reasons for these procedures and explained the questions that might be asked by the committee. He helped them prepare their report. . . . In working out the agenda with the chairman he had suggested that the chairman give some background of the Alonzo Home proposal, pointing out not only the questions, but the positive things such as the expressed interest of the Board in the community. . . .

The worker himself was alert to tenseness in the meeting and by his remarks and attitude was able to ease tensions and to create a feeling of satisfying interrelationships. . . .

The worker also was alert to the need for movement on the part of the committee. Balance has to be achieved between adequate discussion, which allows for airing of feelings as well as full consideration of facts, and decision making, which is necessary both to get the job done and to maintain morale. In this committee the chairman was adept at this. However, at one point, the worker sensed that persons were beginning to repeat themselves and that some of the extremes of opinion were becoming modified. He made a proposal which he believed might meet the objections of the various factions and which incorporated many of the positive suggestions given by the committee members. His suggestion proved a valuable steppingstone toward integration of ideas and arrival at a final decision. . . .

We have not, in our illustration, showed the ending of the Alonzo Home story. It was not our intent to present a complete record. Rather, as indicated earlier, one purpose of using this Alonzo Home case is to illustrate the following remarks which are an attempt to describe what we believe is the essence of community organization process.

The limitations of a flat piece of paper when one is trying to show something that is at least three-dimensional are obvious and unfortunate. We suggest that one method of getting away from the two-dimensional may be to imagine that there are three "planes" that intersect.

For example, there is, on one plane, the sequence of events; what actually happened. In our illustration this would include the Alonzo Home story and the happenings in the Health Division and the Committee on the Aged.

On another plane, bisecting the first plane as it were, there are the various factors which affect the flow of events. These include interpersonal and intergroup relationships, with their causes and effects; community pressures; and national and international influences that color the behavior, interactions, and decisions of the group. We attempted to illustrate these factors by showing in a very limited way the thoughts and emotions that the members had. We did not begin to show all the factors that played upon this one committee meeting or the changing interactions that occurred.

The third plane, trisecting the other two, we choose to call the community organization worker, for by his activity, he interjects into this picture another set of factors which are, for want of a better expression, the conscious factors. We attempted to show this in our illustration by pointing up the professional worker's role.

These three—the sequence of events, the various factors constantly playing upon and modifying what is occurring, and the community organization worker with his conscious use of himself and of a variety of skills—these three elements, inseparable, interacting and infinitely complex, represent to this writer, at least, what we mean by community organization process. Let us examine these three planes more closely.

If we look first at the sequence of events, we are concerned with the steps that occur from the time a problem or need is seen by someone in the community until a program is put into effect to solve the problem or eliminate the need. One or more persons or groups in the community sees a problem and refers this, either directly or indirectly, to the community welfare agency whose function it is to handle it. The problem is then referred to the appropriate subdivision and from there it becomes the concern of a committee, either one already in existence or one formed to deal specifically with the problem. In this committee, attention is given to full exploration of the problem, possible solutions, and a plan of action. The plan of action is then undertaken by the appropriate group, either the committee itself, its parent body, or other authority. Acceptance of the proposed action or program by the appropriate group or agency, either voluntarily or by law, is the final step completing this cycle. . . .

Looking at the second plane, we see the factors that affect the sequence of events, that is, those factors apparently extraneous to the actual problem under consideration, which play upon and affect the characters and their action. . . .

We . . . suggest that the following types of factors be kept in mind: (1) factors pertaining to personality and to interpersonal relationships; (2) factors pertaining to intergroup relationships; (3) factors pertaining to the conditions, patterns, and forces of the particular community; and (4) factors pertaining to the wider social scene, whether local, state, national, or international.

On the third plane, we have the community organization worker, and it is here that we see, in the fullest sense, community organization as a process in social work. For there is a contribution which the professional worker brings to the situation that alters it, that fully identifies the process with social work. The community organization worker is the catalyst which, when injected into the community situation, enables the community organization process as we have outlined it, to occur.

We suggest that the community organization worker brings to the situation the following attributes and that these are indicative of his part in the community organization process and serve to point up the knowledge and skill he needs in order to do his job effectively:

1. A social philosophy that is based on the belief that human beings have a right to freedom and happiness and that social ills can best be remedied through the participation and joint endeavor of the people and groups concerned, rather than through manipulation or direction by one or a few; it implies recognition of the worth of each individual whether of high or lowly station; it implies translation of this philosophy into practice.

2. Knowledge and understanding of individuals and their behavior, groups and their behavior, communities and their behavior; understanding not only of what this behavior is but of its effect upon people and groups and upon the desires and abilities of people and groups to change their established patterns and move ahead; understanding of how such knowledge can be used so that more positive interrelationships are established and community progress may result.

3. Conscious use of one's role as an enabling, helping person who can be of maximum service in assisting individuals and groups in the community to understand their problems and participate in the solution of their problems; who encourages others to take the direct leadership roles; who cares little for personal credit but who is neither timid nor passive when the time comes to be courageous and to push forward; who is as analytical of himself and his role as he is of the community situations with which he is concerned.

4. Ability to work within the existing community structure with-

out being bound by it, to recognize that institutions as well as mores do not change overnight and that there are strong loyalties to groups, to institutions, and to established patterns of living; but to recognize also that it is the people that are of prime importance, not their institutions, and that when the two loyalties conflict, the needs of people rather than of institutions must be of greater concern.

5. Knowledge of the setting; of the community welfare structure, of the fields of service, of the public and voluntary agencies, of the community planning agencies; of the different geographical settings of these agencies and of their purposes and functions.

6. Skill in utilizing the various methods and techniques necessary to the job, specifically skill in administration, interviewing, committee leadership, research and fact finding, oral and written presentation of material, recording, public and personal relations, social education and action, promotion, publicity and interpretation.

30

What Groups Live By [1]

By GORDON L. LIPPITT and WARREN H.
SCHMIDT

Most community organization involves group—or intergroup—
process. Research, then, in group behavior, or "group dynamics," is of
major importance to community organization.

In a small pamphlet, entitled *My Group and I,* two students of group
dynamics have provided a simple but scientifically based guide to "getting the most out of groups." The following excerpt includes two constructive statements: one, a set of "positive assumptions" in the section,
"Principles a Group Lives By"—the other, a number of practical suggestions as to "what you can do," as a member of a group.

Gordon L. Lippitt is program director of the National Training Lab-
oratories, in Washington, D.C. Warren H. Schmidt, formerly assistant
professor of psychology at Springfield College, Springfield, Massachusetts, is now head of the Department of Conferences and Special
Activities, University Extension, and lecturer in the School of Business
Administration, of the University of California at Los Angeles.

[1] Excerpted from *My Group and I* (Arthur C. Croft, Educator's Washington
Dispatch, Washington, D.C. and New London, Connecticut: 1952), pp. 21-23.
By permission of Arthur C. Croft Publications.

Positive Assumptions

1. ANY GROUP CAN BECOME a better group if it focuses some of its attention on the feelings that members have toward each other. Tensions among members waste valuable human energy, prevent the group from examining objectively the proposals of certain members, and in general make the group experience less enjoyable and profitable.

2. Every individual is important and is capable of making some contribution to the group. No "leader" or "executive committee" has a monopoly on good ideas. Because of the wide variety of experience to be found in any group of people, the best decisions and the deepest insights can come only if the group discovers how to use all the resources represented in it. This assumption involves a feeling of mutual trust and respect. It suggests that a primary need in any group is to establish an atmosphere in which each individual feels worthy and respected. Only in such an atmosphere will he feel free to express the ideas about which he is not always too certain.

3. A group has the power to improve its process of operation and its results. No group need be bogged down in apathy or torn by internal strife for an indefinite period. It can, by evaluation, observation, and discussion of its problems find ways of handling them more effectively. Significant problems affecting their morale can be controlled by the group members if they are willing to face them.

4. Leadership is more effective if it is shared rather than concentrated. There is now a new body of evidence that the functions sometimes embodied in the "leader" can be distributed among several people. One member may initiate ideas, another may clarify, another may summarize, another may compromise. Not all these jobs need to be performed by the same person. In the mature group, no single person feels responsible for the direction of the discussion, the success of the program, or the amount of satisfaction felt by the group. This sense of responsibility is shared by everyone if the group recognizes the fact that everyone can contribute to or detract from the group's progress.

5. A group progresses best in an atmosphere of honesty and frankness. The kind of calm that comes from pouring oil on troubled waters is temporary and unrealistic. Where many people are involved, this kind of peace can be attained only by smothering their real feelings. Negative feelings—hostility, fear, guilt—exist among the finest people. To control things so that these negative feelings are never brought into the open will eliminate neither the feelings nor their undesirable effect on group morale and productivity. A group may need an occasional "blow-off" in which members can get rid of some of their tensions. There is little value for a group to try to maintain an illusion of sweetness and light when every member knows there are hostilities and friction underneath.

The responsibility for creating an atmosphere of frankness perhaps rests with the group leaders. By sharing a maximum of useful behind-the-scenes information with all members and by exhibiting a willingness to explain their actions to the group, the leaders can help to create such an atmosphere. One of the subtle ways in which a leader may become a dominator is to withhold certain information from the rest of the group. He then becomes the "authority" on whom the group has to depend. It is particularly important that the leader be honest in explaining how decisions have been or will be made. Nothing is more discouraging to a group than to feel that they have supposedly been involved in making a decision, only to discover that the leader really planned to make the decision anyway.

What You Can Do

. . . It is only as each member realizes his importance and strives to find his role and contribution to the group that an organization will grow and develop. Frequently, members of organizations say to themselves, "But what can I do?"

1. Think and contribute creatively to any action of your group.

2. Encourage others to participate, especially those who do not speak easily, and those who feel too insecure to step forward and accept responsibility.

3. Think clearly and evaluate what you have to contribute before speaking or acting. Try to be objective, simple, and brief as well as efficient in expression and behavior. In this way you can help the group find the hard core of the problem and discover the most practical approach to its solution.

4. Remain loyal to the group. Strive sincerely and effectively to participate even though your personal interests are not the immediate concern of the group.

5. Strive to be fully informed about the subject of the group discussion and action, to think clearly and objectively as an individual as well as a member of the group.

6. Assist in eliminating the destructive influence of personal jealousies and competition between members and co-operating groups. Be a team member of the group and help the group to become a successful team.

7. Develop the "doing" skills of a responsible member by understanding the techniques of successful group discussion and action, and learning how to measure and to evaluate member-behavior of the group as a whole. This may be achieved through membership training institutes and conferences.

8. Help to establish an emotional climate within the group in which every member feels accepted.

9. Listen to all proposals of new methods, procedures, and subjects in an objective manner and co-operate in testing the effectiveness of

these proposals. There is a need to be ready for change, to be adaptable and creative when new ideas are required for group action.

10. Be enthusiastic when you are in agreement with others so that they find strength in your support. Strive to arbitrate differences in opinion before they threaten the strength and purposefulness of the group.

11. Welcome the opinions, information, and suggestions of others so that a full census of ideas is available to the group before action is planned and initiated.

12. Help the group act systematically and objectively when it is ready to act.

13. Refrain from being self-assertive, self-deprecative, bossy and domineering in behavior in either word or act.

14. Refrain from discussion or action which is unrelated to the immediate responsibilities of the group for decision or action.

The individual member is important in building an effective group. When each member is ready to participate fully, then we are ready as an organization to perform in a more effective way.

Through assessment, evaluation, and involvement of the members in the new program, groups can bring about new interest, vitality, and increased membership.

31

Principles of Effective Committee Work[1]

By AUDREY R. TRECKER and HARLEIGH B. TRECKER

Committee Common Sense by Audrey R. and Harleigh B. Trecker is probably the best book on committees that has yet been produced. It is simple, clearly written, well-organized, and comprehensive. In dealing with "the why, when, what, and how of successful committee operations," the authors cover most of the topics which will be of concern to committee chairmen, secretaries, or members.

The following excerpt is from the final chapter of the book, "What Are the Principles of Effective Committee Work?"

IN THIS FINAL CHAPTER we want to present a summary of our material. We will endeavor to answer the question: What kind of committees get things done? To do so we will present the basic principles of committee work as they have been developed out of experience and study. Principles are general laws or truths. They may be regarded as rules of thumb which, if followed, will make for effectiveness and productivity in committee work. We believe in these principles. We think that they will have meaning to you also as you participate in the processes of decision making in committees.

[1] Excerpted from *Committee Common Sense* (New York: Whiteside and Morrow, 1954), pp. 145-153. By permission of Association Press, copyright owners.

1. The Principle of Democratic Values

Effective committees are guided in their work by their belief in and respect for democratic values.

Central to this principle is our belief in the capacity of people to make wise decisions when they know and understand the facts. Committee members who practice democracy believe deeply in freedom of expression and respect the rights of individuals to hold and offer differences of opinion. They know that all of us can learn much from listening to the other fellow. The conference table is both a respected symbol and a dynamic device for democratic decision. "Talking it over" rather than telling people what to think is the underlying source of creative power which makes committees get things done.

2. The Principle of Purpose

Effective committees have a clear statement and a clear understanding of their purpose or job assignment.

It cannot be said too often that clarity of purpose is essential if committees are to produce. Purpose must be understood by the body which appoints the committee and by the members who are to work together. In fact, the job to be done determines the kind of people needed in the doing of it. It also provides the committee with a goal or target and defines the limits within which it shall work. Purpose influences the nature of the facts which will be needed and provides a basis for organizing the work systematically. Furthermore, this clear statement of purpose is essentially the baseline the committee must use in evaluating its work.

3. The Principle of Constructive, Creative Leadership

Effective committees have responsible, constructive, and creative leaders who give continuous guidance to committee process.

Good leadership is basic to all productive group experience. In committee work it is of the utmost importance that chairmen and other responsible leaders be chosen with care and in relation to their qualifications. It is particularly apparent that the chairman carries a heavy responsibility which must be taken seriously. The leading of the process of group thinking requires training, study, practice, experience, and continuous self-examination on the part of the person who assumes the leadership role. The way the chairman conducts committee meetings may possibly be the most important single factor in the success or failure of the work.

4. The Principle of Proper Personnel

Effective committees are made up of carefully selected members who are interested and qualified.

Behind this principle is the conviction that when we are building a committee we are building *a work-group.* To become an effective work-group we must, as individuals, accept responsibility and devote our energy to the task at hand. We must place accent on the skills of co-operation and the arts of collaboration. We must accept the full meaning of the assignment and we must be ready to unite ourselves whole-heartedly in the pursuit of our common goal.

5. The Principle of Planning

Effective committees approach and conduct their work planfully by outlining in advance the logical steps to be taken.

Behind every productive committee is a plan. Because so much of the job is done in an informal setting and atmosphere it may appear to be casual. Actually, this is far from the truth. Every series of committee meetings must unfold with a logical sequence and continuity as a controlling influence. Beginning steps must be followed by successively more complex steps. When the committee begins its work with an over-all plan in mind and when it divides the job into component parts movement and progress become readily discernible. Committee productivity thus emerges as a series of calculated and consciously formulated steps. Each meeting is planned and each meeting flows out of the accomplishments of the former ones.

6. The Principle of Preparation

Effective committees prepare carefully for each meeting and have needed material at hand.

If we are to do any job well we must prepare ourselves in advance. If we are going to bake a cake or wash the family car we must have the materials and tools ready to use in doing the work. The same holds for effective committee meetings. Chairman and members must have the agenda, factual materials, minutes of other meetings, and all of the necessary information at hand. People who are prepared produce. People who are unprepared waste time. Last-minute, thrown-together committee meetings usually fail. Preparation pays off.

7. The Principle of Setting and Atmosphere

Effective committees have a good meeting place and develop an atmosphere of freedom and congeniality.

Committees that get things done have meeting places that are conducive to thoughtful deliberation. Attention is given to both physical arrangements and the psychological atmosphere. In fact, the latter item while often neglected is of the utmost importance. When an atmosphere of freedom, congeniality, and informality is created tensions diminish and people become able to talk together with confidence in one another. While the chairman in large measure is responsible for creating and maintaining this positive climate, every member has the responsibility to function as a "creative improver of the group atmosphere."

8. The Principle of Facts First

Effective committees always begin by asking, "What are the pertinent facts related to our assignment?"

As obvious as this may seem, here we have a principle frequently misunderstood or even ignored by committees. Instead of starting with a look at the facts these committees start with opinions, suggestions, experiences, even motions, and work backwards to the facts! The proven better way is to begin with a look at all of the facts related to the assignment and to ask what additional factual data are needed. To be sure, facts must be interpreted and inferences must be drawn from them and there will always be disagreement as to the exact meaning of the facts. Nevertheless, the creation of a factual base is the foundation and frame of reference needed by all work groups as a starting point. Where are the facts? What do they mean to us? How do we feel about them? In the light of the facts and our feelings (suggestions and opinions) what is the best decision we can make? These are the key questions.

9. The Principle of Participation

Effective committees release and utilize the contributions of members who participate actively in discussion, deliberation, and decision making.

This principle is based on the dual concepts of both *right* and *responsibility.* Simply stated they mean that the committee member must feel that he has the right to participate and furthermore it is his responsibility to do so. This does not mean that everyone will participate in equal amount or frequency in meetings. However, he must be willing to involve himself in the development of the group idea in those ways and at those points where he feels that he has a contribution to make.

10. The Principle of Teamwork

Effective committees do their work according to mutually agreed-upon rules and function as a team rather than as individual performers.

At the conclusion of a successful committee experience the chairman usually says, "We did a good job because the members worked." We should add that they "worked *together.*" This willingness to accept responsibility, to perform a task, to "come through" is fundamental. However, in doing so we refer not to the "solo performer" but to the person who can work in harmony with others as a team member. Effective committees are symphonies of effort rather than collections of solo achievements.

11. The Principle of Progressive Process

Effective committees move through their work assignment in an orderly and progressive manner taking one step at a time.

When one reviews the way productive committees have pursued their course of movement from the beginning to the conclusion of an assignment it is evident that they follow the principle of progressive process. Just as the foundation must be placed first when one is building a house, the committee must put down "factual footings" and build its structure and process upon these footings. By taking one step at a time the committee sets in motion an orderly sequence of action. Decisions are made in a cumulative way with each current decision resting upon prior agreements. As progress is made on the parts of the assignment these advances are in turn integrated with each other and ultimately become the finished product.

12. The Principle of Time and Timing

Effective committees develop a good sense of time and timing and function realistically in relation to time needs and demands.

Sometimes a committee member will say, "Don't worry about us. We will get the job done." We want to ask, *"When* will you get the job done?" Because of their very nature committees must have a realistic time orientation. Almost always the committees which turn out an effective piece of work do it promptly and with regard for total organizational commitments. Such committees utilize the forward movement or momentum which is developed from fairly frequent meetings. They avoid the necessity of starting over and over again because of too long an interval between meetings. This need not imply that work is allowed to become frantic, frenzied, and exhausting, but rather it should mean that a steady pace is maintained with the time goal serving as a help in achieving persistent production.

13. The Principle of Reporting

Effective committees keep adequate records which are used in preparing the final report for presentation to the organization.

The committee report both in its preparation and presentation is a vital part of good committee practice. Committees which get things done keep good records and issue periodic reports of progress. Final reports are prepared with care and in relation to the purpose and assignment. Copies are available for committee members and for the board or organization as a whole. Files are maintained and transferred in good order to succeeding committee chairmen.

14. The Principle of Evaluation

Effective committees look at themselves from time to time and endeavor to improve upon their work by means of systematic evaluation.

The spirit of appraisal which permeates all effective work groups is one of the reasons why such groups do well. The willingness to evaluate and to examine our methods and our procedures is essential if we are to avoid falling into operational ruts. Periodic check-ups on ourselves and our ways of working together will do much to strengthen our understanding of places where we can improve our processes.

15. The Principle of Member Satisfaction

Effective committees provide for their members the basic human satisfactions which come when work is well done.

It is true beyond doubt that each one of us who voluntarily leads or works in committee groups must receive satisfaction from doing so. Committees which get things done develop a sense of pride in their members. This pride of accomplishment is a sustaining force and a crucial factor in all voluntary activity. Individual recognition and full utilization of member talents is important. Even more important is the acceptance which the organization gives to the work of its committees. When members see that their labors contribute to the attainment of large objectives their own feelings of worth and importance increase.

Education, Interpretation, and Public Relations
—Introduction

IT IS AN UNFORTUNATE but apparently well-demonstrated fact that social work in general has a poor press and frequently suffers from unsatisfactory public relations. Indeed, social workers are frequently accused of not being community-minded, and of concentrating on service to clients and the perfecting of techniques with a consequent disregard of their responsibility to the public and a failure to assume broad social leadership. Skilled service is not enough—it is also necessary to promulgate the objectives and ideals of social work; and, since public support for programs is necessary, public understanding is essential. Furthermore, "the public" as an abstraction must be broken up and the specific publics of the agency identified and deliberately educated.

Not only is interpretation and the development of informed public understanding an important aspect of administration in the case of individual social agencies, including the welfare council, but it is even more important, perhaps, in connection with interagency relations and the over-all pattern of community welfare services. It is a major objective of community organization in improving existing resources as well as in the promotion of new services and programs, and hence is a significant aspect of welfare planning. While planning bodies, such as community councils, carry some responsibility for interpreting the services of separate agencies, they are even more concerned with clarifying their own role as intergroups.

In the first of the following two articles the authors analyze and describe the various "publics" to which social welfare programs must be interpreted. In the second, Robert MacRae emphasizes volunteer participation as a primary medium for developing good public relations and better understanding of health and welfare programs and objectives.

254

32

The Social Agency and Its Publics [1]

By HELEN CODY BAKER and MARY SWAIN ROUTZAHN

How can an agency's public be more vividly and realistically envisioned and hence more effectively approached? The authors' answer to this question is to split the composite public into a number of smaller, more specific, and concrete audiences, or publics, and to suggest that these more or less separate and identifiable groups be approached on a differentiated basis. Baker and Routzahn describe eight such publics which are depicted in the form of concentric circles surrounding the agency. Other analyses have been suggested. Wayne Vasey, for example, lists five groups in terms of their attitudes toward the organization, as follows: (1) officials and board members; (2) all interested persons; (3) those who are hostile and regard welfare as a threat to their incomes; (4) the large apathetic general public; and (5) the clientele.[2]

Helen Baker was formerly the associate editor of the now extinct *Survey Midmonthly,* and for twenty-two years was director of public relations for the Council of Social Agencies, of Chicago. Mrs. Mary Routzahn was for a long period of time on the staff of the Russell Sage Foundation and served as director of its Department of Social Work Interpretation. She was a leader in the founding of the National Publicity Council for Health and Welfare Services, and an instructor in the New York School of Social Work.

---

[1] Excerpted from *How to Interpret Social Welfare,* A Study Course in Public Relations (New York: Russell Sage Foundation, 1947), pp. 10-13. By permission of the publisher.

[2] Wayne Vasey, "Public Relations—An Inescapable Obligation in Social Welfare," *Social Service Review,* xxvii, No. 4 (Dec., 1953), pp. 394-398.

AT THE CENTER OF THE CHART on the opposite page stands the health or welfare agency, surrounded by the publics from which, at one time or another, it seeks understanding; good will; financial assistance; participation in its program; use of the services it is equipped to give; support for legislative action; or a change of attitude or behavior.

In spite of the steady growth of the federation movement, the individual agency still carries a great deal of responsibility for the public relations of health and welfare work. Even in cities where community chests tell a well-balanced, year-round story on behalf of a number of private agencies, each public agency usually speaks for itself. Councils of social agencies can, of course, tell the whole story—public and private; and some councils try.

However, such a council—or any federation or grouping of agencies that undertakes to plan a public relations program—has its own story to tell to its own publics, as does the Girl Scout troop in any neighborhood, the Visiting Nurse Association of any city, or any county welfare unit or state department of health. Even the Social Security Board has its own general public, bounded only by its geographic limitations, and including a great many smaller publics.

Who are these people who surround your agency? How much do you know about them? What is the basis of their interest in health and social welfare? How deep or how casual is that interest?

You can make your total public seem more real, more knowable, by breaking it down into smaller groups. There are several ways of doing this. The basis may be religion, age, or nationality, or degree of interest. The chart opposite divides the general public into circles, each representing a smaller public with which your agency has some special kind of relationship. This study course begins with the inner group of those closest to your work and moves outward, through circles of diminishing intimacy.

It is in circle one that the heart of your work really beats. Until every member of the professional and clerical staff thoroughly understands an agency's purpose, takes pride in it, and can talk about it accurately and interestingly, public relations have not even begun. When this is accomplished and when, in addition, every member of a private agency's board (or of a public agency's advisory committee) keeps closely in touch with its work and believes in it wholeheartedly, you can almost call the job half done.

For the purposes of this discussion the term "board members" will include, not only the directors of any gift-supported organization, but also the group which stands in somewhat similar relationship to the tax-supported agency: the state or county commissioners, perhaps, or an advisory or steering committee.

To you as an executive or a professional social worker, these men and women are both your policy-forming partners and your first and most important public. It is your responsibility to keep them closely in

256

touch with the day-to-day work, so that in both capacities they will be well equipped to do their share.

This is more than a question of making it possible and pleasant for them to contribute the best they have to give. It is an important step in public relations; for board members who are thoroughly informed and keenly interested will carry the informal type of interpretation . . . into many of their own daily contacts.

Next come your volunteers. Whole armies of new ones were called to the defense of the home front during the war, reinforcing the seasoned workers of prewar days. Think of the millions—literally—of child-care aides, recreation aides, nurses' aides and Red Cross volunteers who stepped into this circle, along with the regular army of civilian

The Agency and Its Publics *

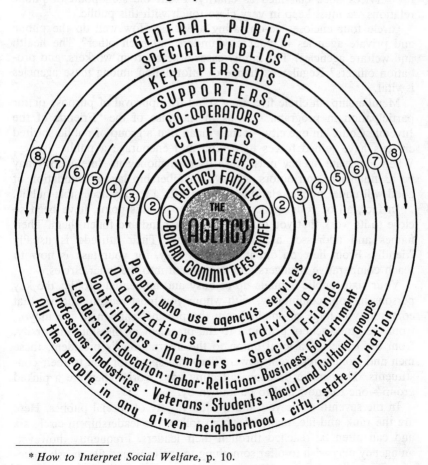

* *How to Interpret Social Welfare*, p. 10.

leaders who have always been the mainstay of our Boy and Girl Scouts and of many other agencies. Often carefully trained in the specific service they are asked to give, but frequently overlooked as possible spokesmen for the whole program, volunteers are one of our least understood publics and one of our greatest sources of potential strength.

Although the third circle carries the label "clients," it includes all the people whom social agencies serve: boys in the Y swimming pool, patients leaving the hospital, mothers receiving aid to dependent children, and neighbors of the community center. Each is a possible ally or critic.

But our relationships with these men and women, girls and boys, are changing day by day. We are living through one of those shifting times when new attitudes and values emerge overnight. The clients of family agencies, in many cities, have become supporters by beginning to pay for services once classified as charity. From the standpoint of public relations we must keep in very close touch with this public.

Circle four encloses co-operating agencies. How well do the public and private agencies in your city understand each other? The health and welfare agencies? The family caseworkers, group workers, and probation officers? Regular exchange of information among these agencies is vital.

Membership, in circle five, may stand for approval of purpose or for participation in program. Or—as in the case of the "Friends of the Juvenile Court" in one city—it may mean that a group of public-spirited citizens have joined forces to defend and encourage a public agency. When a private agency must raise its own money its "members" may be its financial contributors. Always, membership lays a foundation of good will under public relations and provides a readily accessible public.

In fact, all of your agency's publics, up to this point, have been so close to its work that you can put out your hand and touch them. Their names and addresses are known to you. Their attitude is usually friendly. From here on out it is not so easy, for your task is now to reach comparative strangers and draw them into the inner circles.

Your sixth public is made up of busy and influential people: the key persons in your community, with whom you must reckon whether that community is large or small. From the precinct captain to the mayor, from the grade-school principal to the president of the state university, from the leader of a local union to the international's president, these men and women represent power. They can speak for you to their constituents. They make decisions affecting your work. They are a picked group—one to know and to be known by.

In the seventh circle you find a wide variety of special publics. Here are the rank and file, many of whom follow the leadership in circle six and can often be reached through their leaders. Frequently, however, an agency may wish to offer something to the rank and file or ask something of them as individuals. This usually can be done through their organizations, if they are organized.

But housewives, for instance, or unorganized industrial workers, as well as many other special publics for whom there is no space on the chart, must be sifted out from the eighth circle. This is the great mass of unassorted people who read newspapers, listen to the radio, see the posters of the community chest, and attend motion pictures. You may break down this great audience by keying your broadside techniques to the specific interests of some special group or, if you use the radio, by timing your program to catch their attention. Perhaps you can think of other methods .

Of course, this general public, being largely composed of voters, is vitally important to the tax-supported agency. But private agencies cannot afford to neglect the outer circle, since the whole picture of health and social welfare is sufficiently important to hold a place in the public thought. Neither should the tax-supported agency overlook the inner circles; for "everybody's job" may easily become nobody's job unless a few warm and close friends stand firmly in the agency's defense.

33

Citizen Participation and Public Relations [1]

By ROBERT H. MACRAE

How to promote broader and better public understanding of
social welfare without which the future of social work is uncertain, is
the question posed by the director of the Welfare Council of Metropolitan Chicago. The answer, he says, is to encourage citizen participation
and volunteer service in connection with direct service agencies, the
community chest, and the welfare council. This short article reviews
some of the basic principles that underlie an effective program of good
public relations, principles that are the particular concern of the professional community organization worker.

THE SMOLDERING CRITICISM of public welfare . . . will have
served one useful end if it wakes up social work to one great truth:
that the future development and growth of health and welfare services,
public and voluntary alike, depends upon public understanding and
approval. Indeed, in the present crisis, some valued elements of our
social welfare structure may not survive unless public understanding is
broadened.

If such understanding is basic, the question is, "How can we secure
it?" To my mind the answer is citizen participation. Citizen participa-

[1] Excerpted from "The Public: Friend or Critic?", *Community,* Vol. 27, No. 7
(March, 1952), pp. 123-125. By permission of *Community* Magazine, United
Community Funds and Councils of America, Inc.

tion does not just happen. It must be sought energetically and imaginatively and developed continuously. This is a job never completed.

Citizen participation in social welfare operates at two levels—passive and active. Most of the adult public is at the passive level—the newspaper reader, the radio listener, the nominal contributor to Community Chest campaigns, the taxpayer. Here participation tends to be casual and without any great depth of interest. It may swing this way or that—favorable and friendly as people hear of some service that has helped a child, a family, a neighborhood; sharply critical, as they read in their newspapers of social welfare waste, inefficiency, and "chiselers." Yet social work cannot ignore this passive group. It is our constant challenge to move people from the passive to the active level.

This active level marks the point at which citizens assume a vigorous personal interest in social welfare by serving on boards of directors, budget committees, public commissions, and fund-raising teams. It is this level at which social welfare really gets into the blood stream of these volunteers, so that they take on its causes as their own, work to advance its objectives and are able and eager to defend it from its detractors.

It takes hard work to keep the public at the most elementary passive level of participation. Some social agencies apparently believe their good deeds will "shine like candles in a naughty world." Unfortunately, candles throw a very small beam in a world currently illuminated by piercing searchlights. Community services must compete for attention with . . . congressional didoes and new automobile models. Little wonder our candle flickers but dimly among all these foreign and domestic pyrotechnics.

Perhaps what health and welfare needs is an overhauling of its lighting system. The best generator of both light and power is an adequate program of public relations. Let's look at some principles that underlie such a program.

Basic to any attempt to create favorable public attitudes is a "good product." The agency must fill a demonstrated need, its services must be soundly planned and competently operated. It must inspire confidence by the evident skill with which it performs its job. The public won't buy on faith indefinitely. It is quick to suspect a phony article.

Gaining Public Acceptance

Granted that health and welfare services are a good product, how then do we win for it wide public acceptance, approval, and use? Ah, public relations, of course! Every social agency had better wake up to the fact that public relations can't be farmed out to a department, nor can it be dismissed with a regretful "We have no money for public relations," implying that only a heartless budget committee forcibly restrains the agency from the public's affection. The fact is that everybody connected with the agency constantly influences public attitudes toward the agency, for better or worse—the janitor, the telephone operator, the receptionist, the caseworker, the nurse, the executive, and the president of the board. But unless all the power for good will, exercised by "everybody," is consciously recognized, administered, and guided into good and fruitful channels by "somebody"—an executive, a committee—who makes it a major concern, it may well trickle away or dry up. The job of gaining public acceptance has to be *somebody's* business.

From Passive to Active

Assuming that an alert sense of public relations on the part of agencies, chests and councils, has brought Mr. and Mrs. Citizen to the level of passive participation, how do we move this splendid couple over onto the active list? I would remind professional staff of two tried and tested methods:

1. Wider use of volunteers. Let us use committees wherever and whenever there is a real job for them to do. . . . Seek participation in reaching policy decisions. Don't ask a committee or board to simply ratify staff decisions—this is the surest way to kill a committee! Public agencies could learn something from the voluntary in the use of advisory committees. Many public agencies make no use of citizen committees, and to their sorrow, since nobody is so lonely as a "bureaucrat" who has failed to cultivate friends. Public agencies might be surprised and pleased to discover how many people would be impressed with the opportunity to serve on public agency commissions and advisory bodies.

2. A dose of democracy. Let us inject a liberal dose of democracy in policy-making boards and committees. *Noblesse oblige* is definitely "old hat" as a philosophy to undergird social work. The public no longer wants the man in striped pants and the dowager from the social register to have the sole say-so about the policies of their social agencies. Voluntary agencies need to remember that the broadening of the base of financial support about which we speak proudly, must be accompanied by an equally broad base of representation on boards and committees.

Growth in Participation

The growth of labor participation during the past decade is a story with a moral. At a recent meeting of CCC's Labor Participation Department, it was reported that 50,000 labor union members now serve on chest, council and agency boards and committees, compared to 5,000 in 1947. This has been brought about because labor people have been sought out, urged, and given a chance to participate. Surely labor is not the only group ready and willing to participate helpfully and constructively, if we give them the same kind of chance.

Professionals Please Note

We professional leaders have a responsibility to secure this kind of participation and I humbly suggest some steps to that end:

1. *Get and give the facts.* We must be prepared to give the public the facts about needs, services, and budgets. Fact finding, research, evaluation, must be bywords in the vocabulary of our administrators and leaders. These are technical processes, to be sure, carried on by professional experts, but they must be done with the aid and backing of citizen committees, which are involved every step of the way. Research has been called the "radar of social work." It seems to me that in the years immediately ahead, social work had better use its own "radar" pretty diligently to detect any inefficiency or shortcomings that may be blocking its true course of usefulness.

2. *Pull together.* We must develop better attitudes and stronger cooperative relationships between public and voluntary agencies. Too many public agency people feel that voluntary agencies are frivolously wasting funds on piddling little ventures. Too many voluntary agency people look down their noses at public agency programs as "mass services," intimating that the genuinely qualitative job is being done only by the voluntary agency. Such people will view attacks on public agencies as matters of no concern to them. As a matter of fact, public and private agencies are in the same boat and the quicker we admit it the better. An attack on either public or voluntary agencies is an attack on all social work. . . .

3. *Have faith in ourselves.* Before we can succeed in any effort to gain public understanding, we social workers will have to gain a little more faith in ourselves. At present, when attacks are directed at social work we mutter and fulminate among ourselves, but we seldom conduct a vigorous or effective defense. We have become public scapegoats, submitting supinely to attacks on the very basic principles underlying our profession. Every tin-horn legislator assumes the right to speak authoritatively on social work operations. We do not rise very vigorously in defense. Yet we do possess important insights into human behavior. We are able to bring expert testimony to public debate. We have made many significant advances in increasing the health and happiness of mankind. If we are to represent those inarticulate ones we serve, we must have greater faith in ourselves and speak out in temperate and reasoned tones.

4. *Be more than technicians.* Finally if we are to gain public understanding and support, we must recapture the quality of idealism that once was paramount in social welfare activities. In the process of becoming professional, we have lost something—a deep abiding faith, a sense of dedication. In our eagerness to eliminate the silly sentimentalism, the patronizing condescension of some social work of fifty years

ago, we have come dangerously close to becoming people with a technique but with no sense of ministry. We speak of such dedication and devotion with some embarrassment. We have become technicians instead of professionals with spiritual overtones in our jobs. We must recapture idealism and restore it to its rightful place as an essential part of our professional outlook. We must be ready to speak of this idealistic content of our work in helping people find the good life, the abundant life. The public will respond, for in this matter-of-fact, mechanistic world, it is hungry for idealism. Let us not be ashamed that we are ministers to the common good.

Fund Raising
—Introduction

TODAY WE ASSUME that mass needs will be more or less adequately met by tax-supported governmental programs. How to develop financial support for voluntary agencies and services, however, is a different question and a fundamental concern of community organization. The two selections below are devoted to the solution of this problem, mainly through the device of joint, or federated, annual drives at local, state, and national levels. Campaign procedure is analyzed as a process in community organization: the elements involved, the methods used, and the principles underlying successful operation are described, and the relative merits of federated *versus* independent campaigns are evaluated.

The reader's attention is also called to Part IV and particularly to Selection 51, "Chest, Council, and Agency Relationships," where the same controversial subject is discussed in terms of the organizations and services involved. See also Selections 56, 57, and 58.

34

Fund Raising[1]

By F. EMERSON ANDREWS

Over $3,000,000,000 was contributed to educational, religious, health, and welfare institutions and agencies by living individuals in 1949. Still more is being given today. How should these enormous sums be raised, is the question discussed by the author in the first selection below.[2]

Numerous methods of collecting money by amateur fund raisers are described in the original chapter from which the selection is taken. The excerpt itself is devoted to professional fund raising by commercial firms and to federated financing as developed by community chests and united funds. It should be noted that since this material was published the policies of some of the national organizations with respect to participation in united fund drives have been modified. In April, 1955, the American National Red Cross approved such participation in local campaigns. On the other hand, the American Heart Association and the American Cancer Society, which were formerly included, have moved toward withdrawing from united funds throughout the country.

Philanthropic Giving, from which a part of its Chapter 8 was excerpted, is a comprehensive and informative review of voluntary giving in the United States, an activity which is described in the Foreword by Donald Young, general director of the Russell Sage Foundation, as "the emotional and disorderly field of benevolence." It is, however, a field in which a new era has recently dawned.[3]

---

[1] Excerpted from *Philanthropic Giving* (New York: Russell Sage Foundation, 1950), pp. 134-159. By permission of the publisher.

[2] For 1958 United Fund campaign results the reader is referred to Selection 57.

[3] *See* John R. Seeley, *et al., Community Chest—A Case Study in Philanthropy* (Toronto: University of Toronto Press, 1957) for perhaps the most detailed and critical study to date of the functions, possibilities, limitations, and principles of mass fund raising in a typical large city.

F. Emerson Andrews was a staff member of the Russell Sage Foundation from 1928 to 1956, and is presently the director of the Foundation Library Center. He was the co-author with Shelby Harrison in 1946, of *American Foundations for Social Welfare,* and in 1956 he published *Philanthropic Foundations.* Other significant works include *Corporation Giving,* 1952, and *Attitudes Toward Giving,* 1953.

IN MOST COMMUNITIES at the present time residents may expect one major charitable drive or another about once a month. In the winter and spring come the big health agencies and Red Cross, autumn is the usual season for the community chest, and any chinks left in the time schedule are filled in by drives for new hospital wings, churches, and university buildings, or supporting a wide variety of special agencies. In addition to the personal solicitors who call at one's home and place of business, the mailman brings all through the year a flood of appeals, reaching highest tide just before Christmas.

Fund raising is necessary for nearly every voluntary welfare agency, though the chore may be delegated to a chest. Its costs vary from zero, where all the work is volunteered, to 100 per cent in the outright rackets. Its methods are as various as the combined inventions of all the many thousands of men—and women—who annually engage in this $3 billion activity. Many volumes have been written on its specialized techniques, and upon the programs of interpretation and public relations which are its usual adjuncts. Here, no more can be attempted than a description of various types of fund-raising efforts and organizations, with a view to helping the giver distinguish between the desirable and the dubious.

Campaigns that run into the millions, as do those for many educational institutions and national agencies, are usually conducted by special fund-collecting firms whose sole business is organizing solicitation.

Such fund-raising campaigns are highly organized. Operatives are often in the offices of the agency or university six months before the solicitation begins, getting into the spirit of the organization, working on local lists, preparing the elaborate printed pieces which both precede and accompany a major campaign. The fund-raising company takes no part in the actual solicitation of givers, its name appears on none of the literature, and the giver is usually unaware of its existence. But it prepares every detail of a campaign that, at least on paper, should work with clocklike precision.

All potential contributors are listed, with an estimate of their incomes and how much should be expected from them. A special-gifts committee secures in advance a few large contributions, which can be mentioned at appropriate moments. Trained operatives of the fund-collecting agency visit team captains in the larger cities, and instruct them in the organization of lieutenants and actual solicitors. The advance literature goes out. The team captains hold organization dinners— "The menu should be simple to eliminate the mental reaction following heavy eating," one such organization says in its 12-volume guide to standard practice. There follow kick-off dinners, report luncheons, and perchance a victory dinner. "Spread the work" is the principle, perhaps because a solicitor, even if he calls on as few as three people, can then scarcely avoid being also a contributor.

If we are distressed at this degree of organizing generosity, the professional firms can point to their excellent record. It does work. The poor showing in the United States of the 1948 United Nations Appeal for Children was attributed to "amateurish organization," and an editor hoped that the 1949 Appeal would get off to a good start "with full and bold support undertaken by professional fund raisers." [4]

The Federation Idea

An important development in the field of fund raising was the formation of federations, of which community chests are the outstanding though not the only examples. Such federations of social agencies often have functions of planning and community organization of great significance, but it is their fund-raising and distributing functions which are the necessary focus of this chapter.

It was pointed out . . . that growing complications in the social field resulted in attempts to "organize charity" about the turn of the century. The attempts to plan and co-ordinate services did not extend to financing until World War I, except in isolated instances. In 1887 a group of relief agencies in Denver formed a federated plan, and the following year a number of them began uniting their appeals for contributions. But the first real community chest is considered to be the Federation of Charities and Philanthropy organized in Cleveland in 1913.

During World War I the multiplication of appeals of all sorts, including those for relief of sufferers in Europe, induced some 400 communities to organize war chests for joint solicitation of funds. Many of these were disbanded after the end of the war emergency, but the idea had been firmly planted; permanent chests began to increase in number in the early 1920's.

In 1918 the chests formed a national association known first as the American Association for Community Organization, now Community Chests and Councils of America, Inc. Under guidance of this agency,

---

[4] *New York Times* editorial, April 5, 1949.

experience has been exchanged and fairly uniform policies adopted; since 1945 most chests and their participating agencies which are affiliated with the national organization have been using the Red Feather as a common symbol. There are now some 14,000 participating agencies of local chests.

In essence, the community chest ("fund" and "federation" are alternative names) is a citizen-and-agency-controlled organization which has the principal duties of acquiring and spreading information on welfare needs; co-ordinating the work and reviewing budgets for the participating agencies; campaigning for voluntary contributions to meet the chest's accepted share of these budgets; and disbursing these funds to the agencies.

The chest form of money raising, it is contended, has substantially increased both the number of givers and the total amounts contributed to social welfare. In support of this contention the chests present figures for many communities showing increases for the first chest year, often more than 50 per cent above collections by the agencies themselves the previous year. Since, obviously, a chest would put forward a major effort in its first year, these figures are not entirely conclusive, and certain other evidence will be examined later.

Chests believe that programs of the participating agencies are favorably affected by their requirement of annual review and by budgetary control. Duplications with other agencies are often eliminated, economies in operation effected, and sometimes needed extensions of service suggested. In addition, the service agencies do not themselves need to devote staff time and money to fund raising; they can concentrate their attention upon program.

Community contributions for welfare are apportioned by an informed budget committee (after budget hearings for the agencies and the right of review by the board of directors) in proportion to need as judged by this committee rather than on the basis of skill in fund raising or the "heart appeal" of the particular cause.

Typically, community chests are manned chiefly by volunteers. In small communities there may be no paid personnel except possibly for secretarial services during the period of the active campaign. In larger communities the chest has usually a paid all-year executive and sometimes a small staff. If the chest is combined with the council of social agencies, a larger staff is probable.

Most chests endeavor to include all local fund-collecting agencies of approved status, and local chapters of national agencies which conduct local programs—as, for example, the Boy Scouts and the YMCA. Many of them invite state and national agencies, and some of them regard so seriously the competition of outside "drives" by national and other agencies that strong pressures are exerted to bring them in.

It is a fundamental principle of chest operation that agencies which participate must agree not to conduct within the given year other fund-raising drives in the community, with exceptions sometimes permitted in behalf of drives for capital expenditure, such as a new building, and solicitation of their own membership. The contributor is therefore promised "immunity" from further solicitation by these agencies. In recent years the mounting number of drives by agencies outside community chests has severely reduced the value of this immunity.

Opposition to Federation

Giving through community chests or other types of federation has been sharply challenged. Some of this opposition is individualistic, on the part of agencies that believe they can raise larger sums independently than they would receive as their portion of chest campaigns. Nearly all chests have experienced withdrawals of dissatisfied agencies. Some of them later came back, but others have remained outside.

The American National Red Cross formerly was included in many chest campaigns, but the national organization now forbids its locals to join other organizations for federated fund raising.[5] Other national organizations that conduct large campaigns usually independent of chests are the American Cancer Society, National Foundation for Infantile Paralysis, National Society for Crippled Children and Adults, and National Tuberculosis Association.

It is probable that any one organization with an appealing cause, be it local or national, can raise more money than it is likely to be assigned from a federated drive for all agencies. But can it continue to do so if great numbers of other agencies also conduct independent drives? And is ability to collect a satisfactory basis for apportioning contributors' dollars?

Federated fund raising is more fundamentally challenged with the contention that it does not and cannot raise enough money to meet the reasonable needs of all philanthropic agencies. Typically, chests conduct a single campaign, usually in the autumn. Most people, probably, will contribute a greater total amount if they are asked for money perhaps eight or ten times in the year, instead of just once. Chests try to meet this difficulty by arranging for installment payments. But in the house-to-house canvass, the installment plan has not been notably successful; most contributors make a single contribution, and many of them regard the community chest drive as simply another "appeal," similar to other drives for single agencies; their contribution to the whole group of chest agencies may be even less than to the single agency if that agency happens especially to interest them. In industry the chests have had better success with installment payments. Where both labor and management have strongly favored a federated drive in place of numerous plant solicitations, it has usually been possible to arrange

---

[5] The reader's attention is called, however, to the editors' statement on page 266, second paragraph.

pledges covered by payroll deductions once a month, or even weekly.

To the contention that giving should be proportioned to the varying abilities of the givers, and not on the basis of a march of dimes—or of dollars—from everybody, the independents which have used the mass appeal point out that it works. Christmas seals for tuberculosis, March of Dimes for polio, individual memberships for the Red Cross, these and similar campaigns have raised outstanding sums. These three causes collected a total of $113 million for 1949, as compared with the 1949 chest total of $188 million for 1,152 chests.[6]

To the arguments that federation is necessary because multiple drives have become an intolerable nuisance to givers, are a heavy drain on volunteer workers, and are costly, the opponents of federation make these replies. Givers need to be prodded hard and often, for giving is at a shamefully low level. Volunteer workers can still be obtained—one sampling revealed that only one-quarter of all people have been volunteer workers in fund raising, and 30 per cent of the remaining said they were willing to serve—and recruiting and training such workers introduces the agency to an important additional public. Finally, while the costs of raising these separate funds are considerable, some of these expenditures might properly be charged off to education of the public concerning the particular disease or social condition involved.

The National Foundation for Infantile Paralysis points out that it has a "spreading the risk" function. When a disease becomes epidemic in a particular locality, that locality may be unable to bear all of the heavy costs from its 50 per cent of March of Dimes funds. The national organization sends in money from its 50 per cent share, part of which is allocated to epidemic relief, and in emergencies may augment this by contributions, from localities which have had few cases. The national also combines funds received from all localities for research and professional education needed by all.

Chests point out that they also are usually open to inclusion of national agencies, and already do include many. The new state chest idea would prove useful in spreading the load.

"Distribution in proportion to proved need" is another strong plank in federation platform. The independent fund raisers have refused to submit to the procedures of the National Budget and the National Quota Committees. They take the position that no cause has yet received all the financial support it could usefully employ; that they are entitled to put their cause before the public as effectively as they can, and to receive what the public, rather than an "authoritarian body of officials," decides they should have.

---

[6] Comparable campaign results for 1957 were as follows: National Tuberculosis Association, $26,310,400; National Foundation for Infantile Paralysis, $44,034,000; and American Red Cross, $85,109,377; or a grand total of $155,-453,777, in comparison with approximately $379,000,000 raised by 1,986 chests and united funds.

Preservation of the giver's choice in the destination of his gift is one of the chief stumbling blocks in federation's path. The giver favorably disposed toward a particular cause, either because of some experience of his own or because of the agency's superior publicity, may reasonably desire the whole of his gift to go to that special purpose. He may refuse to contribute to the chest if this agency is not included. Even if it is, the budgeted amount may seem to him too small. Probably the chest permits him to designate the whole of his gift for this agency, but this is an illusory privilege; unless the contributions designated for this particular agency exceed its budgeted total, it will get no more than if no designations were made.

The more ardent attackers of federation have lately engaged in broad charges. "We are reaching the point," said Basil O'Connor,[7] "where there is going to break out an open warfare between the school of federated financing and the school of independent financing. . . . Frankly, I cannot personally go along with what I refer to intentionally as the communization of either health or welfare activities or in fund raising in connection with them."

Limited Federation?

Givers have not, in general, been much concerned over this warfare between the embattled camps of federation and antifederation in fund raising. Many have not been aware of its existence. But the decision will be made by givers, through the tightening or loosening of their purse strings. It is quite likely that this decision will vary with the size and degree of industrialization of communities, and with their habits of thought and action.

Welfare needs that affect a large majority of the population and are capable of mass handling will probably remain under, or drift toward, governmental auspices. These include care of dependent children, education for all children, unemployment insurance, health and dental care, assistance to the needy blind and other large groups of the handicapped, relief up to a subsistence level, and pension plans or outright aid for the aged.

To these causes we "give" through taxation or, in the insurance-type plans, through enforced and often matched contributions. Our control is the very remote one of influencing legislation by the ballot and by pressures. In most of these fields some private agencies will still be needed to supplement program and to serve as pilot plants for new experiments and measuring rods of governmental performance—much as private schools continue to serve useful functions.

Beyond the present or probable orbit of government a vast variety of

---

[7] Address before National Social Welfare Assembly, May 6, 1947. Mr. O'Connor is president of the National Foundation for Infantile Paralysis.

needs remain, many of them appealing and important, some of them important but with little pull on the heart strings, and some of them, alas, merely appealing. For the needs which are important, support must be found. In spite of efforts at mergers and combinations, the number of agencies in all but the smallest communities will remain large. No giver will have either the knowledge or the time to consider all of them on their merits. Besides, individual campaigns would be prohibitively expensive and burdensome. In this situation federated fund raising has been a useful device in the recent past and is likely to remain so.

Community chests will lose ground if they permit themselves to become professionally controlled, agency-minded machines for presumed efficient giving, taking the public into their confidence only once a year, when the annual drive is due. They were invented as an aid to givers, to bring order and understanding into the chaos of multiple appeals. To the extent that they remain responsive to the giver, speaking his language, and inviting his participation, to that extent the chests are useful to the giver, and may expect his larger support.

Most chests were started by the people on the wealthier side of the railroad tracks. Many of them have taken pains, especially recently, to represent the whole community by including labor and other groups on their boards. They have been less successful in interpreting to the contributor the wide variety of agencies they represent, and in making him feel that his own dollars are going to causes that are important to him.

Possibly the chests will find a formula by which the individual contributor may select two or three agencies within the chest (instead of the 15 to 400 the chest may include), be kept in close touch throughout the year with the work and the needs of these particular agencies, and designate half his chest contributions to that work, with the remaining half left to the discretion of the budget committee. Such a formula might restore the keen interest and sympathy of individuals who now give perfunctorily or not at all, lost in the maze of agencies the average chest tries to represent equally; it might stir the chosen agencies to a better job of interpreting their work, and still give the chest enough flexibility—with the aid of undesignated corporate gifts—to perform its important function of distributing funds in accordance with community needs.

Chests are troubled by the number of independent drives, usually by national agencies, that compete with their own campaign. In theory, chests would like to see all welfare agencies brought into the common fund-raising effort, and subject to the budget controls that seem to them reasonable and desirable. In practice, chests sometimes do not open their doors soon enough to new causes that capture the interest of givers. Even if they do so, a strong independent may regard its own case as unique, requiring special consideration not likely to be received from a general budgeting committee, or act on the still simpler premise that it can collect more money, even if at a high collection cost, by going it alone.

Since communities differ widely in their organization and in their traditional attitudes, it seems unlikely that the "open warfare" predicted by Mr. O'Connor between the forces for and against federated giving will become general, or will at any near date reach a decisive conclusion, nationally. Highly industrialized communities, like Detroit and Pittsburgh, are likely to find single plant solicitations, with periodic wage deductions, so efficient and convenient a device that even the most resistant independents will find it necessary to federate to this extent. Small residential towns with a leisure class for volunteer workers may support a chest covering many local and a few state and national agencies, tolerate a number of independent drives, and still have ample resources for solicitations by universities, hospital building funds, and many special causes. The village and the farm may continue to do much of their giving through the local church and by simple neighborly action.

In view of the difficulties of collecting sufficient funds from householders in one solicitation, federation itself may find division desirable. For example, family service and recreation (character-building) agencies might join in the regular fall chest drive. Health agencies, national and local, might conduct a federated spring drive. At another convenient season the hospitals might join in a United Hospital Fund solicitation.

The giving we do through government by way of taxes is a duty, with our portion decided by law. The giving we do through voluntary agencies is a privilege, with the amount and channel of the gift determined by our understanding of the need. Since givers differ, no one "right" channel exists. Ample opportunity should remain for the individualist who sees one particular need as more important than all others. Givers should have full information on the advantages and disadvantages of the various methods so that, community by community, the ends of giving in terms of human welfare may be well and willingly served.

35

The Successful Fund-Raising Campaign [1]

By HAROLD J. SEYMOUR

The National War Fund (1943–1947) represented a new high in fund-raising organization for welfare purposes in the United States. Contributions from 43,000 contributors were collected for aid to 126 foreign countries. Valuable lessons in campaign and budgeting procedures were learned from this experience many of which are applicable to all types of voluntary giving.

In the following selection the author, who served as general manager of the Fund, defines clearly what is meant and not meant by a fund-raising campaign, describes what he considers to be the five essential elements, and states ten laws, or principles, of successful fund raising. These, he considers, constitute a "workable pattern for raising money for any cause with a universal appeal, national or local." [2]

FIRST, . . . , LET US SEE what we mean when we say "fund-raising campaign." For while we Americans use those words more often than any other people in the world, there is still far too little enlightenment or agreement on what the words involve. Here, for instance, are five common misconceptions about effective fund raising:

[1] Excerpted from *Design for Giving: The Story of the National War Fund* (New York: Harper & Brothers, 1947), pp. 45-49. By permission of the publisher.

[2] Seymour, *op. cit.*, p. 45.

1. *The William Jennings Bryan Complex.* Before World War I, you oldsters may remember, Mr. Bryan thundered his rebuttal to the preparedness warnings of the great Teddy Roosevelt by the confident assertion that "a million men would spring to arms overnight." People who wish to raise money sometimes make the same costly mistake, by assuming happily that if the cause is well publicized, and the people are told where to leave their gifts, the money will roll in.

2. *The Mike and Ike Delusion.* Rube Goldberg's "Mike and Ike— They Look Alike" was a great cartoon idea, as Lewis Carroll could have easily prophesied. But the concept is just so much virulent poison to effective fund raising, whenever people begin to have the bright idea that everyone should give a dime or a dollar, or that a hundred should give a thousand, or come up with any of those apparently easy schemes that raise money merely by long division and the multiplication table. To be sure, you can raise some money that way, but usually at shockingly high cost.

3. *The Saturday Night Shave.* You'll know what we mean by this if your shave of Saturday morning doesn't look so good when you get ready to go out in the evening; you just give it "the once-over lightly." That's all right with a beard, but it is almost always fatal in a fundraising campaign, for the basic reason that success never comes the easy way, and always requires careful planning and preparation and a lot of hard work.

4. *The Cinderella Dream.* You can call this the Cult of the Ostrich, and it will mean the same thing—a blind hope that everything will come out all right. People responsible for fund-raising campaigns are fooled too often because the first response comes easily, and because realism and objectivity are lost in the clouds of starry-eyed wishful thinking.

5. *The Pattern of the Losing Football Coach.* When you can't win, it may be comforting to reflect that you are building character. But those who want nothing less than victory in a fund-raising campaign should always take heed, if not actually do a little viewing with alarm when the campaign managers start talking about "the larger, long-term gains in making new friends for the institution." To be sure, a fundraising campaign is a public relations operation from start to finish; the design, however, should be for giving.

The trouble with these and similar misconceptions about fund raising, all of them cobwebs we must first strike aside if we are to see clearly what a campaign really is, is that they fail to take into account the five essentials for successful fund raising, and certain of the laws or principles which no campaign can ever escape.

Cobwebs aside, then, we can define a fund-raising campaign affirmatively as "a planned mobilization of the friends of a cause or institution, for a voluntary solicitation of proportionate gifts from an informed constituency; always toward a specific goal or objective, and usually within a specified period of time." Neither Webster nor Churchill might approve of that phraseology, but we think it covers the ground.

Five Essential Elements

Under that or an equivalent definition, an organized fund-raising campaign comprises five basic elements. You need the four to make the watch, and you need the fifth to make it tick:

First, in chronological order rather than in order of importance, a good campaign needs a strong and timely case; an aim plainly in the interest of those who will be asked to give—rather than merely in the interest of an agency or institution *per se*—and a program reasonable enough to let the mind rationalize what the heart prompts the giver to do.

Most important of all, but placed second because you usually have to have a good case to get it, is active and influential leadership. Without such leadership many a good cause has withered on the vine; with it, you can accomplish almost anything. You need it at the top, in terms of the first-class attention of a first-class man, and you need it all the way through the campaign organization, at each successive level—leadership that is active and influential, by getting out in front and leading, in a way others will be willing and ready to follow.

Third, a successful campaign needs a sufficient number of informed and enthusiastic volunteer workers—the sales force to sell the cause. The right kind of volunteer worker is someone with some good reasons for giving liberally and proportionately to some good cause, and who is enthusiastically determined, at some particular time, to see someone and ask for some money. Persons who fail to qualify are those who "just can't say 'no' to the team captain," those who are really terribly busy but might be willing to "take a few names," and particularly those who do nothing more than write a few begging letters. How many volunteer workers are needed, of course, depends on how many people are to be solicited, with variations in the usual proportion of one worker to every ten prospective contributors, depending on the ease or difficulty of personal access and how big a load the workers are ready to carry. (The ladies, God bless 'em, will usually take more names to see than the men will.)

The fourth essential is a campaign constituency, or field of support, in which the known giving potential is commensurate with the campaign goal. A good list of such potential contributors is one in which every name has been carefully selected, all pertinent data accurately transcribed, each card rated by competent volunteers for its individual quota or amount to be sought, and all cards finally classified for easy assignment. All of which requires (1) a good reason for the inclusion of each card, (2) painstaking research, (3) meticulous typing and clerical work, (4) volunteer rating committees, and (5) some simple and economical system of card control.

The fifth essential, for lack of a better term, we'll call campaign dynamics. If you've made a good watch by qualifying your campaign on the first four essentials, this is what you need to make the watch tick—the catalytic agent to put the mixture to the boil. In its essence, campaign dynamics involves the routines of planning, timing, direction, and operation. But you could just as well say that it involves the skillful manipulation of the laws of human behavior by competent campaign management.

And now, assuming agreement on what fund raising really is, and what its basic essentials are, let us look at the main body of the law—the rules or principles which have been found to affect all such voluntary campaign efforts.

Principles of Fund Raising

One of the pleasanter aspects of the profession of one who makes fund raising his vocation is that the wiser such a man gets, the more he shrinks from being called an expert. He comes to feel, after a time, that the more he learns the less he really knows. Which, after all, is as it should be. For fund raising, such an old-timer would tell you, is more of an art than a science, and an art in a relatively primitive stage.

Nevertheless, when you see such and such an effect invariably follow such and such a cause, over a long period of time, you come to share the privilege of the Messrs. Boyle and Charles—you can say you have observed a law, which your colleagues or contemporaries are at liberty to challenge if they can.

Here, then, are ten such laws of raising money, with which the fund-raising fraternity are believed to be in virtually unanimous agreement:

1. The quantitative result of every fund-raising campaign varies directly with the quality and devotion of the leadership.

2. The effectiveness of any campaign organization can be measured by the extent to which responsibility is decentralized, by the planned distribution of assimilable work units.

3. Personal contact, whether for the enlistment of workers or the solicitation of gifts, should be established on the same or higher level.

4. Duly proportionate quotas or goals, whether for dollars or units of work, should be established and accepted for every part of the total campaign structure: for every division, every team, every worker, and every prospective contributor.

5. In any multiple fund-raising effort, where there is likelihood that some units will succeed and some will fail, total success can be assured only by adopting in advance either one or both of two measures: including in the goal an extra amount as a cushion or safety factor against

unit failures, or an agreement that successful units will either pay the full amounts raised, regardless of quotas, or will share such oversubscriptions in some equable proportion.

6. Campaigns are best conducted in an atmosphere of universality—a general public impression that everyone will benefit and that nearly everyone will wish to participate in a certain way, and at a certain time.

7. The effectiveness of campaign organization is limited by the law of diminishing returns: the wider its periphery, the lower the returns and the greater the proportionate cost.

8. To paraphrase Shakespeare, if a campaign were to be done, 'twere well it were done quickly; in communities, as in kindergartens, attention periods have their limits.

9. You can't raise money without spending money; within reasonable limits the return is likely to be commensurate with the investment.

10. Every good campaign is essentially a public relations operation—an aggregate of the tremendous trifles by which any enterprise wins and holds public approval: good manners, pleasurable experiences, recognition for achievement, and proof that all the sacrifice anyone made was worth far more than its cost.

Social Action
—Introduction

THE FOLLOWING SECTION on Social Action is included for convenience in this Part on "Community Organization in Practice," although some of these selections might equally well be considered under Part II, "The Process of Community Organization."

Of the three selections that follow, the first deals with the nature of social action as defined by various writers, and the second and third describe two significant aspects of the subject. Geneva Mathiasen's paper is devoted to the methods employed in social action, particularly in initiating such action; Kenneth L. M. Pray discusses the important question of the relationship between social work and social action.

*   *   *   *

To act collectively is according to the spirit of our institutions.

Henry David Thoreau: *Walden*

36

What Is Social Action? Selected Definitions

Definitions of social action have usually been broad and sometimes vague. In the seven more or less typical definitions that follow—ranging over the period from 1922 to 1957—the chief common thread is the idea of improving mass conditions (Richmond), enhancing social welfare (Solender), solving mass social problems (Hill), influencing "basic social conditions and policies" (Pray), or changing the environment (Coyle). Two definitions describe social action as furthering "desirable objectives" (Fitch, Hill), while one writer (Lee) defines it as "any effort to promote social welfare outside the direct and indirect media represented by our service agencies, national organizations, etc." For Solender, on the other hand, it must conform with the philosophy, and harmonize with the methods of social work.

Some of the issues which are left open by various definitions are these: (1) What is meant by "mass" conditions or problems? How large a group must be concerned as the object of the social action? For example, would efforts to enact legislation to benefit a small racial minority group be concerned with "mass" conditions? (2) If social action must seek "socially desirable objectives," who is to say what is "socially desirable"? Whose value-judgments are to prevail? Can there be "social action" on both sides of a violently controversial issue—such as proposed legislation regarding the giving of contraceptive information to married couples by public clinics, for example? (3) What is the relation of social action to the field of social welfare and to the process of community organization?

The other forms of social work, all of which interplay with case work, are three—group work, social reform, and social research. . . . By a method different from that employed in either case or group work, though with the same end in view, social reform seeks to improve conditions in the mass, chiefly through social propaganda and social legislation. Whether the immediate object be better housing, better health, better working conditions, better use of leisure, or a long list of other objectives, the main purpose in these different social reforms still is to advance the development of our human kind by improving social relations.[1]

PORTER R. LEE   **1937**

In this discussion I am taking the term social action to include any effort designed to promote social welfare outside the direct and indirect media represented by our service agencies, national organizations, etc. Social action seems to suggest efforts directed toward changes in law or social structure or toward the initiation of new movements for the modification of current social practices. Promotion of the idea of crime prevention as a public obligation is social action. Activity on behalf of a political party—republican, democrat, socialist, communist, or labor—when undertaken in the belief that the party's success would result in a greater measure of social welfare is social action. The organization of special-interest groups to achieve through the class struggle a shift in the control of economic power, with the same belief behind it, is social action. Participation in movements to achieve social security or the abolition of child labor by legislation is social action. Safety campaigns and the promotion of the co-operative movement are social action.[2]

GRACE L. COYLE   **1937**

Social action as a part of social work is, I suppose, the attempt to change the social environment in ways which we believe will make life more satisfactory. It aims to affect not individuals but social institutions, laws, customs, communities.[3]

---

[1] Quoted from *What Is Social Case Work? An Introductory Description* (New York: Russell Sage Foundation, 1922), pp. 223-224. By permission of the publisher.

[2] Quoted from "The Social Worker and Social Action," in *Social Work as Cause and Function* (New York: Columbia University Press, 1937), p. 270. By permission of the publisher.

[3] Quoted from "Case Work and Group Work. II. Social Workers and Social Action," *Survey Midmonthly*, LXXIII (May, 1937), pp. 138-139.

JOHN A. FITCH   1940

Social action is legally permissible action by a group (or by an individual trying to promote group action) for the purpose of furthering objectives that are both legal and socially desirable.[4]

KENNETH L. M. PRAY   1945

For the purpose of this discussion we shall define social action as the systematic, conscious effort directly to influence the basic social conditions and policies out of which arise the problems of social adjustment and maladjustment to which our service as social workers is addressed.[5]

JOHN L. HILL   1951

[Social action] might be described as organized group effort to solve mass social problems or to further socially desirable objectives by attempting to influence basic social and economic conditions or practices.[6]

SANFORD SOLENDER   1957

Social action in the field of social work is a process of individual, group, or intergroup endeavor, within the context of social work philosophy, knowledge, and skill. Its objective is to enhance the welfare of society through modifying social policy and the functioning of the social structure, or working to obtain new programs and services.[7]

---

[4] Quoted from "The Nature of Social Action," *Proceedings, National Conference of Social Work,* 1940 (New York: Columbia University Press, 1940), p. 488.

[5] Quoted from "Social Work and Social Action," *Proceedings, National Conference of Social Work,* 1945 (New York: Columbia University Press, 1945), p. 348.

[6] Quoted from "Social Action," *Social Work Year Book,* 1951 (New York: American Association of Social Workers, 1951), p. 455.

[7] Quoted from "Social Action," *Social Work Year Book,* 1957 (New York: National Association of Social Workers, 1957), pp. 517-518. By permission of the publisher.

37

Initiating Social Action[1]

By GENEVA MATHIASEN

This is one of the most practical papers on methods of social action that has yet been written. It was presented originally at a regional institute on methods of social action.

The author assumes that the social actionists are agreed upon their goal, and that "we are going to talk about carrying the project through to completion and my part is to talk about how we get started." The discussion centers about four questions—mobilizing resources, overcoming apathy, developing interest by individuals and groups, and changing attitudes.

Mrs. Geneva Mathiasen is executive secretary of the National Committee on the Aging, of the National Social Welfare Assembly. Her previous history includes five years as headworker of the East End Neighborhood House, in Cleveland, Ohio (1939–1944), and one as executive secretary of the Governor's Committee (Ohio) on Youth in Wartime. From 1945 to 1950 Mrs. Mathiasen lived abroad, in England and Switzerland.

[1] Excerpted from paper of same title, *Proceedings,* Institute on Methods of Social Action, New Orleans, Nov., 1953 (National Conference of Social Work and Louisiana Conference of Social Welfare, 1954), variously paged. By permission of National Conference on Social Welfare.

How to Mobilize Community and State Resources

1. ON THE BASIS *of the project decide who should be mobilized.*
There are very few projects which demand or can secure complete mobilization. In organizing youth centers during the war, I remember we listed organizations and/or individuals whose support was *essential* and others were on a supplementary desirable list. Without the backing of the school superintendent or high school principal, the pastors of the churches, some organized parent groups, the youth-serving organizations, and in some cases the juvenile court—the prospects for success were dim. Other groups might be important—trade unions if a certain type of work were necessary, the Elks Club if they happened to have a useful hall, and so on.

There may also be a time element in involvement. In establishing a clinic for retarded children in New Jersey, a group of parents felt that they must first work out a plan by themselves. Later they involved doctors, psychiatrists, educators, and social workers. It was a long time before they felt strong enough to go before the total community.

In one Ohio city a group of personnel directors met regularly under the aegis of the Welfare Federation for over a year before they felt ready to present to the community the employment problems of older people.

In considering the questions of compulsory retirement, the National Committee on Aging selected representatives of business and industry, labor unions, the Department of Labor, and other governmental agencies, industrial relations departments of universities, the medical profession, including industrial psychologists. Other groups, such as fraternal bodies, and the clergy, and medical social workers and teachers were not included in the initial stages, though their participation and influence were immediately sought in a project to improve standards in institutions.

In a project in a Western city involving getting out the vote, someone had the imagination to enlist the interest of the taxi drivers who became a primary factor in the success of the venture.

2. *Choose leadership with care.*
In this kind of group it would be a waste of time to labor this point. We might keep in mind however, the wisdom of seeking out and developing new potential leadership rather than imposing too heavily on a few who carry more than their share of community responsibility. Interest, enthusiasm, and time to give may in the end be more valuable assets than a name already known.

It may be important to establish at the outset whether committee members represent an organization or act as individuals chosen because they represent particular interests or areas of competence.

3. *Give careful consideration to possible opposition to the project, and*

calculate carefully the risks of antagonism of individuals and/or groups.

Sound plans can afford to present or have presented arguments on the other side. At our conference on retirement we felt it was essential to include those who were in favor of compulsory retirement. One of those said afterward, while reconfirming his belief in compulsory retirement as a tool in industrial relations, "Perhaps we should try to determine industry by industry or even job by job, what that age should be— whether 60, 65, 70 or 75." We thought that represented progress.

4. *Remember that people like to be asked to take part in worth-while ventures, and that there are few human experiences so gratifying as working with others for a common cause.*

The most dramatic example of this I have experienced was in England immediately after the war. I was frequently invited to meet with community civilian defense units who were trying to carry their organizations over into peacetime. On nearly every occasion they would reminisce about their experiences and often someone would suddenly remark, "This must sound to you as if we *enjoyed* the war." And one man somewhat sadly said, "It was worth the war, the working together." Every unit I visited was trying to find a peacetime substitute for civil defense.

5. *Form a firm alliance with representatives of public relations media, and respect the technical skills of the public relations profession.*

Among the expressions heard so often among social workers as to become almost platitudinous is that "we are so poor at public relations." For a profession whose success depends so largely on public interpretation, I have always found this admission of incompetence difficult to understand.

Some social agencies recognize the wisdom of making some investment in professional help in this field. Even if employed only on special occasions, a public relations technician can help a staff to carry on the rest of the time. And if there is no money in an agency budget to employ such a person, many of the techniques can be studied and applied. The art of simple direct statement in nontechnical terms is not to be despised by any profession. This is not to deny the usefulness and often the necessity of special professional vocabulary, but all such words and expressions are confusing and hence irritating to lay readers or audience. In a good many communities, newspaper editors and writers as well as radio and television staff serve regularly on committees involving social action. They are thus in a position to interpret the plan to the public with complete knowledge of the aims desired. By whatever means it is important to make sure that the local newspaper, radio, and television personnel are fully informed about the social welfare goals in the community and understand the functions and program of social agencies.

How to Overcome Apathy

1. Since apathy would appear to imply a lack of emotional interest, it can best be overcome, if at all, by an appeal on the emotional level.

In analyzing the motivating force in the twenty-five case histories in the radio series, "The People Act," it was evident that in many instances an unsatisfactory situation was allowed to continue until some incident touched off a mass emotional reaction—fear, anger, pride, sense of justice, outrage.

For example, a town did not act to provide recreation for its young people though there was ample evidence of the need. Finally a high school student wrote a letter to the governor which eventually found its way into the local paper. Their pride injured over an appeal to the governor which seemed to intimate that the town couldn't take care of its own problems, the citizens at last formed a committee to investigate the possibility of a youth center. Similarly a town was indifferent to the needs of the men in a near-by air base until it was labeled in an article in a national magazine as one of the worst communities in its relationship with Army personnel.

Another town for years paid no attention to the efforts of a juvenile court judge to secure help for youthful offenders. Then a young man was brutally murdered in a cell block in jail where by law he should not have been confined. Public indignation reached a high emotional pitch, the National Probation Association was asked to make a study with recommendations, and the necessary funds voted to put the recommended program into action.

2. The dramatic incident may be used effectively but with restraint when necessary.

In one town eight killings failed to arouse a town to change its gangster-ridden government. Then a popular school teacher was killed on her own doorstep and nobody felt safe. A group of women organized for action and, by keeping the incident alive during a grueling election campaign, succeeded in getting a new government for the town.

The use of the dramatic incident wisely without allowing excited mass demonstration to get out of control, however, requires skill and wisdom.

Often a dramatic incident may be purposely created to stimulate action. In a Western state a "farm of maximum effectiveness" was created from the desert in a day, raising the value of the property from zero to approximately $50,000 in a single day. Irrigation ditches were dug, brush cleared, land plowed, fertilized and planted, a six-room house built, trees and shrubs set out, 1500 workers co-operated with 411 pieces of equipment. This was dramatic enough to rouse a whole country to reclaim the land and make a new way of life, where illustrated lectures, exhortation, and appeals to reason had failed.

How Can Interest Be Developed in Individuals and Groups?

This can best be accomplished, it seems to me, by developing a program of action in which individuals and groups have something specific to do to contribute to the common goal.

As an example of this I should like to describe in some detail a program of action at present under way in the state of Kentucky.

This bold venture is designed to raise the state from 47th place in the nation to first place in providing free library service in a single year. Some leaders in the state were shocked into action when 33 per cent of Kentucky's young men called to Service last year had to be rejected as functionally illiterate. The plan calls for 100 bookmobiles to bring books to *all* Kentuckians. A descriptive folder points out that Georgia has 40 bookmobiles; Missouri, 50; and North Carolina, 89. The initial cost of $300,000 plus $200,000 a year state appropriation for books and professional supervision of the plan divides the job into categories, defines function of citizens, corporations, local communities, and the state government, and suggests definite ways whereby every citizen can make a contribution. A corporation or individual may give a bookmobile with an appropriate inscription; a club can buy a wheel for $30, a child can buy a bolt for eleven cents. On a certain Saturday morning every theater in the state will have a special motion picture show for children, admission two books. A citizens' march for books is being held during American Book Week in Louisville and other communities. Any family with books to contribute leaves his porch light on, the teamsters union will transport the books to the fairground where volunteer librarians and trained volunteer assistants will sort and catalogue them. Every person in the state will receive an attractive folder giving full information in simple terms. Attached is an addressed envelope with a form listing seven things each person may do in addition to giving money. All he needs to do is check the card, sign, and post the envelope. The folder says, "If successful, it would be one of the greatest adventures in social progress of our time."

The same principle of interesting people on the basis of their *doing* something is equally true of any project regardless of its scope. If a person votes, gives a dime or a dollar, makes a telephone call, writes a letter to a friend, or a congressman, rings a doorbell, addresses cards, wraps packages, makes a speech, drives a car, serves coffee, attends a meeting—the project is his.

At the moment the National Committee on the Aging is having a very sobering experience with the Advertising Council. This is the medium through which the advertising profession makes its contribution to good causes. It has been suggested that their services be used to alert the country to the needs of older people. The council is willing to give the idea consideration if we can reduce it to advertising technique. This means addressing the individual directly and suggesting that he *do* something. What definitely do we want individuals to do about old age, their own or someone else's? "If you only wanted to raise money," say the advertising experts, "it would be so simple."

How Do You Influence People to Change Attitudes?

. . . What does the person lose if he gives up a prejudice? [Goodwin Watson] points out . . . that not many individuals or organizations know the techniques of work with "subcultures" (characterized by ignorance and narrowness of experience and outlook) where prejudice is intense.

Without therefore assuming to answer the question, I shall comment on some attempts to influence attitudes in the field with which I am presently concerned, attempts to change some of the stereotypes about older people. The only effective method I know about is demonstration that an attitude is false—and that doesn't always work. Exhortation I believe has little effect.

A radio program in the Northwest was designed to combat the idea that old people can't work. It is entitled "Shooting for a Hundred." The main feature of every program was an interview with an elderly person who was at the time actually carrying on a responsible job. One of these was the vice-president of a local bank who had taken on the job after being retired as a newspaper editor. Another was a woman employed as a model in a department store—demonstrating that neither personal charm nor attractive appearance is the sole prerogative of the young. Still another "worked" her own gold mine during the summer months. A second part of the program was an interview with an older man or woman seeking work. The candidate was allowed to set forth his experience and qualifications and to explain the kind of job he felt he could do. Often his "references" were on hand to speak on his behalf. Not one of the persons seeking work through the program failed to get a job during the ensuing week. At the same time the employment needs and contributions of older people were effectively dramatized. This program, growing out of a community institute on the needs of older people, was sponsored at the outset as a public service. It continued for nearly two years on the basis of its popularity rating, against all theories about what makes for popularity in radio.

Another device in common use and sometimes effective is the oblique approach. A council of social agencies in a Western city was concerned with suspicion, antagonism in a section of town containing separate nationality and racial groups—Chinese, Japanese, Filipino, Negro, white. Instead of a frontal approach on trying to correct mistaken attitudes, a frontal attack was made on the number one health problem of the community, tuberculosis. In organizing a plan for mass X ray, followed by a clean-up campaign and a well-baby clinic, the groups mingled in a natural way, rid themselves of some erroneous ideas, and gradually became an integrated community.

At best, changing attitudes is a slow process, and we are not sure of the amount of time we have. And in closing I would like to say a few words outside of my assignment about the need for social action and the place of the individual social worker. Our country, unprotected by any kind of "curtain," lives today in the full light of world public opinion, under the glare of searchlights whose long piercing fingers seek out every nook and cranny for evidence of social ills which may be made the subject of powerful propaganda. More serious than their use for propagandistic purposes, which are now well recognized and evaluated accordingly, are the honest who have not yet decided under what kind of social and political system they wish to live if permitted to choose freely. Every report of racial discrimination, every eviction or photograph of substandard housing, every manifestation of youthful lawlessness, undermines our influence in world affairs and makes more difficult the task of our representatives in embassies and consulates.

Brock Chisholm, former director of the World Health Organization, has, I think, admirably stated the responsibility of the individual: "Whoever is reasonably informed on any aspect of human emotional, mental, or social development, whoever can do something to clarify thinking even a little and very locally, whoever can remove a prejudice, soften a hate, increase the total of understanding and tolerance in the world by that knowledge, training, insight and ability is made responsible to do what he can in all possible places. Whoever can get at people in homes or schools, PTA, clubs, youth groups, by talking or writing, through any channels of communication, is obligated by his ability to serve the human race where he can to the limit of his equipment."

38

Social Work and Social Action[1]

By KENNETH L. M. PRAY

Following the Lane Report on Community Organization to the National Conference in 1939 (see Selection 5), John Fitch presented a pioneer paper defining "The Nature of Social Action," at the Conference of 1940. A year later he followed this with the first *Social Work Year Book* article on "Social Action." In the years that followed, social workers in general seemed to become more "social-action conscious," in the sense that they recognized social action as something that social workers needed to know about, think about, and perhaps do something about!

In 1945 came this vigorous and forthright paper by Kenneth L. M. Pray on "Social Work and Social Action." Social action is (according to one's point of view) either an integral aspect of community organization or a process closely related to it. It is doubtful that anyone has yet equaled this analysis and discussion by Kenneth Pray of the relation between social work and social workers on the one hand and social action on the other.

Mr. Pray was president of the National Conference of Social Work in 1946, and his presidential address, on the theme of "Social Work in a Revolutionary Age," embodies some of the thinking which was earlier expressed in the present paper on social action.

[1] Excerpted from paper of same title, *Proceedings of the National Conference of Social Work,* 1945 (New York: Columbia University Press, 1945), pp. 348-359. By permission of National Conference on Social Welfare. Included also in the volume of the author's collected papers, *Social Work in a Revolutionary Age and Other Papers* (Philadelphia: University of Pennsylvania Press, 1949), pp. 37-52. A related paper, by the same author, on "Social Workers and Partisan Politics" was published in *The Compass* for June, 1945.

FOR THE PURPOSE OF this discussion we shall define social action as the systematic, conscious effort directly to influence the basic social conditions and policies out of which arise the problems of social adjustment and maladjustment to which our service as social workers is addressed. This definition itself may not satisfy all of us to begin with, for it has at least one debatable limitation. While it does not deny, neither does it specifically acknowledge or emphasize the potential and actual indirect influence upon the total social scene which may emanate from the specific services social workers render to particular individuals and groups, through the traditional primary task of helping people to find and use their own strength and the resources around them for the solution of their own problems and the fulfillment of their own lives. I am inclined to believe that the importance and value of this indirect social action, inherent in our day-to-day service, are often unduly minimized or even forgotten in our discussions of social action. But for the present, it is not really in controversy, and I am quite sure that none among us would want to limit our professional service, either in scope or method, so as to preclude these potential, indirect, social gains. It is in relation to the direct, deliberate application of our effort to general social change that our problems and our differences principally develop.

With reference to this issue, let us state some of the disturbing questions plainly.

First of all, the basic question: Does social work as a profession bear any specific responsibility to apply its knowledge and skill to the end of adjusting social institutions and arrangements to the needs of human beings, or is its responsibility limited to helping people find the utmost of satisfaction and achievement within the social circumstances that surround them, whatever those circumstances may be?

If the profession does have some responsibility to participate in social change, what are the boundaries of that responsibility? Has it any real boundaries? Can it be defined or measured in such a way as to differentiate the responsibility of social work in social action from that of other groups devoted to other forms of human service? Or is our responsibility unlimited, all-inclusive, subject only to a constantly changing and expanding definition of what constitutes social need and social betterment?

If, as a profession, we have an inherent, definite responsibility for participation in social action, is it a universal, individual responsibility, borne by every one of us, each in his own place and station? Or is it essentially a collective responsibility only, to be discharged primarily by chosen representatives of the whole profession, on behalf of all? Or is it, perhaps, a responsibility to be delegated by all of us to a few especially interested and competent individuals, employed in agencies devoted to this particular purpose?

Under any of these concepts, can the discharge of this responsibility

292

be brought under anything like professional discipline? What is the relation of the performance of these tasks to other aspects of professional performance? How does it affect, for instance, our direct service relationships with clients? Can this primary professional service relationship be used in any way as an avenue for discharge of a professional responsibility for social action?

And how does our professional relation to a particular agency—which is an almost uniquely significant factor in the performance of our professional function—affect the scope or nature of our responsibility for social action? Does it define, control, limit, or modify this responsibility?

What is the place of the professional association in this whole problem? Is there anything in its function or its composition, or in our relation to it, that determines or defines the use we can make of it in discharging our responsibility for social action? And what of the union? Can we use it—how or to what extent can we use it—for this professional purpose?

Finally, what of our professional relation to political action, especially partisan political action? What part, if any, can we play as professional people in this recurring contest between opposing social interests and concepts and those that represent or uphold them? Does such participation necessarily violate professional standards, because it involves the abandonment of our primary obligations or the destruction of essential professional relationships? In this regard, does it make a difference whether we act as individuals, or in groups, or as a total profession? Can we, indeed, act as individuals or as groups, without involving our whole profession or entangling our primary professional services with divisive and extraneous public issues?

The history and the generally accepted basic philosophy of social work point to a definite answer to our first question. Social action, once more commonly called social reform, has always been an integral and often a decisive element in social work practice as a whole. From the early days of the charity organization and settlement movements in England, down to the mental hygiene and public welfare movement of our own time, there has never been a moment when professionally conscious social workers have been content wholly to separate their day-to-day service of particular individuals and groups from some measure of responsibility for controlling or preventing some of the broad social factors that caused, complicated, or intensified the problems with which they dealt. And the reason, I believe, is that there is no possibility of such separation in fact. In accepting responsibility for administering particular services, social workers accept, also, the inherent obligation to see that those services find their mark, so far as possible, in the lives of those that seek and use them. The special knowledge and skill and discipline upon which the professional character of our whole function rests are directed precisely to that end. Otherwise it would be empty pretense. But suppose, in that effort, we discover circumstances beyond the immediate control of ourselves or our clients which frustrate or obstruct the full and fruitful use of our service? That cannot absolve us from our inherent responsibility to make our service available and useful in fact, as well as in theoretical purpose. And how can we discharge that full responsibility without undertaking somehow to help in removing the obstructions that confront us and our clients? And what is this but social action?

In affirming this basic concept that social work, as a profession, necessarily involves and includes social action as a professional function, we are brought close to an answer for our second question, as to the nature and scope of that responsibility. Social work is not the whole of social welfare enterprise. It is not the exclusive custodian or captain of social progress. The social welfare, in a true sense, is the common ultimate objective of every social institution; it is the characteristic aim of many parts of our modern culture. Social work cannot possess, it can only share, that objective. We have learned through experience the essential practical value, as well as the theoretical validity, of a limited and defined function as the basis of our direct professional service to clients. We know that we need that limitation as the focus of our own development in skill and knowledge, and as the solid framework that sustains and sanctions our helping process. We know that the client needs it, too, among other reasons, in order that he may know whether the service we offer meets his need, and whether he can use it with satisfaction and success. The same principle applies with equal force to that secondary aspect of our task which concerns our participation in helping the community effect broad change in itself. We need to know the limits within which we can truly help, as a basis for the development of our own skill and the formulation of our own criteria of the validity of change. The community needs to know the area of our special knowledge and capacity, as the basis of its discriminating acceptance and use of our help.

What, then, defines the province within which, as a profession, we carry responsibility for social action? It cannot be bounded once and for all, by the range of the human problems with which it is concerned, in terms of the aspects of human living with which those problems are identified. One decisive characteristic of social work as a total professional field is the fact that there is no problem of human living in society which is not likely, appropriately, to come within the orbit of some of its professional practitioners. Problems of health, work, play, education, of family life, parenthood, childhood, of every social relationship within which people must find their place, are grist to our mill. Yet, obviously, that cannot mean that our specific professional capacity and responsibility extend to the understanding and treatment of all the infinite ramifications of human life as a whole, or of any of these problems in their entirety.

There is, however, one focal point to which all our professional services do converge, whose specific significance sets off our tasks from every other part of social welfare enterprise. That is our concern with the actual impact of any or all of these problems upon the individual life, and the way in which human beings face and meet these problems, and thus attain, through social relationships, their mastery over them. We do not know, for instance—we have no way to find out through our own professional service or training—what constitutes a good and complete health program in any community, in terms of the technical components of such a program. We do know and we must know, because we are responsibly helping people to face their health problems as factors in their social adjustment, what stands in the way of the maintenance of health and the full use of health resources. We know the effect upon individual people of inadequate or inaccessible health resources, inadequate provision for meeting the economic hazards of illness, inadequate appreciation and, therefore, inadequate provision of integrated treatment, of the interacting physical, social, and emotional factors of illness. We know some of the conditions, mechanisms, and processes that are prerequisite for the attainment of recognized standards of health. With respect to these aspects of the community's health problem we have a clear professional responsibility to make our help available, not only in the realization, but also in the formulation of its own health standards and health program.

Take another example: We do not know, nor can we conceivably learn—as a part of our own professional study and practice—all that must go into the organization and operation of an adequate and satisfying economic system. But we do know the impact of economic factors of life upon individual human beings and groups, and we know the problems that people face in the actual process of adjusting to these fundamental realities of social living, because we have been responsibly and studiously engaged in helping people through that actual process. We do know, therefore, not only the fact, but the meaning to real people of inadequate income, of intermittent employment and unemployment; we know the meaning to the individual of real work, of creative, free, self-respecting participation in the economic process and in the determination of his own working conditions. This does not entitle us to prepare or to endorse a detailed blueprint of a total reform of the economic system. It does obligate us to contribute of our special knowledge and our professional judgment to the formulation of acceptable criteria of the validity of economic arrangements, and to exert our influence toward the introduction into our economic structure of those mechanisms and processes that make it possible for people continuously to find positive satisfactions, through sound relationships, in all their working life.

The province of professional social work, then, either in its direct service or in its social action, does not encompass the total life problem of anybody, not the whole of any problem. We are concerned with social process—the impact of social structure and policy upon individuals, and the process by which people are enabled to meet and master the problems this impact presents.

It is obvious, if this be true, that the responsibility of social work for social action is both an individual and a collective responsibility. It cannot be entirely separated from individual practice; it cannot be wholly entrusted to a special group of workers charged exclusively with the specific set of tasks involved in social action; it cannot be delegated by each of us to a few chosen representatives of all of us. Each of us carries a dual responsibility: first, to perform with all the competence and faithfulness we can muster the particular services which are entrusted to us by the particular agency with which we are identified; second, to contribute steadily of our understanding and skill, derived from this experience, to help the community constructively to relate its institutions and arrangement and services to the fundamental needs of human beings as these are disclosed in our service relationships. No one of us can know all about all these needs; each of us can and must know a part, and each of us must be responsible, therefore, for contributing his own part to the larger whole.

There are four kinds of relationship within which this responsibility must be defined and controlled, if professional standards are to be discovered and upheld. There is the client-worker relationship; the agency relationship; the relationship to the profession as a whole; and the relationship with other organized forces of social change and control in the larger community.

It seems clear that the client-worker relationship must be held clear for service, and for service only. Any use of that relationship for the attainment of any goal other than that to which it is dedicated in advance—the service of a particular need upon which the agency has offered help, through the worker—is a betrayal of the client's confidence, of the agency's purpose, and of the worker's professional obligation. The process of service itself, by helping to discover and release strength and energy in clients, which they may ultimately turn, along with others, if they choose, toward the conscious change of social policies that affect them, may, it is true, indirectly promote social change. But this must always remain one of the incidental, unpredictable, and undesigned outcomes of service—never its goal.

The professional social worker's agency relationship is of another order. Here he is somewhat freed to participate directly in social action affecting the problems encompassed within agency function. As an individual he discharges this aspect of professional responsibility in helping the agency to mold its own part of the total social structure to the needs of those who seek its help. By the consistent and continual registration of the worker's actual experience, and the circumstances surrounding the client's need and his use of agency service, through the established agency channels, the worker contributes responsibly to that alert awareness of, and readiness for, change, which is the hallmark of every effective social agency. By sensitive and discriminating participation, at every appropriate time, in the formulation and expression of progressive agency policy, geared to clients' needs, the individual worker helps to mold this little part of the total organized community. This is no negligible contribution. Given an agency under professional leadership, in which there is a constant two-way flow of creative interest and experience, among board, administration, and professional staff, the habit of sensitive response to the changing needs and new meanings of its own service is bound to grow into an expanding concern for factors beyond agency control that cause or complicate the problems with which agency service is concerned. And that kind of agency is going to feel an obligation to contribute, as a whole—not only through its professional elements—to the pool of community feeling and understanding out of which new and more serviceable social structure and policy will emerge. I venture to affirm that every social agency expressing, as it must, in its own function, the community's purpose to meet a specific need, is obligated to help the community to fulfill that purpose completely, by removing the obstructions that prevent the service from reaching its mark in the lives of people, and by relieving the conditions that steadily augment or intensify the need.

But it is also true that every agency necessarily carries, in practice if not in theory, a limited function. Its responsibility for social action— and, hence, the opportunity of professional workers to discharge their responsibility through it—is limited to the area of need with which it is functionally involved. Furthermore, the agency is composed of both lay and professional elements. It can act, as an entity, only within the area of its own internal agreement. It may not, at a given time and place, be ready to act, or capable of acting effectively, toward ends that its professional staff, or some of its members, consider to be necessary for the full discharge of their professional responsibilities. Does this circumstance absolve the individual professional worker of all further responsibility? Or, to put it another way, is the professional staff member stopped from further professional social action beyond that which he can discharge through the agency or within it?

On the contrary: professional responsibility is individual. It cannot be surrendered or evaded. Within the bounds of one's direct functional service, the professional worker is, of course, the representative of the agency and faithfully applies its policy, expressing his own professional self in the process of helping clients use agency function and policy to the utmost for their own good. Beyond those boundaries, one still carries one's own individual professional responsibility to free oneself for professional performance in accordance with one's own professional standards. It is here that the professional association, as an instrument of professional social action, serves an indispensable purpose.

Here the limitations of an individual service responsibility, and the limitations of a particular agency function, are erased; here, as a member of the total professional group, the worker finds an avenue through which to bring to expression his whole professional self, in behalf of the highest professional standards.

As a united body, pooling the experiences and the resources of all its members, the profession is free to establish its own criteria of social structure and policy, to articulate its own total contribution to the guidance of social change, and to participate in social action to that end in accordance with its own deliberately accepted standards and methods. The circle of individual responsibility and influence is thus widened; one's own interests and purposes and standards are measured and tested against others. In the end, one can join confidently and helpfully in support of professional interests and aims even far beyond those bounded by one's own specific experience. To help the professional association serve that useful purpose, with courage, with foresight, with consistent determination, in social action, is one of the solemn obligations professional workers accept with their membership in the association.

Here again there are prerequisite conditions that must be observed and maintained. The association unites professional workers around one basic interest—the discovery, progressive development, and consistent use of the highest professional standards of service. It is concerned with the actual performance of social workers, through the acceptance and enforcement of such standards. Its members are not asked to check their religious, their political, even their economic and social convictions and differences at the door. They are asked to join in support of certain common standards of performance, whatever other differences may divide them. The usefulness of the association as an instrument of social action is necessarily limited by that primary functional concern with professional standards. Even within this area of interest, its practical usefulness depends upon the degree of its actual internal agreement. It is foolhardy and dangerous for the association to presume or pretend to speak for the whole profession upon any issue, even those affecting or affected by professional standards, when actually professional agreement does not exist. It is sound principle and serviceable practice that have led the association usually to limit its undertakings in social action to those which, after study and discussion by the whole membership, command the convinced support of a clear majority.

There is, of course, danger in this concept of the limitation of association responsibility. Endless study, aimless talk, may become an easy refuge from the perils involved in clear conviction and decisive action. The boundary between intelligent discretion and unconfessed cowardice is sometimes difficult to draw, but we must depend upon a growing, vital sense of true professional responsibility to protect us against yielding to ignoble fears.

We can also depend upon vigorous individual and group action, supplementing united association effort; for, just as the individual's professional responsibility for social action is not completely absorbed into agency function, so the individual's responsibility is not completely submerged in the professional group. Each of us continues to carry that responsibility for living up to our own standards, and for finding a way to discharge this responsibility, whether or not the whole profession supports and sustains it. It is right here that the union in social work finds a suitable and effective place in the discharge of individual responsibility for social action. The union opens, in a way, a still wider circle of interest and effort and influence than that of the association. As the professional association breaks down the barriers of individual specialization, of experience, and of agency function, in relation to the worker's responsibility for social action, so the union levels the walls enclosing a narrow professionalism. It unites professional workers, not only with other workers in social agencies, but also with the whole wide labor movement. It may thus open avenues for the effectual application of concerted conviction upon matters about which all professional workers are not now and may never be united. It offers, therefore, to groups of professional workers an instrument for effective use on matters beyond the area of association function and association agreement.

Here, again, there is a true functional limitation. The union in social work, like any other labor union, is united around common economic interests. It is an appropriate and effective instrument for protection or realization of those interests. It is certainly not the most appropriate agency for the determination or formulation of professional standards, nor for the articulation of programs involving the application of professional standards. That is a professional responsibility for which professional workers are accountable to their peers, and which they cannot share with nonprofessional colleagues. As the professional association more and more consistently and courageously represents truly professional interests in social action; as it recognizes the value, even to itself, of freeing groups of its members to unite with other workers in promoting causes, upon which the whole profession is not and probably cannot be united—it is to be hoped that the union need no longer seem to be an intruding competitor in professional circles, but an additional instrument through which individual professional workers may promote some of their legitimate professional interests, in social action.

Upon the same basis rests the validity of individual and group action of professional workers in the political arena, where many social issues come inevitably to final settlement. It is perfectly obvious that a social agency, dedicated to a specific service, about which, alone, its sponsors and its supporters are united, cannot ethically or practically expend its energies or resources to ends not directly related to that service. Its social action must be confined to the interpretation of its own experience, in terms of chosen objectives, accepted principles and incontestable facts, commended on their merits, as factors in the determination of community policy affecting its service. It cannot take responsibility for measuring the relative importance of this aspect of public policy, as compared with others, as decisive factors in a political contest. It would be wholly inappropriate for an agency, therefore, to espouse a particular party cause or candidate.

The professional association is in a somewhat similar position. It is united upon objectives and principles, on the basis of professional standards. In all but the rarest instances, it cannot command the judgment of its members, or bring them to agreement, as to the relative weight to be assigned to these agreed concepts, as compared with other issues involved in a political campaign, nor as to the relative capacity and determination of opposing candidates to carry these concepts to realization in public policy. It would be utterly inappropriate, it seems to me, for the association, as such, to throw its influence in behalf of one or another party or candidate in a political contest in which other than strictly social issues were at stake.

Does the same set of limitations bind the individual professional worker? To answer that question in the affirmative seems to me to threaten the integrity both of the individual and of the profession as a whole. The individual not only can but must exercise his judgment as to the relative weight of issues at stake; he must make a final choice, as a citizen. If, in his honest and considered judgment, social issues are paramount, and if his choice is made between parties or candidates on the basis of their position on these problems and of their relative capacity and determination to solve those problems by measures that conform with professional principles, must he stifle those convictions, remain silent, and refuse to make his judgment as a social worker available to anybody else? And because the professional group as a whole is prevented by its collective responsibility and function from direct participation on the political level, must social work have no voice at all in the moment of decision? The individual must, if he is true to his own professional responsibility, remain free to act as an individual beyond the level of agreement of all his colleagues. It is that freedom, that personal obligation of the individual to be an independent creative unit, which is the essence of professionalism. It is likewise the source of the progress and achievement of the profession as a collective whole.

It is of special consequence to the profession of social work that this freedom should be conserved and protected. It is of the nature of professional social work practice that the individual practitioner shall not be completely free in the performance of a specific service. He is, and must be, the representative of a social agency, bound to operate within its policies, which cannot always express his own highest ideals of service since they must incorporate, also, the differing viewpoints of nonprofessional sponsors and supporters. He is protected against the loss of professional integrity, in this complete identification with agency, by his active and responsible participation in the development of agency policy, on the one hand, and by his membership in the professional association, where standards are sustained, on the other. If, however, his identification either with agency or with association limits or nullifies his independence as a professional person in the realm of social action in pursuit of professional objectives, then he has no further means of protecting his professional integrity—the fulfillment of his own sense of professional responsibility. His independence even as a citizen is qualified and limited.

There is risk in this individual freedom which we affirm—risk to the individual, to the agency, and to the profession. But that risk is as nothing compared to the danger of placing social workers and their profession under the suspicion that any considerations other than honest conviction and the analyzed outcomes of their study and experience can determine the part they shall play in decisive struggles for the realization of social ideals. The perfect pattern of political action affecting social work would be achieved, I firmly believe, only when every administrator, every board member, every practitioner of every rank, in every social agency, would regard it not only as a privilege, but an obligation, frankly and openly to relate the knowledge and judgment derived from his own social work experience to contested public issues, and thus to make his special sincere contribution to the formulation of enlightened public judgment and decision. I would have no fear of divided counsels in the field. I would welcome them in the open forum, where differences could be defined and tested, and where, in the end, social work would surely find a voice worthy of its own potential role in human affairs.

Recording in Community Organization
—Introduction

SYSTEMATIC RECORDING—aside from minutes and a few other accepted administrative records—has been a generally neglected area in community organization. As for a published literature on community organization recording, it has been almost nonexistent up to the last few years.

This section brings together five of the most useful discussions of records and recording which are currently available.

The first of these is Campbell G. Murphy's brief but useful discussion of the subject in his *Community Organization Practice*. Next comes a more specific consideration of the "why" of records, from a report on Recording issued by the Los Angeles Chapter of the Association for the Study of Community Organization.

C. F. McNeil, in a paragraph in the *Social Work Year Book*, 1954, distinguishes between "administrative" and "process" recording. The latter is an aspect of community organization recording which has awakened a good deal of interest and some experimentation in recent years.[1] Trecker's discussion of the nature of process recording in administration is included, since it may be applied in large measure to community organization recording also.

Finally, there is a thoughtful analysis of "process recording as a technique"—a contribution by Gloria Roman to a Community Chest and Councils workshop report on *Evaluating the Effectiveness of Councils*.

---

[1] For some examples of published process records, see: Helen D. Green, *Social Work Practice in Community Organization* (New York: Whiteside, Inc., and William Morrow & Co., 1954), Ch. VIII; Frances Goodall, *A Narrative of Process in Social Welfare Organization: Step by Step Through a Project in Community Organization* (St. Louis: Washington University, George Warren Brown School of Social Work, 1948).

39

Community Organization Recording[1]

By CAMPBELL G. MURPHY

Campbell G. Murphy is executive director of the Health and Welfare Council of Metropolitan St. Louis. His previous experience includes service as the executive of the Community Welfare Council of Dayton and Montgomery County, and as a member of the faculty of the School of Social Work, of the University of Denver.

PROFESSIONAL SERVICES of almost all kinds have developed systems of record keeping. In any professional program involving the use of a highly disciplined skill, it is essential that the worker have certain past data at his command in order to meet the current need, and in order to project future plans of service or treatment.

Social caseworkers have developed highly skillful methods of recording which have become essential tools in most programs of high standards. The core of this record material is the "running record" covering interviews between worker and client, supported by documents such as files of correspondence, copies of court orders, records of financial payment, and such. The running record and the movement found in service or treatment give the worker, his supervisor, and any consultants a basis for evaluating the professional service given, and a basis

---

[1] The selection from Campbell G. Murphy, *Community Organization Practice,* 1954, pp. 299-301, is reprinted by permission of and arrangement with Houghton Mifflin Company, the authorized publishers.

for planning the future course of service or treatment. It is also of inestimable value when a new worker is assigned a case.

In group work, record keeping of the same type is beginning to be used in some highly skilled programs. But the records in many group work programs tend to be confined to supporting documentary material. More detailed "process" records of what actually happens in the group situation are generally limited to those developed for teaching purposes.

In community organization practice, record keeping on the whole is in a primitive stage. A very practical problem is that the wide range of activities in which the community organization worker is engaged would require a tremendous amount of recording if anything realistic regarding the "process" or "movement" or "relationship" were to be properly recorded. Thus a record might become so monumental that following it, writing it, and doing the job might be more than most practitioners could handle. Records are also limited because perhaps most of the more experienced community organization workers have had considerable experience in casework or group work, and have gained considerable skill in evaluating and planning on the basis of a minimum of written material.

Recording in community organization is largely limited to files of correspondence and memoranda and minutes of meetings, plus occasional summaries of important interviews. Detailed process records have been developed in a few agencies for teaching purposes, but not many of these are available.

It is only in the past decade that professional process, partly in common with casework and group work, and partly distinct from them, has been recognized as basic in community organization practice. As a result of this development, much more recording is needed than is currently done, even though the kind and amount of detail found in the better casework recording would not be practical in community organization except for teaching purposes.

On assuming the position of executive in the Community Welfare Council in Dayton, the writer found prepared by his predecessor a system of record keeping for a local community welfare council which was more adequate than any he had seen before. For each project or committee in which the Council is active, a separate loose-leaf minute book is kept which is available in the current record file of the staff member to whom it is assigned. In the minute book is kept first of all a basic log or chronology on all activities related to the committee or project. For each meeting, conference, telephone call, piece of correspondence, et cetera, an entry is made in this log. In addition, three files of relevant materials are kept. Attached directly to the log are copies of all material it refers to. Thus the minutes of all meetings, memoranda on telephone conversations, correspondence, and the like, are filed in back of the chronological record in the order in which the material appears.

In addition to the chronological log and the primary file, there is a secondary file of certain supplementary materials, such as supporting correspondence not referred to in the chronology. Additional data, such as newspaper releases, rosters of persons interested in the project, and other miscellaneous material of importance, are kept in a third file. All three files are kept in the minute book. When the project is completed, or at the end of a year's activity in a continuing program, the material is removed from the loose-leaf notebook and transferred to a back correspondence file in a permanent loose-leaf binder, or is bound for the permanent record.

Such a record is somewhat like the case records that may be kept on an individual client or a family in a casework agency and the records on a club group in a community center. But to be properly useful in community organization work, this type of record must be available at least to the chairman of the committee involved, and at times to other members of the committee. Therefore, certain types of observations or critical comments or evaluations which might be included in a case or group record cannot appropriately be included.

40

Why Records?[1]

By LOS ANGELES CHAPTER, ASCO

VIEWED BROADLY, RECORDS are kept in community organization for two main reasons:

1. For the community group itself and other groups and individuals in the agency and the community. Thus, minutes are kept for the committee. Reports are written for the committee itself, for a board to which it reports, for dissemination to interested parties, as a basis for action, and so on.
2. For the internal administrative processes of the agency. In this connection, the records are used for supervision and for education and benefit of the worker himself.

These two broad purposes are, of course, not completely separated from one another, since records in community organization may serve several, in some cases, interrelated purposes. Thus, the minutes of a meeting are helpful to the committee itself, but also aid the community organization worker in watching developments, evaluating his own role in the process to date, and so on.

Since the purpose of records in community organization, in many cases, overlap, it may be fruitful to list the different usages:

1. As a record for the community group or committee itself.
2. To inform other committees or boards within the agency itself to whom the committee reports and as a basis for action by the agency itself.

[1] Excerpted from *Recording in Community Organization in Social Welfare Work.* A report by the Los Angeles Chapter of the Association for the Study of Community Organization. (New York: ASCO, Community Organization Materials, No. 2, 1951; mimeographed), pp. 9-11.

3. For educational and interpretative purposes to individuals, organizations, and community groups closely associated with the agency and the problem under discussion.
4. More general educational and interpretative purposes in the community, such as for newspaper releases, material for conferences and forums, et cetera.
5. As a basis for action by boards other than the agency board, making decisions about laws and ordinances and concerning allocations.
6. To provide the agency with necessary data so that it can provide an accounting to its supporting public for what has transpired. Statistical data, annual reports, reports of progress of committees and conclusions they have reached are illustrations of the end products, gathered from more detailed records within the agency.
7. For supervisory and administrative staff to know what is happening; whether activities of a given group are consistent with the purposes and policies of the organization and with the assignment; whether the community organization worker has been effective and the points at which he can be assisted in becoming more effective.
8. For teaching and research purposes, with the teaching purpose closely related to supervision.
9. For the worker himself so that he acts in accordance with assignments and is able to perform his role more effectively out of increased insight based on review of the records. (Therefore, the worker often finds it fruitful to have for himself a fuller record of a meeting than goes into the minutes sent committee members.)
10. For a succeeding worker so that he can know what the developments have been to date for a given problem, project of committee, and be able to pick up the strands most effectively.
11. For various staff members to keep acquainted with developments and provide a more co-ordinated agency operation, by circulating some records.
12. As a basis for legal accountability; as a corporation or public board, the minutes, especially formal actions, meet this legal requirement.

Correspondence, reports, and minutes for committee members are already well-established elements in community organization recording. These are all primarily for the community group itself.

More detailed or even verbatim minutes, memoranda to the file, periodic summaries, statistical data, observations concerning movement, and reports to agency administration, are illustrations of community organization recording having primary value within the staff itself. . . .

41

Administrative and Process Recording [1]

By C. F. MC NEIL

SOME TYPE OF ADMINISTRATIVE recording is in use in every agency engaging in community organization. Minutes, annual reports, project progress reports are examples of some types of essential administrative recording. There is less experience with the more complicated process recording, in which the aim is to get a verbatim recording of attitude, manner and expression, and intricate interactions of personalities upon personalities and groups upon groups. Process recording is still in its experimental stages, but current experience forecasts better understanding through its wider application.

[1] Excerpted from "Community Organization for Social Welfare," *Social Work Year Book*, 1954 (New York: American Association of Social Workers, 1954), p. 124. By permission of National Association of Social Workers. For biographical data concerning C. F. McNeil see Selection 11.

42

Process Recording[1]

By HARLEIGH B. TRECKER

WHAT ARE WE ATTEMPTING to record when we are recording *a process?* This is the most important question to answer and understand. Partial answers are found in the following list of items:

1. When we record a process we write about persons and their responses to each other in a given situation.
2. We write about the type and extent of participation of persons working together to solve a problem.
3. We put down the origin of ideas and the development of ideas, including acceptance and rejection by the persons involved.
4. We put down exactly what the executive does, what he thinks, feels, and hopes to accomplish.
5. We put down movement, growth, and change of individuals and the group as a whole.
6. We write about the relationships between groups and the formal and informal communication that takes place.

Recording the administrative process means, then, that we concentrate upon these factors:

1. *Individuals* working together in group situations.
2. *Relationships* between individuals as reflected by their participation.
3. *Interaction* within the group and between groups.
4. *The worker* who is exercising a helping role.

[1] Excerpted from *Group Process in Administration* (New York: Woman's Press, rev. ed., 1950), pp. 303-305. By permission of the copyright owner, Association Press. [See Selection 26 for biographical data concerning the author.]

We may restate this as (1) *who?* (the members of the group), (2) *what?* (the things they do together), (3) *how?* (the way they do things together), and (4) *why?* (the reasons that certain things happen or fail to happen).

The executive in writing the process record will find that his task consists of (1) alert observation—becoming sensitive to what is happening, (2) selection of what to include, (3) organization of material selected, (4) analysis of the material, and (5) interpretation, stating implications. The actual writing of the record is thus an expression of the underlying skills in administration. Persons who have not done process recording should be encouraged to be inclusive at the start. It is far better to put down everything at first. Selection can take place later.

With regard to style it must be kept natural and informal as opposed to prescribed and formal. Workers should write their records in the fashion which is easiest for them. The only restriction on style would seem to be at the point of separating the *who, what,* and *how* from the *why.* Evaluation, analysis, interpretation, and comments written by the worker should be so labeled and kept separate from the body of the record. This reflective section may be the most difficult part to record because it shows the worker's thinking about and into what is happening. It gives the record its dynamic quality and reflects the worker's sensitivity to the underlying tone of the relationships.

43

Process Recording as a Technique[1]

By GLORIA ROMAN

IF WE PUSH THE NOTION of process recording back far enough, we may say it is a technique to preserve situations which may not occur again. Basically, any process record is an eyewitness account of a series of events which lead to some end or result. The series of events leading to a result is the process; the eyewitness account is the record. When a researcher is given the problem of analyzing changing situations, or situations which will not occur again in precisely the same fashion (such as a Council operation) he has two alternatives. One is to analyze "on the spot." The other is to preserve the situation so that he may analyze at his leisure. To attempt to analyze "on the spot" has obvious difficulties. Often the real meaning of events taking place within a process does not become apparent until the process itself is completed. The other alternative is obviously preferable. With the total situation before one, each event may be observed in the light of all other events and in terms of the end product.

The problem, then, is how to preserve the situation. The closest approximation to preserving the *total* situation is with sound films. As we move from sound films to sound records, verbatim stenographic notes, summarized notes, we progressively record less and less of the total situation. The recording becomes more and more selective.

It may be that we do not wish to record everything that goes on. When we ask a student to write the minutes of a meeting, we are often

[1] Excerpted from "A Perspective on Process Recording," in *Evaluating the Effectiveness of Councils:* Report of the 1954 Research Workshop (New York: Community Chests and Councils of America, Inc., 1954, 59 pp. mimeo.), pp. 44-48; 50. By permission of United Community Funds and Councils of America, Inc. The author of this paper was the assistant director, Research Department, Welfare Planning Council, Los Angeles Region at the time the report was written.

surprised at the length of his minutes. He has six pages where we normally have two, or at the most, three. We may fume and fuss that "they ought to teach students to write clearly and concisely"—or, "students nowadays don't know how to use English." The real problem is that the student doesn't know what to include and what to leave out. He doesn't have a cognitive framework which deals with writing minutes for meetings. As he develops one, his minutes become shorter and more selective. This is also true in process records. Often we may be selective without destroying meaning.

This gets us out of our first difficulty into a more critical problem—how we decide *a priori* what aspects of the situation are relevant.

As with all research instruments, we may take two general approaches to process recording. We may do our thinking before we start to collect the data, before we begin recording. We may do our thinking after we collect the data, after we do our recording. In other words, we may set down the categories around which we record before we begin (come to the data with a cognitive framework)—or we may attempt to pull these categories out of the record itself (develop our cognitive framework from our data).

1. Using Process Records to Develop a Cognitive Framework

In a discipline where procedure has not been codified, process recording may serve as an aid in codification. Typically such records are kept by an observer who is also a key person in the process. The observer has no set of categories clearly in mind as the record is kept. Everything that seems important to getting the job done is set down. As such, the record provides insights in the same way that living through an experience may. The major asset is that outside the line of fire, the observer is able to relive an experience.

If such records are to be kept of council committees, they would include minutes of some sort of committee meetings, correspondence memos, records of out-of-committee contacts between staff and committee members. Such records enable us to:

Concretize and find empirical content for concepts that are given verbal expression in the literature of community organization.

The process record gives some clues by answering, for one situation, the specific question. Sustained relationships means communications, directly or through intermediaries. Communication takes place in person, by telephone, by letter or memo. Lines of communication are developed and kept open with committee members, other staff, members of the community interested, and directly involved, in the problem, or potentially influential. As this is spelled out in the record, the notion "concurrently maintain different sets of sustained relationships" is given empirical content and thereby becomes more meaningful.

Generalize. This is a corollary to the first. Having developed empirical content, we may then generalize. Consider the problem of staff role in the community organization process. A process record of a council committee's progress will provide specific data related to staff role. We will find that the staff person works with both the committee as a group and with members of the committee individually. What is the nature of the community organizer's relationship to the individual? A record will show how the worker behaves in relation to individuals. This may then be generalized and tested in other situations.

Modify concepts developed elsewhere. In general it is accepted that in social work community organization, the group determines its own goals and procedures. A process record may show that the group does not enjoy full self-determination. Self-determination operates within the limits of the planning structure, of the job assignment, time limits, financial limits, and so on. When there is clarity about these limits and an acceptance of them, there appears to be a complete self-determination. However, when certain members of the committee are not clear on these limits, it is the staff person's function to state these limits and thereby restrict the area for self-determination.

Informally test out concepts developed elsewhere. The social sciences have developed a number of concepts relevant to social work community organization. Process records of community organization experiences are an ideal place for informally testing the applicability and usefulness of these concepts.

2. Using Process Records to Test a Cognitive Framework

Process records can be used to test relationships derived from theory or experience. To use the technique this way, a good deal of thinking must be done before recording begins. In order to adequately test notions about phenomena, it is necessary with process recording, as with any other research technique, that we are very clear on (1) the notions we want to test and (2) the empirical phenomena related to these notions.

As a tool . . . process recording tends to be somewhat cumbersome. The only available technique for analyzing the data is content analysis which is time consuming. Similar results may be attained by using observers to code the behavior as it occurs. The content analysis is then completed as the behavior takes place. This technique has been used by Bales and others. It requires trained observers—but seems to be as reliable as a content analysis of written material.

PART FOUR

AGENCIES

AND

PROGRAMS

Introduction

THE COMMUNITY ORGANIZATION PROCESS finds its expression in and through many types of agencies and a variety of services and programs. Part IV is devoted to these agencies in which community organization is practiced, to their objectives, policies, relationships, functions, and methods, and to the structures and devices through which they operate.

The selection from Bradley Buell's *Community Planning for Human Services* serves to introduce the reader to the complex pattern of welfare services in the modern city. Buell and his associates point out that programs have expanded rapidly without any definite plan and that more attention has been paid to promotion, administration, and professional techniques than to the orderly development of an integrated community program. As a result little has been accomplished in the direction of preventing and reducing welfare needs and problems.

The authors also describe the purposes and general plan underlying their research study of welfare services in St. Paul, Minnesota, a report that has strongly influenced the direction of community organization thinking in recent years. The classification of problems, agency functions, and service structures, which served as the framework of their investigation of dependency, ill-health, maladjustment, and recreational needs, in this, the first of a series of studies, is also presented. Hypotheses developed in the St. Paul survey in connection with three of these areas—dependency, health, and maladjustment—are now being tested in a number of communities throughout the country. These relate to the importance of the family unit as the basis of investigation, co-ordination of services and agencies, the use of scientific knowledge in prevention and treatment, and to the role of national leadership in achieving local community integration.

The remaining selections are grouped under four headings, devoted to the kinds of agencies engaged in community organization at different levels. Certain controversial issues will be seen to emerge from these materials. What is the proper function of neighborhood planning and action groups, and what should be their relationship to the central community welfare council in metropolitan communities? What responsibilities do direct-service agencies carry for community organization? Again, chests and councils being the two major local agencies specifically engaged in community organization, a good deal of controversy revolves around the question of their respective functions. What should be their relationship to each other and to the individual agencies they serve?

Perhaps the most heated arguments occur between the advocates of federated or joint financing of welfare agencies and those who prefer independent campaigns. Again, through what kinds of agencies is community organization on nonlocal levels carried on, and what are the appropriate functions of such state and national bodies? Community organization is also taking place at the international level through various programs of the United Nations. In Part VI some reference will be made also to community development in recently developing countries which generally involves international co-operation. Facts and opinions from various points of view on these and other issues are presented in the readings.

44

Problems of Community-Wide Planning and Prevention [1]

By BRADLEY BUELL and ASSOCIATES

The Problem and the Setting

FROM PIONEER DAYS, the spirit of America has been in protest against anciently conceived ideas about the inevitability of human trouble. The rights of the individual to life, liberty, and the pursuit of happiness have been linked inextricably with a common duty to "promote the general welfare." During 300 years of our history we have been constructing a vast network of community-supported services whose purpose affirms this intent.

Many of these services, originally founded for the benefit of the disadvantaged, have now become indispensable to everyone, regardless of his means. Almost all the services have the intent to provide protection for anyone upon whom life's hazards may fall too heavily. The early pauper lists and poor farms have grown into a system of public assistance and insurance. From the first institutions for the sick poor has come the modern community hospital. The ideas which found expression in the gaol, the stocks, and the whipping post have been supplanted by quite different notions of criminal justice and correction. For the mentally abnormal of an early day there were only a few institutions, and these were to protect the community against the so-called "criminally" insane. Today a host of mental hygiene, casework, and other agencies strive to aid those whose circumstances and behavior handicap their adjustment to society. Not so long ago, abun-

[1] Excerpted from *Community Planning for Human Services* (New York: Columbia University Press, 1952), pp. 3-11, 411-412. By permission of the publisher.

317

dant nature surrounded nearly every doorstep. Now, in urban America, carefully planned parks and playgrounds must serve a common purpose for many thousands of city dwellers. Today we pay through taxes, contributions, and fee payments about $13 billion annually to support a gigantic, sprawling, and complex network of community-provided services that we have welded into the structure of our society to protect ourselves as best we can against the historic inevitabilities of human trouble.

The Challenge of Complexity

The structure of community services was built largely without benefit of blueprint. Different parts were constructed at different times to meet different needs. Moreover, because their foundations were fitted to particular communities, they differ widely in surface appearance from one community and one section of the country to another.

In the last three decades all the parts have expanded rapidly, sprawling out in many directions. The prosperous 1920's encouraged great private philanthropic expansion. The depressed 1930's demanded large-scale additions to governmental service. Both of these phenomena accelerated the natural growth of community-provided services to meet the pressures and complexities which accompanied the change from the social independence of a rural agricultural society to the necessary interdependence of an urban industrial society.

Out of this turmoil of rapid expansion and social pressure has emerged a large-scale enterprise, progressively specialized in its professional personnel and in the organization of its many separate agencies and units. At this turning point of the twentieth century it presents a picture of such complexity that it can scarcely be comprehended as a whole. The authors of this book are convinced, however, that it must be so comprehended.

Community welfare has deep meaning for Americans. In the scores of communities studied during the past twenty years by those who participated in the preparation of materials for this volume, there was found an abundance of sincere citizen belief in the importance of services designed to contribute to the common welfare. But everywhere we discovered confusion and mounting frustration about what that design should be and why. The vital spirit of America's protest against the inevitability of human ills is in danger of becoming lost among protests against irrationalities in its organized expression. The phenomenal growth of voluntary and public services has compounded bafflement with bewilderment. The truth is that many facets of community administrative machinery are separate in origin, purpose, and tradition. Professional and agency specialization now pose problems of service relationships that are only slightly less confusing to professional leaders than to the citizen leaders of their communities.

One who peers beneath the complex structural surface will see that the sources of confusion are profound. Public policy regarding our community services has its roots in a welter of misconceptions, fears, and conflicting traditions, complicated by great gaps in precise knowledge. But to the present authors a more important reason for this incoherence is that in the past three decades these services have been increasing rapidly in volume, variety, and cost, without corresponding gains in purposeful direction. As more people are served at more cost in connection with more manifestations of trouble, the heart of the problem to be attacked becomes obscured, and the organization and administration of service functions move dangerously close to becoming ends in themselves.

Analysis of the community-wide characteristics of the problems creating the need has not kept pace with the promotion of resources for their remedy. Study of methods to reduce the prevalence of certain problems has been neglected. Research into the causes of problems, a move which might produce the key to their prevention has, in many areas, taken a minor place. Scientific evaluation of the results of service has been bypassed. On the other hand, matters of auspices, administration, financing, and professional techniques have risen in importance.

The Road to Prevention

This book [*Community Planning for Human Service*] is based on the premise that our historic duty to promote the common welfare carries not only the intent to care for people with problems but to prevent their occurrence and protect the community against their deteriorating consequences. It has been written out of a deep belief, engendered by three decades of intimate knowledge of American communities, that the prevention and reduction of these ancient ills is a realistic possibility. Further, it is believed that the very pursuit of this aim can begin to dispel the frustration arising from the present complex pattern.

Our thesis is that the vast networks of health, welfare, and recreation services can and should be more effectively planned and organized to prevent and reduce these community-wide problems. The task is to set this great community enterprise on the road leading in this direction, and to shift gears for more efficient travel.

The research project upon which this volume is based was designed to produce a definitive treatise on the major issues underlying community organization efforts in four large interrelated areas of community service: dependency, ill-health, maladjustment, and recreational need. It was carried out by Community Research Associates, Inc., and underwritten by The Grant Foundation. The approach was threefold: (1) extensive research into the history and literature of each field; (2) careful analysis of the problems and organization of the community services, in consultation with experienced specialists; (3) a comprehensive statistical study of the four areas of service in a typical urban American community.

The statistical study made in St. Paul, Minnesota, was an attempt to measure, for the first time, the shape, size, and interrelatedness of these problems on a community-wide basis. With the co-operation of 108 public and private agencies in the four service fields, data were obtained about the problems presented by and the services rendered to every family under care in the month of November, 1948. Cross-tabulations established reliable unduplicated figures for the numbers of families being served simultaneously by agencies in the same and different fields of service, and the specific problems for which they were being served.

Those who participated in the research project are well aware that the size, although not the form, of human problems differs from community to community, from section to section, from region to region. We believe, and in these pages attempt to show, that much of the necessary knowledge of cause and method of treatment is at hand. We recognize, too, that there are great gaps in learning and have tried to show where they are, and how they handicap our purpose. But after three years of intensive study and analysis of this gigantic community phenomenon, we are convinced that our communities have much more knowledge than is being effectively put to work; that we are allowing inherited ideas to interfere with common sense and scientific fact; in short, that we know better than we do.

A Problem of Logistics

Planning and organizing the community's services for an attack upon the major problems of dependency, ill-health, maladjustment, and recreational need is essentially a matter of logistics. In terms of what is known about the characteristics of these enemies, their methods of community infiltration, and the nature and disposition of their forces, the right services in sufficient amount must be brought to bear at the right places at the right time with a maximum of efficiency and economy. The fruits of victory are the preservation and enhancement of individual and family capacity for social self-maintenance and self-sufficiency.

We believe that comprehension of this problem of logistics can come only with a philosophy which encompasses the following understandings:

1. The community is in truth the battle area.

2. Systematic community-wide knowledge about the characteristics of these problems and the total resources available to meet them is a necessity.

3. There are active interrelationships between the major human problems.

4. Within the family group these destructive forces move continuously to reinforce each other.

The Community-Size Pattern

It is always well to remind ourselves of the simple truth that it is in the community that people have troubles and seek solution for them. The community is the place where people benefit much or little from services provided in their behalf. Here must converge all the particular ideas about what these services should be, what degree of protection they should afford against the hazards of modern living, and what enhancement they should bring to family and personal well-being. This is true even when the services are paid for out of a federal or state pocket and carried out by a hierarchy of ascending administrative levels.

Today some measure of the welfare of two-thirds to three-quarters of the families in a community may depend in a single year upon the manner in which its health, welfare, and recreation services are provided. The St. Paul study showed that in a single month 41,000 families, 40 per cent of all the families in the community, were being served by the city's 108 public and private agencies. A previous study, made in Syracuse, New York, established with considerable accuracy that about 100 community agencies and administrative units had collectively rendered services to approximately 70 per cent of the city's families during the year 1941.

Finally, there is the compelling fact that about three-quarters of a community's service cost is met directly from local funds. In St. Paul for instance, the annual cost for community services is about $17 million. Over half of this is local money paid in fees or in voluntary contributions and over half the tax money comes from city-county taxes. About $1.5 million, mainly money for public assistance, comes from federal sources.

The Community-Wide Picture

The intent to promote the common welfare, by very definition, does not distinguish among different segments of the community population. Neither are human problems, especially under the pressure of modern living, respecters of particular persons. The nature of the problem and its volume, the segments in the population which it attacks with greatest ease, the measure of serious social fatalities flowing from it—these and many other matters of knowledge concerning its community-wide characteristics are essential to a sound strategic plan for prevention and control. An effective program, then, will be community-wide in nature. Before it can be designed, both the problems and the services set up to meet them must be seen and comprehended on a community-wide scope. The parts of neither problems nor services can be seen in perspective until they are seen in relation to the whole.

The Vicious Circle

It is a matter of common observation and experience that one trouble leads to another. Professional health and welfare workers have long been aware that human problems set up a vicious circle within individuals and family groups. In the strategy which underlies the plan of logistics, it is of the greatest importance to see the interrelatedness of these problems in measurable terms, for it is in this relation that the person comes back into true perspective. We see what we have always known, but forgotten in the specialized complexity of our times, that his life's success or failure stems from a composite of his assets and his liabilities.

The Family Setting

Modern psychiatry teaches us that many of our human problems grow out of faulty family soil. Moreover, professional workers of all kinds know that family strengths and weaknesses constitute powerful assets and liabilities in the treatment and cure of many different kinds of problems. But strangely enough they sometimes forget or overlook the family in preoccupation with a part of its problem. It is not that particular troubles do not enlist their sympathies. The caseworkers, doctors, psychiatrists, nurses, public welfare workers, probation officers, prison wardens, club leaders, recreation directors, and the rest whose services will pass in review in this volume, all draw upon great wellsprings of sympathy and understanding in dealing with human problems and human suffering. Indeed, without these qualities of spirit such workers would be unable to perform their daily tasks. But the mind is sometimes prone to forget that in most cases this difficulty has arisen in a *family* where each member is dependent on the others, each looking to the family as a whole for the strength with which to solve his own problems.

Among the 41,000 families under care of St. Paul agencies in November, 1948, about 7,000—7 per cent of the community's families—were dependent, nearly 11,000 had problems of maladjustment, well over 15,000 had problems of ill-health, and almost 19,000 were being served by public and private recreation agencies. It can be seen at a glance that some families had more than one kind of problem. Seventy-seven per cent of the dependent families also had problems of ill-health or maladjustment. Fifty-eight per cent of the families with problems of maladjustment were known to agencies in the other service fields. Thirty-eight per cent of the families with health problems also had other problems. The most dramatic evidence of the vicious circling of problems in St. Paul's families came with the discovery that a group of 6,600 families, about 6 per cent of the city's families, were suffering from such a compounding of serious problems that they were absorbing well over half of the combined services of the community's dependency, health, and adjustment agencies.

The troubles of humanity and the particular things professional workers seek to do to help are now divided into such small segments that the family framework fades quietly from view. We believe that in the forefront of sound strategy must be a realistic concept of the family's relationship to the particular problems which the community program must attack.

Framework for Study

From the start, the conduct of the research project which produced materials for this volume posed a basic problem of classification. Some framework for study and analysis was needed to bring order out of the complexities of our health, welfare, and recreation operations. Its devising was not easy. The whirlwinds of expansion and specialization, almost within a single generation, have scattered widely the seeds from which our present multiplicity of welfare activities have grown. The working tool which we finally produced is a relatively simple classification of problems, functions, and structure (see Chart on following page). We would be the last to proclaim its enduring perfection. But it has enabled us to search coherently for widely scattered materials about the strategic characteristics of the problems toward which the different facets of our community programs are directed. It has assisted us in critical analysis of the functions indispensable to prevention of these problems and protection against their consequences. It has guided our evaluation of the structure most appropriate to the administration of these essential functions. From this composite of basic factors has come stimulation to precise thought about the avenue for productive movement toward coherent community-wide planning and action. It is within this framework that we attempt, in the final chapter of this work [*Community Planning for Human Services*], to synthesize the results of this assembly as it is presented in the four sections of the book.

Four Major Human Problems

The foundation for this classification rests on four major types of human problems toward which our community-supported services are directed. Three of these—dependency, ill-health, and recreational need—are self-descriptive and have long been terms in common usage. The fourth, maladjustment, serves a purpose for this project which is new in the annals of health and welfare; for here are grouped together symptoms of crime, delinquency, child neglect, mental and emotional disturbances that traditionally have been regarded as separate entities. The term maladjustment comes into usage in tacit recognition of psychiatry's teaching that the roots of these disorders lie deep in the same teeming soil. Correctional, mental health, and casework agencies are putting this teaching into practice by increasingly requiring some combination of the same three professional skills—psychiatry, psychology,

PROBLEMS	SERVICE FUNCTIONS	SERVICE SYSTEMS
	DEPENDENCY	
Economic dislocation (unemployment)	Determination of need	The insurances
	Provision of maintenance	Assistance programs
Personal disabilities	Economic rehabilitation	
	ILL-HEALTH	
Communicable disease	Community-wide disease prevention and control	Public health
Hazards of maternity, infancy, and childhood	Diagnosis and treatment	Organized medical care (hospitals and clinics)
Chronic disease	Nursing	
Chronic handicaps	Control of the environment	Private medical practice *
General morbidity		
Environmental hazards		
	MALADJUSTMENT	
Behavior disorders: Mental defect Mental disease Antisocial behavior Social failure	Diagnosis and treatment of behavior disorders	Correction
	Situational treatment	Mental health
Situational difficulties	Community-wide prevention and control of behavior disorders	Social casework
	RECREATIONAL NEEDS	
Recreation satisfactions: Sports and games Social occasions The arts Informal education	Provision of facilities for public use	Municipal recreation
		Private youth agencies
	Organization of activity interests	Federal-state parks and preserves
Group association	Organization of friendship interests	Religious-social-fraternal organizations *
		Commercial recreation *

* Not community-organized systems with financial support from taxes or community-wide campaigns.

and casework—to diagnose and treat the basic problems which underlie these several symptoms of disturbance.

The reader will note that we have characterized these problems negatively, or as one might say "according to their pathology." Some no doubt would prefer a phraseology couched in terms of more affirmative human aspirations—economic security, health, social adjustment, recreation.

Our own use of the pathological terminology is deliberate, however, because we believe it is conducive to more precise thinking. Pathological conditions exist; it is possible to get data about them, study their causation, observe and test efforts to correct them and prevent their occurrence. The practical danger of using more optimistic-sounding phrases lies not only in the fact that the concepts may be more vague, but also, and more importantly, in fact that a program which does not accept ultimate responsibility for the prevention or protection against pathological conditions is removed from the compulsion to measure specific results. The essential difference is not in goals, but in the degree of realism in methodology.

The Human Picture

In the pages of this book, the problems of people are dealt with in the aggregate, as they must be to serve the interests of community-wide planning. But we should remind ourselves that the very form and substance of such terms as dependency, ill-health, maladjustment, and recreational need are drawn from the troubles of the people who live side by side in all the communities of America. . . .

The Agency Systems

The reader will note that the community-supported services which are today at the disposal of these community neighbors have been classified in broad groupings for the purposes of this project.

The use of the phrase "agency systems," however, is for generic and descriptive characterization rather than to define a precise structural or administrative unity. In fact, there is very little of the latter. An exception is found in the federal-state program of relief for the aged, the blind, and dependent children, which does have a good measure of organic and administrative unity. In our characterization of the "public assistance system," however, we also have included "general assistance," which is not part of the federal-state program, as well as the small amount of private relief which communities now provide. These agencies, separately administered and financed though they may be, are, nevertheless, part of the "system" through which communities provide for people who are in need of food, clothes, and shelter.

The degree of organic and administrative unity among the other "systems" of our classification is much less, and in some cases entirely, nonexistent. Nevertheless, some device is necessary to achieve orderly thought about the literally thousands of different agencies, departments, and service units that are serving the people of this country. The groupings in our framework have behind them a good deal of rule-of-thumb usage. In all instances they deal with a common basic problem. In many of these systems large segments meet in common conferences and conventions. In most, although not all, a profession or a basic program philosophy supplies a cementing factor. . . .

Significance of the Findings for Community-Wide Planning

Throughout the preceding pages we have assumed that inherent in the culture of America is a belief in a progressively better way of life which would minimize continuously and realistically the ancient hazards of poverty, disease, social abnormality, and of unrewarding leisure.

Our purpose has been to show what now is involved in better methods of preventing and protecting the community against the consequences of these hazards. Throughout, we have been guided by the fact that when both problems and services are seen from a community-wide vantage point, compelling reasons appear for establishing a carefully planned interrelationship between the principal fields of present service. One value of this approach has been the identification of many gaps in knowledge and experience; wherever we have felt qualified to do so, we have indicated directions for the research and experimentation needed to fill them.

Our materials make it quite apparent that the services as now organized and rendered to the people of our communities do not offer a purposeful, comprehensive, well-integrated program. Certain segments have behind them a tradition of community-wide objectives and of functional integration. Others do not have such a tradition. Many of the agency systems, or movements, through which these services are provided have interests and objectives not easily accommodated to a unified community plan.

It is our expectation, however, that the trend toward coherent community-wide planning, within and among the major fields, will accelerate in the years immediately ahead. Therefore, it seems useful to summarize our materials from the standpoint of two principal factors that will affect this trend. The first has to do with the basic ferment necessary to real progress. The second concerns the realistic elements in the present status that have special significance for the task ahead. . . .

We believe that the preceding pages make it clear that the pace of integrated community planning depends upon (1) a greater unity of purpose, (2) better scientific and professional disciplines, and (3) more coherent national leadership in terms of community-wide guidance and stimulation. . . .

Neighborhood and Area Organization in
Urban Communities
—Introduction

TURNING FROM THE PROBLEM of community-wide welfare needs and planning we look next at the agencies responsible for community organization in the modern city. Starting at the lowest level, that of the neighborhood and the subcommunity, we note that the process in such areas differs somewhat from that in the city or larger community. In urban neighborhoods, as well as in small towns, as will be seen in Part VI, planning and action tend to be horizontal rather than vertical, inclusive and comprehensive rather than specialized and segmented, and may be directed toward the solution of any type of problem or to meeting almost any kind of local need. They attempt to involve the whole area and to include representatives of all organized groups as well as social agencies. Such an over-all approach is not feasible in the greater city with its many separate planning and promotional bodies, with the result that decentralized community organization on a neighborhood basis has developed rapidly since the depression of the thirties. Furthermore, even with respect to specialized needs and services such as those in social welfare, this return to local participation and determination is in accord with the basic democratic principles of community organization.

The necessary structure may be simply an informal group, a local committee of a national organization such as the Boy Scouts, a joint and expanded board resulting from the merger of several neighborhood centers, such as the recently established "Neighborhood Service Organization" in Detroit, or a district or area (community) council. Such councils are found today in increasing numbers in metropolitan areas like Seattle, St. Louis, Cleveland, Pittsburgh, Chicago, and Detroit.

The nature of the process as carried on under these conditions is twofold: (1) program planning to improve the immediate situation, whatever it may be, and (2) the incidental and consequent development of group co-operation, consensus, and neighborhood integration—in other words, community growth—through the habit of working together to meet a common problem. Both functions are important, but the latter is more significant from the standpoint of social work since it involves the development and strengthening of groups.

In the large urban community, on the other hand, community organization for social welfare is apt to be more specialized, both with respect to the groups involved and the objectives sought. The structure, generally a welfare council, or central council of social agencies, with its various divisions, is more complex, and membership is more narrowly limited to citizens with a particular interest in health and welfare. Program planning and social action is, therefore, more specifically directed to these areas than to broader concerns such as adult education, better business, civil defense, and general civic improvement. Furthermore, the process of group integration is confined largely to the membership of the council, or to the so-called "welfare community," rather than to the neighborhood as a whole.[1]

As already noted in the *Introduction* to Part I neighborhoods and small urban subcommunities are parts of the larger city community, and many of their interests are mutual, interrelated, and interdependent. The district council links these interests of the local area with the similar interests of the various central planning bodies, including the welfare council, which often provides staff service to the neighborhood groups. District councils, in turn, serve as outposts for the central planning organization providing valuable information on social problems and the opportunity for limited experimentation.

The two following selections discuss the role of local area organization in general and the functions of the neighborhood council in particular.

---

[1] Murray G. Ross, *Community Organization, Theory and Principles* (New York: Harper & Brothers, 1955), pp. 41-42.

45

The Functions of Neighborhood Organization [1]

By SIDNEY DILLICK

In this selection from the first comprehensive study of neighborhood community organization as such the author describes what he conceives to be the five unique functions of the district council and indicates the reciprocal relationship that exists between such bodies and the central planning council. He stresses the distinctive and valuable contributions that neighborhood organization has made historically, and is still making, to welfare planning and points out that in the last analysis service programs and social reforms must all be tested at this level.

Dr. Dillick served as secretary of the Division on Recreation and Informal Education of the Welfare Council of Toronto from 1945 to 1946. In 1948 he became secretary of the Group Work Division, of the Council of Community Services of Providence, Rhode Island, and in 1955 was also named as secretary of the Community Councils' Bureau of the same city. The following year he was appointed executive director of the Council of Community Services which position he now holds.

THE BACKGROUND of neighborhood organization since the Civil War shows that many of our fundamental social problems have persisted since the industrial revolution. . . .

[1] From *Community Organization in Neighborhood Development,* by Sidney Dillick, copyright 1953 by Sidney Dillick, by permission of Whiteside, Inc.

Vigorous efforts are needed today in neighborhood organization to make services available, to offer integrated patterns of services to meet the varying needs of neighborhoods and districts, to co-ordinate services to prevent overlapping and overlooking, to provide opportunities at the neighborhood and district levels for people to form groups through which they can act together, and to provide channels for groups to act together to change social goals and create new ones. In carrying out these functions the keynote must be the participation in these processes of people in their neighborhoods—where families live, shop, go to school and church, and where they vote.

Health and welfare agencies have developed specialized functions and have tended to operate out of central offices with consequent disadvantages as well as advantages. Quite often this has cut off valuable close contact with the organizations and agencies within the neighborhoods and districts of the area served. . . . Centrally administered direct-service agencies can help to prevent this by making their services available to people in neighborhoods on a decentralized basis. District advisory committees can provide a channel through which the neighborhood supporters and users of the services can participate in policy making and help to make the services available. These committees can be represented by delegates on the district community council.

We have lost some of the values inherent in the integration of services in neighborhoods and districts which were realized by the charity organization societies and the settlements. These values might be regained today through the development of the potential of settlements and community centers to make available a variety of services, under many auspices, in one place in the neighborhood or district.

In addition to making available a variety of health and welfare services the settlement can develop recognition of a need, set up a new service on a demonstration basis, and then seek permanent auspices for it. This function has brought into existence many of our basic health, welfare, and recreational services. Another major contribution of the settlement is to help people to form groups through which they can act together and say what they think is needed for the welfare of the community. Such groups as neighborhood associations can play a significant role as constituent groups in a district community council. The settlement can help those interested in the formation of a district community council to take their initial steps and can itself participate as a member agency. . . .

It took a great deal of experimenting on the part of councils of social agencies and later community welfare councils before it became clear that district community councils represent a significant and, in many cases, a necessary form of organization through which their work might be made more effective. Community welfare councils, as centralized co-ordinating and planning bodies which co-ordinate the activities of a large number of voluntary and tax-supported health and welfare services, need district community councils to facilitate citizen participation in action to change social conditions and to make available in neighborhoods and districts the services of city-wide agencies.

The district community council, as a co-ordinating, interorganizational body related functionally to the community welfare council, is a means through which the direct-service · agencies in health, welfare, recreation and education, and citizen organizations may work together within the larger context of the city or metropolitan area as a whole. The co-operative effort of citizen organizations and social agencies on problems in neighborhoods can be the beginning of work which may be extended to as broad an area as a solution may require. The district community council can help to meet today's need for neighborhood organization, not only by virtue of its own activities as an interorganizational body but also by the activities it can stimulate in direct-service agencies and citizen groups. Because of this, the district community council has a key place in neighborhood organization today.

Some of the unique functions of a district community council, as set forth by professional staff workers from a number of cities,[2] are as follows: (1) Co-ordination of health and welfare services at the neighborhood level; (2) helping people to become articulate about their needs and enlisting their participation in meeting them; (3) serving as a medium for the interchange of ideas among rank-and-file professionals; (4) serving as a medium for joint planning and action by agencies and civic groups; (5) providing a means for communicating to the city-wide level the neighborhood view of problems.

When it is seen in this light, neighborhood organization is of value, not only for "problem areas," but for all areas served by a community welfare council—urban, suburban, and semi-urban. It offers to councils of social agencies another way of broadening into councils that are not only concerned with, but are representative of, the welfare of the whole community. It is neither possible nor advisable for a city-wide council to attempt to impose an elaborate scheme of neighborhood organization upon a metropolitan area. It is possible—perhaps even advisable—to have a considered policy for developing neighborhood or district councils, because they can strengthen the work of a community welfare council.

Neighborhood and district organization may prove to be a significant approach to the community organization problems of metropolitan areas. Such areas are made up of numerous separate communities in many of which there is an intense feeling of local pride. Although to democratic institutions this is often a source of great strength, in community organization it has made difficult the development of a large enough unit to warrant the specialized staff that is needed today. A

---

[2] "Minutes of meeting of neighborhood council secretaries of community welfare councils at the National Conference of Social Work," August 5, 1946.

metropolitan council in which the constituent communities have their own district councils may make it possible for smaller communities to do their own planning within the larger framework and to have available the specialized staff and committees of the functional divisions of the over-all council.

In a district community council it is possible to bring together the representatives of the various agencies and organizations that exist in a district. It is often possible to get participation of groups and organizations that are rarely reached at the city-wide level. Furthermore, it is the lower echelons of leadership that are reached in the agencies and organizations. These are the leaders who work directly with the people of the community, for example, the local librarian, the leader of the parent-teacher association, the school principal, the trade union official, the parish priest, local ministers, the president of the fraternal order, the caseworker, the group worker, the playground supervisor, and the district nurse, among others.

The distinction between neighborhood and district which was made some time ago by settlement people is deserving of wider acceptance. A neighborhood is roughly the area served by an elementary school. It may be an eighth- to a half-mile in extent. A district, however, includes several elementary school areas and is roughly the area served by a high school. The so-called "neighborhood council" is often not an interorganizational body because the neighborhood is too small an area in which to find enough organized groups. Local interorganizational councils need the larger area of a district in which there exists a sufficient number and variety of organized groups.

Enthusiasm for a neighborhood project often carries the district council into the sponsorships of direct services. But if it develops such a program it will get into conflict with the agencies whose function it is to offer services. A district community council can be more effective if its efforts are focused upon getting appropriate agencies to assume these responsibilities. . . .

In bringing together the various organized groups in the district the council should be instrumental in stimulating discussion within the constituent groups. To do this effectively, the council should be composed primarily of delegates of the organizations of the district. The thinking of the community can be more adequately expressed by representatives of organized groups than by selected individuals who are "leading citizens." Often the effectiveness of the latter stems from their conscious or unconscious representation of groups. It is hazardous for a district council to reflect the personal sentiments of certain individuals rather than those of the organizations of the community.

Workers in the field have expressed the conviction that the professional staff of district councils should concentrate on helping neighborhood groups in their relations with other groups and with the agencies of the community. Delegates of local groups should be helped to report back to their groups on the matters discussed and on the decisions made in local council meetings. In this way the community will participate in determining its needs and in taking action through the district council. Skill is needed in helping delegates work out differences amid tensions. Staff people are needed who have the knowledge and skill to help a great diversity of groups, see their common interests and work together on them. A positive appreciation of ethnic, racial, religious, and other differences is important. The breadth of representation that district councils can potentially attain may help overcome the social barriers that have excluded significant groupings from community planning activities. . . .

Neighborhood councils need a degree of autonomy in keeping with their local character. They need complete independence in matters of a purely local nature and an appropriate part in making decisions that affect other neighborhoods in addition to their own. . . .

Throughout this study we have seen how neighborhood organization takes form in social welfare activities. In every period we have seen that it has had a significant place. The neighborhood and district levels of organization have their places among city, county, state, national, and international levels. In fact, neighborhood organization makes a unique contribution to social welfare, since efforts to solve the problems of social well-being are ultimately tested in their ability to meet the common human needs of individuals and families in their neighborhoods.

46

The Role of District Community Councils[1]

By VIOLET M. SIEDER

In this paper, presented at the 78th Annual Meeting of the National Conference of Social Work, Violet Sieder stresses the need for welfare planning and action by those who are most immediately concerned, namely, the citizens of the local area. City, state, and national agencies may suggest and stimulate specialized programs, but these must be accepted locally and articulated with numerous other needed services or they become ineffective or even disorganizing. The problem, as the writer aptly points out, is how to preserve the values of specialization as well as those of participation and co-ordination.

Miss Sieder notes that planning on a district or area basis has been neglected in the modern city and describes a number of "channels" through which the average citizen can participate in neighborhood improvement and gain personal satisfaction at the same time in helping to solve health and welfare problems. Among these channels is the district community or neighborhood council with whose organization, activities, and relationships with metropolitan planning bodies the selection is primarily concerned.

Violet Sieder, at the time this paper was presented, was associate director of the Health and Welfare Planning Department of Community Chests and Councils of America (now United Community Funds and Councils of America). For additional information concerning her the reader is referred to Selection 15.

[1] Excerpted from "Solving Health and Welfare Problems Through Neighborhood Participation," *The Social Welfare Forum*, Proceedings, National Conference of Social Work, Atlantic City, 1951 (New York: Columbia University Press, 1951), pp. 311-322. By permission of National Conference on Social Welfare.

IN YOUR COMMUNITY, are you faced with a wide, if not shocking discrepancy between professional social work know-how and actual practice in meeting the health and welfare needs of people? . . . This is doubly important today because we cannot afford the luxury of a society weakened by inadequate individuals upon whom the success of our democratic system depends; nor can we undertake the financial burden of costly treatment made necessary by lack of preventive services. In short, . . . the urgency of developing and applying social science knowledge to community social services must be recognized as of equal importance to the continued growth and development of the physical sciences so important to industry. . . .

Inherent in a democracy is the provision of opportunity for its members to exercise their responsibilities, rights, and privileges for determining, maintaining, and improving community services, and for creating a healthy social atmosphere for personal and family life. This ideal is hard to achieve in our industrial age when the individual is overwhelmed by the sheer bigness of government, industry, labor, and religious and social institutions, and when he is dependent upon many types of expertness in our economic, social, and political life. He is prone to blame "them" in Washington, the state capitol, or city hall, or the economic or political system as the great impersonal forces responsible for his state of impotence. He tends to feel or express no personal responsibility for the ills of his community. Such an individual is ripe for the seducements of a new political system in which he is promised an easy cure-all for his complaints; or he may become dependent upon men of influence; or buy favors at the price of a vote. . . .

It is significant that during periods of national stress or crisis—be it depression or war or defense—we become intensely aware of the discrepancies between the ideals of a democracy, which we want to preserve, and their practical application in our social institutions. We expect every man, woman, and child to rise to the defense of a way of life and are shocked by attitudes of lethargy or passive inaction. The truth is that we can hardly expect a show of strength in our body politic if its members have never had an opportunity to flex their muscles in the exercise of democracy. Going to the polls once a year is important, but, as we all know, it is not the full answer.

When folks lived in small towns, each person had an opportunity to make an important place for himself in his community, could express his viewpoint at town meeting, and keep in personal touch with the programs of his school, church, government, and other social institutions. Today we live not only in a society of organized bigness but also in a number of communities. Our community has become variously the world, the nation, the metropolitan area, the county, the city, or the neighborhood in which we live. Each of these communities is interrelated and interdependent. It is futile to hope for a strong world organization if any one of the links in his chain of communities is weak.

335

In the past, local communities have attempted to meet the health and welfare problems of their citizens largely through city-wide or county-wide agencies, or by metropolitan planning councils. Even the location of neighborhood centers, or decentralized branches of an agency, has been determined by city-wide leaders working through such community planning organizations as the community welfare council, city planning commission, housing authority, or through centrally administered agencies such as nursing services and family agencies. What is more, even after neighborhood programs are established, they are administered in most cases by a "downtown" board with little, if any, representation of the point of view of citizens for whom the programs were designed. Usually guided by outstanding citizen leaders of recognized reputation, by experts and specialists, and backed by powerful interest groups, plans for community services are too often developed for rather than with the citizens whom they are designed to serve.

This approach is patently a violation of a basic social work premise, namely, that successful treatment of social problems must be based on a recognition of the problems and a willingness to do something about them by the people most concerned. . . . The dynamics of community planning is not found in a perfect blueprint master-minded by experts. It is found in an understanding and acceptance of the plan which can be achieved only through participation in its making and execution. The broader the understanding, the greater the chance for assuring the desired results, both in terms of use of the services and of their financial support.

If we accept the principle of starting where people are—physically, mentally, emotionally, spiritually—what are some of the other guideposts to solving health and welfare problems which may be traced to our growing body of social work knowledge about people and the communities in which they live? First, social work as a profession has been constantly pushing back the problems to their causes. Great emphasis is placed on preventive services. . . .

Second, more and more emphasis is given to mental hygiene. We realize the need for ego satisfaction through opportunities for self-expression and a sense of being an important participant in a group to which we have a sense of belonging. The concepts of interaction of individuals within the group and the art of group development are expressed in the current interest in group dynamics.

Third, social work has always been dependent upon other professions, such as medicine, law, psychiatry, sociology, and nursing. More and more it recognizes the interplay between housing, employment, city planning, law enforcement, education, religion, and race relations as important to the social problems with which it treats.

If we agree, then, that social work of the future is not an isolated professional practice, but is an integral part of the social life of the community, we recognize that its effectiveness in solving welfare problems depends upon strengthening all aspects of community life through programs of prevention, practical application of mental hygiene concepts, and interpreting welfare broadly to include work with all related fields. The various social forces and programs which are treated as specializations at the national, state, or city level merge in the district or neighborhood of the city where they directly affect the lives of people. Here such concerns as health, delinquency, recreation, housing, rat control, family and child welfare, liquor control, old age, street lights, employment, and zoning make up the warp and woof of the pattern of life of the family and individuals. These interests, representing variously needs or services, are interrelated and inseparable parts of the whole and together describe the kaleidoscopic variations between communities or their subdivisions or districts.

Out of our specialized approach to welfare problems there is a tendency to develop programs centrally which are directed to the various districts or neighborhoods of a city. This vertical approach to planning frequently results in a multiplicity of planning organizations, each promoting a special interest, vying for the same local leadership, and becoming competitively destructive of each other through needlessly working at cross purposes. Regardless of where we start with special needs, the interrelatedness of social problems inevitably leads to a broad or horizontal approach to planning in the neighborhood, the least common denominator of practical social organization for a democratic society. Experience indicates that a council through which all groups and interests can work together must be staffed by a central planning body and not by any one operating agency—be it schools, courts, recreation, welfare, health, or any other field of service. An agency-sponsored council which attempts to plan and act on problems broader than the function of the sponsoring body runs the risk of becoming advisory to a program or causing confusion in the city-wide planning picture. The problem is how to preserve the strengths of specialization and at the same time assure a well-rounded welfare program with the full participation of folks concerned as users, contributors, and policy makers.

By and large, the neighborhood or district of a metropolitan area as a social planning unit has been greatly neglected. It is true, of course, that in a modern city, much of our life is organized around our special interests on a city-wide or metropolitan basis rather than in terms of where we live. . . . It is equally true that we have other ties to the community in which we live, shop, play, send our children to school, and vote. Our political life is still related to our residential district. As governmental services assume an ever greater importance in our lives, it becomes necessary to develop more direct channels of organized community expression between the electorate and the elected representatives. Political reform is possible only through informed citizen action expressed in terms of the neighborhood in which we live. Public officials and legislative representatives are more prone to pay attention to their voting constituents than to pious resolutions of a city-wide planning body.

Improvement of local playgrounds, streets, traffic regulations, sanitation, and other services are an immediate concern. Through the Parent-Teachers Association (PTA), the citizen keeps in close touch with the schools. He also works through church groups, social clubs, local businessmen's associations, fraternal groups, and social agency boards, committees, and group activities for the mutual interest of himself and his neighbors. All these interests are a personal concern because he actively participates in them, shapes policies, plans programs.

On the other hand, the social services offered by professional workers through agencies directed by prominent city-wide boards are remote from the average citizen, even though they are provided for his benefit. At times, these services are even resented by him. How often have we seen welfare programs established by the local PTA, the church, the social club, or the civic association without benefit of professional staff or guidance and in violation of recognized good practice? Could it be that social workers and their boards are violating the basic concept of how to help people when they plan for and not with them? People use services they believe in and understand. This is best achieved through participation in planning program, shaping policies, and financing. Along with such responsibility goes a sense of local pride and a promotion of the use and support of services. . . . The neighborhood as a planning base offers an opportunity to multiply the number of citizens who can effectively participate in the management of their social life and welfare.

Just what are the opportunities for solving health and welfare problems in a neighborhood? Specifically, what are the channels through which the average citizen can get these satisfactions in the neighborhood in which he lives?

The *first* channel is through participation in neighborhood organizations which carry on projects affecting the welfare of his community. These include the PTA, church, civic organizations, union, business associations, fraternal groups, and others.

The *second* is through participation in social agencies, on local advisory committees and boards either as a volunteer or as a program participant. Scout troop committees long ago demonstrated their effectiveness as interpreters of a program. Local committees of YMCA and YWCA branches and community centers are also effective. . . . Settlement houses and community centers, on the other hand, which serve only one neighborhood, offer to local citizens a number of avenues for participation. . . .

A *third* and increasingly effective method of neighborhood participation is through the district community council. . . . These councils, whose membership is drawn primarily from delegates appointed by organizations and agencies, and includes other interested citizens, serve a geographical subdivision of the city or county for the purpose of improving its social and civic life and of giving the citizens an opportunity to contribute to the welfare of the whole community. A single council frequently covers several cultural, ethnic, or racial groups and cuts across economic and social status lines. The size of the area served is determined in part by topography, main thoroughfares, and shopping centers and also by whether it is large enough to encompass a good cross section of organized groups, such as churches, PTA's, business associations, social agencies, neighborhood or block associations, and other civic groups. In larger cities a high school district frequently determines the area served by a council.

District councils are most effective when they are spread over many sections of the city, including wealthy, middle-income, and poor areas. What do they do? They work for better housing, use of school buildings as community centers, tuberculosis case finding, health institutes, improving race relations; they attack divorce through courses on family life and arrange for counseling services through established agencies; they extend day care and playground facilities; they improve city services, such as police protection, garbage disposal, street lights, transportation facilities, and enforcement of zoning. They are both a device for prevention of social problems through education and the elimination of social and physical hazards and for development of new or changed services to meet existing problems. . . .

Fourth, and finally, to achieve its greatest potential, planning in the district or neighborhood cannot be carried on in a vacuum, but must be related through established channels to city-wide planning bodies. This is important to prevent extremes of local self-interest and chauvinism, to keep neighborhood leaders aware of community-wide planning objectives, and to temper city-wide planning with the expressed needs and attitudes of local citizens. Such organizations as city planning commissions, housing authorities, boards of education, civil defense organizations, as well as community welfare councils find district councils a two-way street to the citizens they want to serve and from whom they need support to implement their plans. The district councils have proved an effective action arm for city-wide planning projects.

There are three major channels between districts or neighborhoods and city-wide planning bodies: (1) the vertical flow of information to and from district advisory committees and their city-wide public and private agencies and membership organizations, which, in turn, are represented in city or metropolitan planning bodies; (2) the direct channels between autonomous councils and central planning bodies; and (3) the formal relationships between an association or federation of councils and central planning organizations.

The purposes served by a federation or association of district councils include the following:

1. There is an opportunity to exchange experience on methods for tackling community problems and district council administration.

2. District councils working on the same or similar problems can co-ordinate their efforts in terms of fact finding, planning, and action. By careful timing of approaches to community-wide agencies, or to public officials, they can achieve more effective results with less confusion.

3. The attention of district councils is focused on the over-all needs of the metropolitan area, and perspective is given to the special needs of each district. Priorities for projects can be established jointly and in a statesmanlike way.

4. Leadership discovered within the district councils has an opportunity to develop and gain recognition through participation in the association of councils and thus to supply new and valuable citizen participation in city-wide agencies and organizations.

The devices to facilitate a two-way flow between central and district planning include direct representation, specialized consultation, and staff service from generalists in community organization to district councils. In some cities, district councils hold membership in community welfare councils and are represented in council divisions or committees. They serve on city-wide planning bodies for such special interests as housing, race relations, and civic improvement. They seek advice from specialists in the fields of health, recreation, family welfare, housing research, and public relations on local planning problems. . . .

Experience indicates the great importance of professional community organization staff in helping local citizen leaders develop studies, seek out appropriate resources, co-ordinate competing activities at a level where status and credit are all-important, educate neighbors about services and standards, and take effective action to bring about change. Staff skill is required to keep the district council from succumbing to the temptation of operating a community service program and thus lose its identity as a planning organization. The big problem is not how to stimulate such councils; for there is plenty of evidence that neighbors are getting together to plan and operate services, with or without the benefit of skilled advisers from the social work "clergy." The problem is to time advice and be a step ahead by offering a helping hand at the points of sound planning rather than to spend endless hours and money later, patching up or redirecting misguided efforts.

If we are to meet the problems of an expanding population in the suburban and county areas adjacent to our cities with tested programs, which are up to recognized professional standards . . . we had better create some modern machinery to make it possible. To reach out to "each individual," involve every interested "autonomous organization," and achieve a maximum of participation, understanding, and responsible action, we must build, not only through a central planning organization, but also through the neighborhoods or districts of our great metropolitan areas. . . .

Direct-Service Agencies and Community Organization
—Introduction

WITHIN the greater city, as well as in neighborhoods as noted earlier, organization and promotion for welfare purposes is also carried on by agencies whose primary responsibility is for direct service to individual clients and groups as well as by community welfare councils. In fact, a large part of welfare planning and action results from the interagency activities of caseworkers and group workers, with or without the assistance of a professional community organization practitioner, as might be expected in view of the generic nature of all social work. These interagency activities are sometimes referred to as "secondary" functions of direct-service agencies though they are of no less importance to the community. Such functions include the community-wide efforts of board members and executives, the services of workers on interagency committees, co-operation on joint projects, and their participation in council activities in general. In group work agencies, particularly, social action is a traditional and persisting responsibility.

Before presenting material on the more highly specialized welfare planning and financing bodies two excerpts are introduced which emphasize the important role of direct-service agencies in the total process. The first of these concerns the role of family service agencies in urban community organization, and the second, interagency co-operation in general.

47

Participation of the Family Agency in
Community Planning[1]

By FAMILY SERVICE ASSOCIATION OF AMERICA

Family agencies historically have taken the lead in demonstrating the need for new community welfare services and in promoting their establishment. In 1950 the Family Service Association of America appointed a study committee to evaluate its program. The report of this committee submitted three years later included two parts, the first on general objectives, or scope, and the second on casework methods.

In the following excerpt, taken from Part I of the report, a distinction is made between "complementary" services designed for clients of the family casework agency, and "parallel" services, which, though administered by the family agency, are available on a community-wide basis. Many such services are eventually separated from the sponsoring agency and set up under independent auspices.

FAMILY SERVICE AGENCIES, from their inception, have included, as a major function, responsibility for community planning. The development, over the past three decades, of various joint planning councils and financing bodies has brought about changes in the form that the agencies' activities take, but has not altered the field's commitment to work toward the improvement of social conditions.

[1] *Scope and Methods of the Family Service Agency* (New York: Family Service Association of America, 1953), pp. 9-11. By permission of the publisher.

The commitment to improve living conditions and to better the social climate is shared by many more groups at this point in social work development than was true in the early pioneer period of the family agency movement. Organized social work has greatly expanded and has drawn into its ranks large numbers of lay and professional participants. The programs of various civic and industrial groups, of neighborhood organizations, of other professional organizations, and often of such public services as the press, radio, and television, encompass activities directed toward achieving various social and educational goals.

Improvement of Social Conditions

The family service agency has a particular responsibility to take leadership in working for the improvement of social conditions and the establishment of adequate community welfare and treatment services. Because of its intimate knowledge about the negative effects of low living standards and inadequate resources on individuals and families, the agency should play a prominent role in the community's planning activities. The responsibilities include study of existing needs, presentation of the findings to appropriate planning groups, and educational and interpretative efforts.

Board and committee members, as well as the professional staff, have a role to play in these activities. Usually the evidence of unmet needs is gathered, studied, and documented by the professional staff. Board and committee members, however, as well as staff, have the responsibility of presenting the findings in appropriate ways to community planning groups, to legislative bodies, and to the public.

Although the family agency may channel many of its activities through the local, state, or national planning bodies of which it is a member, it should not overlook its obligations to speak for itself. Cooperative efforts should be effectively supplemented by independent activities.

Establishing New Services

Family agencies, historically, have undertaken to demonstrate the need and value of new services or resources. Many of these services subsequently have been established as separate community services under other auspices.

If these agency services are designed to serve the total community (and not only the persons receiving casework service from the agency), they may be described as *parallel* services, as distinct from the *complementary* services described earlier. Many family agencies currently operate one or several parallel services. Parallel services, like the complementary services, include tangible resources such as foster homes or camps, or counseling help such as vocational guidance. The distinction between parallel and complementary services is an administrative one. Parallel services are designed to offer service on a community-wide basis; they are operated as separate units with their own intake policies. It is important for agencies to keep this administrative factor clear in planning budgets, assigning staff, and so on.

The particular type of parallel services that a family agency may decide to establish will be affected by several factors, such as its concept of function (whether it is a multiple service or a family casework agency) and the structure of community services. Some variation is to be expected. The family agency should, however, be in the vanguard in calling attention to unmet needs and inadequacy of resources and in taking responsibility, when appropriate, to demonstrate the need for and value of new services. It seems likely that some of the new services and projects undertaken by family agencies will be those which lead to collaboration with other professional disciplines, in the interest of extending technical knowledge and skill. The techniques of research should serve as a resource to add validity to the findings that may emerge from such demonstrations.

48

Interagency Relationships [1]

By RAY JOHNS and DAVID F. DEMARCHE

Not only do direct-service agencies, such as family welfare bureaus, engage in community organization, but a great deal of community-wide welfare planning and programing is carried out on a joint or interagency basis. In the following selection by Johns and DeMarche examples of joint program in such fields as service to the handicapped, recreation, work with unmarried mothers, civil defense, capital fund campaigns, and community center programs are given, as well as illustrations of co-operative relationships between casework and group work agencies, and between caseworkers and visiting nurses. The authors are careful to point out that such co-operation is essential for effective community work and does not necessarily lead to mergers.

Community Organization and Agency Responsibility, from which the excerpt was selected, is based on a study of the experience of some 500 workers in thirty different organizations in approximately sixty communities. It is concerned with various aspects of co-operative relationships and the principles involved in good interagency practice.

Ray Johns has had some thirty years' experience both in direct-service agencies and in interagency work. David F. DeMarche's experience includes work in local, metropolitan, and interstate areas. For additional biographical comments see Selection 11.

[1] Excerpted from *Community Organization and Agency Responsibility* (New York: Association Press, 1951), pp. 162-173.

Services for the Handicapped

A CO-ORDINATING SERVICE for crippled children was established in the Department of Health in New York City, with an advisory council of recognized leaders in various services to. insure community representation and responsiveness. The Committee for the Study and Care and Education of Physically Handicapped Children of the New York City Board of Education also recognized the need for co-ordinating educational and other services to physically handicapped children as indicated in this statement:

> "To modernize the program and to co-ordinate the various aspects of the work, it appears desirable to have the educational provisions for all groups of physically handicapped children placed under the administration of a single official who is qualified for this position and who is assigned to devote full time to it. It should be the responsibility of this official not only to co-ordinate services within the Department of Education, but also to secure appropriate co-operation from the other city departments, particularly the Department of Health, the Department of Hospitals, and the Department of Public Welfare." [2]

In commenting on the foregoing co-ordinating efforts for the physically handicapped in New York City, Stanley P. Davies pointed out some of the essentials of such joint efforts. "What we need to make sure," he said,

> "is that co-ordination is not just at the top. The setting up of advisory and co-ordinating councils . . . will serve the intended purpose only when the discussion of common problems translates itself into an interrelated and integrated direct-service program. The practical machinery for co-ordination of local direct service consists of the continuing joint case conference in which the various disciplines come together for the planning and execution of combined action in each particular case. Whether this case conference is held in the hospital, the public school, the public health nursing agency, or the social agency will depend largely on the nature of the handicap and the problems in the particular case.
>
> "Such a plan means unification but not uniformity. It does not discourage specialization and the further development of different professional skills and techniques; on the contrary, it encourages them by integrating them as parts of one program to serve one individual." [3]

---

[2] Stanley P. Davies, "Co-ordinating the Efforts of Agencies Serving the Physically Handicapped," *Proceedings, National Conference of Social Work* (New York: Columbia University Press, 1941), p. 468.

[3] *Ibid.*

Settlements and Public Recreation

An experiment in Cleveland between public recreation agencies and privately financed social settlements illustrates another type of inter-agency relationships. The Neighborhood Settlement Association of Cleveland, formed in 1948 as the joint and central administrative agency for three settlements, approached the co-ordinator of recreation of the Joint Recreation Board of the city of Cleveland and the Cleveland Board of Education about possible joint relationships in an area then served by both groups. The Board of Education had been sponsoring a community center at the junior high school in an inter-racial area, one evening for adults and one for teen-age youngsters, under the direction of untrained, part-time staff. Parents and business-men had complained about the youngsters' destructive behavior. A few blocks away, one of the settlements participating in the Neighborhood Settlement Association had operated a small settlement branch, with limited program and staff, in inadequate but expensive rented quarters.

A new joint plan was developed. The settlement branch was discontinued. The junior high school became the headquarters for the joint project. The Neighborhood Settlement Association provided a clerical worker and office furniture. Both groups agreed upon the selection of a well-experienced settlement worker as joint director of both parts of the project, one-fourth of whose salary was paid by the Board of Education on a per-session basis and three-fourths by the Neighborhood Settlement Association. Part-time workers for each part of the program were paid by the two groups. The total memberships, interracial and interreligious on all levels, soon grew to over one thousand, two-thirds of them under eighteen. Twenty-five social clubs and twenty-eight recreational interest groups soon developed.

Similar joint projects were later established in other sections of the city, except that different proportions of the director's salary were paid by the participating organizations.

What does such a plan mean to the objectives and functions of the public recreation agencies and the settlements? "We are convinced," the director of the Neighborhood Settlement Association stated, "that it maintains and strengthens both, and increases and improves the actual services to the community which sees only the total program and is less confused by separate sponsorship." [4]

Casework-Group Work Relationships

Working relationships among caseworkers and group workers have for years been considered as among the most potentially valuable rela-

---

[4] Henry Ollendorff, "Public Recreation and Settlements," *Recreation*, Dec., 1950 (National Recreation Association, 315 Fourth Avenue, New York), p. 391.

tionships social workers can develop in the interest of more effective service for individuals. Joint case conferences, such as those referred to earlier in relation to work with the physically handicapped, have been utilized in many communities. Referrals between caseworkers and group workers have also been utilized to an increasing degree. Three general categories of casework-group work relationships have been identified: (1) the supplementary type, where caseworkers or group workers utilize in their own program techniques usually needed in the "other" field; (2) the referral type; (3) the integrated type, where caseworkers and group workers jointly provide the needed service.[5]

The referral process was analyzed by the Casework-Group Work Committee of the Greater Boston Community Council in 1948–1949. Their report stated the common objectives of casework and group work in these terms: "Casework and group work both seek to stimulate people to achieve the best possible adjustment to life. These processes are socially creative and disciplined in that they require interaction between the person and the human situation." [6] Casework and group work were both described, and ways in which each can make use of the other's services were outlined.

Suggestions were made for caseworkers referring persons to group workers. Average persons may be referred to provide opportunities to make normal separation from parental environment, to enrich life by helping individuals learn how to get on with other people, to assume citizenship responsibilities, learn self-respect and respect for others, and awareness, appreciation, and acceptance of social and religious differences. Individuals without special problems may also be referred to help counteract environmental factors which might lead to individual breakdown, or to help satisfy an individual's special interests. People with special needs can be referred, when their capacities and readiness to enter a group indicate possible help from selected and guided group relationships. It was suggested that persons unable to relate to others and those who would endanger the health and safety of other individuals in a group should ordinarily not be referred. The types of information the caseworker should obtain regarding the group work services, necessary steps in the referral process, and follow-up procedures were also outlined.

Group work-to-casework referral considerations and steps were also suggested. Families or individuals who request help with personal or social problems beyond the function and resources of the group work

---

[5] *Group Work-Casework Co-operation,* a symposium sponsored by the American Association of Group Workers (New York: Association Press, 1946), pp. 18-19.

[6] *Considerations and Steps in Making Referrals Between Casework and Group Work* (Greater Boston Community Council, reorganized in 1949 as part of the United Community Services of Metropolitan Boston, Inc.), Feb., 1949, mimeo., p. 1.

services should be referred, it was agreed, for casework service. Consultations should be held between the group workers and caseworkers regarding possible referral of families or individuals whose behavior becomes a matter of concern to the workers, but whose need of referral to a casework agency is in doubt. In exceptional cases, where instances of cruelty, neglect, or dangerous psychotic behavior is evident, referrals may be made to an appropriate casework agency, even without the consent of the individuals involved. Ordinarily, individuals who present problems, but who have indicated that they are determined not to accept such help, ought not to be referred. Some problems can be dealt with best by the group workers, in the group work setting, sometimes in consultation with a caseworker. (Steps for referrals to casework agencies, outlined by the study committee, can be noted in the document listed in Footnote 6.)

The basic factors involved in casework-group work relationships have been outlined as follows:

"First, a recognition that we have common objectives and are working toward the same end . . . to help people to the most satisfactory personal and social adjustment. Second, a recognition that we are on common ground in that we are serving the same communities and many of the same kinds of people in them and, since this is true, that we make a more significant contribution if we work together than if we work independently . . . third . . . fundamental concepts as to the confidential nature of material exchanged, use of such material only as it relates to dealing with the individual in a professional relationship, a nonjudgmental attitude based on recognition of causative factors in behavior, and the right of self-determination of the individual. . . . A fourth factor necessary to the working out of co-operative relations is that we keep the focus of attention and effort on the individual and not upon the service to the other agency or the workers in it. . . . A fifth factor . . . was a feeling of respect for and confidence in the effectiveness of the contribution of one's own field. . . . The sixth factor . . . is an appreciation of and respect for the contributions of the other's work which result in a wish to learn about it. . . ." [7]

Co-operative Services for Unmarried Mothers

The way in which a number of cities have developed co-operative services for unmarried mothers illustrates a set of interagency relationships in another field. For example, in Chicago, the Welfare Council, after years of study of the problem, requested the United Charities of Chi-

---

[7] Mary Hester and Dorothy G. Thomas, "Casework and Group Work Co-operation," *Proceedings, National Conference of Social Work* (New York: Columbia University Press, 1939), pp. 339-341.

cago, the major family casework agency in the city, to establish a specialized service. The Woman's Service Division was organized, and co-operative arrangements were set up with all agencies dealing with the problem. If a Catholic, Episcopal, or Jewish client applies, she is informed about the sectarian agency available. Working arrangements are maintained with medical and health agencies, maternity homes and shelters, the Juvenile Court, and Court of Domestic Relations, and with children's agencies for service in connection with adoptive placement and long-time foster care.

This centralized, specialized service has resulted, it is reported, in a general improvement in casework service and planning for unmarried mothers, in a greater knowledge and skill by caseworkers in using community resources, and in a general improvement in co-operative relationships between agencies.

Civil Defense Relationships

Civil defense planning, in a number of cities, has furthered interagency relationships. In Cleveland, during World War II, the Welfare Council took the leadership in civil defense planning, and voluntary agencies and tax-supported agencies worked closely together. When the Korean crisis and other aspects of the international situation stimulated civil defense plans, co-operative planning of emergency social services quickly developed again. For example, in Boston an executive committee for the social services division of the Civil Defense Organization, composed of representatives of the Department of Public Welfare, the American Red Cross, and the United Community Services, was established. Each section—information and referral, census, evacuation, emergency, social services, financial aid, and emergency housing—was headed by a chairman and two vice-chairmen from each of the three groups, with the chairman appointed from the group which would most appropriately take the primary responsibility. A crisis situation, when the resources of all agencies are obviously needed, usually gives considerable impetus to joint efforts.

Visiting Nurse and Social Caseworker Co-operation

An investigation of the methods and channels by which two important family services might become more effective in their joint effort for furthering the health and well-being of families both were serving was made through the co-operation of the Family Service Association and the Visiting Nurse Association of Cleveland.[8]

---

[8] Annikki M. M. Ahla, *Referred by Visiting Nurse* (Cleveland: The Press of Western Reserve University, 1950).

The common goals of the two organizations were summarized as follows:

"They both aim at the maximum good of the basic unit of the community, the family. They are concerned with the family's health as well as its social adjustment. They deal with people in need, work for the good of the whole community, and are supported by citizens. In both fields the workers have an intimate relationship with the family, the client asks for counsel on a variety of personal matters, and the work is based on knowledge derived from common sources such as medicine, psychiatry, and education. Both professional groups use the interview as a tool and keep records of their work. . . . Social casework may be utilized whenever people's satisfaction in their ordinary relationships has disappeared. . . . The helping process of social casework consists of three important steps: study of the problem, establishing the social diagnosis, and treatment. In order to help, the worker must know the needs and resources of the client's total situation as well as the weaknesses and strengths of his individual personality. . . . The public health nursing profession has also been sharpening its tools and revising its objectives. The original function of providing bedside care for the sick in their homes has been extended to include the prevention of illness and promotion of health. . . . Often [the public health nurse] may find health problems other than those for which she was called. To render effective service to the individual she has to consider the health and the relationships of the family as a whole. . . . The nurse instructs individuals according to their specific needs and their ability to use health information. . . . She attempts to evaluate attitudes and relationships within the family which may be operating for or against satisfactory care." [9]

Eight of the thirty-seven cases referred by the Visiting Nurse Association to the Family Service Association in 1946 were studied. The eight cases were selected from those which were accepted for major casework service and were those which were new to the FSA in 1946. These cases were closed by January 31, 1948.

The analysis of the cases made clear the differences in original emphases, the barriers which arise, and the steps toward mutual understanding and co-operative work. The social caseworkers were described as "psychosocial practitioners" who deal with people in trouble, "enablers" who help clients understand their situation better and use available resources. Public health nurses help restore the sick, alleviate suffering, and prevent disease. The training is different. Lack of mutual understanding of each other's goals and methods, and neglect of the principle of a two-way channel were noted as the chief barriers

---

[9] *Ibid.*, pp. 1-3.

to effective relationships. Steps toward mutual understanding were identified as (1) information about each other during the period of professional training, (2) staff education inside an agency, (3) interagency activity. The study concluded that

> "two agencies with common interests and goals certainly are interested in co-operation. The definite differences in their functions do not diminish this interest. On the contrary, it may be through these differences that both may work out professional co-operative relationships and effectively serve those who need their help." [10]

Joint Agency Capital Fund Efforts

Joint efforts in a number of communities to secure capital funds for new facilities or to improve and expand existing structures represent an important set of relationships. In San Francisco a number of youth agencies, including the YMCA, the Boy Scouts, and the Boys' Clubs, conducted a joint capital fund effort in 1948. They thus reduced the number of campaigns, and although the total goal was not reached in the first effort, it was possible for them, according to reports, to secure contributions from corporations which would have opposed separate campaigns. Rochester, New York, conducted a successful joint YM-YWCA capital effort in 1947.

Joint Agency Community Centers

Community centers, jointly sponsored and managed by two different agencies have been experimented with in a number of communities, following the USO joint agency operations of World War II.

The experience in different cities has varied. In one city several experiments were started, but one was discontinued because the identity of the two agencies seemed to be lost. The other efforts in that city, functioning under more favorable conditions, have continued. In another city, the staff situation was unsatisfactory to both agencies for a time but later was changed, and relationships improved. In another city, joint title to all property was worked out, and working relationships regarding board and staff responsibilities, finances, program, and other aspects of the work were agreed upon in advance. Joint operation involves close and sometimes complicated relationships. A great deal of similarity in objectives and methods, and considerable flexibility, are needed. It is one of the ways by which integration of experience and service may be achieved. Further experimentation, objectively evaluated, seems merited.

---

[10] *Ibid.*, p. 5.

Relationships Which Resulted in a Merger

Close relationships, based on increasingly common purposes and services, resulted in one community in a merger of two separate organizations. The Hampden County Children's Aid Association and the Family Service Association of Springfield, Massachusetts, had operated for over seventy years as separate organizations. As each agency came to develop a rounded program for families and children, and as they participated together for years in community planning and in joint fund raising, informal discussions developed about the desirability of merging their services. A joint committee studied statements of the aims, philosophies, and services of the two agencies. They investigated the results from a merger in a near-by community and considered legal and financial problems of amalgamation. The staffs were kept informed and were consulted. The joint committee came to the conclusion that merger services would (1) provide better service because the client's whole problem could be considered; (2) more flexibility would result in the combined budget, and better use of the community dollar would thus result; (3) better administration would be possible through combined case records, clerical services, and broader opportunities for staff members.

Interagency relationships, it should be emphasized, are not necessarily forerunners of mergers. In fact, most relationships should probably not result in merged services. Agency individuality has been one of the most valuable aspects of American community social welfare services. But effective relationships among different agencies dealing with the same people, and working on similar community problems, are necessary. When, in exceptional cases, the aims and services of two or more agencies are found to have become fundamentally the same, such as with child care and family agencies, mergers can well be considered. Interagency relationships should not be considered a threat to agency identity. They are one of the necessities of modern community social welfare services. Through them, an agency's special emphasis and individualized service can be made most effective.

Community Welfare Councils and Community Chests
—Introduction

IN CONTRAST with direct-service agencies, welfare councils and chests are generally considered to be the major specialized, or "primary," community organization bodies in cities and metropolitan areas. Although both play important roles in determining the focus and direction of local welfare planning, particularly of voluntary programs, they are not actually in most communities the dominant or controlling power in the shaping of social welfare development in general due not only to their lack of complete coverage, but also to the operation of other important nonwelfare forces. The problem is to make them more effective and more representative of *all* important groups in the community. The first two selections, "Code of the Chest and Council Movement," and "Community Planning for Social Welfare" present what might be termed the "official" philosophy and policy of the national organization of chests and councils.[1]

It should be noted, further, that the number of councils in United Community Funds and Councils of America, Inc., is much smaller than that of chests and funds, and has even decreased somewhat since 1953, but that the growth of the last two has been spectacular. In view of the essential planning function of the council and of its more representative nature this increasing disparity may be significant.

Both organizations are found in nearly all urban centers with a population of 100,000 or more, but in the United States as a whole chests outnumber councils more than four to one. In 1950 the number of

---

[1] The first five selections were originally published under the auspices of, or by, Community Chests and Councils of America, Inc. Early in 1956, however, the title of this association was changed to United Community Funds and Councils of America, Inc.

councils listed as members by Community Chests and Councils of America was slightly over 400.[2] The number increased to 450 in 1953 but decreased to 434 in 1956.[3] In contrast, CCC listed 1270 chests in 1950 and by 1956 reported a total of 1,994 chests and united funds, not including those in Canada. Including the latter, the figures for 1956 stand at 2,063 for chests and united funds, and at 461 for councils. With respect to the latter (as well as the former), it should be noted, however, that the number includes only those councils which are members of United Community Funds and Councils of America. While the exact number is unknown there are probably nearer 700 councils concerned to some extent with welfare planning in American communities today.

How welfare councils facilitate teamwork in a community and what characteristics determine an effective council are discussed in two selections from UCFC publications, entitled respectively, "Community Welfare Councils—What They Are and What They Do," and "Criteria for a Good Welfare Council." In general, community welfare councils may be defined as intergroup bodies composed of delegates or representatives, of member organizations and of the public. Institutional membership includes both chest and non-chest voluntary agencies and public departments.

Three main types of councils may be distinguished: (1) traditional councils of social agencies, (2) community welfare councils, and (3) specialized councils. The first tends to be limited to social welfare agencies and other organizations with committees or departments specifically concerned with social welfare. Perhaps the majority of metropolitan welfare councils today are of this type. Community welfare councils, on the other hand, include a larger proportion of individual members, lay and professional, and have a broader base of organizational representation. They are concerned with social welfare in a comprehensive sense and frequently engage in social action as well as in efforts to co-ordinate social agencies and improve health and welfare programs. Specialized councils may be functional divisions of either of the other two types, that is, subcouncils, or independent organizations. They are found in such fields as family and child welfare, recreation and group work, health, mental hygiene, rehabilitation, juvenile delinquency prevention, youth services, and the like, and may be sponsored by sectarian, labor, or other special groups.

Councils are voluntary bodies with no administrative control over their member agencies. Their major functions include: fact finding, planning, stimulation of discussion, co-ordination and the improve-

---

[2] *Social Work Year Book,* 1951 (New York: American Association of Social Workers, 1951), p. 605.

[3] *Ibid.,* 1954, p. 614, and *1956 Directory* (New York: United Community Funds and Councils of America, Inc., 1956), p. vi.

ment of teamwork and agency efficiency, consultation to neighborhood councils and to agencies, interpretation and the improvement of public relations, and promotion and social action. In addition, they may administer certain common services such as research, information and referral, volunteer bureaus, and the social service exchange. The function of the last service, or device, is reviewed by Frank Greving and Stephen Angell in the selection on "The Social Service Exchange and Agency Co-operation."

Many problems confront welfare councils today in addition to that of their relationship to chests, which is noted below. Some of these are discussed in the following selections; others are referred to in previous and later excerpts. The following questions relate to some of the major current issues. How can the council be reconstructed to incorporate the more powerful and controlling forces in the modern community? How may its program be geared more effectively to total community planning? How can governmental agencies be involved more actively than at present? How can councils receive sufficient funds to carry on effective welfare planning, supported entirely as they generally are, by chests? What other sources of financial support might be tapped to free councils from this dependency and encourage independent research and comprehensive planning? Finally, to what extent, and in what connections, should councils engage in social action?[4] The future development of councils is dependent to a great extent upon finding the answers to these and other pertinent questions.

Two selections on fund raising as an aspect of community organization were included in Part III. In Part IV we are concerned with the structure of chests and the problems of federated financing as carried on by chests and united funds. One of the most phenomenal developments in community organization in recent years has been the rapid growth of joint fund-raising organizations as previously noted. These fall under two heads, local community chests and united funds or "extended federations," which include one or more of the "Big Six" national appeals (Red Cross and five national health agencies). In 1956 United Community Funds and Councils of America listed a total of 2,063 chests and united funds in the United States and Canada.[5] The 1,994 in the United States raised a total of $322,186,544 for 1956, and the sixty-nine in Canada, $17,519,523, or a grand total of $339,-706,067, a substantial increase over the preceding year. Furthermore, the total raised during the past five years has increased by nearly 60 per cent, or $127 million. Much of this spectacular growth has been due to the "United Fund Movement" which started in 1950, is now found in 821 cities, and accounted for 59 per cent of the total raised

---

[4] See Part III, Selections 36, 37, and 38 above.

[5] *1956 Directory* (New York: United Community Funds and Councils of America, Inc. 1956), p. vi.

for 1956.[6] In over 2,000 of all types of campaigns in the United States and Canada for 1958 over $412,000,000 was raised, three-fourths from United Fund drives.[7]

Community chests have two major functions: campaigning annually for the support of member agencies, and distributing the funds raised through joint budgeting. Through the allocation of funds, the chest, of course, exercises considerable control over agency personnel, services, expansion, and planning in general. The issues involved in this connection are more controversial than those associated with councils, and include the problem of agency participation in budgeting, the preservation of the freedom of the individual agency, local *versus* national appeals, and the ultimate limits of federation. Ralph Blanchard, in the selection, "Why Federation," projects the future of the movement in optimistic terms. The *pros* and *cons* of united fund raising are presented by Albert Nesbitt and Rome Betts, respectively.

In terms of planning, perhaps the most significant question concerns the relationship between chests and councils. Since the member agencies are also involved, this becomes a three-way problem which is examined in the document entitled, "Chest, Council, and Agency Relationships." Structurally there appear to be four possible patterns of relationship between chests and councils. They may be combined into a single integrated agency with one board and a common staff; they may be partly united as a chest-council organization under the same board but with separate, specialized staffs; they may be separate agencies with independent boards, but served by a joint executive staff; or finally, they may exist as entirely separate and independent bodies with their own boards and staffs as in the majority of large cities today. Does the merging of chest and council functions in a single agency strengthen or weaken the council as a planning body? This issue is analyzed in the selections by Charles Birt and Whit Pfeiffer. Finally, in terms of function, and irrespective of structural organization, there are additional problems associated with the division of labor between chest and council and with the respective responsibilities of each for such activities as admission to the chest, budgeting, research, publicity, and other central services which are also referred to in the various readings that follow.

---

[6] Esther Moore, "Federation: In Tune with the Times," *Community* (New York: Community Chests and Councils of America, Inc.) Vol. 31, Jan., 1956, pp. 83-87.

[7] Kenneth Wood, "Autumn Harvest: $412,000,000," *Community* (New York: United Community Funds and Councils of America, Inc.), Vol. 33, No. 4 (Jan., 1958), pp. 63-66.

49

Code of the Chest and Council Movement [1]

By COMMUNITY CHESTS AND COUNCILS OF
AMERICA, INC.

All professions and many other occupations have their officially
approved codes of ethics and the American Association of Social Workers adopted such a code for all social workers in 1951. The following
statement of beliefs, objectives, and standards of professional practice
was approved by Community Chests and Councils of America in 1953
as a code for community organization workers, particularly those
employed in the chest and council field. Harry McElhinney Carey, who
drafted the twenty-five propositions, has been director of the United
Community Services of Metropolitan Boston since 1949. He was chairman of the Personnel Committee of CCC from 1939 to 1941, became
president of the Massachusetts State Conference of Social Work in
1949, and served as chest and council specialist in Germany for the
U.S. State Department in 1952.

THREE YEARS AGO the executives of the ten largest Chests stated
their desire for a code that would express formally the ethics of practitioners in the Chest-Council field. C. Raymond Chase of Boston appointed the first Code of Ethics Committee in October, 1951, with
Robert H. MacRae of Chicago as chairman. Harry M. Carey of Boston was appointed to draft such a code. During the past year Mr.

[1] Adapted from article of same title, *Community* (New York: Community
Chests and Councils of America, Inc.), Vol. 28, No. 8, April, 1953, pp. 160-161.
By permission of United Community Funds and Councils of America, Inc.

Carey's draft has been reviewed and strengthened by a special committee of CCC. The code was accepted by CCC's Board of Directors at its March meeting [1953], and is now being made available to the whole country.

Basic Concepts

We believe that:

1. Each individual has a responsibility to meet his own needs to the extent of his ability. People are interdependent, however, and the welfare of each affects the welfare of all. It is, therefore, desirable and necessary that people form organizations to work for their mutual benefit.
2. The necessity for community organization for social welfare arises from the needs and desires of all people. All interests and elements of the population have a right and a responsibility to participate.
3. Community organization for social welfare is concerned with the welfare of the community and of each individual as a part of that community.
4. Fundamental to community organization for social welfare is acceptance of change and development of health and welfare services and a firm belief in the value of preventive measures. This point of view is essential in order to keep pace with changes in social and economic conditions, with growing insights into social problems, and with evolving concepts of human well-being.
5. The Chest and Council movement, whatever its expression in organizational form, is a co-operative undertaking of individuals, health and welfare agencies, and citizen organizations, working together to meet human needs through voluntary and tax-supported services.
6. The participation of citizens broadly representative of all community interests is a right which must be exercised if the Chest and Council movement is to realize fully its objectives.
7. The Chest and Council movement can and does serve as a means of translating into creative action the concept of human brotherhood.

Objectives

In recognition of these basic concepts we seek to:

1. Promote preventive measures of social welfare in the interest of strengthening the general welfare of society.
2. Secure a balanced health and welfare program.
3. Foster co-operation among all voluntary and tax-supported health and welfare agencies.
4. Bring into effective participation all constructive forces in the community.

5. Create awareness and understanding of human needs and community problems which lead to continuous improvement in health and welfare services and a consequent strengthening of community life.
6. Encourage adequate support of an orderly, efficient and humane system of essential voluntary and tax-supported services.

Obligations of Professional Conduct

In order to carry out the basic concepts and achieve these objectives of the Chest and Council movement, professional personnel employed in Chests and Councils are obligated to:

1. Maintain high standards of personal and professional integrity.
2. Respect individual differences of race, national origin, religion, political affiliation, social status and personal characteristics, realizing that our culture is enriched and strengthened because of its diversity.
3. Assist board members, other volunteers and professional associates in gaining wider perspective and understanding of local, state, and national health and welfare needs. Stimulate appreciation of the total community health and welfare program and the relationship of its component parts. Encourage citizens to assume their responsibility in the interests of the common good.
4. Hold a firm commitment to the goals and objectives of the Chest and Council movement, and encourage a similar conviction in others.
5. Accept assignments with due regard for one's own limitations and the appropriate purposes of the organization.
6. Be thorough and objective in assembling and presenting information and facts.
7. Inculcate a spirit of partnership in working with voluntary and tax-supported health and welfare services, and endeavor to resolve differences in an atmosphere of mutual respect and confidence.
8. Strive continuously to grow in knowledge and skill and contribute to the advancement of the profession.
9. Assume responsibility for sharing knowledge with and contributing to the professional growth of colleagues.
10. Discipline the desire to seek personal recognition and acclaim.
11. Be alert and receptive to the ideas and suggestions of all those with whom we work.
12. Provide an accurate accounting of our stewardship.

DEDICATION

As professional workers committed to the Chest and Council movement as an important means of strengthening community well-being, we subscribe to these obligations of professional conduct and pledge ourselves to the realization of these goals.

50

Community Planning for Social Welfare—a Policy Statement [1]

By UNITED COMMUNITY FUNDS AND COUNCILS
OF AMERICA, INC.

This statement was prepared originally for Community Chests and Councils of America by a special committee of the Advisory Committee on Health and Welfare Planning, and was approved by the Board of Directors of CCC, September 28, 1950.

Preamble

THE EXPERIENCE OF OVER 1,200 communities has established the soundness of certain principles and procedures in the field of community organization for social welfare. A need has been expressed in the Health and Welfare Planning Advisory Committee for a statement, formally approved by the Board of Directors, covering the objectives, philosophy, principles, and procedures of community planning. While no such statement ever could be considered final, it is clear that the community organization movement has reached a stage of maturity which permits the drafting of such a position of policy for the guidance of local communities and of Three C's staff in its consultation work.

Upon recommendation of the Advisory Committee on Health and Welfare Planning the Board of Directors has approved this "policy

---

[1] Adapted from publication of same title (New York: Community Chests and Councils of America, Inc., 1950). By permission of United Community Funds and Councils of America, Inc.

statement" with respect to community planning for social welfare. It is thought that agreement upon these possibly self-evident objectives, principles, and methods will sharpen thought, improve practice, and narrow differences in the community organization field. The relation between what is now called "planning" and "financing" will thus cease to be identified with particular structures but will become a set of defined functions, the performance of which would be facilitated and protected in various ways, depending on local conditions.

The term "social welfare" as used in this statement refers to the well-being of people in the broad sense, encompassing health, social adjustment, recreation, and environmental conditions. Social welfare programs include preventive and treatment services in health, welfare, and recreation, whether under governmental or voluntary auspices.

I. *Philosophy*

1. Each individual has a basic responsibility to meet his own needs to the extent of his ability. But people are interdependent; the welfare of each affects the welfare of all. It is natural and necessary, then, that people form organizations to work for their mutual benefit.
2. The need for community planning for social welfare stems from the wants and desires of all the people; and all interests and elements of the population have a right and a responsibility to participate in it.
3. Community planning for social welfare is concerned with the welfare of the community and the total life of the individual, taking account of his physical, mental, emotional, and spiritual needs.
4. Fundamental to community planning is acceptance of change and development of social services to keep pace with changes in social conditions, in knowledge of social problems, and in concepts of human well-being.
5. While agencies and organizations in the American system are self-determining and autonomous they are mutually interrelated. They come together in a joint co-operative effort in community planning. Community planning, then, is a democratic process in which agencies and organizations, as well as individuals, participate through representatives of their own choosing.

II. *Objectives*

1. To enable citizens to work together to determine needs and to develop the social welfare resources to meet these needs.
2. To bring about community recognition and understanding of the needs of people, and to stimulate interest and participation in meeting them effectively.

3. To bring about an orderly development of a well-balanced social welfare program.
4. To work for prevention and elimination of social conditions which cause social problems.
5. To promote the highest possible quality and efficiency in the operation of services.
6. To promote effective co-ordination of effort.
7. To make services readily available to all people as and when they need them.

III. *Principles*

1. Sound community planning encompasses the whole range of social welfare needs and considers all available resources— governmental and voluntary, local, state, and national—for serving these needs.
2. Sound community planning focuses on the needs of people and is concerned with efforts to meet these needs as effectively as possible rather than limiting itself to a series of adjustments of existing services.
3. Community planning must take into account the administrative and specialized planning which is done by service agencies, groups of agencies, and other organizations in the community. The community planning organization has no administrative authority over participating agencies, organizations, and individuals. Action in community planning, then, depends primarily on full participation, mutual agreement, and education.
4. Effectiveness in securing results depends on broad representation of all community interests, consideration of all pertinent points of view and the joint participation of both laymen and persons engaged in professions related to social welfare.
5. Good community planning requires use of objective, accurate, and comprehensive research into the nature of the needs of people and the most effective means of servicing them. Fact finding provides a solid basis for the group thinking which is essential for decision and action.
6. Community planning takes into account the means of financing social welfare services, whether from governmental or voluntary sources. The amount of money needed, the methods of securing the funds, and the allocation of funds are essential elements. This means that effective working relationships must exist between community planning groups and federated financing groups, governmental appropriating bodies, and other financing bodies.
7. There should be effective working relationships between planning for social welfare and planning that is done with respect

to the physical, cultural, and economic aspects of community life.

8. Local, state-wide, and nation-wide planning are interrelated, and there must be effective channels of communication and productive interaction among them.

9. The successful application of these principles requires the services of professionally qualified community planning staff.

IV. *Methods and Procedures Essential in Community Planning for Social Welfare*

1. The membership of the community planning organization should include all voluntary and governmental agencies which conduct programs having a sincere purpose of social welfare as defined in the preamble, other organizations directly interested in community social welfare, and interested individuals. To be eligible for membership an agency, organization, or individual should subscribe to the purposes and objectives of the community planning organization.

2. The member agencies and organizations should be represented by delegates of their own choosing in the delegate assembly in which the ultimate authority of the community planning organization resides. Such individuals have a responsibility to bring to co-operative planning the knowledge and points of view of their organizations and to promote knowledge and interest of their constituencies in community planning problems and activities.

3. There should be a governing board democratically elected by the constituency through the delegate assembly. This board should be representative of the various interests and geographic areas served by the community planning organization. It should include able leaders who are well informed about community needs and services chosen from among both the boards and staffs of member agencies, from other organizations, and from the community at large.

4. Members of the governing board should serve on a rotating basis with a definite limitation on the length of continuous service by any person. Similarly, there should be turnover in the membership of committees, and in other ways a breadth and variety of participation should be fostered.

5. The community planning organization should serve as the central clearinghouse on program planning for social welfare through its use by operating agencies, civic organizations, and other groups planning in special fields.

6. The community planning organization should continuously and systematically gather significant facts about the community,

its social welfare needs and the adequacy and effectiveness of services to meet those needs.

7. Any specific recommendation or decision should be based on adequate fact finding and careful analysis of significant data using good research methods and qualified professional consultants to assure sound judgments.

8. The internal structure of the community planning organization should be such as to insure that each decision is arrived at as the result of group thinking which includes the participation of persons representative of the principal interests affected by the the decision. Participation need not be limited to the formal constituency.

9. The community planning organization should develop plans for needed new services, elimination of outmoded or duplicating services and readjustment of existing services better to meet current community needs.

10. The community planning organization has a primary responsibility for the promotion of action which will result in the successful application of conclusions reached through its studies, projects, and committees. In promoting action the community planning organization needs to use methods which in the end will result in the most favorable reception to recommendations which require decisions by the groups concerned. Among such methods are the following: maintenance of full and continued channels of communication, active association in the study process by groups and individuals concerned, progress reports to interested groups, preliminary informal clearance of findings, support of legislative proposals and appropriations, and consultation with those who put recommendations into effect.

11. The community planning organization should seek to improve the quality of community services by promoting community acceptance of good standards of work; providing opportunities for agency staffs and volunteers to come together for understanding and sharing viewpoints, and working together on community problems; providing consultation services; conducting institutes; and other means.

12. One of the appropriate functions of the community planning organization is to provide common services to member agencies which will help them do a better job and which no one agency could provide so well or so economically for itself. Among the possible services of this kind are the following: social service exchange, volunteer service bureau, information and referral bureau, Christmas bureau, directory of community resources, common building and office space, joint insurance or purchasing plans, central bookkeeping.

13. The community planning organization should sponsor public meetings, publish studies and reports, and use the various media of public information to quicken public awareness of community problems and develop an understanding of how voluntary and governmental agencies are dealing with these problems.

14. The community planning organization for social welfare should develop definite channels for two-way flow of information and productive interaction with other planning organizations whose functions are outside of but closely related to social welfare, such as physical, cultural, and economic planning bodies.

15. The community planning organization should have an executive secretary who is qualified by professional competence, personal integrity, leadership qualities, and social vision, and who is able to command the confidence and respect of professional agency workers and lay leaders. Other professional staff members should have similar qualifications.

16. Since the community planning organization must be on a stable and continuing basis, financial support should be provided by federated financing and other major financing bodies, public and private.

17. It is essential that conditions exist which will promote two-way flow of information and productive interaction between community planning and financing, whether the financing is through federated campaigns, taxation, or other methods. Among these conditions are the following:

a. In relationship to all kinds of financing:

(1) Recognition that expenditures should be based on a study of community needs in relation to the total financial resources of the community. Financing groups should look to the community planning organization for studies of needs and recommendations about program priorities. The planning group, in turn, should look to financing groups for advice about financing potentials.

(2) Recognition that both planning and financing are concerned with promoting better social welfare services to meet community needs.

(3) Recognition that both planning and financing are interested in developing citizen awareness of social needs and an attitude of community-mindedness.

(4) Recognition that one of the functions of the community planning organization is to identify needs to be met by government and by voluntary effort, and present such findings to the service agencies and to the

appropriate financing body whether it be government, federated financing, or a group financed independently.

(5) The active participation of representative and influential lay and professional leadership in both community planning and financing groups.

(6) Mutual understanding and respect between the people involved primarily in community planning and those involved primarily in fund raising, including both those who are professionally engaged and those serving as volunteers.

(7) Some key leaders who are actively involved in both planning and financing so as to provide direct channels of communication between the two activities. The governing board of the community planning organization should include representatives of voluntary and governmental financing groups.

(8) Awareness by community planning of the problems of fund raising and the attitudes of the contributing public and of the fiscal and taxing problems of government.

(9) Strong support of community planning methods and objectives by financing groups.

b. Special factors in relationship to federated financing:

(1) Freedom of both community planning and federated financing from control by any special interest group.

(2) Acceptance of goal setting and allocation of funds raised in federated financing as a joint responsibility of community planning and federated financing. In this joint participation, the fund raising group has final responsibility for disbursing funds, and the community planning group has the basic responsibility for determining program needs to be financed. Each has a responsibility to make its findings and decisions known to the community.

(3) Acceptance of the principle that community planning needs to have a realistic understanding of fund-raising possibilities but cannot be dominated by factors of campaign expediency.

(4) Recognition that professional staff service is needed in both community planning and federated financing.

(5) Recognition that federated financing should provide financial support for the community planning organization.

c. Special factors in relationship to governmental appropriating bodies:

(1) A clearly defined policy in the community planning organization in regard to the channels and methods of taking a responsible stand on public issues, including legislation and public appropriations.

(2) Active participation in community planning by administrators of public programs, members of public boards, and key public officials such as commissioners, municipal and county managers, councilmen, legislators, fiscal agents, and others whose responsibilities for budgeting, policy making, financing, and legislation affect the work of tax-supported agencies.

(3) Recognition that it is appropriate for governmental funds to be allocated to the community planning organization.

d. Special factors in relationship to groups financed by other means:

(1) Recognition that groups financed independently have a responsibility to participate in co-operative efforts to study all community needs and weigh their relative importance.

(2) Recognition of ultimate agency autonomy in decisions on financing plans, as in other administrative matters.

(3) Acceptance of joint responsibility for determining program goals and the funds needed to achieve these goals.

(4) Recognition that independently financed groups have a responsibility for sharing in the financial support of the community planning organization.

18. Various structural arrangements are possible for the relationship of community planning and financing groups provided that the above outlined methods and procedures are adhered to. No single pattern is applicable to all situations, and the most important thing is to have effective co-operation.

V. *Methods and Procedures in Developing or Revising Structures*

In any consideration of structural arrangements or working arrangements between community planning and federated financing, both interests should participate on an equal basis in the approach to the problem, in the study of it, in the formulation of conclusions, and in subsequent action. The knowledge and desires of contributors, agencies, civic organizations, and the general public should all be given full consideration. Tradition, community attitudes, and general acceptance of one plan or another are factors to be considered in arriving at a practical arrangement which will promote a high degree of mutual confidence and satisfactory working relationships.

51

Chest, Council, and Agency Relationships[1]

By STUDY COMMITTEE, SIDNEY HOLLANDER, CHAIRMAN

If harmonious relationships between the individual agencies and the central planning bodies, the welfare council and the community chest, are disrupted, as they sometimes are, tensions and disagreements may arise. In order to discover the nature of the inciting forces involved in such situations and to recommend solutions, Community Chests and Councils of America and the National Social Welfare Assembly in 1949 set up a study committee composed of 11 lay and professional members. Sidney Hollander, who served as chairman, was at this time a member, not only of the boards of the two sponsoring agencies, but also of the National Urban League and the Family Welfare Association of America.

The report of the committee published two years later has lasting value. It reviews first the developmental background of welfare agencies, including central planning and financing bodies, and then examines specific problems. The main areas in which tensions most frequently occur appear to be: (1) organizational relationships, (2) financial support of agencies, (3) conflicting national and local pressures affecting agency programs, and (4) division of responsibility for interpretation and public relations among the groups involved. Typical problems with suggested solutions are discussed under each head.

---

[1] Excerpted from *Toward Improved Chest-Council Agency Relations*—An analysis of current relationship problems among Chest-Councils and member agencies and suggestions for solution based on experience (New York: Association Press, 1951), pp. 1-36.

Organizational Problems and Sources of Misunderstanding

MISUNDERSTANDINGS and tensions between chests and their member agencies have sometimes arisen because of a lack of mutual understanding of the extent and nature of the responsibilities of each. Sometimes they are due to a conflict of purposes. Operating methods and procedures have also been a source of misunderstandings. This section of the report attempts to identify some of the major problems of organizational relationships and to suggest some ways by which such problems may be solved.

I. *Problem:*

The functions and responsibilities of agency boards and their freedom to discharge those responsibilities, together with the extent of the authority of the chest and council, need clarification.

For example, it is charged that some chests are guilty of undue interference in the management of the internal affairs of participating agencies. Strict "line-by-line" budgeting has been a source of tension.

The problem will yield to solution as there is an increased awareness and understanding of the functions and responsibilities of chests and of individual member agencies. The basic purpose of chests, Edward L. Ryerson has said, is "to help build the best possible program of health and welfare for our American communities . . . chests must never forget or leave out the agencies, which are senior partners in this great co-operative enterprise . . . without their active and enthusiastic co-operation no great gain can really be made and consolidated." [2]

Participating agencies need to be aware that if chests are to discharge their function of trusteeship to the giving public, they must be concerned with the quality and character of the service given by agencies. The chest cannot evade the responsibility of assuring itself that the funds are spent for the purposes approved and that they are spent efficiently and wisely. Budget review is an essential process. Chests also have a responsibility for the development of a balanced program of community services. These responsibilities, however, cannot be met by dictatorial action on the part of the chest.

The community welfare council provides a mechanism through which joint planning can occur in an earnest effort to eliminate duplication and by which maximum effectiveness of services can be gained. All agencies have an obligation to the community to use the community

---

[2] Edward L. Ryerson, "Freedom Within Federation," *The United Way in Financing Health and Welfare Services* (New York: Community Chests and Councils of America, Inc., 1950), p. 8.

welfare council and to help make it an effective instrument for the improvement of community services. . . .

This chest-agency relationship is a partnership of equals. It has the strengths and weaknesses of all partnerships. Like all partnerships it is fraught with the hazards of serious misunderstandings. Some misunderstandings can be reduced if budget policies and procedures are determined jointly and outlined in a written statement. Such a statement should be the result of the deliberations of committees representing the agencies and the chest administration. The statement should outline the rights and responsibilities of both parties in the relationship. . . .

Understanding will be furthered if there is a procedure established to set the campaign goal on the basis of actual agency needs, combined with shrewd judgment about how much money can be raised in any given year. A goal should be both challenging and realistic.

Understanding will also be furthered by the attitudes which govern the annual budget review. The review should be conducted in the spirit of a conference, not an inquisition.

It is important that necessary budget adjustments be arrived at through joint discussion and consideration. When downward revisions are necessary, agencies are entitled to expect an individualized examination of needs rather than to be subjected to the easy device of flat, horizontal cuts. Courteous and understanding consideration of painful necessities builds good will. The right of agencies to appeal decisions of the budget committee to the board of the chest must be maintained.

The budgets of the central services of the chest and council should be subjected to the same policies and the same reviewing processes as those applied to participating agencies. . . .

In order to make board membership attractive to able men and women, there must be a maximum of freedom, within the necessary limitations of membership in a federation, for the board to develop the agency program. Strict "line-by-line" budget operation, under which an agency cannot make even minor adjustments between items in its budget, seems an unnecessary infringement on agency-operating responsibility.

While such freedom of action is essential to the development of vigorous agency programs, there must, however, be limitations placed on that freedom. The following limitations seem to be necessary for membership in a federation:

1. Agencies should be prepared to operate within their agreed-upon program and budget;

2. Agencies should refrain from making future commitments without consultation with the central planning body and the chest budget committee;

3. Agencies should weigh the effect in the community of their involvement in issues on which there are sharp differences of opinion. . . .

II. *Problem:*

Chest and council boards should represent community-wide interests. Some chests and councils do not observe this principle adequately.

Chest and council boards which secure and maintain community confidence must be representative of the principal elements in the community. . . .

III. *Problem:*

The failure of chests and councils to understand the relationship of local affiliates to their national organizations is one of the causes of misunderstandings and tensions.

. . . Local affiliates have a responsibility to inform their chest leaders of the structure and policies which guide or govern the local affiliate in its operations. Local affiliates have a responsibility to their national organization to follow agreed-upon national policies. . . .

The budget review process . . . offers one of the most useful opportunities for explaining and clarifying these relationships. While the primary purpose of the budget process is the review of financial data, the financial needs cannot be fully appreciated without knowledge of program and policies underlying financial plans.

Chest and council people have a responsibility to make a conscious and continuous effort to inform themselves regarding the policies of national agencies and the recommended procedures for the guidance of local affiliates. Only as chest and council leaders inform themselves on these matters can they deal intelligently with the problems which inevitably arise in the competition for limited funds.

Chest-council personnel will find national agencies to be useful sources of information, advice, and counsel, as they together develop a sense of common purpose. As the national agencies relate to local needs and local planning processes, they will increasingly aid in the development of balanced local programs. . . .

IV. *Problem:*

The lack of agency understanding and acceptance of chest-council policies and procedures is a frequent source of tension and difficulty. Active resistance to these policies and procedures on some occasions by some agencies has led to open conflict.

. . . Chests and councils have an obligation to adopt policies and procedures consistent with the best prevailing practices. These policies should be made known to all participating agencies. Among these policies and procedures are the following:

1. formal budget conferences with committees which really represent different community and agency interests

2. opportunities to discuss financial problems throughout the year
3. equitable treatment
4. the right of appeal
5. support by the chest of high professional standards of agency practice and readiness to meet salary scales which will attract and hold trained personnel
6. proper accounting and financial reporting. . . .

V. *Problem:*

> *In some chests and councils it is believed that the policies of some national agencies are developed without proper regard for local needs and without adequate consultation with their local agencies and with local planning bodies.*

Greater confidence would be developed if more local participation were sought and secured in the formation of national policies and programs. Encouragement should be given by national agencies to the development of channels through which the local community point of view can be given expression in national agency deliberations. There should be an effort to secure points of view of local community leaders along with agency points of view of needs in the local community.

. . . National agency programs at their best grow from a broad awareness of the needs of the nation and of the world as a whole. Yet these programs must also be based on and related to the needs of the local communities, and integrated with local services. Conflict and tension arises if an over-all view of the local community's need is ignored in developing agency programs.

Thoughtful chest-council leadership, on its part, needs to recognize that national policies generally tend to be developed from an expression of local community needs. Chest-council leadership must also realize that national standards tend to improve the quality of local agency service. Mutual confidence and mutual respect will lead chest-council leaders and national agency leaders to recognize their essential partnership in building sounder community life.

VI. *Problem:*

> *Local affiliates of national organizations sometimes seem to find themselves in conflict with local planning bodies as a result of policies adopted by their national organizations.*

. . . There is no easy solution of this problem. It is important for an agency to be loyal to its constituency and to its own purposes. At the same time it must be deeply aware of local community needs across the entire front. . . . Opening and maintaining channels for local participation in national planning will be an important aid. Freedom to modify programs on the local scene in light of local needs helps prevent conflict. Inflexibility, on either side, leads to hostility between local affiliates of national organizations and their chests.

Chest-council executives have a responsibility to make known the facts regarding community needs as revealed in their planning processes and in the policies of the chest. In co-operation with the local affiliate (member) they should avail themselves of the opportunity for face-to-face discussion with field representatives of the national agencies and share with them knowledge of local situations.

On the other hand, national agency representatives when requested by or in co-operation with their local affiliate (member) have an obligation to discuss with chest-council executives their aims and objectives as they affect local communities. Face-to-face discussion and sufficient flexibility to modify national programs in light of local needs can reduce such conflicts and tensions and develop satisfactory solutions.

VII. *Problem:*

> *The "channels of communication" between chests and councils and national organizations are not always clearly understood. . . .*

Conferences from time to time by national representatives of chests and councils and national agencies will provide a medium for improved understanding of objectives and plans of national agencies. In some of the conferences, representatives of local chests and councils and of local operating agencies can well participate to make sure that local points of view are taken into full account. . . .

Financial Relationships and Tensions

Financial problems have been the cause of many misunderstandings and tensions between chests and their member agencies. This section will seek to identify and analyze some of these problems and to suggest ways in which they can be solved.

I. *Problem:*

> *Funds provided through chests have in some communities been inadequate to finance essential services on an effective basis. This problem has two aspects: (1) Operating budgets have been considered inadequate by some agencies . . . ; (2) Provision has been inadequate for sufficient reserves for necessary major maintenance and equipment replacements, and for meeting capital needs. . . .*

The following suggestions merit consideration by chests and by agencies:

1. Review of the fund-raising machinery by the chest; setting a goal by the chest that will produce the greatest possible amount of money; building up the strongest possible campaign organization;

2. Responsibility by the chest for making the community aware of unmet needs;

3. Hearty participation in and support of Red Feather Campaigns by member-agency board and staff members. This step assumes a type of campaign organization in which agency representatives can participate effectively;

4. Understanding by the agencies of the many factors, such as unfavorable economic situations, which may affect the amount of money which can be raised;

5. Review by chests of their policies toward givers, so that the chest will give leadership for adequate financing of a sound community social welfare program, rather than primarily providing "protection" for givers.

6. Fair budgeting processes and allocation of available funds to types of services and to individual agencies and the avoidance of across-the-board percentage cuts;

7. The necessity of "deferred maintenance and equipment reserves" for agencies with extensive building facilities, particularly for income-producing units, as residences, food services, and so on, should be recognized in order to maintain continued earnings and prevent the absorption of capital assets through current use.

8. Steady progress in overtaking capital fund needs by member agencies with campaigns timed properly after clearance with the chest. Chest-council leaders should give all possible support to approved capital efforts conducted by member-agencies;

9. Increased agency self-support through membership and other fees based on higher costs for service through charges to those able to pay in whole or in part; serious consideration by the agency of economies and changes recommended by chests. (This is not intended to apply to registration fees of membership organizations.)

II. *Problem:*

> *Some agency leaders and some chest-council leaders feel that local budget review processes are not yet satisfactory.*

1. The basic principles of budget conferences . . . should be observed. Budgets are ways of achieving balanced programs, as well as ways by which agency services are financed. Campaign goals and campaign efforts must be based on agency needs for adequate services; but budgets must be related realistically to fund-raising expectations as well as to needs. Fair and competent representation of different points of view must be provided. . . .

2. A plan for regular turn-over in a portion of budget committee personnel can well be considered. . . .

3. Effective presentation of needs by agencies is essential. Agencies should develop greater ingenuity in describing their services and their needs to budget committees.

4. Budget committees should welcome suggestions for budget procedure changes by agencies.

III. *Problem:*

   Some agencies have been pressing plans for supplemental fund raising for operating budgets.

1. The philosophy and the advantages of federated financing can well be reviewed periodically with participating agencies by chests. The hazards of certain kinds of supplemental fund raising on the federated campaigns should be realized by agency leaders. Independent, supplementary campaigns for operating funds may jeopardize the federated financing process. At the same time, chest leaders should recognize that some people wish to support particular services and will give more generously if they know that their contributions will help support these services more adequately. Adequate goals, effective campaigns, and sound planning and allocation procedures will help build such confidence. Federated financing can be a way of providing more adequate financial support for individual agencies and a means of achieving a sounder community wide program.

2. Mutually acceptable definitions and agreements should be reached about supplemental fund-raising efforts, including individual memberships, if such efforts are to be held. Bona fide membership efforts should be encouraged. They can be a source of strength to individual agencies and to the whole community service structure. They ought not to be financial campaigns in disguise. . . .

IV. *Problem:*

   How can order be brought into the confused situation of financing national services? . . . Can a system of quotas be developed which will be equitable for communities and yet provide adequate funds for national services? . . .

1. Continued search and research can well be made for equitable quota plans which can be applied both to organizations which provide nation-wide health and social welfare programs and to national membership organizations. . . .

2. General acceptance should be sought of the principle that chests should support national agency services. . . .

3. Mutually acceptable ways of helping validate soundly prepared budgets of national organizations must be developed. . . .

The national budget review process has weaknesses, its proponents concede. A sound basis for appraising national agency services has not yet been developed. Many chests have ignored the recommendations of the National Budget Committee. Some national agencies which have submitted their budgets for review have not found an appreciable increase in support from chests. The chests which support the national budget review process believe, however, that it has resulted in better relationships and more adequate support from some chests. . . .

Program Relationship Problems

A number of problems of relationships between chests and their member agencies center around the programs and services the agencies provide and wish to extend.

I. *Problem:*

> *How can a balance of services, in light of needs and resources, be achieved? . . . The total needs and resources of the community —local and national—should determine the specific and total services. . . . But in practice, the application of this basic principle has proved difficult.*

Greater acceptance by agencies and contributors alike of the principle of a balanced community plan of services would greatly aid in putting the basic principle more generally into practice. Broad and realistic community planning, with both governmental and voluntary resources being utilized, is essential. . . .

This process requires for its best functioning the development of criteria for judgment of needs and service performance. Local and national organizations and planning bodies should join in the development of these criteria. Different sets of criteria for different types of need (for example, for material relief and for leisure-time services) will probably be needed. . . .

The process of obtaining balance requires a consideration of both local and national forces and factors. Therefore, joint planning locally and nationally by local and national interests is essential. . . .

II. *Problem:*

> *How can a disregard for balance of local service be handled? Some national organizations have at times imposed program, standards, and budgets on their local affiliates without reference to the balance of services locally. On the other hand, some chests and councils have also, at times, imposed program, standards, and budgets without bringing the agencies concerned into consultation and without reference to the balance of services.*

The basic starting point in dealing with this problem is understanding and good will. . . .

Disregard of the balance of services locally may be reduced or removed by appreciation of the values in the "greatest good to the greatest number" of people, which can be achieved through a balanced program.

A sincere regard for a balanced program will flow from understanding of what a balanced program is and of its value to the chest, the agencies, and to the whole community. Active participation by agency representatives in council planning processes is essential. Councils and chests must, on the other hand, interpret and develop support for unmet needs. A broad view of community needs and resources must always be the "backdrop" against which service priorities are mutually determined.

III. *Problem:*

> *How can normal development of new services and growth of existing services be made possible? The problem is to find ways of attaining this normal development and growth without ignoring or violating sound community planning. . . .*

Voluntary social welfare's very existence rests upon free action by organized groups. The pioneering of certain agencies is responsible for many of today's essential services. Imagination and free initiative must be encouraged, but they must not run riot. There must be orderliness in meeting human needs, within the resources of a community. Consequently, the task is to find the balance between freedom and orderliness in social programs. The council can be used to achieve such balance. This goal must be recognized by both chests and agencies. It is as important to avoid chest and council suppression of new and needed services as it is to prevent organization of new services without reference to an over-all community plan. . . .

IV. *Problem:*

> *How can higher standards of performance and practice be encouraged? On the one hand, national organizations at times have been slow to deal with substandard local affiliates; and on the other hand, chests and councils have at times stood by inordinately long in the presence of indefinite continuation of marginal-need and substandard services. Who is responsible? How will such weaknesses be corrected?*

Basic standard setting for programs and for personnel is a primary function of national organizations, if it is based on local experience. It is also an appropriate concern of local agencies and chests and councils. The primary local responsibility is for the determination of the extent and quality of service in the light of generally accepted standards. National organizations concerned with higher standards can be helpful in local consultation regarding the application of their own standards. . . .

National qualifications for professional staff workers, however, may well be regarded as requisites for local affiliates. Unavailability of qualified workers or inability to finance qualified staff may, under extreme conditions, make employment of workers who meet national qualifications impracticable for a time, but ordinarily, national qualifications should be met.

Unilateral or independent action in these matters by either chest, council, or agencies is to be avoided. Consultation is mutually advantageous.

Similarly in program standards, basic national responsibility for their determination is balanced by local basic responsibility for determining the extent and quality of program in the light of the national standards.

The maintenance of good standards of personnel, of program, and of organization may be facilitated by a joint chest-agency agreement on a "timetable" for improvement and for periodic appraisal of needs and performance in the light of standards. Evaluation of services may be done through local surveys and studies and through national organization examination. . . .

Interpretation Questions and Tensions

Interpretation to the public of the total community program of social welfare and health services, and of the services of individual member agencies has been one of the particularly difficult problems involved in federated financing and joint planning.

Most of the tensions discussed in this report have been, at their core, problems of "internal" public relations, which is to say, human relations between people in chests and agencies. This is a form of public relations that should not be confused with publicity or public information. Yet relationships and attitudes within a federation's family are inevitably reflected, for better or worse, in the attitudes of the general public, and so have a direct effect on public interest and support. The public is not usually sympathetic to "jurisdictional disputes," no matter where they occur. When serious tensions arise in situations involving chest budgeting, goal setting, agency autonomy, and so on, they are generally due, not to lack of understanding by the public of agency services or reluctance to support federation, but rather to the faulty practice of federation by the federators themselves. All of this points up the fact that public relations is a clear function of "top administration." It cannot be relegated to a publicity department or committee but must always be the responsibility of chest and agency boards and executives.

It should also be noted that the basis of any sound public relations program is effective service by agencies and by the chest-council.

I. *Problem:*

Some agencies complain of a "power complex" on the part of their chests; some chests complain of a "me-and-my-agency" complex on the part of some of their agencies.

A frank review by both chests and member agencies of the principles and purposes of federation should be made periodically; the teamwork involved; the wide, democratic participation required; the sacrifices and compromises that may be called for; the rewards federation offers to those who *want* it to work, and who resolve to *make* it work; the alternatives to federation; study of successful chest-agency relations as they exist in many a community. Channels for expression of agency points of view must be opened and kept open; thus the machinery for policy making will be an effective reality.

II. *Problem:*

It is difficult to interpret to the public the total community program of health and welfare, and at the same time do full justice to the services of individual agencies. . . .

1. Interpretation to the public, both of the total program and of individual agency service, should be recognized as a joint responsibility of chest and agencies. Neither can do it alone; it is a job for teamwork. . . .

2. Chests can help public understanding by emphasizing in their campaign publicity that they are *not* direct-service agencies, by using such phrases as "Give *through* your Community Chest" (not *"to"*); and by giving to the fullest extent possible visibility and audibility to its member agency services. . . . A continuous year-round publicity program is clearly needed. The best year-round interpretation will be done by agencies, themselves. Chests should be alert to assist them, and to supplement their efforts. . . .

3. Agencies should, for their own sakes and that of their fellow agencies, lose no opportunity to let the public know by their own testimony that they are bona fide members of the chest. Failure to do so puts the whole burden of identification on the chest, and at best can be only fifty per cent successful. . . .

III. *Problem:*

Agencies sometimes sense a conflict between the interpretation program of their local chests and that of their national organizations.

1. This problem should be discussed by national agencies, . . . at the highest executive levels and a sincere effort made to reach some definite conclusions and policies. . . .

2. (a) National agencies should lend cordial support to local chest campaigns by editorials in their publications, reminding their local affiliates of the stake of the agency in local federations and urging active participation in local campaigns. (b) Whenever possible, they should include some mention of the fact that their local units are members of community chests in their own national publicity programs, via radio, magazines, newspapers, and so forth, particularly during nation-wide observance of agency anniversaries, special "weeks," and so on. (c) National agencies could include in the program packets they send their members more materials designed to increase co-operation between chests and agencies, with practical how-to-do-it suggestions based on current good experience. (d) Several national agencies have brought out a new design for a symbol, combining the agency symbol with the Red Feather for use when appropriate.

3. CCC, as the national association of chests and councils, should seek the co-operation of national agencies in giving visibility and audibility to various Red Feather services in the material it produces for use by its member chests. The series of pictorial campaign posters and year-round leaflets, prepared with the help of national agencies and featuring Red Feather services, with the legend "Give to the Girl Scouts (YWCA, YMCA, Boys Club, Family Service Society, et cetera) through your Community Chest," was a step in the right direction. CCC should step up its year-round promotion of good chest-agency relations through its monthly public relations kit, press releases, news bulletins, national public relations clinics, conferences, and so on.

In Conclusion: Chests, as exponents of sound community organization, should be keenly aware of the responsibilities that go with financial strength, and realize that such strength can be properly exercised only if there is full opportunity for participation by member agencies in all the functions of a chest, be they fund raising, planning, standards setting, or interpretation.

Obviously, chests and agencies both exist for one basic purpose: the welfare and growth of people. This is a goal that should be approached in an attitude of co-operation. It will never be reached by the propaganda of words. It will require the propaganda of deeds.

52

Community Welfare Councils—What They Are
and What They Do[1]

By UNITED COMMUNITY FUNDS AND COUNCILS
OF AMERICA, INC.

Selections 52 to 55, inclusive, are concerned with the nature and functions of councils and their organizational relationships with chests. This, the first in the series, was published by CCC (now UCFC) as a practical guide for community leaders interested in establishing a council or improving one already in existence. It deals with such questions as membership, organization, activities, and relationship to the chest and the local government. The reader may also be interested in *Miracles Every Other Tuesday,* a collection of thirty-four short and lively "success stories" of councils in action.[2]

On Getting Things Done

NOT LONG AGO A YOUNG GERMAN rediscovered America. A refugee from fascism, he had found work here in a social agency. Coming back from a Community Council meeting one day he had a gleam of excitement in his eye. "I have just discovered what is so great about Amer-

[1] Excerpted from *Teamwork in Our Town Through a Community Welfare Council,* rev. ed. (New York: Community Chests and Councils of America, Inc., 1954), pp. 1-31. By permission of United Community Funds and Councils of America, Inc.

[2] Community Chests and Councils of America, Inc., now United Community Funds and Councils of America, Inc. (New York: 1953), 47 pp.

PROBLEMS AND SERVICES: A FRAME OF REFERENCE

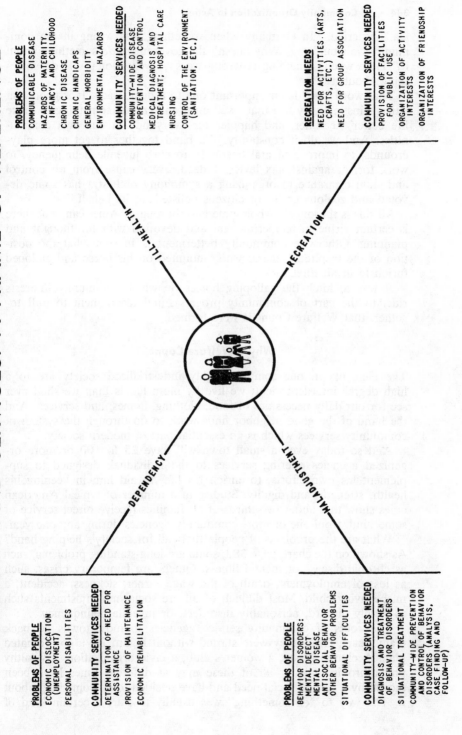

PROBLEMS OF PEOPLE

COMMUNICABLE DISEASE
HAZARDS OF MATERNITY,
    INFANCY, AND CHILDHOOD
CHRONIC DISEASE
CHRONIC HANDICAPS
GENERAL MORBIDITY
ENVIRONMENTAL HAZARDS

COMMUNITY SERVICES NEEDED

COMMUNITY-WIDE DISEASE
    PREVENTION AND CONTROL
MEDICAL DIAGNOSIS AND
    TREATMENT; HOSPITAL CARE
NURSING
CONTROL OF THE ENVIRONMENT
    (SANITATION, ETC.)

RECREATION NEEDS

NEED FOR ACTIVITIES (ARTS,
    CRAFTS, ETC.)
NEED FOR GROUP ASSOCIATION

COMMUNITY SERVICES NEEDED

PROVISION OF FACILITIES
    FOR PUBLIC USE
ORGANIZATION OF ACTIVITY
    INTERESTS
ORGANIZATION OF FRIENDSHIP
    INTERESTS

ILL-HEALTH

RECREATION

DEPENDENCY

MALADJUSTMENT

PROBLEMS OF PEOPLE

ECONOMIC DISLOCATION
    (UNEMPLOYMENT)
PERSONAL DISABILITIES

COMMUNITY SERVICES NEEDED

DETERMINATION OF NEED FOR
    ASSISTANCE
PROVISION OF MAINTENANCE
ECONOMIC REHABILITATION

PROBLEMS OF PEOPLE

BEHAVIOR DISORDERS:
    MENTAL DEFECT
    MENTAL DISEASE
    ANTISOCIAL BEHAVIOR
    OTHER BEHAVIOR PROBLEMS
SITUATIONAL DIFFICULTIES

COMMUNITY SERVICES NEEDED

DIAGNOSIS AND TREATMENT
    OF BEHAVIOR DISORDERS
SITUATIONAL TREATMENT
COMMUNITY-WIDE PREVENTION
    AND CONTROL OF BEHAVIOR
    DISORDERS (ANALYSIS,
    CASE FINDING AND
    FOLLOW-UP)

ica," he cried. "In Germany when something was wrong in the community we would say, 'Why doesn't the government *do* something about it?' Here when something is wrong we say, 'Why don't WE do something about it?' "

That word "we" is an important one to a democracy. It is good that citizens instinctively feel that "we" must and *can* do something to make life better, healthier, and happier for everybody in our own communities. And we do it constantly. We band together to get more playgrounds, to improve mental hospitals, to curb juvenile delinquency, to work for, or against, tax levies. Indeed, every cause from rat control and slum clearance to organizing a symphony orchestra has some devoted and zealous group of citizens enlisted on its behalf.

All this is thoroughly wholesome and thoroughly American. But there is certain virtue in tempering zeal and devotion with forethought and planning. Otherwise community betterment is in somewhat the position of the inspired General who "mounted on his horse and galloped furiously in all directions."

It was to hitch the galloping horses on which community interests ride, to the cart of community progress, and teach them to pull together, that Welfare Councils were formed.

Why a Welfare Council?

The elements in our complex highly industrialized society are to a high degree interdependent; we live by more hands than we shall ever see for our daily necessities of food, clothing, homes, and services. And the hand of the good neighbor finds work to do through the system of community services which is an essential part of modern society.

And so today even a small town will have 25 to 100 or more organized agencies offering services to the individual, designed to supplement his own efforts, to enrich his life, to aid him in keeping his health, strength, and dignity. Studies in a number of typical American cities show that about two-thirds of all families receive direct service of some kind, from one or more community agencies during any one year.

What are the problems of people that call for society's helping hand? As shown on the chart, page 383, some are long-standing problems, such as chronic disease or mental illness. Others are temporary crises, such as loss of employment, death of the wage earner, sickness, accident, a misbehaving child. Most difficult of all are social maladjustments such as family discord, personality disorders, or juvenile delinquency.

The roots of community service agencies in most towns go back many years. Often they were started without regard for a co-ordinated plan. A church group, a women's club, a civic organization, a wealthy philanthropist, any or all of these may at different times have been moved by a certain social need and have decided to do something about it. The way to "do something" was usually to start a certain kind of agency. From time to time the city, county, and state governments, too, established health and welfare agencies. Assuming that all of these agencies were at one time needed, is it not sensible for a community to ask itself: Are they still needed to the same degree? Are they working together effectively? Do they seem to duplicate each other's efforts? Are they keeping their programs up to date? Have new needs sprung up that our town has been neglecting? Are the specialists—the doctors, lawyers, social workers, teachers, nurses, psychologists, counselors and others—working together as a team? Answers to questions like these will be found only as citizens get together to find the facts and act upon them.

Social services are expensive. A study made in 1952 shows that a total of $57.81 per capita was spent for health, welfare, and recreation services in 15 typical urban communities. A town of 100,000 may be pretty sure that its people get between four and six million dollars worth of these services each year.

Each individual has a personal stake in the health, welfare, and recreation services of the community. He may participate in one of these ways:

(1) *as a direct consumer,* through use of a clinic, a playground, a family agency, for example; or through membership in such organizations as the Scouts, the YMCA, or YWCA;

(2) *as a professional worker* who operates a service (a social worker, doctor, lawyer, nurse, psychologist or other front-line worker);

(3) *as a volunteer* who serves on a policy-forming board or committee of an agency or assists in program activities;

(4) *as a financial supporter.* Literally everybody, directly or indirectly, supports health and welfare services, many by voluntary contributions, and all by the payment of taxes.

All this natural flow of interest by organizations and individuals will accomplish more good if somewhere in town there is a clearinghouse for ideas, plans, and action; a piece of common ground where in good democratic fashion the many groups concerned can come together to look at the whole picture of community needs, evaluate present services, and agree on next steps in achieving an orderly and adequate program of health and welfare.

Nearly 500 cities and towns have found that clearinghouse, that common ground, in their Community Welfare Council.

Such a council can co-ordinate the work of existing agencies, both voluntary and tax-supported; can locate unmet needs and find ways and means to meet them; can eliminate duplicating or outmoded services and improve the quality of those that remain. It can work for the *prevention* of social ills as well as their treatment. And in the doing of all these things, it will constantly be fulfilling its own highest purpose—to promote richer, happier, more productive lives for all the people.

Who Will Belong to the Council?

Since we have seen that practically every organization and every individual has a stake in health and welfare services, it is clear that any Council worth its salt will have a very broad and inclusive membership. It will be democratic from the ground up. The first step in making it so is to get these three groups in the Council's membership:

1. Representatives from the boards and staffs of tax-supported and voluntary health, welfare, and recreation agencies
2. Representatives of civic and professional organizations
3. Individual citizens chosen because of their interest, knowledge, and competence.

What Does a Council Do?

If so many groups take part in community planning, how does anything ever get done? The answer is that things get done *because* of this broad participation. Councils have a remarkable record of practical accomplishments, using only the power of facts, group opinion, and agreement on what is best for the common good.

Here are just a few things that one Council did in a recent year:

Studied and approved a plan to establish a community center.

Worked out plans for continuing essential parts of the service of an agency which was terminated.

Developed a plan for establishment of a new state-wide health agency and secured agreement that it absorb an existing local agency.

Made studies which led to the revamping of two agencies.

Secured adoption of a Standard Ordinance and Code for better restaurant sanitation.

Secured an effective city program for inspection and licensing of foster homes.

Carried out a demonstration project which showed that with better staff service, half of the girls in an institution could be returned to their homes or homes of relatives.

Worked out a plan for better co-operation between public schools and social agencies.

Made numerous agency studies at the request of the Community Chest Budget Committee and other groups.

Operated a Social Service Exchange, a Christmas Clearing Exchange, a Central Information Bureau, and a Volunteer Service Bureau.

Sponsored over two dozen public meetings for discussion of current issues.

Organization Chart for a Typical Council

| Public health, welfare and recreation agencies | Private health, welfare and recreation agencies | Civic and professional organizations | Interested individual citizens |

COUNCIL DELEGATE BODY

This is the basic membership body. It is made up of two delegates from each member agency and organization, plus individuals serving as members at large.

Nominating Committee

BOARD OF DIRECTORS

Majority elected by delegates

Chairmen of divisions and departments

Representatives of Community Chest and local government

ADMINISTRATIVE COMMITTEES

Executive
Membership
Budget
Personnel

FUNCTIONAL DIVISIONS

Such as:
Health
Family and Child Welfare
Recreation and Group Work

DEPARTMENTAL COMMITTEES

Such as:
Research
Volunteer Service
Public Relations
Social Service Exchange
Information and Referral

PROJECT COMMITTEES

Such as:
Services to the Aging
Rehabilitation
Study of Court Services

NOTE: A simpler structure is desirable in small communities.

The programs of no two Councils will be exactly alike. However, the specific activities of a well-organized Council can usually be grouped under six headings: (1) Co-ordination; (2) Fact Finding; (3) Joint Action; (4) Improving Quality of Service; (5) Providing Common Services, and (6) Developing Public Understanding.

How Does a Council Work?

Planning and co-ordination don't just happen. Conscious and carefully guided effort are necessary, for there is no Aladdin's Lamp in community organization work. Citizen leaders will need to give much thought and time to the day-by-day process of promoting community well-being. But there must be an organized way for channeling their efforts.

Since organization is a means to an end rather than an end in itself, the machinery should be kept as simple and flexible as possible. Councils must guard against the danger of absorbing too much volunteer and staff time in matters of organization. The following are generally considered minimum requirements for the operation of a Council:

1. Articles of Incorporation
2. A constitution and by-laws
3. A basic membership body
4. A board of directors and officers
5. Committees, divisions, or departments to undertake specific projects
6. A professional staff, if possible
7. Financial support

A sample organization chart for a medium-sized Council is suggested on the preceding page. Don't use it as a set pattern. Work out your own "tailormade" organizational plan. A small community, for example, may not need permanent "divisions" in the three major fields of work. It may operate entirely through short-term project committees, each appointed for a specific purpose and discharged when the project is completed. A very large community may need more machinery than the chart indicates. When a city combines the jobs of joint planning and joint financing in one organization there would be additional departments of fund raising and budgeting. Most Councils, however, follow the general plan of the sample organization chart.

The board of directors is the Council's direct governing group. It decides which problems should get the Council's attention and which projects should be undertaken. It reviews committee reports and makes final decisions. By all means make the board a real governing body. It may delegate to an executive committee responsibility for handling emergency matters between board meetings, but such a committee should not usurp the board's own responsibility.

Because the board is the nerve center of the Council, it must reflect the major elements of the Council's membership and include its best leadership. A well-balanced board will always include the following six elements:

a. Well-informed citizens who are serving on the boards of member agencies in each field of work
b. Other citizens qualified to represent the points of view of major religious and racial groups, management, labor, the professions, and other civic interests
c. Capable professional workers from the staffs of member agencies in each field of work
d. Officials of local government
e. Community Chest leaders
f. Chairmen of Council standing committees, divisions or departments.

Small communities will find that much of the Council's business can be tackled directly by the board itself, thus making standing committees unnecessary. Many small Councils, and also a few large ones, make no attempt to set up standing program divisions or committees. Instead, the board of directors acts as the clearing point on matters in all fields of work, appointing special committees as needed. Councils following this plan will do well to schedule frequent meetings of the delegate body. The educational and co-ordinating objectives of the Council will be served by regular participation of the entire membership.

Larger communities are likely to need the kind of structure portrayed in the sample organization chart. In adidtion to the usual committees on administrative matters, such as membership, budget, and personnel, there will be standing "divisions" or committees in each broad functional field, advisory committees for the service departments, and project committees to undertake specific jobs.

Professional staff service is essential for best results. The executive secretary of a Council is the one who sees that the organization operates smoothly. Besides handling administrative details he contributes knowledge of health and welfare services, and skill in the processes of bringing about community improvement. He gathers or directs the gathering of facts needed by the Council. He cultivates the interest of citizen leaders and helps them apply their interest where it will do the most good. He keeps records and assures continuity in the Council operations.

The executive secretary should be qualified by training, temperament, and experience to practice sound methods of community organization. He should be familiar with problems and practices in all fields of health, welfare, and recreation. He will need imagination and vision and an appreciation of long-term values, in addition to the administrative abilities and personal qualities expected for a position of such importance in the community. He should be able to gain the confidence of volunteer leaders, and be himself accepted as a leader by professional agency workers.

Small communities may find it difficult to finance the full-time services of a professionally qualified executive. In considering the cost of staff service it is well to keep in mind that the Council's work, covering as it does all community needs and services, whether financed from governmental or voluntary sources, amounts to a very substantial enterprise. In an area of 50,000 population, for example, expenditures for health and welfare services will likely exceed $2,000,000. Measured against this figure or against the demonstrated value of staff service in communities which have it, the cost is relatively small.

If a full-time executive secretary cannot be employed, then an effort should be made to secure part-time service. Sharing an executive with the Community Chest is a common practice. This plan has the advantage of helping to bring together the closely related functions of planning and financing. The chief danger in such a setup is that campaign duties may absorb so much of the executive's time that the Council's program is neglected. If an executive is shared with the Chest he should be chosen jointly by the Chest and the Council and should be qualified for both money raising and community planning.

In communities of less than 25,000 population some other arrangement will probably be necessary. In some instances part-time service may be secured from a faculty member of a near-by university, or from a local resident who has had experience in health or welfare work but is no longer actively employed in it. Other possibilities are: arranging with a Council in a near-by large city for staff service; engaging a professional consultant for part-time service; joining with two or more neighboring Councils to employ an executive; sharing staff with some other local organization.

The Council, the Chest, and Local Government

Community planning inevitably affects distribution of funds, for program changes will require either increases or decreases in appropriations. Conversely, groups responsible for allocating funds make decisions that have program significance.

"How shall the Council be related to the Community Chest or United Fund?" This is a natural question, for the Chest or Fund is bound to be drawn into community planning.

The task of joint planning is so closely akin to that of joint financing that some communities have established a single organization to do both jobs. Such an organization will have a campaign section, a planning section, a budgeting section and such other sections, divisions, or departments as are needed. Some communities have chosen the name "United Community Services" for this type of operation, to indicate that it is concerned with planning and co-ordination of all services, both governmental and voluntary. A combined Chest and Council can be successful as the over-all planning organization only if the structure, the board, and the staff are established in full recognition of this broad concern. If the organization is set up primarily for financing the voluntary services, with a section added for planning, it will not be in a position to do the job. Whatever the plan of organization, it must recognize the interests of the agencies which provide the services, and of the public which both uses and supports them. The executive of a combined Chest and Council must have had training in both planning and financing.

The combined plan of organization has several advantages: (1) It helps assure unity in financing and planning activities, bringing together agency and contributor interests; (2) It requires less organizational structure and simplifies staff responsibility, especially in small communities which must rely upon a single staff for both financing and planning functions; (3) It may stimulate the interest of campaign leaders in planning as well as fund raising.

The more usual plan is to establish the Chest (or United Fund) and the Council as two distinct organizations. The Council is set up to be the central co-ordinating and planning body for all community welfare activities. It develops working relationships with the Chest or Fund as well as with other financing groups.

The separate plan of organization has the following advantages: (1) The planning function is more likely to get proper emphasis and less apt to be subordinated to the money-raising operations; (2) Full participation of public and other non-Chest agencies is easier to achieve; (3) The general public is more likely to view the Council as an impartial body not affected by factors of campaign expediency.

Often the Council and the Chest jointly employ one executive to serve both organizations. This arrangement has some of the advantages of both the combined and the separate organization plans in that while each organization retains its identity, close co-operation is assured. The disadvantage is that while the executive is responsible to two boards, the general public may not understand these relationships. However, the joint executive plan has proved practical, especially in smaller cities and towns which find it easier in this way to employ staff of high caliber. Of course, the selection of the executive must be done jointly and he must be qualified for both planning and financing responsibilities.

Whether entirely separate, jointly staffed or combined in one organization, the Council and the Chest will need to work together harmoniously. Certainly their objectives come together in the budgeting of funds raised annually for agency services. Usually the budget committee is a committee of the Chest, although some Councils carry direct responsibility for the review of agency budgets. However it may be set up, the budget committee should seek the advice of the Council on all matters of agency program and relationships. The Chest and Council will want to co-operate, too, in other activities such as public relations and research.

To facilitate close working relationships the following practices are in common use:

1. The Chest president and budget committee chairman are ex-officio members of the Council board.
2. The Council president is an ex-officio member of the Chest board and budget committee.
3. The Council selects some of the members of the Chest board and budget committee.
4. Staff service and office facilities are shared.
5. Joint committees on public relations and research are established.
6. The constitutions of both Chest and Council provide for using the Council in program planning matters.

"How shall the Council be related to local governments?" That is a question that should be asked more often than it is. More than half of all health and welfare expenditures come from tax funds. Departments of local government are key elements in the total community program. Teamwork between the public and voluntary agencies is, therefore, essential. The Council can hardly plan and co-ordinate community services without the full participation of the public agencies. Public officials should be able to turn to the Council as the central clearinghouse on health and welfare needs and services. For these reasons special attention should be given to securing the active participation of public agencies and of officials who have policy-forming and budget-making responsibilities.

How the Council Gets Results

A membership, a board, a sound organization plan, leadership—essential as all these are to a successful Council, they are only means to an end. Much of the Council's achievement will be intangible: the gradual growth of the spirit of teamwork; clearer allocations of responsibility; more skillful professional service; better public understanding of social needs and services. But the average citizen, including the contributor, will want to know about the more tangible accomplishments—new services started, old ones revamped and rejuvenated, duplications eliminated.

How does the Council get improvements such as these actually into effect? When a problem is recognized and decision is made to do something about it, there is a logical sequence of steps to be taken. They might be in this order:

1. Define the problem.
2. Get the facts about it, measure it, understand it.

3. Consider all opinions and all possible solutions.
4. Reach agreement among all concerned upon a plan of action.
5. Get action on the plan.

Number five is, of course, the stickler. When a plan of action has been agreed upon how can the Council get community acceptance and action? It has no authority over any of its agency members. Each of them is autonomous and administers its own affairs. Actually the Council itself does not *co-ordinate* or *plan for* organizations; rather it is the medium *through which* its members agree to plan and work together. The most solid successes may come from changes that have occurred in the attitudes of people as they have participated in the planning process.

But there will be times when the proposed improvement will depend upon action by persons who have not participated or who have not concurred with the majority opinion. What does the Council do then? The answer is that it must rely upon the power of facts, group thinking, and public opinion. This is the reason fact finding must be objective and thorough, participation broad and representative, and leadership devoted and able. But even these are not enough. There must be much patient negotiation, persuasion, and a meeting of minds based on the logic of the situation before the proposed improvement becomes an accomplished fact.

53

Criteria for a Good Welfare Council [1]

By CONFERENCE COMMISSION ON STRENGTHEN-
ING COUNCILS

In January, 1953, the first national Conference of Community Welfare Council Leaders was held in Cleveland. Some 375 industrial executives, business men, and representatives of various professions from all over the country were present, and participated in nine round-table discussions. The following report on principles of planning, the conditions necessary for success, and recommended methods of work for councils, summarizes the conclusions of the nine laymen constituting the Conference Commission on Strengthening Councils.

Six Principles

1. COMMUNITY PLANNING is a democratic process, and therefore all major community groups should be included in its activities. The Council should include governmental and voluntary agencies, lay and professional interests, and citizen organizations having a concern in health, welfare, and recreation. The Council should respect and build upon the autonomy of agencies and organizations.

[1] Excerpted from "What Makes a Good Council? A Summary Report of the Conference Commission on Strengthening Councils," *Community* (New York: Community Chests and Councils of America, Inc.), Vol. 28, March, 1953, pp. 126-127. By permission of United Community Funds and Councils of America, Inc.

2. Councils are concerned with the entire range of community services, whether under voluntary or governmental auspices.

3. Practical long-range goals for the improvement of community services, including broad priorities, in which all recommendations are related to community resources, should be established. These goals should be positive, and should represent an attack upon the causes of social problems. They should also be flexible and continuously re-evaluated.

4. The Council has a responsibility to work for expansions, retrenchments, and changes to bring about a balanced, efficient community program.

5. Planning and financing go hand in hand; a close liaison between the two is essential.

6. Local conditions should determine organization and structure; no one master plan can be applied in all localities.

Conditions for Success

Broad participation . . . Top-grade leadership . . . Good staff service . . . Equal status for planning and financing . . . Acceptance by the community of the value of planning.

Methods of Work

The following suggestions were commended to all local communities:

. . . Keep far enough ahead of the community to be progressive, yet close enough to be practical.

. . . Endeavor to interest many people, and particularly the most able people, in Council activities, including both "progressives" and "conservatives."

. . . Be sure the Council leadership is representative of broad community interests and not limited to narrow segments of the community.

. . . Give people an opportunity to take an active part in fact finding and decision making; eliminate "spectatoritis."

. . . Tackle issues of public importance even though they may be controversial. . . .

. . . Provide opportunity for all points of view to be heard. Be sensitive to the attitudes of individuals and groups; be tactful; be patient.

. . . Strive to reach agreement among groups concerned as a basis for action. . . . Base decisions on facts.

. . . Define problems carefully and set clear objectives. . . . Establish time schedules and set deadlines.

. . . Be practical—relate recommendations to community resources.

. . . Follow through on findings and recommendations.

. . . Use imagination in getting action; sometimes wide publicity is required, sometimes quiet negotiation.

. . . Keep the public informed. The Council's work is public business. . . . Use clear, simple language in reports and recommendations.

. . . Relate planning to budgeting. . . . Involve some of the same people in both planning and financing.

. . . Avoid excessive expenditure of time and energy on matters of organization and structure. . . . Have both long-range and short-range projects.

54

Chest and Council Relations—Where Chest and
Council Are One [1]

By CHARLES J. BIRT

Another moot question concerns the structural relationship that
exists between the chest and the council. This controversial issue is discussed in the following two readings, 54 and 55, both of which may be
considered reasoned statements. In the larger metropolitan areas these
organizations are generally separate, but communities are constantly experimenting and switches from one form to the other are not infrequent.
In the first selection the shift from two separate bodies under a joint
executive to an integrated structure, which occurred in St. Paul, Minnesota, in 1947, is described by Charles Birt. In this article the author
plays up the council component in the consolidated agency, the permeating influence of its planning services, and the values of co-operation. On the basis of this experience he concludes that effective unity
under a single board is possible without the loss of independence or
responsibility on the part of the council.

Charles J. Birt was formerly executive secretary of the Madison,
Wisconsin, Chest and Council, a position which he held for some fourteen years. During this period he also served as a field representative
for the Federal Emergency Relief Administration under Harry Hopkins,
directed a number of surveys, and did some lecturing and teaching in
addition. In 1940 he became associate executive secretary of the Council of Social Agencies, of Minneapolis, where he remained until 1943
when he was commissioned as a major in the Army's School of Mili-

[1] Excerpted from "Where Chest and Council Are One," *Community* (New
York: Community Chests and Councils of America, Inc.), Vol. 24, No. 9, May,
1949, pp. 167-169. By permission of United Community Funds and Councils of
America, Inc.

tary Government. In July, 1946, he was appointed executive director of the Greater St. Paul (Minnesota) Community Chest and Council.

ST. PAUL IS ONLY ONE of many cities which are experimenting with their council structures. On the whole we all face essentially the same kinds of community social problems, strive for the same objectives, and have much the same potential material with which to work. The fact that some of us are adherents of a unified chest-council structure, while others are not, is not too important. Many roads lead to Utopia. None of us will probably ever reach it, but it adds zest to our daily jobs to keep trying.

The heart of our council experiment during the past fourteen months is the fact that we have tried to make "grass roots" knowledge and influence concerning social work in our city an integral part of our total community social planning structure and policy making.

We set out to prove that Chest and Council can be one rather than two separate organizations or two organizations connected by remote control. It is our belief that Mr. Citizen Leader is a better community leader if he is not segmented. We also hold to the belief that Mr. Practical Conservative Chest is no less concerned by the social conditions in his community than is Mr. Idealistic Liberal Council. If we are to have strong welfare leadership in our community, Mr. Chest and Mr. Council will develop this leadership more quickly if they face together the common community problems around the same table.

It would be folly, of course, to fail to recognize the fact that people are conditioned to look upon things differently. However, a community program is no stronger than its weakest member; and if teamwork and understanding are its essence, then we should get these qualities into our approach to community problems. Through constitutional provisions, whereby co-ordinating councils are assured representation, participation, and autonomy, we have found that unity is possible without minimizing the Chest's responsibilities or stifling the Council's activities and independence.

The need for streamlining our chest-council structure was apparent for several years before it was actually accomplished in January, 1947. The drafters of the new constitution realized that structure alone would give no assurance of a sound program. However, they felt that if the ideas that had grown out of our accumulated experiences related to representation, autonomy and participation were incorporated into the new constitution, the chance of providing a base for a sound program would be assured.

Today we have in our council-chest structure 135 organizations, agencies, and divisions. Approximately 480 lay and professional persons guide our health, welfare, recreation, money-raising, and publicity programs, under the direction of a representative board of thirty-two persons. The board is responsible to a corporate membership which meets annually. We have three co-ordinating councils—Casework, Health, and Leisure Time—which we consider the "grass roots" of our community program. They have 216 members, 105 of whom are lay board members and 111 staff workers. These members come from 28 governmental and 80 voluntary agencies, 39 of which participate in the federated appeal of the Chest. During 1948, despite insufficient staff and lack of familiarity with new operating rules, the co-ordinating councils undertook 18 projects in addition to their regular programs, and completed seven. The others are being carried into 1949, except one which was discontinued.

This article concerns itself primarily with the structure of four council groups: the Corporate Membership Body, the Board of Directors, the Planning and Research Council, and the three Co-ordinating Councils. Budgeting, campaigning, public relations, and research are equally important in our structure, but they cannot be discussed here.

The Corporate Membership Body is made up of three groups: contributors, honorary members, and organizations, either affiliated or participating. This body meets annually to hear reports, approve any changes in the corporate provisions, and elect 15 of the 32 members of the Board of Directors.

Nine other members of the board are elected by the Planning and Research Council, and three serve by virtue of being chairmen of the co-ordinating councils. The board may select from its own membership or may appoint nonmembers as chairmen of the Planning and Research Council, and of the campaign, budget, nomination, and public relations committees. Nonmembers, when appointed, serve as board members. It also appoints 15 members to the Budget Committee and three to the Planning and Research Council.

The Planning and Research Council is composed of 26 members: the chairman, the three chairmen and nine vice-chairmen of the co-ordinating councils, three members elected by the board, and six more selected by the Council itself from the public at large. Other members are the president of the board and the chairmen of the budget, campaign, and public relations committees.

The task of the Planning and Research Council is to co-ordinate the programs of the three co-ordinating councils and to serve as the connecting link between them and the board on all matters except money raising and budgeting, which subjects are taken up only on request. However, since the Council elects 12 members to the Budget Committee, its ideas are registered in budget procedure, policies, and decisions. In addition, the fact that council staff serves the subcommittees of the

Budget Committee, and that research responsibilities are lodged with the Council tends to integrate the budgeting, planning, and research processes.

Our constitution spells out three areas of operation for the co-ordinating councils. These areas are designated as (a) "Independent," (b) "Interdependent," and (c) "Dependent." Autonomy of operation, that bugaboo of conscientious council workers down through the years, is defined in clear and certain terms in the clause related to independence. This clause gives the three councils power to act independently on public questions and social legislation, provided that the boards of the participating or affiliated agencies which wish to take action in the name of the Council, state this decision in a motion filed in the council office. Matters relating to the budgetary needs or problems of the chest-federated agencies come within the "dependent" area and must be referred by the councils to the Budget Committee and the Board for decision. Matters pertaining to programs, research projects, and special studies fall within the "interdependent" area and are usually settled by the co-ordinating councils or referred to the Planning and Research Council for decision.

Representation has been mentioned as an unusual phase of our co-ordinating councils' structure. The "garden variety" of council usually includes two members from each participating or affiliated agency. Our councils follow a similar plan except that each one elects an executive committee of six and a chairman. The chairmen cannot be on the payroll of a public or private welfare agency. These chairmen automatically become members of the Board of Directors. In this way some "grass roots" of community social processes are transplanted from the working organizations to the authoritative policy-determining body. There are three vice-chairmen in each co-ordinating council. They must be elected from a governmental agency, a non-chest agency, and a chest agency respectively. The remaining three members are elected at large.

Each co-ordinating council has drafted for itself a statement of organization which fits within the provisions set forth in the constitution of the corporate organization. This statement allows each council to add a certain number of persons to its membership.

Possibly the outstanding test of the value of the new structure and the extent of co-operation realizable among our co-ordinating councils was demonstrated last year in one important undertaking—The Family Unit Report System project. Working through an over-all steering committee, chaired by a volunteer and composed of subcommittees representing each council, it was possible to compile approximately 56,000 complete family schedules during the month of November, 1948. This number represents practically every family served in Ramsey County that month. Services were classified according to economic need, maladjustment, health, and recreation by 126 reporting units representing 108 voluntary city, county, state, and federal agencies. The report on this project, which is being directed by Community Surveys, Inc., and financed by the Grant Foundation, will be released in September, 1949. It is the first time in the history of social work in the United States that such a complete picture of one town's community services has been obtained.[2]

While this over-all description of structure may sound as if we had more harness than horse in some areas, it has proved after a year's operation quite suitable for our needs. It does take time, of course. But when, for example, an agency study report is completed, we have the satisfaction of knowing that the best minds in the fields concerned have expressed their opinion of it. Again, with this way of working, the councils with representation balanced among lay and professional persons, voluntary and governmental agencies, and with independence of action assured on public questions, become the formers of public opinion and not mere followers.

---

[2] See Selection 44.

55

Chest and Council Relations—The Case for Separate Councils[1]

By C. WHIT PFEIFFER

Nearly seven years after the changes described in the preceding selection, and following three years of intensive study, a representative citizens' committee in the Los Angeles area voted to establish the new "Welfare Planning Council, Los Angeles Region," as a legally separate organization from the Welfare Federation which formerly had included both the chest and the council. Whit Pfeiffer, author of the following article, describes the transitional process and lists the major reasons for the change. These may be summarized as (1) the existence of basic differences in scope, areas of interest, function, and methods; and (2) the fact that the administration of either is a big enough job to require a separate board and an independent executive. Underlying this writer's position is the premise that while either the chest or the council may dominate the integrated organization theoretically, the former is more apt to do so. Hence separation is necessary to enable the latter to perform its full function.

Whit Pfeiffer has had many years of executive experience in community chests and community welfare councils. He was executive secretary of the Welfare Planning Council of the Los Angeles Region until his retirement in January, 1957. His previous record includes a variety of activities. From 1916 to 1920 (excluding 1917–1918, when he participated in the War Camp Community Service program) he was assistant secretary of the Public Affairs Department of the St. Paul, Minnesota, Association of Commerce and served as secretary of the committee

[1] Excerpted from "A Vote for Separate Councils," *Community* (New York: Community Chests and Councils of America, Inc.), Vol. 29, No. 6, Feb., 1954, pp. 103-106. By permission of United Community Funds and Councils of America, Inc.

which recommended the establishment of the Community Chest in this city. Appointed as the first executive secretary of the new chest, Pfeiffer continued in this position from 1920 to 1930. From 1930 to 1941 he was executive director of the Kansas City, Missouri, Council of Social Agencies and secretary of the Charity Fund. He held his recent position from 1942 to 1957 when he retired. Mr. Pfeiffer holds degrees from Carlton College and the University of Minnesota, and is a member of the Phi Beta Kappa Society.

SHOULD CHESTS AND COUNCILS be legally separated? Los Angeles has recently voted "yes," and by that vote has created the new "Welfare Planning Council, Los Angeles Region," structurally and legally independent of the Welfare Federation, fund-raising body for the area.

This decision did not come about fortuitously, as has happened in some cities where the Chest has been succeeded by a superfederated financing organization; it was the result of more than three years of study, discussion, and organizational planning.

As we all know, the question of separate or united existence for Chests and Councils has long been a subject for debate, and practice varies widely throughout the country. As the national Statement of Policy [2] issued by the Three C's in 1950 puts it: "Various structural arrangements are possible for the relationship of community planning and financing groups provided that the outlined methods and procedures are adhered to. No single pattern is applicable to all situations and the most important thing is to have effective co-operation."

Let me say at the outset that I accept that statement because I know that successful planning is being done under various structural arrangements. People are more important than structure. Good people have made poor structure work well, and inadequate people have not been saved by excellent structural arrangements. Our experience, however, has convinced us that it is easier to achieve the desirable "methods and procedures" outlined in the Policy Statement when the two functions of federated financing and community planning are carried out by two separate organizations.

The process of study that led to our decision went through three stages.

The first stage involved fifteen months of study by a Citizens Study Committee appointed by the Welfare Federation to analyze the Federa-

---

[2] *Community Planning for Social Welfare—a Policy Statement.* See Selection 50.

tion, which embraced both Chest and Council, and to make recommendations for improvements. . . . Its field service was done by a firm of management specialists and its conclusions reflected the management point of view, supplemented by a limited "public opinion poll" carried on by the firm of management consultants. Its most important recommendation was that Chest and Council be separated.

That recommendation led to the second stage in the process. The idea of separation was not received with enthusiasm by either Chest or Council, but they did carry out promptly a proposal to create a Joint Steering Committee made up equally of Chest and Council members. The Citizens Study Committee wanted this joint committee to develop a new, legally independent planning organization. But when the Joint Steering Committee was created, it was instructed to pass on the merits of separation before undertaking to accomplish it. So the committee put in a year of intensive work before it finally recommended separation and worked out basic terms and agreements between Chest and Council.

The third stage in the whole process was the job done by a subcommittee of the Joint Steering Committee known as the Organizing Committee, which spent another year of hard work, including conference meetings with representatives of the Board of Supervisors, the City and County Welfare Departments, the Board of Education, the "Big Six" national health agencies, organized labor, and other Chests and Councils in Los Angeles County. Also consulted were the co-ordinating councils, representatives of state agencies, department heads of local health and welfare agencies, and numerous other groups. After months of such conferring, this committee was augmented by new members named by the Board of Supervisors, the City Council, the Board of Education, other Chests and Councils in the county and by the President of the County Federation of Co-ordinating Councils. The Organizing Committee then developed Articles of Incorporation and by-laws and lined up the first Board of Directors in accord with the by-laws. Foundation plans were then laid by the new organization, which held its first board meeting November 18, when it adopted by-laws and started the new Council on its way.

Such thoroughgoing procedures naturally focused attention upon and stressed the importance of the real reasons for structural separation. Here, in brief, are the reasons:

In the first place, as our Citizens Study Committee recognized, the scope and area of concern of community planning and federated financing are different.

Difference in Scope

It has often been said that the two are so interrelated that they are like the opposite sides of the same coin and therefore should be a part of the same organization. This line of reasoning is specious. In a coin, both sides have the same diameter, the same area. This is not true of federated financing and community planning. While community planning, of course, does not do all the planning that goes on (a point which is recognized in the Policy Statement), its concern must necessarily be with the *total program* of health and welfare no matter whether it be financed through federated financing, through other voluntary contributions, or through taxation. The primary concern of a Chest, on the other hand, must be with the agencies it finances. . . . The Citizens Study Committee put it this way:

> There is an incongruity in combining responsibility for over-all planning with that of financing a small minority of total health and welfare services. A sound, proved organization principle is that responsibility and authority should be co-extensive. This principle is violated in the current arrangement between Council and Chest.

One of the results of this "incongruity" which was pointed out by representatives of the Citizens Study Committee was this: The close connection between the Welfare Council and the Chest, and the fact that the Council was a part of and legally responsible to the Welfare Federation Board which operated the Chest, led non-chest agencies to feel that the Council was not sitting in a "neutral" corner. For that reason, non-Chest agencies did not participate in the old Council as wholeheartedly as was desirable and necessary for effective over-all planning.

Many members of the Joint Steering Committee were skeptical about this point. But now that separation has been effected, with strong representation on the new Board of Directors having been named by the County Supervisors, the City Council, the Board of Education, state organizations which belong to the Council and by other groups, there can be no further argument about the correctness of that point made by the Citizens Study Committee. The fact is, the enthusiastic, interested, and broad participation which the new Council is receiving not only goes far beyond any comparable experience in the old Council but is exceeding everyone's expectations. It may, of course, be simply the rosy hue of the honeymoon but it certainly promises well for the future.

Difference in Function

In the second place, the functions of planning and fund raising are quite different. The job of federated financing is to raise and allocate funds for a specific group of health and welfare agencies. As the Citizens Study Committee report points out, "the Council encompasses a much larger scope." Its task is to bring together representatives of a wide variety of interests to the end that by research, study, joint consideration, mutual agreement and follow-up, their co-operative efforts will bring about good community conditions and appropriate community services as needed, no matter from what source they may be financed.

Difference in Method

Because of these differences in function, there are significant differences in methods. Federated financing involves a most intensive selling job with high-powered organization. At campaign time, in particular, it becomes a high-pressure operation. Prospects, many of them tough, must be convinced; pledges must be signed; the campaign must be completed on a sharp time schedule. It is all highly dramatic.

On the other hand, while Councils, too, have their share of pressures, time schedules and hard, grinding work, community planning is essentially a slower, less dramatic business. This was recognized by the Citizens Study Committee, which commented that "the Council is perhaps necessarily a cumbersome and deliberative form of organization." While selling and organization are needed, and while drama is not lacking, the differences between the two, including the difference in tempo, are so marked that they become a difference in kind, not simply a difference in degree.

It was stated at the Laymen's Conference on Community Planning in January, 1953, that in Cleveland, which has, it has always seemed to me, the most effective planning organization in the country, it takes about seven years from the time of inception to the time of actual implementation of any major project. Imagine trying to run a Community Chest campaign on that kind of time schedule! On the other hand, what would happen to a planning organization if it tried to put the "bee" on a member agency the way in which a determined chest solicitor may handle a particular prospect?

We must also remember that community planning is definitely nonauthoritative. It cannot compel anybody to do anything. It has no control over anyone. Federated financing, on the other hand, necessarily imposes many controls on its member agencies. It seems perfectly clear that there are fundamental differences in function, and consequently in method, between federated financing and community planning.

Finally, both jobs are big enough and important enough to require the best brains and ability that they can recruit, plus the all-out attention and consideration of the people who are primarily interested in one or the other. When both functions are put under the direction of one board and one executive, the two are likely to get in the way of each other. The Citizens Study Committee put it this way: "The mixture of responsibility for both financing certain private agencies' services, and for over-all planning, results in a dilution of top management's attention and energies so that the job done in either or both fields may be completed." In other words, one function or the other is very likely to suffer. It is interesting to note that the Citizens Study Committee believed, although this does not appear in its report, that the Chest suffered more than did the Council from this situation in Los Angeles. Whether or not they were right on this point, it is my judgment, based on observation over many years, twenty-two of them spent as a chest executive, that generally it is planning that suffers.

When you try to place them on the two sides of a single coin, federated financing is likely to be heads, planning, tails. Campaigning is demanding. It is insistent. It is time consuming. When a combined organization is in the midst of its federated financing job, everything else for the time being has to go by the board, planning included.

Under a joint arrangement, the situation is likely to work out in the following manner. The chest board recognizes that it must hire a good executive. He has to be an expert salesman, a top-flight organizer. He must be able to talk to the top men of both management and labor and to other people of influence in the community. He should know something, of course, about the health and welfare programs he is promoting, and believe in them. A man of this calibre does a good job. He raises money. He gets a substantial salary, and earns it, since the ability to stimulate and direct the raising of funds is a rare asset with a high market value. He would be less than human if he did not feel the sense of power that the control of money inevitably brings.

Then he realizes that along with fund raising goes the need for planning. So he promotes the organization of a committee or department devoted to community planning. There may be some agencies he thinks should be merged; others that he would like to eliminate. Perhaps a Council could help him accomplish those ends. So he engages an assistant who is assigned to work on Council matters. But the chest executive still "calls the shots." Is it any wonder, under such circumstances, that people are asking why planning organizations continue to devote 75 to 90 per cent of their time to community chest affairs to the neglect of broader community problems? Or why, except in very few communities throughout the country, community planning has not attained the stature which it ought to have?

There are, of course, chest executives with social work training and genuine interest in and competence for community planning, who understand its somewhat subtle but very real differences from federated financing. Such men may feel perfectly able to carry both responsibilities. If it comes to a choice, however, few would be willing to give up the higher salaries of chest work in order to concentrate on community planning.

Granting that there are always exceptions to any general rule, the situation which seems to us in Los Angeles more likely to produce the best results, especially in larger communities, is one where there are two organizations, one concentrated on federated financing, one on community planning. Each is free to do a good job in its field, respecting the other, helping the other, neither one trying to dominate the other, both working together in properly co-ordinated relationships for the common good. As our Citizens Study report said, "The task is large enough in each field that it appears sensible to provide for specialization and separation. Co-operation and co-ordination can still be maintained on less formal and integrated a basis than currently."

56

The Future of Federation [1]

By RALPH H. BLANCHARD

The following statement regarding the outlook for federation gains significance by reason of the facts, first, that it is the considered opinion of the executive of the national organization representing chests and councils, and second, that it was issued just on the verge of the period when "united funds" began to emerge as one response to the vexed problem of "multiple appeals." The 1000 chest and council cities spoken of by Mr. Blanchard in 1949 had risen to nearly 2000 cities with federated financing in 1955.

Ralph Blanchard has served on the staff of United Community Funds and Councils of America (formerly Community Chests and Councils of America) since 1928; he has been executive of the organization since 1943. In 1948–1949 he served as president of the National Conference of Social Work.

IN PROPHESYING THE FUTURE of federation, I would remind you of one thing: that time is indivisible. You can't thrust it into three convenient pigeonholes labeled Past, Present, and Future, and expect it to stay there. Time doesn't stay *anywhere*—it moves and flows; its elements merge and intermingle. If you would attempt to prophesy the future of one man, you must first take a look at his past record, and try

[1] Excerpted from *The Future of Federation* (New York: Community Chests and Councils of America, 1949), pp. 3-14. By permission of United Community Funds and Councils of America, Inc.

to estimate his present capacity for growth and achievement. It is the same with an *idea*—and federation is a very big idea. Its past, we know, is deeply rooted in the good earth of democracy. And I believe that the facts of its present show a tremendous capacity for future growth in service to the American people.

Facts of the Present Situation

What are some of the facts of the present situation that point to a bright future?

1. There are now over 1,000 chest and council cities and towns listed in the directory of Community Chests and Councils of America, Incorporated. It is estimated that there are at least 300 more in small communities which are not listed.

2. The number of adult chest givers had risen from a 1936 figure of 8,400,000 to over 20 million in 1948—more than 22 per 100 of the total population.

3. These givers will provide more than 185 million dollars to support the services of the voluntary agencies in 1949. This is nearly double the total given in any prewar year.

4. The number of Red Feather service agencies supported by these contributions is now more than 12,000.

5. Probably a million and a half volunteers serve these Chests and Councils—as campaign workers and as year-round volunteers.

Steady Growth

All this has happened in less than half a century. From the earliest days the growth has been steady and irresistible, with the greatest spurts coming in times of stress and strain.

But the greatness of the chest-council movement is measured not in statistical terms—but in the service it has rendered:

   . . . in spreading the load of giving and developing new types of givers, such as corporations and labor groups

   . . . in eliminating wasteful and costly competition in the raising of voluntary funds, thereby releasing more dollars for actual health and welfare services

   . . . in raising more money than was produced by individual agency appeals

   . . . in conserving volunteer leadership and manpower

   . . . in saving the time of contributors and campaign workers

   . . . in freeing agency directors and staff to concentrate on their major job—operating the health and welfare services.

Community Values

The greatness of the movement is still further underscored by chest-council contributions in:

. . . stimulating over-all community planning
. . . introducing budget analysis into the health and welfare picture
. . . providing an educational force for social betterment
. . . bringing balanced growth, better quality and co-ordination into the programs of service
. . . developing community spirit and a sense of unity by bringing together citizens of all racial, religious, political and economic backgrounds to work for a common purpose.

Beginning of Federation

But these facts, impressive as they are, serve only to confirm the logic of the evolutionary developments which preceded Chests and Councils in this country. In Colonial days the "social work" of the community was done on a neighbor and kith-and-kin basis. Grandparents of almost any of us can recall the nursing visits to neighborhood farms or the crop-gathering parties to help an injured or sick neighbor or relative. Later, as cities began to develop and people had more leisure and means, the practice of "friendly visiting" became more highly developed. Gradually the combination of greater need and an increasing sense of community responsibility led to the establishment of agencies which could more effectively meet the need and more efficiently raise sufficient money to do the work.

Finally the agencies became so numerous that their programs often overlapped, conflicted, or competed. Efforts had to be made to co-ordinate their work. And so we saw the development of the Social Service Exchanges and the Charity Organization Societies—forerunners of the community organization movement as we know it today. All these developments led naturally and normally to the establishment of federations in the form of Chests and Councils to plan, co-ordinate and finance the social welfare activities which had become so widespread throughout the country. And as some of these activities, up to then considered the province of voluntary agencies, were taken over and operated by various units of government, the need for such planning and co-ordination became even more pronounced.

Nation-Wide Extension

In the meantime, Councils and Chests were growing until they were everywhere—in cities of all sizes. But it was not until World War II that the values of federation were extended generally to all parts of the country—rural as well as urban. Then, under the whip and spur of war-generated needs, these federations were extended to every county in every state and to the states themselves, and finally to the nation as a whole. Always these developments have been characterized by a voluntary spirit with full recognition of the right of local self-determination—hallmarks of democracy in action in America.

All of these developments are written on the records of the past for everyone to read. They are facts—the true history of the situation. We accept them, not only for what they tell us of the past, but for what they predict for the future. And we accept the Chests and Councils which have resulted from this kind of social evolution, not as forms of organization to be worshiped nor as sets of rules to be followed slavishly, but as ideas—ways of life—which can bring greater health and happiness to all our people.

We have faith to believe that this evolutionary development will bring still better things in the future. It can do so, if we have the character to master the problems that face federation right now—and if we have the courage to push ahead.

There Are Dissenters

Unfortunately we must have character and courage for more than ourselves—because there are some who do not have our faith in federation—nor the courage to face the facts of evolution. Undoubtedly there are many varieties of these "dissenters," but three of them are outstanding. First are those individuals I would call *"Backward Facers,"* who identify themselves by greeting Chest solicitors with the answer: "I prefer to give my charity directly." Some of these people, perhaps, are using this answer as a blind for not giving at all. But some are sincere, and one can only feel sorry for their inability or unwillingness to face the facts of life as they are today and not as they seem to wish they were. For these persons are only expressing their vain and wistful longing to return to the old days when life, they feel, was simple—days which are gone forever.

The second group I would call the *"Pretenders."* It is made up of those health and welfare agencies which have yielded to local pressures to join Chests and Councils and which pretend to believe in the principles of federation. However, when a real issue arises, such as a difficult budget situation or a campaign setback, they quickly show their true colors, for they are essentially "agency-minded," not "community-minded." The true community spirit and point of view are outside their understanding, and their sole interest is their own agency and their own point of view. They don't know what you mean when you talk about a "co-operative way of life."

The third group of "dissenters" from our co-operative or federated way of life, I shall call the *"Isolationists."* This group is more noisy than the other two, more aggressive, more negative, and more divisive in its effect. Its members go part way on the evolutionary path but stop short at the point where they fancy their own interests, their own agencies, are being threatened. They refuse to join Chests and many times will not take part in council activities, saying that federation repre-sents the "communization" of health and welfare activities and is, in essence, "monopolistic."

These are the people who have been saying for a long time that fed-eration will spell the doom of private health and welfare, only to see the ground swell of federation continue its relentless progress toward the very organizations whose leaders vainly command the progress to cease. These people talk about their organizations as though they were the ultimate developments, and would march into eternity unchanged and unchangeable. Yet the very arguments they use are, in fact, an-archistic, in the sense that they deny all social growth and, if followed to their logical conclusion, would prevent the existence and mainte-nance of the very agencies they seek to protect.

These "Isolationists" are true cases of arrested development; they are willing to *start* along the evolutionary road but they deny that the road has been going anywhere. They overlook or refuse to admit the proven gains made by federation in the last thirty-five or forty years and, curiously enough, while they attack its virtues, they seem to be unaware of some of its faults and weaknesses which you and I know exist. This may be due to the fact that they are really not students of federation at all—they just don't know the facts. Or it may be due to the fact that the weaknesses and dangers that exist in federation, as you and I know them, are many times more weak and more dangerous in the form of organization which they support. Probably it is due to a mixture of the two but, in any case, I'm sure you will agree with me that it would be refreshing to hear a "good case" made against federa-tion by its enemies, instead of the flimsy fabrication of untruths and half-truths which seems to be the fashion these days.

The fear and panic which seem to possess some of these foes of fed-eration become all the more difficult to understand when one realizes the high quality of the agencies which they many times represent—agen-cies which gallantly and successfully attack some of the greatest enemies of mankind, and which obviously do not need the type of overpro-tection which they are getting.

The People Want Federation

Of course none of these dissenting groups can stop the evolutionary de-velopment which resulted in Chests and Councils. They can't stop it for the best reason in the world, which is that Councils and Chests exist and grow because they serve the people and the people want them. The people will continue to want—and to have—them as long as they are useful social instruments, and no longer.

Chests and Councils will not continue to grow and prosper because Three C's or some other group or individuals scheme that way. We aren't that smart, and social progress doesn't come that way. Chests and Councils are here to stay because they are useful to people—lots of people—all the people. They will stay and grow for the same reason.

What Kind of Federation?

And so the question is not shall we have federation or separation—but rather what kind of federation shall we have? And what can those of us who have a positive attitude toward federation do to make it work better and serve more effectively? What improvements, what further advances can we help bring into the picture?

First—it seems to me that we can and must speed up the process by which our Chests and Councils are representative of all the people and in which representatives of all the people participate. One has only to study campaign and other records of local Chests and Councils to know which ones are really securing participation of all leading community groups—labor, nationality, civic, neighborhood—in their planning, operating, and financing efforts. We have made some good beginnings in this area, but they are only beginnings. We need to speed up the process and help extend it to our Red Feather members as well. This is indispensable to the future usefulness of Chests and Councils—not only to raise more money in campaigns, but also because it is only through broad participation that the people will come to know the health and welfare needs of their communities and what should be done by both public and private agencies to meet them.

Second—we must develop far better methods for educating the public about people's needs and what social welfare agencies can do about meeting those needs. Opinion polls have shown conclusively that people overwhelmingly want the services of voluntary agencies. Unfortunately the same polls also show that the public does not identify the chest member agencies as the ones which can give them the services they want. How to bring about identification, in the public's mind, of Red Feather services with the Chest is one of the central questions facing us today. How to create and foster the willingness to support such expensive multiple function services is another. And our practical giving ceilings will remain maddeningly low until we begin to find some of the answers.

We Must Remember

One of the great difficulties with federation today is that its constituent elements, and especially the member Red Feather services, are by no means united on the best ways to proceed. We must recognize the fact that we are living in a period of revolt against central planning and of impatience with restrictions and disciplines of all kinds. Inherent in our type of federation are certain restrictions and self-imposed disciplines, even though federation has always recognized the individuality and autonomy of the group or agency participant in the planning or financial process. We must remember, too, that we are dealing for the most part with agency leaders, with contributors and taxpayers who represent a new generation—one which has never lived under the chaotic conditions which existed when there was no federation. Again, we need to remind ourselves that we can hardly expect enthusiastic support from the general public if those who are in the "inner family circle," so to speak, are disaffected to the point where they hold back in the traces or even revolt.

Teamwork Needed

This is a situation which must be corrected at once; the solution will no doubt call for action on both local and national fronts and involve both public and private agencies. In the meanwhile, we who believe in federation must present a united front to the public, with all elements in the federation team pulling together. We in the chest-council corner must make it clear that we are not irrevocably committed to a particular pattern of federation—that we want rather the kind which will do the best job. And then we must share with our member Red Feather services the task of creating such an organization. Such action will call for the greatest flexibility, a quality which is unquestionably one of the key elements in the future usefulness and success of federation. From its earliest days, federation has had to contend with inflexibility. Chests and Councils have been established all too often in local communities as "giver revolts," with agencies, who should have been natural leaders, withholding their full co-operation through resentment, fear or unwillingness to change their patterns of thought or work.

Federation Is Flexible

It is not federation which has been inflexible, but rather those who should have been closest to it and most ready to adapt it to changing need. Federation itself was flexible enough to get its first great impetus from World War I, but to have its first long period of growth in the peaceful but hectic 1920's. It was flexible enough to take on unemployment relief as an extra load in 1930 and 1931, until government could step in, but elastic enough to discontinue such relief when it became apparent that government really was doing the job. Federation was flexible enough to take on its share of the National War Fund load during World War II—that is, more than 60 per cent of the total—and at war's end to adapt itself to peacetime conditions, modified sharply as they were by inflationary factors.

Federation has operated successfully in towns of 15,000 population and in metropolitan areas peopled by millions; it runs without participation of this or that group in city after city—and all the time it produces by serving the people. It has done everything it has been asked to do—not perfectly, but better than it had been done before. If there is something radically wrong with federation it is more than likely centered in those of us who are supposed to be closest to it! And here is where we, the Chests and Councils, must exercise great care lest we unwittingly keep federation from fulfilling its destiny.

For every time we have a Chest which is narrow and restrictive in its setup, which denies the right of participation to some legitimate community group or groups; every time a Chest operates in violation of principles which we have learned over the years to be sound; every time a Chest assumes an overlord attitude toward the Red Feather services or toward the community itself—then that Chest is denying to federation its full birthright.

Where a Council becomes merely an academic debating society; where it is an exclusive group of private agencies with public agencies and citizens groups left out; or wherever a Council is operated with the primary thought in mind of preserving the present status and resisting change *regardless*—then the chest-council movement is in trouble—and by just that much is being kept from fulfilling its destiny.

The Road Ahead

What is the destiny of federation? In my judgment it is destined to serve every local community, large and small, in every state in the union. And since the effectiveness of its local service will be largely influenced by state considerations, this will mean that federation, planning as well as financial, will ultimately be extended to every state. And finally, logically and inevitably, it will be applied to the nation as a whole, not in an overlord position but as a helper and enabler for state and local federation.

Sign Posts

Events are now happening in local communities, in states, and in the nation which may well be the forerunners of other events to come. And these ultimate developments are not so very remote either—the time is later than we imagine! As an illustration, witness the courageous and significant experiment now going on in Michigan which has organized a state-wide United Health and Welfare Fund, and in Detroit which has its United Foundation. Other states are watching Michigan, and making their own decisions. Such experiments and demonstrations should have not only our academic interest but our enthusiastic help, not because we necessarily agree with all their operating policies, but because they are headed in the right direction.

Barriers

To me one of the great regrets during the present period of experimentation and demonstration is that again so many powerful agency groups, instead of taking their rightful positions of leadership, are holding back. Even some of our own organizations and personnel are holding back too! On the other hand, there are increasing numbers of leaders in national and state agencies and in Chests and Councils who are determined that federation shall not be sold short but rather shall be placed in a position where it can deliver up to its full potential. The experiments will continue, with some succeeding and some failing. But whatever the outcome they will go on persistently until every barrier is cleared and the right road appears through which every community—local, state and national—can be served.

Trail Blazing

They will go on more swiftly, more soundly, far more constructively or more surely when the natural leaders, the agency leaders and workers, assume or resume their rightful positions of leadership. I hope and believe that they inevitably must and will do this. They are the people who have had the most experience; they have proved their concern for human need; they will be gladly followed when they assume the lead. For this trail blazing, these historic developments, which are even now beginning to form and take shape, must proceed in an atmosphere and climate of harmony and unity in which only one consideration will be uppermost—the health and welfare needs of all the American people.

The Future of Federation? It is limitless! For federation is not a piece of machinery, an "agency," nor any set of petty rules. It is a philosophy, a way of life that is part and parcel of our political, social, and economic structure. And the problems that beset it today are certainly not confined to our little field of health and welfare. Our own United States Government, and the United Nations, are struggling to apply the principles of federation to the political field on a national and international basis.

Federation is an idea and an ideal. It restrains selfishness; it builds the common good. Its strength is its voluntary quality, not fear or compulsion. And its staying power is its universality, not its restrictions. It helps people—all the people.

57

Where Do We Stand in United Fund Developments?[1]

By ALBERT J. NESBITT

Viewed from the standpoint of an informed layman the united fund movement represents merely the application of community chest principles to national appeals, and is definitely "on the march." The author, however, is in no way a dogmatic advocate, unsympathetic to local opinion, or unaware of the objections of some of the national agencies. In fact, he warns against inflexibility on the part of united funds, against overemphasis upon campaign techniques, decisions based on expediency only, and neglect of the "spiritual content" of the movement, and insists that the major concern should, instead, be the welfare of the people involved.

Albert Nesbitt is an engineer by profession and president of the Philadelphia manufacturing company that bears his name. In the federation field he was early active in the local chest and became the first president of the Philadelphia United Fund. He has served CCC for many years in various capacities and became its president in 1954.

Federation has marched forward rapidly since Nesbitt enunciated the following basic principles in 1954, primarily as a result of the expansion of united funds. Between 1952 and 1957 the number of united fund cities more than tripled reaching approximately the number of those with community chests.[2] By September, 1957, the thousandth fund had been established in Wausau, Wisconsin, and toward the close of the year it was estimated that federated campaigns of all types would

[1] Excerpted from "Federation Is on the March," *Community* (New York: Community Chests and Councils of America, Inc.), Vol. 29 (March 1954), pp. 127-129. By permission of United Community Funds and Councils of America, Inc.

[2] *1957 Experience in United Funds* (New York: United Community Funds and Councils of America, Inc., Bulletin No. 193, 1957), p. 3.

produce a total of over $400,000,000 for the support of voluntary health and welfare services throughout the nation during 1958.[3]

WHEN WE SPEAK OF United Funds, we are speaking of Community Chests as well. All of the United Funds of which I have knowledge are organizations that have applied the chest principles of federation to national appeals. The United Funds are just another step in the evolution of federation.

This process of evolution, now going on in many communities throughout the country, will inevitably result in changes and adjustments, not only in the policies and practices of national agencies, but also in those of Chests and United Funds.

Thus, I believe that this process will cause many national agencies to re-examine their present policies and, where they are found to be in conflict with local thinking, make such adjustments in national policies as may be indicated in a democratic society of free men. For free men resent *too much rigidity,* even though the cause is good.

Not all of the "give" must come from changes in national policy. Local federations have, in my opinion, a responsibility to accept to a far greater extent than in the past, national budget and quota allocations for the national appeals which they include. The work of the National Budget Committee and the National Quota Committee is important in this connection.

Certainly, there must be ground rules that are applicable to all participants. What is essential is that there be *agreement upon basic fundamentals* and that the measure of our effort should not necessarily be strict uniformity of rules for both national and local agencies.

There are principles of federation that I hold more dearly than uniform budgeting or uniform budgeting procedures. In certain situations we have observed that United Fund campaigns are limited to the place of employment, with the national agencies free to solicit at another time of the year at places other than the place of employment. This method has served well in some communities, including my own city of Philadelphia.

The success enjoyed by the United Funds has caused some communities to establish such Funds on an expediency basis. Here I am not

---

[3] "The Thousandth United Fund," *Community* (New York: United Community Funds and Councils of America, Inc.), Vol. 33, No. 2, Nov., 1957, p. 24. Actually a total of approximately $412,000,000 was raised for 1958, three-fourths by united funds. See introduction to this section on "Community Welfare Councils and Community Chests," page 357.

critical. Our major concern must always be for the welfare and growth of the people, and the raising of adequate funds in order to carry out such a program might very well justify the expediency of the moment. But in such situations there should be a return to sound principles of fund raising and fund allocation as soon as these objectives may be achieved. I am quite willing to define sound principles as those set forth in the CCC publication, *Organizing a United Fund.*

With the exercise of tolerance, understanding, and confidence, problems can and, I believe, will be resolved between the local and national organizations. The high purpose to be served in a sound working relationship at the local and national levels is so compelling as to overcome differences related to method.

Certainly the desire for a successful campaign is an understandable and high aspiration. The desire to reduce the number of solicitations in a community and at the same time to raise more money for worthy causes, are strong motivations. Indeed, these are the very motivations that have brought into being so many United Funds.

To what extent have these motivations been justified by campaign results? For the answer to that, let me quote from the analysis that appeared in the January, 1954, issue of *Community:* United community campaigns for 1954 set an all-time high, but the principal gains one sees over the past several years have occurred where *new* United Funds came into operation. Greater numbers of people participated and the increase in dollars, generally, was about 22 per cent more in total than the combined results of the last independent campaigns.

While not as much of an increase is generally experienced in the second and third years of United Fund operations, there is a sound basis, statistically, upon which one can conclude that the percentage of increase each year after the first year was above the average of a straight Community Chest campaign increase.

Yes, federated fund raising is on the march! In our first Philadelphia United Fund campaign in 1950, I frequently used the expression that the United Fund was "an idea that had come to its time." When I first used the phrase (and it was not original with me) the "idea" to which I referred was the combining of major national appeals with that of the local agencies. But as the campaign went on and I saw the sincerity with which business, professional, and labor leaders were dedicating themselves to making that campaign succeed, I realized that the idea that had really "come to its time" was that the success or failure of a campaign was the individual responsibility of every person identified with the task. This brought a sense of rededication that was spiritual, not material. Yes, we developed highly, as many of you have done, the techniques of fund raising, such as payroll deductions, budgeted giving, plant rallies, inspirational reporting luncheons. Indeed, our technology embraced all of the best that was available in federated fund raising. But beyond all that there was present this sense of spiritual rededication.

It is well-known that technology operates on the surface, but that spiritual concepts penetrate below the surface and into the hearts of men. And this brings me to a trend which I seem to have noticed and which gives me some concern. This is the overemphasis which I see being placed on the technology of fund raising and the neglect of spiritual content. If this trend continues, the honeymoon of greater federation will soon be over, because unless in this process we capture and retain the hearts of men, we will ultimately fail in this cause.

We carefully prepare statistics to show the average gift for industry and the professions. We carefully prepare statistics to show proportionate giving for corporations. Presumably, we do all of this in order that we may establish for the giver a frame of reference. . . . A major task in all fund raising is to develop a spiritual frame of reference in people's hearts. The story of the Good Samaritan is a story of people who beat other people up, people who pass them up, people who lift them up—and too many are still going through life passing them up, and too few are lifting them up.

We need to emphasize the importance of men participating in and contributing to our Chests and United Funds because of man's humanity for man; man's love for man. If we do not recapture the spiritual initiative which we seem to be losing, our cause will be doomed to failure.

What I am trying to say is beautifully pictured in the four murals that may be seen in New York City's Rockefeller Center, depicting the onward march of man: First, man is shown laboring painfully with his hands, yet determined to survive. Next, the maker of tools is shown extending through his skill the comforts of his civilization. Then, one sees the master of the machine harnessing to his will the forces of the material world. Finally, the fourth mural portrays the scene of the Sermon on the Mount.

Then, under all four, these words are engraved:

> "Man's ultimate destiny depends not on whether he can learn new lessons or make new discoveries and conquests, but on his acceptance of the lesson taught him close upon two thousand years ago."

It might just as truly be said that the ultimate destiny of federation depends not upon new discoveries, not upon new techniques, but upon how well we apply the lesson taught us some two thousand years ago.

58

Free Choice in Giving [1]

By ROME A. BETTS

Federated versus "independent" financing of voluntary social welfare agencies is one of the major controversial issues in American community organization today. Proponents of the community chest and united fund movement have stated the case, at various times and in various ways, for joint fund raising. Most of the arguments in favor of the preservation of independent financing have come from representatives of certain of the leading national health agencies.

The Heart Fund Story, from which the following article is excerpted, is a four-page broadside in which "the American Heart Association seeks to present a factual and objective explanation of its support of the independent fund-raising concept." An editorial statement indicates that the Heart Association is not opposed to "the community chest principle, which is devoted to the support of purely local agencies. We have no quarrel with any fund-raising plan so long as the agencies are free to come in or stay out, so long as no element of compulsion is aimed at the giver, and so long as the contributor remains free to support those causes he favors and reject those in which he has no concern." Writing from this point of view the author states the case for independent fund raising and "free choice in giving."

Rome Betts was general secretary of the American Bible Society from 1942 to 1948 and has been executive director of the American Heart Association since 1949. He is also vice-chairman of the Broadcasting and Film Commission of the National Council of Churches,

[1] Excerpted from an article, "Will Giving Be Regimented? Or Shall We Retain Free Choice?" In *The Heart Fund Story* (New York: American Heart Association, 1955), pp. 1-4. By permission of the publisher.

and a member of the board of the Central Atlantic Area of the YMCA and of the Youth Program Committee of the National Council, YMCA.

MANY AMERICANS RIGHTLY FEAR the dangers of regimentation, collectivism, and undue restriction of individual freedom of thought and action. They applaud competitive free enterprise, and, with equal vigor, they deplore any trend toward monopoly. Suggest to them that all insurance agencies unite, so as to make operations more efficient and to spare themselves the bother of duplicate solicitation, and they will treat the suggestion with the contempt it probably deserves.

Should charity be regarded differently? In the minds of some it would appear so. Many honorable and well-intentioned individuals, who zealously defend competitive free enterprise as it applies to our social, political, and economic philosophies, favor its exact opposite when applied to the field of philanthropy.

To me it seems unfortunate that many of our finest leaders have failed—at least up to the present—to perceive the hazards on the road down which so many of our communities have started to travel. There are not too many freedoms that are left within the individual's own choice and determination. One of them is the freedom to select to whom we shall give or to what cause we shall give. This freedom, I submit, is worthy of strong defense.

Most individuals wish to preserve some ability to choose. For personal reasons, one man may wish to support Heart, another to support Cerebral Palsy. Yet another may wish to support Cancer, not Polio. These are things of deep personal concern. But, when you contribute to a united fund, you have no choice. You give to them all.

In some united funds there is still preserved the fiction that you may designate your contribution. Generally, however, designation means nothing. Every dollar that you designate for Heart or another individual designates for Cancer is simply included in the general pie, which, at the end of the campaign, is sliced in exactly the same ratio as if nobody had designated a nickel. That's the way it works. Your so-called ability to designate is not in effect a reality.

Another myth concerns the ability of federated funds to show a consistent growth in income. After the initial wave of enthusiasm that always accompanies a new idea has worn off, the giving to a united fund tends to level off and frequently actually to decrease.

What does that mean to young growing organizations with important causes to serve? What does it mean to the Heart Association specifically or to the Cancer Society? It simply means that if you wish to increase your program, the only way in which that income may be increased is either for the united fund to raise more money or to take it away from other organizations already in the united fund.

When a united fund has hit its plateau or begun to move down, an agency can't ask for more money and expect to get it. The united fund can't raise it. If you suggest that it be deducted from some other agency, you're not going to be very popular with those other agencies.

Therefore, it is becoming increasingly true across the country, that when a national voluntary health agency enters a united fund, in effect, it enters a strait jacket. This statement can be documented with many case histories, which leads to still another difficulty.

New Areas of Service

When you go to the united fund and ask for an increase for your particular cause, which as a young agency has now begun to move into new areas of service, you will, in most cases, be required to sign an agreement that you will undertake no new service until you have the united fund's consent. Then, after you present your budget (assuming that you document your case and say you need more funds) the united fund may tell you: "We think you can eliminate this item. We don't think this is necessary."

In other words, almost inevitably there is going to be budget control by people who know little about your program or about the nature of the problem at issue. Here's another thing that is strange but true: In a recent survey of about twenty united fund communities involving national agencies we found that in every instance, the united funds have budget committees which are composed of groups of ten to a dozen local citizens. Only two of the twenty included a doctor who would be able to express any kind of intelligent judgment on the Heart Association's budget request. Also, *these small budget committees consisting of only a very few people are expected to make up your mind and my mind as to how our gift dollar is going to be divided.*

Again, there is a tendency in united funds to make a tax out of what should be a gift. Let me explain: In a midwestern city, there is one company which will refuse to hire a new employee unless he agrees to give a fixed percentage of his weekly paycheck to the united fund as a condition of employment.

It is difficult to see how this process differs from that of having Uncle Sam collect money from your pocketbook. To me, the logical conclusion of the trend in which the united funds are moving us, is to make giving a tax.

Even where giving to a united fund is not a condition of employment, it has become so much a matter of moral suasion that only a brave person will stand up and say, "I'm not going to give the recommended percentage. I'm going to give something different." When the time comes that we have to be told that we must or should consider giving 1 per cent, 1½ per cent, or whatever it may be of our weekly paycheck, we're in bad shape. One man may be taking care of an aged mother, whose expenses are running very high, another may have none of those responsibilities and can well afford to give his 1½ per cent.

Many "Ask-Its" Inevitable

Consider now the slogans of united funds. They say to us, "Give Once for All," or "Put All Your Begs in One Ask-It." It sounds wonderful, but what they're really appealing to is your desire to avoid nuisance, to get rid of the whole business as quickly and with as little thought as possible. When has charity or help for one's neighbor been predicated upon the avoidance of nuisance?

Yet united funds are not truly all-embracing as the term implies. As long as the United States Post Office operates under the present laws of this country, you will never have a completely united fund.

Regrettably, the united fund movement has made targets of the major health agencies because of their obvious appeal. Through pressures that have frequently bordered on compulsion, they have sought to force them to come in, so as to be able to call it a united fund. Yet, as noted, so long as Uncle Sam's postmen continue to function, the goal of an actual united fund cannot be achieved.

To me the argument of too many appeals and chaos in fund raising has little real meaning. This is being loudly shouted by a few social planners and fund-raising professionals, who arrogate to themselves the prerogative of deciding how much every voluntary agency in a community should receive. Let us agree that some volunteers have been overworked and let us not lack sympathy for those who have been like whirling dervishes rotating from one good cause to another and pursued by all for campaign leadership. The answer to that problem, however, is not a united fund. Instead it is the unearthing of new leadership.

Then there is the united fund argument that people are tired to death of working on these drives. That is not the experience of the American Heart Association. More than 500,000 Americans went out on Heart Sunday, in February, in all kinds of weather, visiting their neighbors in behalf of the Heart Fund. Nobody compelled them to do it. Most of them were enlisted by telephone. Many of them told us *they had never been asked to help in such a cause before*.

There is an even more compelling reason for worrying about the united fund trend for those of us who are interested in the heart as a nation-wide and community health problem.

It is a well-known fact that more than half the deaths in the United States are caused by the cardiovascular diseases. They represent a very serious health problem even to those who are in the prime of life. Furthermore, considering incidence, the best estimate is that about 10,-

000,000 persons living in the United States today have some form or another of heart disease.

This is not a local problem. This is not a state problem. It is a problem national in scope. The proponents of cancer or mental illness can give you much the same kind of picture. This is something in which we have more than just a humanitarian interest. It is a matter of self-interest. It is something more than a welfare cause. It is a medical and scientific cause upon which depends the future health of millions of Americans.

If we're going to do anything about this problem, we need new knowledge, we need research into the essential causes of rheumatic fever and rheumatic heart disease, hardening of the arteries and high blood pressure, which cause 90 per cent of all heart diseases.

Without this new knowledge, everything else that we do by way of educational and community service efforts to ameliorate the condition of those who are already suffering from heart disease is of marginal value. Of course, something can be done with the knowledge that we have, and we are applying it as rapidly as it comes. Still, our great task is the support of fundamental research. Since the best kind of research program has been demonstrated to be one nationally planned and executed, more than half of the funds that are received by the American Heart Association are devoted to the support of fundamental studies. Local budgeting committees find it difficult to understand the significance of a national research program. Most especially do they resent use of local funds to support research in other communities. Yet logic dictates that the fruits of research have a universal application. It still is going to benefit you and me ultimately, regardless of where we live.

A More Appropriate Aim

In talking about dollars, let us think in terms of what those dollars do and of our ability to spend them wisely. Let us not raise money just for the sake of raising money. A more appropriate objective, I submit, is that of finding answers to the causes of heart disease. Let us remember the 10,000,000 people who have heart disease. Let us consider how we can prevent another 10,000,000 from getting it in the years to come.

59

The Social Service Exchange and Agency Co-operation [1]

By STEPHEN L. ANGELL and FRANK T. GREVING

The future of the social service exchange has recently become a controversial issue. Historically, as well as in terms of the current concept of an integrated approach to community welfare problems, the exchange has had an important role to play as a device to facilitate joint effort. On the other hand, it has been attacked by many psychiatric and other highly specialized social work practitioners. A recent CCC survey reported that although 50 exchanges have been closed since 1951 this fact alone cannot be regarded as establishing a trend since 219 remained in operation.[2] Undoubtedly, however, many exchanges, though officially open, are not now being widely used.

In the following excerpt the authors review the history of the exchange and of recent attacks upon it. They identify the basic issue as one of effective and sympathetic communication between agencies engaged in a common task, and attempt to show that the exchange is an essential device for interagency co-operation and a necessary one if a fragmented approach to community welfare problems is to be avoided.

Stephen Angell, formerly associate director of the Delaware County District, of the Health and Welfare Council of Philadelphia, Delaware, and Montgomery Counties, is currently executive director of the Lehigh County Community Council, Allentown, Pennsylvania. At the time the article was written Frank Greving was assistant executive director of the Brooklyn Bureau of Social Service and Children's Aid Society. He is

[1] Excerpted from "A New Look at the Social Service Exchange," *Social Work Journal,* XXXVI, Jan., 1955, pp. 13-17, 33. By permission of National Association of Social Workers.

[2] Kenneth I. Williams, "Social Service Exchange Roundup," *Community* (New York: Community Chests and Councils of America, Inc.), Vol. 30, No. 6, Feb., 1956, pp. 108-111.

now associate director of Community Research Associates. Both authors were members of CCC's national Advisory Committee on Social Service Exchange.

RECENT PRACTICE AND CONCEPTS regarding the use of the social service exchange have fluctuated in a seemingly confused pattern. There are those in the profession who believe the exchange has no logical place of merit or importance within the social work structure and have therefore advocated and, in several instances, succeeded in bringing about its abolishment. There are others whose acceptance and use of the exchange, at least in a quantitative sense, has become so routine as to resemble a mechanical performance. Between these extremes there are about as many variations as there are agencies.

In order to understand the concern and confusion which has been expressed, a review of some of our traditional social work philosophy may be in order. The use of the exchange has in many ways reflected the growth and development of the profession as a whole. We would like to show in this paper how a social service exchange can and in fact must fit into the redefined concepts of social work today. If our position is tenable, then it must derive from sound social work policy as applied to the best in today's practice.

Development of the Exchange

In the period of greatest quantitative usefulness of the exchange, the depression years, policy was based upon a desire that funds entrusted to agencies (voluntary and public) be applied without duplication. While far from foolproof, the exchange did provide some assurance that the assistance programs were being administered with reasonable accountability. . . .

At an earlier period, before the major impact of public assistance, the mainstream of social work was largely represented by the voluntary agency. Separation of the so-called "worthy" from the "unworthy" was then of primary concern in the use of the exchange. At the same time, its use as a means of interagency communication—for helping one agency to know the service record and pertinent facts possessed by another—was gaining acceptance, and the rationale for this was often work-economy and better planning. . . . A statement circulated by 26 Philadelphia citizens in 1878 as a charge to a commission which formed the Philadelphia Society for Organizing Charitable Relief and Repressing Mendicancy (now Family Service of Philadelphia) read as follows: "To discuss and, if possible, determine on a method by which idleness and beggary, now so encouraged, may be suppressed and worthy, self-respecting poverty be discovered and relieved at the smallest cost to the benevolent."

The search for a specific body of knowledge which could become a part of teaching and practice and which could achieve its own definition of purpose made great strides after the voluntary agency was freed from its major material assistance job. This development led us into many bypaths, and we found our inevitable affinity to other professions—sociology, psychology—and particularly to psychiatry. Since we were concerned with the welfare of the individual, we recognized that to work effectively with him we would need to deepen our understanding of the many cause and effect factors which appeared to determine his adjustment. Perhaps, we thought, psychiatry, psychology, or sociology could provide this. Psychiatry, with its tremendous contributions to the dynamics of individual adjustment, served to complement our own growing awareness that focus upon the individual might yield a more effective casework methodology than we had had.

While it is not the purpose of this paper to elaborate upon this phase of our development, we believe that the effect of psychiatry upon the formulation of casework methods and concepts has had both positive and negative results. A positive effect is that our knowledge of individual motivation has increased and enabled us to apply our services more appropriately, while at the same time we have become far more aware of the client-worker relationship, its assets, and its hazards. A negative result has been an overidentification with the goals and often with the methods of psychiatry, so that we have lost some of the concern for the "social" in social casework.

What is important with respect to the social service exchange is that the second of these trends, if followed to its ultimate conclusion, would obviate the need for the functions of an exchange. In the extreme, one might say that the more social casework practice moves in the direction of individualization of the client, as in the private practice of psychiatry or psychoanalysis, and the greater the emphasis is upon intra-psychic conflict, the less important are considerations of environment *per se,* be they family, economic problems, housing, or other needs on the periphery of adjustment. Or to state this another way, the farther casework practice becomes removed from the community concern for a broad approach to social problems, the more it isolates itself; the less it will require the use of the social service exchange. If we develop in the direction of an isolated counseling service, then we will not need the exchange any more·than does the practitioner who is in private practice for himself and the individual patient. In this instance we will have ceased to be a community agency within the meaning by which we seek and get community support for our services.

Perhaps the basic question involved is whether or not it is important that our social and health agencies work together in providing services to people of the community. This working together boils down to a question of whether agencies communicate with one another or, as previously suggested, become isolated service entities.

The modern exchange should be a tool for facilitating the casework helping process by making possible interagency communication with the least possible waste motion and in an orderly manner. There is no essential ethical difference between use of an exchange to facilitate communication (provided standards of professional social work are adhered to) and communication without the exchange. There is, however, a tremendous difference in efficiency and effectiveness of one approach as opposed to the other. Therefore, what we must decide is whether in the interests of the client, who needs the most help that our combined services can give, and in the interests of the community, which subsidizes almost totally these services . . . we will make every effort to work as a team interested in the whole individual and the family of which he is a part.

This is a dilemma currently faced by much of social casework practice. A reorientation to basic social work goals and responsibility has begun. As the pendulum swings back, it undoubtedly will not go all the way to the past. We will find that social work will retain its new knowledge, but that its gain will be through an integration of the new insights with a view of the individual and his family as a composite social structure rather than as an individual entity. This means that we will change from intensive treatment goals (in the sense of remedying psychopathology, which is the prerogative of the medical profession and medical practice) to social goals for families and individuals. It will require all of the understanding of individual and interpersonal dynamics we can muster, but we will apply this knowledge to the individual in relation to the cause and effect factors operating in his total environmental setting.

We have already undertaken a number of important steps in this direction. Such studies of family breakdown as have been conducted by Bradley Buell and associates have greatly advanced our knowledge about the long-standing concern we have had that our community services are not measuring up to full effectiveness. A small hard-core segment of a community's problems has consumed a major portion of our available resources. This has occurred in an unco-ordinated, disjointed way, which can only lead to the conclusion that many of our facilities are being wasted in unproductive effort.

Our great stress upon specialized but often unrelated social work practice has contributed to this problem. The preoccupation with specialization itself has paralleled an intensification of practice akin to the goals of individual therapy.

In almost any community one can find in the files of the social servive exchange cases currently known to a large number of agencies. Examination of these will reveal a noteworthy lack of communication among the different agencies concerned with special areas of interest in the same case. The extent to which the exchange may have been used for the purpose that one agency might know that another is or has been interested in the same case does not by itself demonstrate co-ordination or integration of planning.

Interagency communication is concerned not only with the fact that two or more agencies may have been in touch with one another about a mutual client, but also with the manner in which they have communicated with one another. Has real communication taken place— or has insufficient time and thought been given to the case discussion? Has either agency been holding back pertinent information for fear of revealing errors in practice? Has discussion centered on pertinent aspects of the case, or ranged into irrelevant areas? All of these and many more factors are involved in purposeful and effective interagency communication.

From this brief description of a part of what is involved in communication it can be seen that the skill of communication "is a part of practice—a discipline learned and developed as other social work skills are learned and developed—through experience." [3] This practice of interagency communication is closely related to the swinging back of the pendulum from a rather exclusive concern with the individual to more attention to the family unit as a whole, representing as it does the most basic social structure in our society. . . .

Future Role of the Exchange

What, then, is the future role of the exchange? How can it best serve the community interest?

The foremost purpose of the exchange has been and should continue to be facilitating communication between our communities' health and welfare services. Clearing of information in order to know among the specialist agency practitioners about the service each is giving in a particular case situation, which is the somewhat restricted limit to which this concept of the exchange's responsibility for interagency communication has many times been confined, is but a beginning in the job that might be done.

We believe that the newer concepts of integrated social work practice introduce another facet to the exchange's responsibility, namely, that the exchange itself not just be "used" but become an active agent in its own right, and a force which can greatly accelerate the integrative process. In this view the future of the exchange would become part

---

[3] Quoted from Bulletin No. 44 published by the Philadelphia-Camden Social Service Exchange, "New Ideas in Interagency Communication, A Study of Multiple Registrations," p. 2.

and parcel of the continuing development of social work itself. Of course, this presumes agreement on the development of the social work purpose of the community agency. Social work practice which emphasizes the intra-psychic conflict areas to the exclusion of the total socioeconomic adjustment will not have as much need for the exchange as other agencies. But if community funds are given and allotted for social work purposes in the broad sense, and if the integrative forces now at work in the field of practice gain momentum, then the exchange must be considered one of the important media to accomplish this, and participation in the exchange by even the more specialized services is important to its fulfillment.

How, then, can the exchange become a more dynamic force than heretofore? This, we believe, can take place in at least two ways: First, as mentioned above, when agencies accept the full implication of their social service role, and second, if the exchange can become more effectively related to the center of responsibility for total community planning. Since the interest in total community planning for social services is only a development of recent years, it is not surprising that greater recognition of the new role of the exchange has lagged.

As a central service the exchange has often been under the administrative umbrella of either the community financing or community planning bodies (that is, the chests or the councils). Chests and councils, however, have been slow to recognize that their exchange operation is just as much in need of skilled professional administrative assistance as is the local family agency or as is the chest budget committee. Nominally an exchange may be under a professionally trained administrator, but in actuality its operation has been left primarily in the hands of a clerically trained employee who can handle the mechanics of the indexing operation and see that it functions smoothly.

There is no question that if the exchange is to continue to exist it must be a part of professional social work practice. As such it must receive active administrative leadership from a professionally trained executive, it must be attuned to the needs of its member agencies, and as a tool for the professional social worker it must do its job in accordance with present-day standards of social work practice. It should have the help of a continually active professional advisory committee, drawn from the member agencies, which will consider exchange practices in the light of current philosophy and aid the executive and governing body in resolving organizational and operational problems in keeping with principles of professional practice.

Furthermore, it will not be possible to reach the specified goals unless more professionally developed and specific membership standards are adhered to than exist in most of our exchanges today. The inclusion of such organizations as housing authorities, courts without probation departments, and draft boards has been found in many communities to be inconsistent with current exchange philosophy and use of the exchange as a tool of the professional worker. . . .

Not only is it important to have thoughtful discussion of the exchange on the community level but also on the individual agency level. Member agencies should have their policy for use of the exchange clearly defined, and such a policy should be subject to periodic review and evaluation. An agency policy must take into consideration three main factors: (a) what use of the exchange will be most helpful to the agency in aiding its clients and the community; (b) what aspects of its use might benefit the client or community as a result of other agency use of the exchange; and (c) how its use might affect the exchange's function to serve as an active agent in the integrative process.

In their job of community planning, councils have seldom used the exchange as the ready-made research medium which we believe it can and should become. There is no single agency in any community which has a more accurate record (granting the adequate participation of member agencies) of the duplication, waste motion, uneconomical procedures, and the "run-around" to which clients are often subjected, than has the exchange. It offers a continuous method of research based upon registrations, clearings, and the appropriate case analysis of services actually provided, referrals made, and rejections and reapplications in the same and other agencies. Community welfare councils, the budget committees of chests, and the agencies themselves could, through the use of such exchange data, develop a more objective approach to sound planning and research in the social service arrangement. This would help tie together the meanings of social service for the contributor and the consumer.

Community Review

When there is question about the usefulness of an exchange, such doubts as exist should be opened to review by the total community concerned, public and voluntary, professional and board member. . . . The exchange is one of the main tools we have for developing better integration and collaboration in agency services. When we have a better tool we would certainly want to adopt it, but until then the exchange is badly needed in order to make our social welfare programs most effective.

State-Wide and National Agencies
—Introduction

THE LANE REPORT in 1939 (See Selection 5) pointed out that community organization could be practiced at any geographical level—state, national, or international—as well as town, city, or county. Selection 60 below describes the process at the *state* level, and the other three, 61, 62, 63, deal with welfare planning and organization on a *nation-wide* basis. On the *international* level, community organization is one of the concerns of such bodies as the United Nations, the International Co-operation Administration, and the Social Security Administration, and so several selections in Part IV, on Community Development in the United States and Other Countries, reflect certain aspects of such programs.

The decade 1940–1950 brought important developments in community welfare organization at the *state* level: enlarged activity by state conferences of social work; the increase of state planning bodies in the areas of health and of children and youth; major changes among the state-wide citizens' welfare associations; and the rise of the state war chests. Community Chests and Councils of America followed these developments closely, and in 1949 CCC published a Directory of state-wide agencies which was invaluable as a factual guide to state-wide planning and co-ordinating bodies.

Selection 60, from a paper delivered by Arthur Dunham at a meeting of CCC at the National Conference of Social Work in 1950, uses this Directory as a starting point in discussing current types of *state-wide* community organization agencies, state-wide tasks that need to be accomplished in this area, and a set of suggested "guideposts" to state-wide organization.

National agencies are one of the most striking features of social welfare in the United States. They are also an aspect of community welfare organization, for most national agencies are community organization agencies. Few of them give direct service, but nearly all are concerned with fact finding, planning, program development, education, and the rest of the elements that make up community organization.

On the national level, as on the local, there are both governmental and voluntary agencies. The governmental agencies include the Federal Department of Health, Education, and Welfare, and a score or more of other federal agencies and organization units. The voluntary national agencies include some 250 organizations concerned, in the aggregate, with almost every imaginable aspect of health and welfare.[1] Taken together, these federal and voluntary agencies play an incalculable part in community welfare organization in this country.

Selections 61, 62, and 63 relate, for the most part, to *national* voluntary agencies. Selection 61, a brief excerpt from the *Manual* of the National Budget Committee, gives the rationale of national agencies in a nutshell.

George W. Rabinoff, in Selection 62, taken from the *Social Work Year Book,* 1954, goes further in exploring the philosophical, sociological, and historical bases of national agencies. Mr. Rabinoff has had strategic opportunities for knowledge of and participation in national agencies: he served for fifteen years on the staff of the Council of Jewish Federations and Welfare Funds; he headed a national bureau for advanced study in Jewish communal service; and since 1951 he has been assistant director of the National Social Welfare Assembly.

Selection 63, from an article by Edmund deS. Brunner in *Adult Leadership,* discusses particularly the functions of national agencies. Dr. Brunner has been for many years a national leader and an author in the fields of rural life and adult education; he is a member of the graduate faculty of Teachers College, Columbia University, director of the Special Projects Division, and chairman of the Bureau of Applied Social Research. Though he writes this article primarily from the standpoint of adult education, almost everything he says is translatable into terms of social welfare.

---

[1] For listings of national agencies, both governmental and voluntary, see the Directories in the *Social Work Year Book.*

60

Community Organization at the State Level [1]

By ARTHUR DUNHAM

The State-Wide Setting for Community Organization

THE STATE PROVIDES a radically different setting from the local community for purposes of community organization. The basic differences stem from the factors of geographic area and distance. The area of the state is of course immensely greater than that of the local community. The state contains a variety of communities and types of territory: large cities, small cities, towns, villages, and open country. Location, topography, and climate vary. The total population of the state, unlike the total population of a local community, does not dwell in contiguous territory.

The element of distance is a physical, sociological, and psychological factor of basic importance. Distance frequently means lack of information, lack of understanding, prejudice, and even active hostility. Distance breeds sectionalism, as isolation breeds provincialism. There may be the perennial struggle between east and west or north and south—or between the large city and rural upstate or downstate, as the case may be. A mountain range may divide the state and intensify the rivalry between the first city and second city. Or rivalries may exist between two or more large cities of almost the same size.

State-wide organization is much more difficult than local organization. It is hard to hold meetings, and who can do community organization without meetings? It is difficult, time-consuming, and expensive for people representing all sections of the state to get together for a

---

[1] Excerpted from "State-Wide Community Organization Comes of Age," *The Social Service Review,* Vol. XXIV, Dec., 1950, pp. 484-492. By permission of the publisher.

committee meeting or otherwise. A state organization must depend far more upon the written word and far less upon firsthand contacts than a local organization. Of the firsthand contacts which are made, many can be made only through staff travel, which is expensive and time consuming. Moreover, the state-wide organization's constituency is usually larger, more widely distributed, and more diverse in experience and points of view.

Nevertheless, the importance of state-wide community organization can scarcely be overstated. Governmentally, the state is the basic unit of the nation, as our very name, the "United States," attests. The federal government is a government of delegated powers; the powers not delegated to the federal government are reserved by the Constitution to the states or to the people. The state possesses a large degree of autonomy; even in time of war or economic depression, when federal centralization is increased, most social legislation is state legislation. The state stands midway between the nation and the community. Legally, the county and the municipality are the creatures of the state.

Moreover, the basic pattern today in the field of social welfare is the pattern of public welfare. In the field of the public social services it is the state which plays the leading part in programs of categorical public assistance, treatment of the physically handicapped, mental health, corrections, and frequently in child welfare and general assistance. Most public welfare programs which are in operation today involve one or more of the elements of state legislation, administration, leadership, supervision, or support.

It is true also that it is virtually impossible to reach most rural areas with social services except by means of state-wide programs. Left entirely to their own resources, too many rural counties would have neither the vision, the leadership, the cohesiveness, nor the financial resources to develop social welfare programs adequate to their needs. With state-wide programs and leadership and with the possibilities of state aid and equalization plans to give proportionately greater allotments to poor or distressed counties, there is far more chance of developing something like adequate services to the rural counties.

One characteristic of state-wide community organization, which has already been suggested by implication, is the importance of the promotion of legislation. All public welfare programs rest upon a statutory basis, and many other social relationships which are of concern to both governmental and voluntary agencies are affected by legislative provisions; for example, marriage, adoption, domestic relations, education, public health provisions, inheritance, and many criminal proceedings.

All in all, then, it is clear that on the state level, if anywhere, many of the major battles for social well-being must be fought and won.

The Background of State-Wide Community Organization

In spite of its importance, state-wide community organization for social welfare as we think of it today is a fairly recent growth. In the field of governmental services we may trace it back to what Sophonisba P. Breckinridge used to call the first "state central authority," the Massachusetts State Board of Charities, in 1863; and we may follow it through the Ohio Children's Code Commission, the first of the children's commissions, in 1911; the Illinois Department of Public Welfare, the first modern state welfare department, in 1917; the New York Temporary Emergency Relief Administration, the first of the ERA's, in 1931; and the widespread reorganization of state systems of public welfare, in the years following the passage of the Social Security Act in 1935.

On the side of voluntary organization, we may go back to three developments in the 1870's and 1880's: the founding of the New York State Charities Aid Association in 1872, the establishment of the National Conference of Social Work by representatives of the state boards of charities in 1873, and the organization of the Wisconsin Conference of Social Work in 1881.

Between 1880 and 1940 we should find several important developments. State conferences spread to almost all states; an increasing number of these conferences moved in the direction of becoming year-round "action" bodies, with full-time executives; and an association of state conference secretaries was organized as early as 1924. State-wide citizens' associations grew up in a few additional states; councils of state-wide agencies were organized in a number of states in the 1920's but did not survive; and a large and uncounted number of state-wide promotional and community organization agencies came into existence in such fields as tuberculosis control, social hygiene, crippled children and adults, and mental hygiene.

As far back as the 1920's (possibly even earlier) there were some signs of recognition that the same process which was called "community organization" on the local level might be practiced on the state and national levels also. The Lane Committee report on "The Field of Community Organization," at the National Conference of 1939, made this recognition explicit,[2] and Russell H. Kurtz amplified and illustrated this idea in 1940 in his National Conference paper on "The Range of Community Organization."[3] Since about 1939, part of the working equipment of the modern community organization worker has been the knowledge that the community organization process—in spite of the local sound of its name—may be practiced on any geographical

---

[2] Robert P. Lane, "The Field of Community Organization" (Committee Report), *National Conference of Social Work Proceedings,* 1939, p. 497.

[3] *National Conference of Social Work Proceedings,* 1940, pp. 405-408, 411-412.

level or between any geographical levels. This idea is a natural corollary to the conception of community organization as an attempt to bring about and maintain an adjustment between social welfare needs and social welfare resources. Incidentally, the term "state-wide community organization" in this discussion will be interpreted broadly enough to include not only "over-all health and welfare planning" but also the programs in specific fields, such as crippled children or mental hygiene, where there is a large promotional component in the job.

The Foreground

In a sense, "what's past is prologue" to the current drama of state-wide community organization. Since 1940 there have been several new and exciting developments. The state war chests swept the country during World War II and demonstrated the possibilities of joint financing on a state-wide basis. The number of state conferences with full-time executives doubled—from nine to eighteen—in about ten years. State-wide commissions on children and youth were organized in most of the states. State health councils and associations increased from about six to nineteen. Major changes have been taking place in the state-wide citizens' welfare associations. The Ohio Welfare Council has reorganized. The Public Charities Association of Pennsylvania has established a substantial quarterly periodical, *Currents,* and has changed its name to the Pennsylvania Citizens Association for Health and Welfare—though mercifully preserving the initials "PCA," without which Pennsylvania social work could scarcely survive! In New York Dr. Harry S. Mustard, an eminent leader in the field of public health, has succeeded to the honored place of Homer Folks, who for fifty-three years gave statesmanlike leadership to the State Charities Aid Association. . . .

Moreover, there has been experimentation with a variety of new agencies—particularly in the area of chest and council operations—and also a growth in a number of certain older forms. Within the past two or three years also there has been the development of an informal group of executives of certain state-wide community organization agencies for sharing experience and ideas and for joint thinking and planning.

Along with this has come the beginnings of research and laying the foundations of a literature on state-wide community organization. Here Community Chests and Councils of America, and particularly Lyman S. Ford, have played an important part. CCCA's mimeographed memorandum of April, 1946, on "Community Organization for Health and Welfare on a State-Wide Basis" was a pioneer contribution of great value. The last four years have seen several National Conference papers on state-wide community organization as well as the first article on the subject in the *Social Work Year Book.* Finally, in 1949, Community

Chests and Councils published their invaluable *Directory* of state organizations engaged in planning and co-ordinating activities in the field of social welfare.

State-Wide Community Organization Agencies Today

This *Directory* is the most important compendium of facts about state-wide community organization agencies that has yet been produced. It gives us, by all odds, the best available picture of these agencies as they are today. It is an invaluable tool for anyone interested in state-wide health and welfare planning.

The *Directory* lists 194 state-wide planning and co-ordinating agencies "either totally or partially in the broad field of social welfare." . . .

An analysis [4] of the 194 agencies listed in the *Directory* yields a classification into thirteen categories (Table 1). . . .

TABLE 1

TYPES OF STATE-WIDE AGENCIES LISTED IN CCCA "DIRECTORY"

Associations of chests and councils	9
State chests and review boards	6
State citizens' councils	5
Commissions and associations for children and youth	40
State conferences of social work	47
Development commissions	19
Health councils and associations	19
Planning boards	16
Recreation commissions and associations	9
State-wide citizens' welfare associations	5
Legislative councils	6
Community organization service	1*
Other	12†
Total	194

---

* The Massachusetts Community Organization Service is the only separate agency in this group. Michigan has a community organization service, but it is given by the Michigan Welfare League (state conference).

† The miscellaneous group of 12 agencies listed under "Other" includes: the Welfare Council of Delaware; Florida Federation of Social Workers; Florida Institute of Government; Louisiana Interdepartmental Committee; Extension Service University of Michigan; Mississippi Crime and Delinquency Association; North Carolina Resource-Use Education Commission; North Carolina State Board of Public Welfare (Licensing Program); Ohio Postwar Program Commission; Pennsylvania Department of Welfare, Bureau of Community Work; Rhode Island Public Expenditure Council; and Rhode Island Social Workers Club.

[4] Based on *Directory of State-Wide Agencies,* published by Community Chests and Councils of America, 1949.

TABLE 2

CLASSIFICATION OF STATE-WIDE AGENCIES WITH PROGRAMS RELATED TO HEALTH AND WELFARE PLANNING

No.	Type of Agency	Auspices—Governmental or Voluntary	Area of Interest	Relation to Social Welfare—Primary or Secondary	Community Organization Function—Primary or Secondary
1....	State public welfare departments and related agencies (departments of mental health, departments of corrections, departments of institutions, etc.)	G	Public welfare in general or special aspects of public welfare	P	S
2....	State commissions and associations for children and youth *	Usually G	Children or youth	P	P
3....	State planning boards *	G	Physical and social planning	S	P
4....	State development commissions and associations *	Usually G	Economic-social development	S	P
5....	State recreation commissions and associations *	Usually G	Recreation	P	P
6....	Council of state-wide welfare agencies	V	Social welfare—general	P	P
7....	State health councils and associations *	Usually V	Health	P	P
8....	State conferences of social work *	V	Social welfare—general	P	P
9....	State-wide citizens' welfare associations *	V	Social welfare—general	P	P
10....	State-wide associations of chests and councils *	V	Chests and councils	P	P
11....	State chests and review boards *	V	Federated financing	P	P
12....	State-wide community organization service *	V	Local community organization	P	P
13....	State citizens' councils *	V	General welfare of state	S	P
14....	Legislative councils *	V	Social welfare legislation	P	P
15....	State-wide agencies dealing with specialized problems (tuberculosis, crippled, mental health, infantile paralysis, probation and parole, corrections, association of public welfare or public assistance officials, etc.)	V	Specialized problems or areas of social welfare	P	Usually P
16....	State-wide vocational associations	V	Usually social welfare, general	P	P
17....	State-wide associations of family service agencies	V	Family welfare	P	P
18....	State-wide client-service agencies (child-placing, etc.)	V	Specialized areas (child-placing, etc.)	P	S
19....	Miscellaneous	G or V	Miscellaneous areas	P or S	Usually P

* Listed in *Directory of State-Wide Agencies*, published by Community Chests and Councils of America, 1949.

It seems desirable to go a step further and to attempt a more comprehensive scheme of classification which will include the other major types of state-wide community organization agencies which are omitted from the *Directory*. Table 2 suggests nineteen categories and indicates for each (1) whether the type of agency is governmental or voluntary; (2) what is its area of interest; (3) whether its relationship to the field of social welfare is primary or secondary (for example, a state conference of social work is oriented primarily to social welfare, whereas a state planning board has only a secondary concern with the field of social welfare); and (4) whether the community organization function of the agency is primary or secondary.

Each of these types of agencies (with one possible exception—the council of state-wide agencies) is believed to be currently in operation in one or more states. Additional types which have been known at various times and some which may even be in existence today would include: official study commissions in fields other than child welfare (such as the public welfare reorganization commissions), legislative fact-finding committees concerned with public assistance or other aspects of social welfare, state defense councils, state war chests, and others.

Nobody knows how many agencies there are in all these classifications. There are something like 100 state "overhead" public welfare agencies besides those listed in the CCCA *Directory*. There are state mental hygiene societies alone in twenty-six states.[5] In 1949 in the state of Michigan there were some 40 state-wide agencies concerned with the fields of health or welfare. On the basis of a conservative estimate of an average of five specialized agencies per state, there would be 240 such agencies; adding these to the 100 public welfare agencies and the 194 agencies listed in the CCCA *Directory,* we have a total of 534 agencies. It is highly probable that there are not less than 500-600 state-wide agencies concerned with community organization to a greater or lesser degree.

The Tasks of State-Wide Community Organization

. . . For the area of state-wide community organization we may lay down the general principle that *getting certain functions performed is more important than the precise agency patterns or forms of organization that are used to do the job*. . . .

. . . I suggest nine major functions of state-wide community organization. Those who are familiar with the writings and addresses of Lyman S. Ford will recognize a close parallelism between his analyses and my own.

---

[5] See *Public Welfare Directory,* 1949, and Hugh R. Jackson, "State-Wide Organization in Social Work," *Social Work Year Book,* 1949, p. 508.

1. The *conference* and open-forum function of the state conferences of social work is of basic importance for the exchange of experience and ideas, for education, for the improvement of standards, and for the development of a sense of cohesion and unity among social workers and laymen concerned with social welfare. The United States is too big for one national conference to do all that is needed; on the other hand, a conference should represent ideas and experience from beyond the limits of any one community. So the traditional state conference open-forum function is still vitally needed.

2. *Fact finding* is of course basic to any sound planning for social welfare. This should include the regular collection and dissemination of needed data in respect to needs and resources, the making of special surveys and studies, and the development of a comprehensive long-range plan of research into which specific fact-finding projects can be fitted.

3. *Co-ordination* and integration of effort is required—first, among the state-wide agencies, governmental and voluntary, themselves; and, second, between state-wide bodies and national and local organizations. For voluntary state-wide agencies one prime requirement is the constant maintenance of an adequate liaison with state governmental agencies in the same or related fields.

4. *Joint planning and action* on state-wide problems is the acid test of much community organization effort. This kind of activity at times reaches a climax in the planning and execution of a long-range state-wide program in a particular field such as public assistance, child welfare, health.

5. *Education and interpretation* is an essential aspect of the community organization process on the state-wide level as on the local and national levels.

6. *Legislative analysis, reporting, and promotion* is an immensely important function. Every state needs competent analysis and prompt reporting of current social welfare bills during every legislative session; every state needs, moreover, a rallying point for promotion of or opposition to specific legislative proposals.

7. *The enlistment and mobilization of citizen interest and participation* in matters relating to social welfare is a test of the vitality of the community organization process in a democracy. The state-wide citizens' welfare association and any other agency that attempts a dynamic program of health and welfare planning in a state stands or falls with the effectiveness of its performance of this function.

8. It seems likely that certain functions with respect to *joint financing and allocation of funds for voluntary agencies* should be performed on the state level. The benefits of joint financing are not likely to be gained for smaller communities or counties with scattered populations without some state-wide joint financing organization. It is probable also that state chests or similar agencies may play an important role in

working out the difficult problems of methods of fund raising and the applicability of joint financing to the important national programs of agencies concerned with health and other aspects of social welfare. . . .

9. *Consultation and assistance to local communities* in reference to health and welfare planning, joint financing, and program development in specific fields is a state function of great potential importance. There is a rich field here for experimentation in co-operation between national state-wide agencies with respect to field service and the most effective ways of channeling consultation and help to local communities.

Guideposts to State-Wide Community Organization

Can we draw any conclusions or state any principles that may serve as guideposts to the future of state-wide community organization? I submit these suggestions for the consideration of those who are interested in state-wide community organization.

1. All or nearly all of the nine functions listed above are needed in every state. These functions, then, ought to be covered in each state by some agency or agencies.

2. A state department of public welfare can and should perform certain community organization functions. But the state welfare department, as a governmental administrative agency, cannot properly, and should not be expected to, take the lead in most controversial matters of legislative promotion and social action.

3. For this reason and other reasons, *every state needs a voluntary organization concerned with broad health and welfare planning.*

4. The exact form of this voluntary agency is a matter of secondary importance. But, whatever its form, the agency probably ought to meet the following specifications for any state with a population of a million or more: (a) The agency should be a continuous, year-round "going concern." It must not be merely a "seasonal" legislative agency or an annual-meeting organization. (b) It should have a broad citizen membership and a board composed chiefly of laymen rather than social workers. (c) It should have a skilled staff with at least two professionally qualified workers, and it should have a reasonably adequate budget—probably not less than $25,000. (d) It should perform the major functions among those listed above.

In the largest states this should probably mean a state-wide citizens' welfare association. These agencies deserve more study and attention than they have received. They have achieved some of the most impressive results that have yet been seen in the whole area of community organization, particularly in the realm of mobilizing citizen interest and concern for health and welfare planning.

In a smaller state the action type of state conference will probably have to give the major leadership in state-wide community organization. If it is to be effective, however, the conference will need to measure up to the specifications mentioned above.

It is possible, though by no means certain, that in some smaller states a voluntary "citizens' council," or similar organization (like those in Georgia and Kentucky, for example) with health and welfare planning as one aspect of its program, may give adequate leadership in state-wide health and welfare planning.

5. The interests and, so far as possible, the program of the state health and welfare planning agency should be as broad as the whole field of health and welfare. This would include general public welfare organization, social insurance, public assistance and family welfare, child welfare, mental health, programs for the physically and mentally handicapped, corrections, public health, housing and planning, and recreation. It is doubtful that any existing agency covers all this ground, but such coverage seems a desirable objective. In the interests of integration and economy of effort and increased effectiveness, it would seem desirable that whenever possible, community organization in a specialized field should be carried on through a division of the central state-wide health and welfare planning agency rather than through a separate agency. The New York State Charities Aid Association and the Pennsylvania Citizens Association have indicated some of the possibilities of this sort of organization, in such areas as mental health, tuberculosis and public health, and corrections.

6. Every state-wide health and welfare planning agency which has not done so within the last five years would do well to make an inventory of the needs and resources in each of the fields in which it is active. Needs would include those in the areas of fact finding, education, legislation, and administration. Resources would include the laws, the governmental and voluntary agencies, the adequacy and quality of employed personnel, and current budgets and appropriations. An inventory of this sort would be a basis for examining relative needs in various fields and for establishing program priorities.

7. Every state needs, and it is questionable whether any state has, a comprehensive, long-range state-wide program for the development and improvement of its total public welfare programs and services. Where a state has more than one state public welfare agency, each agency usually feels limited to its own field in planning. Even where there is a single integrated state welfare department, it may not have either the leadership or the freedom from political or administrative commitments to draft bold or far-reaching plans. Any long-range public welfare plan that will be worth anything must be a product of joint thinking and cooperation, but it is likely that the state-wide health and welfare planning agency will frequently be in a strategic position to take the initiative and give leadership in the development of such a plan.

8. Finally, we need more research with respect to history, objectives, programs, methods, and accomplishments in state-wide community or-

ganization. We need also the production of a working literature, beginning with a practical and down-to-earth workbook, "A Guide to State-Wide Health and Welfare Planning." . . .

State-wide community organization has come of age. It is a growing and expanding field. It presents to well-equipped community organization practitioners unrivaled opportunities for pioneering, for social adventure, and for creative leadership in the field of social welfare.

61

Why National Agencies? [1]

By NATIONAL BUDGET COMMITTEE

TODAY OUR NATIONAL and international responsibilities are becoming part of our local responsibilities. This results inevitably from the basic social, economic, and technical changes taking place. National agencies in the field of health and welfare are all part of the whole enterprise which has been built up in this country to serve the people—all the people. They cannot be separated from local agencies and local services.

Effective service in one community inspires similar service in another and another until there is a chain of similar services across the land. Services are provided the other way too. Some services—such as fundamental research, or developing effective programs and standards within special fields—are beyond the resources of most communities. Consequently, many communities, counties, and states pool their resources in support of national agencies, which can do certain things better and more economically than the supporting communities individually could do them.

National health and welfare agencies exist to do those things which can be done best by this particular teamwork approach. The national agency comes into the picture because (1) a number of local agencies in the same field need the co-ordination, development, stimulation, and support that a national association can give them; (2) some general needs, affecting almost all communities, can best be met by a national approach.

---

[1] Excerpted from *Manual,* National Budget Committee (New York, 1952), p. 1. By permission of United Community Funds and Councils of America, Inc.

62

National Organizations in Social Welfare [1]

By GEORGE W. RABINOFF

The organizations of a people are the product of their social, economic, and political development. The circumstances which created the sturdy individual of American tradition created also the mechanisms through which he and his colleagues of like mind could consult with each other. Representing rebellion against established patterns, they brought with them from all corners of the globe their diverse traditions, life experiences, and values. In a strange and undeveloped country it was inevitable that experimentation by trial and error should precede stable social institutions. Stability would have to reflect the amalgam of social factors, voluntarism and individualism would dominate the process, and exchange of experiences would expedite progress. Accordingly, business men and doctors, industrialists and ministers, lawyers, laborers, and scientists joined with kindred spirits, and added the "genius" for organizing and "joining" to the universally accepted stereotype of American character.

Social welfare has gone through the same process. Individuals discovered needs and then organized groups to do something about them. Usually they limited their activities to their local community; sometimes they were sufficiently imbued with zeal to conceive of their program as nationally significant. This pioneering stage continued past the turn of the century. The decades following, paralleling other fields, saw the emergence of standard types of agencies. The stage of maturation, begun in the early 1920's, is manifest in the greater awareness by agencies of the total needs of social welfare and the consciousness of com-

---

[1] Excerpted from article of same title from the *Social Work Year Book*, 1954, Russell H. Kurtz, ed. (New York: American Association of Social Workers, 1954), pp. 360-369. By permission of National Association of Social Workers.

mon broad objectives. These three stages—organization, program, and relationships—co-exist today. Pioneering seeks and finds new fields to conquer; the setting and attainment of standards is still of major concern; but co-ordination and planning are drawing increasing attention. The pace, the attitudes, and the results vary from place to place and between levels, and differences persist; but the process continues.

National social agencies are part of the whole welfare enterprise that has been built up to serve all the people. It is becoming increasingly evident that national services, like local, are the creatures of the communities, responsive in policies and administration to the widening spread of support. National agencies, it is agreed—at least in principle— are required either because local agencies need the development, stimulation, support, and co-ordination they can derive from national association, or because some needs can best be met by a national approach. Acceptance of this mutuality of national and local objectives has developed unevenly. The national agencies have more recently come to accept the importance of full co-operation with each other, and in that relationship, with local communities. Contributing to this development have been, among other factors, the lengthening community conscience and the shortening lines of communication.

Types of National Organizations

The directories of agencies contained in this volume [*Social Work Year Book,* 1954] list some 387 voluntary national and 63 federal welfare agencies. Some of these are foundations or foundation-sponsored; some appeal to limited interest groups; some are associations of professional persons. It is estimated that about 100 seek voluntary support from the general public on a national scale.

The standard national organization functions in one or more phases of the welfare field: family or child welfare, health, recreation and informal education, community organization, or the specialities within these divisions. The programs of some are limited by age groupings, of others by race or denomination. These functional lines of division are tending to blend; for the national agencies are finding, as are the local, that the effective discharge of their specific job requires concern with the over-all person in his family and community relationships. But there are trends toward separation, too, as new groups and ideas come into the field and start the cycle of pioneering, standardization, and maturation.

The national agencies differ in objectives and purposes, structures and relationships, and the focus of their programs, all of which are determined usually by their origins, their dominant personalities, and their sources of support. Over the years, studies of these factors by individual agencies, by co-operative committees, and by other groups have shown that no neat classification is feasible, that the differentiating factors are not related to the functional fields, that the situation is exceedingly dynamic, and that distinctions are not sharp. In many instances the program was initiated out of a similar impulse in one or in a series of communities, either independently or by active promotion from one city to another, culminating in a national body; in others, the idea was launched nationally and projected into local communities. The net product is a national service program in which the binding force is either a religious, spiritual, philosophical, or ideological way of life; for some, the association is based on common interests in a technique or field of work.

Functions of National Organizations

Irrespective of differences in other respects, national organizations use similar methods to reach their goals. In the final analysis, social welfare is concerned with people and people live in local communities, so the local community is the point of impact. Practically every form of local service seeks a national affiliation; few indeed are the local agencies which choose to stand entirely on their own, unrelated through a national bond to their counterparts in other cities.

National agencies provide essential ingredients to local services, with the result that in place of there being a great diversity among thousands of unrelated local agencies, the function and quality of local organizations today are easily recognized. As affiliates of national bodies, such locals can be used with confidence because the trade-mark of national affiliation assures good standards. Such affiliation gives local groups the full benefit of national experience; it enables them to keep pace with national advances in their fields. It provides leadership with opportunities for relating specialized service to the perspective of the total welfare field, and to the ongoing social, economic, and political developments affecting the needs and programs of social agencies.

The national organization carries the torch of its philosophy and techniques into new territories. It stands ready to meet crises, either in service needs or changing concepts. It undertakes research into pertinent problems, program, methods, and relationships to other fields. It maintains a personnel service, recruiting into its field, giving guidance and orientation training for professional and volunteer personnel, and setting standards, personnel policies, and practices. It gathers information from its member agencies and compiles therefrom data for their guidance, for enlightening public opinion on goals and achievements, and on the extent and kind of problems with which the field is occupied. It develops standards of program and administration.

To these ends the national organization employs qualified headquarters and field service staff; it conducts national and regional conferences and training institutes; it publishes technical and popular literature to keep its personnel abreast of development and to educate the public;

where appropriate, it supplies equipment for its constituency. It offers consultation to its local members through all these media and on all phases of operation. Although national staff and board are responsible for national activities, program priorities and policies are formulated through major participation by local personnel in study, planning, advisory, and administrative bodies.

In short, the standard national organization is at the center of a national system of service receiving from and feeding to its local constituencies the materials which result from their joint labors.

63

The Functions of the National Agency [1]

By EDMUND DE S. BRUNNER

First, a national organization can and should determine the over-all objectives of those concerned with its area of interest. It can bring together people from all over the nation, pool local needs and experiences, and arrive at consensus. In so doing it puts behind the local the power of national opinion crystallized with respect to its interest. If such objectives represent some compromises, as they will, they also stress the fundamental and the basic, and protect the majority from a possible lunatic fringe, which left to itself could discredit a movement.

Second, by similar processes, the national organization can arrive at standards of membership and of performance. There are sometimes difficult questions at this point unless membership is open to all who may be interested. Some time ago, for instance, one of the farm organizations decided to limit its membership exclusively to farmers. It also voted to exclude merchants. Complications arose when merchants who were also farm owners applied for membership. What would be the attitude of the Adult Education Association of the U.S.A. if the organization of Schools for Bartenders applied for membership as an adult educational agency?

Third, it is the function of national organizations to suggest programs and procedures to local groups, especially to newer ones which have not yet developed well-recognized patterns of operation. A national organization is the depository of a great deal of experience. It has a history behind it. It knows what has succeeded and what has failed. It should be freely available in organized fashion to membership and local units.

[1] Excerpted from "Why Nationals?", *Adult Leadership* (Chicago: Adult Education Association), Vol. 2, Jan., 1954, pp. 14-16. By permission of the publisher.

The Extension Service of the United States Department of Agriculture has found that this type of assistance is highly appreciated. A small unit in the federal office reads and analyzes each year the annual reports from the states and the 3,000 counties. These are indexed and cross-indexed. Significant programs or events are referred to the specialists who might be interested. Any county or state taking up a new activity, unless it is unique, can find out what others have done and what the results were. Similarly, exceptionally good teaching or promotional materials can be circulated. This, of course, is the co-ordinating function worked out in very practical, operational fashion.

Fourth, it is the function of a national agency to promote the central interests which brought it into being and link it with the local affiliates. This function has two focuses. One relates to intra-organizational activities such as holding conferences, publishing a journal or a house organ. The publication materials can well be a selection of the best of the materials that flow in to the "national" as it collects information about its program, what goes well where, what the locals are doing. It must be stressed that neither of these functions can be performed with maximum satisfaction unless the locals co-operate. It is in the locals where things happen, where members gather most frequently. Reporting worth-while experience is not a favor to "national." It is an obligation to the other locals. "National" operates simply as a middleman in this activity.

The other part of this function is to keep the purposes and work of the organization before the general public as part of the general promotion program. From this, locals presumably can benefit.

A fifth obligation of the national organization is to assist in leadership training. As a minimum this assistance involves the preparation of both recruitment materials and those which can be used to initiate local leaders into the purposes and methods of the organization's operation. If staff are available, this minimum program can be expanded to include workshops or training conferences for the local leaders on a district or regional basis. There are also the most important tasks of the recruitment selection and training of the agency's professional staff and the in-service training of employed personnel. Certainly one of the explanations for the success of the Agricultural Extension Service's recruitment of over a million volunteer leaders a year is the continuing emphasis on leadership training. This is a responsibility of the state and county staff for the local units and, to a considerable extent, of the federal staff in the work with the employed personnel. It is significant that although the state and county units of the Service are very jealous of their prerogative, there has never been any question but that the federal office has the responsibility for organizing and conducting the regional schools, workshops, and institutes and is expected to be represented on the faculty of such training activities.

There are other activities that may be assigned to a national office, particularly research. There are other ways of stating the functions set down. There can be no question but that these functions are necessary obligations of a national office and essential to the effectiveness of the local affiliates.

There is, however, another side. Too often there is more than a modicum of truth in the criticism of national organizations. A national organization is an institution. Inevitably an institution seeks prestige and power for itself. This applies not only to its place in society but also in intra-institutional relations. Local personnel feel that they "are on the firing line," "doing the real work," "acquainted with local conditions." National leaders believe that their position, some would say their eminence, gives them such an over-all view of the field that they can tell local affiliates how to operate. The more strongly national officers feel this, the closer they come to an attempt to dictate both policy and procedure. More unfortunate is the natural tendency of a national agency staff to see no local interest but their own. They are concerned with an institution not with the community in which the local operates.

The first of these tendencies constricts the initiative of the local affiliate. The second in the last analysis leads to competition among organizations for the time and money of the local people, to a degree of divisiveness in the local community as unfortunate and harmful as is competition and overchurching in the field of religion. The community cannot help being weakened when this occurs and the social organizations within it are weakened too.

People do not live life in segments, each separately organized. They live life whole. A community is a complex social organism. The multitude of personal and organizational interactions are not neatly distinguished as on a chart as people move through their waking hours.

People invest time and money in organizations because what is offered meets to some degree, and almost always to an imperfect degree, some need or stimulates some interest they recognize as important for themselves and for the place where they live. The choices they make among the opportunities available reflect their own capacities and concerns. If a national organization permits no flexibility in programs, no adaptation to local conditions, we can only hope that it fails before it does too much harm.

There is much complaint today about communities being overorganized. All over the nation rural social research workers have heard, "There are four meetings every night of the week in this town. We need to get together." What overorganization really means is that in the struggle to institutionalize separate interests (so that national organizations can glow with the satisfaction of reporting more locals and more funds each year), the needs of the community as a whole have been forgotten and the priority of those needs with reference to a particular community neglected. Integrated community life is handicapped, sometimes even becomes impossible. The tragedy is that organizational leaders never realize that in those too few cases where leaders have paused to look at the community first and then moved to allocate organizational resources to meet the needs discovered there has been work enough and prestige enough for all and the community has benefited immeasurably.

Communities differ as to their economic base, the age structure of their population, the occupational distribution, the educational status of their people, their cultural heritage, and therefore their values, traditions, modes of communication. They differ in other ways as well. It is folly to suppose that any standardized program can neatly fit everywhere. It is folly to suppose that every community has equal need for any well-meaning, noble-purpose organization that comes along. The General Education Board found that before it could launch its efforts to improve public education in the South it had to help raise the economic status of the farmers and improve the health of the people.

National organizations we will have. We need them. They work most effectively through local affiliates. The delicate problem is to find out how in each local situation to promote the institutionalized interest so that it will strengthen, not weaken the community. The considerable amount of real harm many national organizations do can be measurably reduced, but only by taking off the institutional blinders, looking at the community first, and then molding the service rendered to the needs discovered.

PART FIVE

Introduction

WHO IS RESPONSIBLE for doing community organization—who are the workers? The personnel situation in this area differs significantly from that in casework, for example, in that both nonsocial workers and lay volunteers are engaged in its practice. In the first respect, community organization resembles social work research in which many social scientists without full professional training in social work are employed; and, in the second, group work, in which large numbers of lay leaders participate. Many workers engaged in community organization in broad social welfare fields, such as delinquency prevention and community development, for example, were trained in the psychological and social sciences, or education, rather than in professional social work, and interested lay citizens participate in all types of community planning and social action projects. Though it is often maintained that casework cannot be practiced in the absence of a professional worker the analogy would not appear to hold in community organization where, it would seem, the process frequently occurs without benefit of any social worker—community organization specialist or other type.

Furthermore, in contrast again with casework, most of the responsibility for community leadership and planning in any locality is carried by direct-service workers in casework and group work agencies rather than by council staff members. In fact, according to various estimates, from a third to a half of the time of casework and group work practitioners and executives is devoted to interagency work and community-wide planning and promotion.

Unfortunately we have little accurate and specific knowledge of the background of community organization workers in the various welfare and closely related fields and only limited data on those identified with

455

professional social work. The number of such practitioners, as in the case of social work research, is relatively small. This fact is partly explained by the comments above, but it has, presumably, hampered development in this area of professional social work. Only a few studies of the "COP" (community organization practitioner) have been made, the first statistical investigation being a thesis submitted to the Institute of Social Work, of the University of Michigan, in 1948.[1] Five years later a survey was made by the Association for the Study of Community Organization of the training, experience, and professional affiliations of the 550 members of the organization at that time.[2]

On the basis of a 50 per cent reply it was found that the mean age of members was 45.5 years, and that 62 per cent were men. Some 80 per cent were members, or eligible for membership, in the American Association of Social Workers, and nearly 90 per cent in one of the then six other professional associations. The group averaged over eleven years in social work experience with a median period of ten years in community organization.

With respect to education, 59 per cent of ASCO members responding had had two years or more of graduate professional training in comparison with 70.5 per cent of AASW members in general. The percentage of ASCO members with this amount of education was also less than that for those in the American Association of Psychiatric Social Workers, the American Association of Medical Social Workers, and the Social Work Research Group, but was higher than that for the group work and school social work associations.

The major issues and questions considered in the following readings relate to (1) the responsibility of all social workers for community organization; (2) the community organization practitioner—the jobs he holds, the roles he plays, and the education he has had or should receive; and (3) the importance of the volunteer, or citizen participant. The first selection stresses the community relations of direct-service workers, the next four, the functions of the professional community organization practitioner as seen during the decade 1947–1956, and the last, the importance of the volunteer in welfare activities. Material on the last subject will also be found scattered throughout the book.

Since the majority of the readings in Part V concern the specialist in community organization, the "COP," some of the principal issues in this connection might properly be pointed up. First, what are the kinds

[1] Robert Irving Hiller, *The Education and Work Experience of Community Organization Practitioners* (New York: Association for the Study of Community Organization and Community Chests and Councils of America, Inc., 1949).

[2] Ernest B. Harper, *Survey of Opinion and Professional Status of ASCO Members,* May, 1953. Unpublished Report to the Association. See also article by same author, "ASCO and Social Work," *Social Work Journal* (New York: American Association of Social Workers), XXXIV, No. 4, Oct., 1953, pp. 182-183, based on same study.

of jobs that require professional education and experience? No completely satisfactory or accepted classification of positions in community organization exists, but this question is considered in detail in Selection 65, "What Is the Job of the Community Organization Worker?" Complete job specifications for positions in local chests, councils, and central services will be found in a later CCC publication.[3] Comparable descriptions for the many nonchest and council positions, however, are needed in addition to the few such positions established under civil service in various states.

The role of the professional social work practitioner in community organization has also been the subject of considerable writing and discussion. Though there is substantial agreement on essentials some divergence of opinion exists when the practice of community organization in nonwelfare fields such as adult education, religion, and agriculture, for example, is considered. In addition to the material included in these selections the reader is also referred to an excellent recent description of community organization in these various areas by Murray G. Ross in which he defines the worker's function as including, at times, the roles of guide, enabler, expert, and social therapist.[4] The same subject is also discussed by Mildred Barry in Selection 29 of Part III.

Opinion is also divided on the subject of professional education. With the growing acceptance of the generic nature of social work training and changing policies with respect to the accrediting of specializations it is coming to be generally agreed that *all* social workers should receive at least minimum education in community organization, including instruction in public relations, as Bower urges in Selection 64. Furthermore, Violet Sieder and others propose the addition to the curriculum of a course, or sequence of courses, devoted to community growth and development, and/or the dynamics of culture and the social process, *per se,* parallel with the currently approved series on human growth and development.

Beyond basic or generic professional education would come the various specializations, not in fields of application, or settings merely, as traditionally, but in the major processes, including community organization. Opinions differ, however, concerning the point at which such specialization should begin, and the level at which field training should be undertaken.

One final problem, that of recruitment for community organization work, is becoming of increasing concern to the profession. One basis for this is the startlingly small number of second-year students in the schools of social work in the United States and Canada with field place-

---

[3] *Job Descriptions for Chests and Councils: Titles, Duties, Typical Tasks, Qualifications* (New York: Community Chests and Councils of America, Inc.), Bul. No. 141, March, 1953, 23 pp.

[4] *Community Organization, Theory and Principles* (New York: Harper & Brothers, 1955), Chapter 8, "The Role of the Professional Worker," pp. 200-228.

ments in community organization. As of November 1, 1957, the 60 schools in both countries reported only 45 students assigned to planning agencies or community organization programs out of a total of 1,882. In contrast, there were 156 placements in group work and 1,612 in various types of casework agencies. Furthermore, there were only 21 placements during the year in the closely related area of administration, and two in research, with 46 unclassified or not reported.[5] In view of such facts the belief is growing that both class and field work in community organization should be initiated earlier than formerly.

The following selections treat various aspects of the questions above with the exception of the last, on which, unfortunately, no adequate study has yet been published.

---

[5] *Statistics on Social Work Education,* Nov. 1, 1957 and *Academic Year,* 1956–1957 (New York: Council on Social Work Education, Jan., 1958), Table 10, p. 16.

Social Workers and the Community[1]

By CHESTER L. BOWER

The occasion for the following paper was the first annual meeting of the newly formed Council on Social Work Education in St. Louis, Missouri, in January, 1953. Its significance for community organization lies in the forceful plea made by a successful council executive to *all* professional social workers to strive to understand the community, identify with its various components, and participate widely in its activities. The writer complains that social workers tend to associate too exclusively with each other and, as a result, are too often out of touch with the "business and industrial community in which they work." The remedy for this situation, he thinks, lies in professional education and he urges, therefore, that the schools of social work place more emphasis on responsibility to the community, on social dynamics, the power structure, and public relations.

Chester L. Bower is currently executive director of the Welfare Planning Council, Los Angeles Region, having succeeded C. Whit Pfeiffer when the latter retired in January, 1957. He was a member of the first board of directors of the Council on Social Work Education and served until 1955. From 1943, until he moved to Los Angeles, Mr. Bower was identified with the Community Council of Houston, Texas, and became its executive secretary in 1945. He has been active in the American Association of Social Workers (now National Association of Social Workers), the former American Association of Group Workers, and the National Conference of Social Work (now National Conference on

[1] Excerpted from "Social Workers and the Community: A Challenge to Education," *Social Work Journal* (New York: American Association of Social Workers), XXXIV, April, 1953, pp. 71-73. By permission of National Association of Social Workers. Also, *Education for Social Work,* Proceedings, Council on Social Work Education (New York: 1953), pp. 46-49.

Social Welfare). He holds a Master's degree from Northwestern University.

. . . I COULD GO ON with dozens of illustrations why it is important for social workers to be community conscious and skilled in community relationships. I hope you agree about the need, which is for *all* social workers—not just the administrators and community organization workers—to be so skilled. But the real question now is, can social work education do anything about it? I believe so, and offer only a few illustrations which I hope will be suggestive of more.

First: The most important thing to be done is to change our point of view in teaching social work concepts, principles, and skills. We must include in that teaching an awareness and accurate understanding of the role the community setting plays in actual social work practice. For instance, when the principle of confidentiality is being taught to students, is the teacher aware, and is he able to make the student aware, of the general community's attitude toward that concept? How does that community attitude modify practice? By what principle is the worker guided in a conflict situation caused by the concept?

When casework is being taught, what concept of the professional worker's total job is in the teacher's mind? Does she teach casework as though the only thing it includes is the worker and client relationship, or does it include the facts of that relationship existing in a social-cultural-economic setting which modifies and in many important respects determines the larger meaning of the relationship?

Social work must recognize that as a profession it is answerable to the whole community, not just to the client. To get this concept clearly identified would help clear the cobwebs from a good many controversial subjects.

Throughout the curriculum—casework, group work, community organization, administration, specialized casework services, and so forth—what is the concept of the "social work job" that is in the mind of the instructor and gets transmitted to the student? Does it include, throughout, the understanding that community activity is as much a part of the job as is the client-worker contact? If social work behavior as I observe it answers the question, I'm sure the present answer is "no."

Nearly any community organization worker is acquainted with the complaint from some agency staff people that they have so many committee meetings they haven't time for *their own jobs*. I quarrel with two things in that situation. First, the committee work ought to be just as much a part of the social work job as the casework or group work assignments in the agency. Second, more social work staff should be assigned to committee and community work so that a few administrators and supervisors are not overburdened with community responsibilities.

Perhaps I am overworking the point, but let me repeat: we need to get the community viewpoint into our faculty and fieldwork staff. It's the primary step in changing practice.

As this point of view is accepted, what changes can be made in what is taught in the classroom that will lead to more and better community participation by social workers? First, the most accurate and scientific material available from the social sciences on social dynamics, stratification, power structures of communities, and so forth, should be in the curriculum and translated into social work understanding. It should be made meaningful to the social work practitioner. In the same way that an understanding of the dynamics of individual behavior contributes to objectivity in casework, so does the understanding of social behavior contribute to the social worker's ability to understand and use his knowledge in dealing with the community.

Second: Let's teach all social workers, not just the group work variety, some skills in discussion leading and participation, at least the rudiments of public speaking, something about the art of readable writing, parliamentary procedures, and other similar skills of social communication. It's not the desire to be democratic that's lacking. It's the skill.

Third: Let's [make a curriculum change and] drop this time-honored, wasteful, and juvenile concept of "supervision" as it's practiced, especially in the casework setting. It results in a duplicate system of administrative responsibilities which is costly in both professional skill and money. It keeps the individual social worker from growing up to the place where he is able to make decisions on his own. The essence of professionalism is the skill and ability to make decisions based on knowledge, not to make decisions under supervision. If the doctors can bury their mistakes, we at least should be able to stand up to ours.

There are ways of making this shift without wrecking the profession. Dr. Hollis and Miss Taylor have pointed it out clearly.[2] We need immediately to get at this job of identifying clearly the concepts, knowledge, and skills required for various levels of social work functions, and then assign personnel that is properly equipped for each identified level. This is obviously a basic task requiring the co-operation of school, agency, and the professional organizations. But the results would pay off in economy to the community and maturity to the profession.

Obviously there are field work changes required if we are to take these ideas seriously. Field work assignments must include not only the business of carrying cases and groups, but experiences with agency

---

[2] Ernest V. Hollis and Alice L. Taylor, *Social Work Education in the United States* (New York: Columbia University Press, 1952).

boards, committee meetings, civic organizations, public officials, and a host of other persons and groups that help make the community. Students might learn something about social work and the community by taking an active part in the community chest drive. I grant that these experiences are not easy to create and to be made meaningful—but it isn't easy to have students carry cases or handle groups, either, and we make the necessary preparation and arrangements when we are convinced it's part of the social work job. I'm convinced the *community* is part of the social work job.

65

What Is the Job of the Community Organization Worker? [1]

By ARTHUR DUNHAM

This paper is in the "line of succession" of a number of National Conference papers in the years following the Lane Report of 1939, in which various aspects of generic community welfare organization were analyzed and discussed.

The present selection seeks to examine the broad subject of personnel for community organization, from a generic standpoint rather than from the standpoint of any special types of agencies, such as chests and councils. The discussion includes a suggested list of types of community organization jobs; a consideration of the role of the community organization worker; what constitutes desirable equipment for such a worker; and some brief suggestions regarding the development of the community organization worker to meet the needs in terms of both quantity and quality.

. . . COMMUNITY ORGANIZATION includes a wide range of diverse activities and methods. In this respect, community organization is unlike casework or group work, where there is more intensive con-

[1] Excerpted from the paper of the same title in the pamphlet, *The Job of the Community Organization Worker* (Association for the Study of Community Organization and Community Chests and Councils of America, Inc., June, 1948), pp. 3-14. By permission of United Community Funds and Councils of America, Inc. See also *Proceedings of the National Conference of Social Work,* Atlantic City, 1948 (New York: Columbia University Press, 1949), pp. 162-172.

centration on a narrower range of more nearly similar activities. The caseworker, for example, is always concerned with helping a family or individual to solve certain individual problems; the community organization worker may be engaged in activities as diverse as operating a social service exchange, planning and carrying out a survey, directing a community chest campaign, or promoting a bill to reorganize the state's public welfare system.

It follows naturally that there are many types of community organization jobs, and that these are far more varied and dissimilar than the various types of specialized casework and group work jobs. For purposes of this discussion let us limit ourselves to jobs which are concerned primarily with community organization and leave out of account the jobs of executives of client-service agencies, child welfare and public welfare workers, settlement workers, and so on, where there may be a community organization component in the job, even though the job is concerned primarily with administration, casework, or group work.

The Personnel Department of Community Chests and Councils, Inc. has performed an invaluable service in making a job analysis study of positions in community chests and community welfare councils. On the basis of this study they have drawn up job specifications for seventeen types of jobs in chests and councils. Three of these are definitely non-social work positions—Accountant, Comptroller, and Office Manager. The other fourteen jobs are as follows:

1. Executive Secretary, Chest and Council
2. Executive Secretary, Chest
3. Executive Secretary, Council
4. Budget Secretary
5. Campaign Director
6. Campaign Division Secretary
7. Secretary, Council Division
8. Secretary, Information and Referral Service
9. Labor Representative
10. Neighborhood Council Secretary
11. Publicity Director
12. Research Director
13. Social Service Exchange Secretary
14. Director, Volunteer Service Bureau

Let us hold over for the moment the question of whether all of these are social work jobs. They *are* obviously all typical jobs that are found in chests and councils.

I suggest that at least three of the jobs in the foregoing classification—Publicity Director, Research Director, and Neighborhood Council Secretary (or neighborhood worker, as it might be called)—may be found in other types of community organization agencies, so these may be considered generic types of community organization jobs rather than chest-council specializations.

If we go on from here, I believe we can identify at least eight other types of community organization jobs, all of which are outside of the chest-council field. These are as follows:

1. *Executive of state-wide agency for health and welfare planning.* Carries on general health and welfare planning and usually promotion of legislation on a state-wide basis, through such organizations as a state-wide citizens' welfare association (the New York State Charities Aid Association, for example) or a state conference of social work which conducts a year-round "action program" in addition to the traditional conference program.

2. *Executive of a program promotional agency in a specialized field.* Development and promotion of a social welfare program and improvement of standards in a specialized field. Examples would include a local housing or tuberculosis association; a state society for mental hygiene, crippled children and adults, or the blind; and most national agencies, such as those in the fields of family service, child welfare, health, recreation.[2]

3. *Executive of a national agency for co-ordination and broad health and welfare planning.* Carries on health and welfare planning and co-ordination in the field of social welfare as a whole or in a broad area such as health, youth service, casework. The National Social Welfare Assembly and its divisions, the National Health Council, and, I think, the national professional associations, are examples of such agencies.

4. *Financial secretary.* In charge of or primarily concerned with fund raising for a local, state, national, or international agency. The job sometimes involves direction of a highly organized national or state financial campaign, as in the case of certain national health agencies.

5. *Conference executive.* Carries on the direction of a national, state, or possibly local social welfare conference whose primary function is the holding of an annual conference or convention, and closely related activities. There are relatively few of these jobs; examples are afforded by the National Conference of Social Work and the state conferences in New York and Pennsylvania.

6. *Community organization field representative.* A field representative's job may be concerned with either administration or community organization or both. The worker whom I have called "community organization field representative" carries on field service for a national or state agency where the contacts are primarily consultative, co-operative, and liaison in nature rather than authoritative, administrative, or procedural. The job of field representative for an agency like the Family

---

[2] This would include also certain positions in federal agencies, such as the Social Security Administration in the Federal Security Agency.

Service Association of America which is essentially a federation of local units would be an example. Obviously many public welfare field representative jobs would be primarily administrative in nature and would not be included as community organization jobs.

7. *Legislative representative.* Analyzes, interprets, and promotes legislation for a state-wide or national voluntary agency.

8. *Teacher of community organization.* Teaches community organization in a school for the professional education of social workers. The teacher is of course primarily an educator rather than a community organization practitioner, but he is so intimately related to the training of community organization workers, and there is so much movement back and forth between teachers and practitioners that it seems reasonable to include the teacher's job in this analysis.

If we take into account both of these classifications, several comments may be made.

In the first place, both classifications cover only the executive or primary jobs; they do not take account of assistant or subordinate grades. In practice one would find in many community organization agencies examples of such gradations as executive, subexecutive, senior practitioner, and junior practitioner.

In the second place, I believe that a careful examination of community organization jobs would show that the job of the community organization worker—even that of the senior or junior practitioner—resembles the job of an executive or subexecutive, in terms of its content and types of activities, more closely than it resembles the job of the casework or group work practitioner. If this is true, it has important implications for the training, selection, and supervision of community organization workers.

In the third place, these classifications obviously contain some borderline jobs which require further study to determine whether or not these are primarily social work jobs, whether the persons who hold these jobs should be primarily social workers, with community organization training, or whether we should expect to draw these staff members mainly or largely from other related professional or vocational fields such as social research, public relations, fund raising, and accountancy. The particular jobs which seem to me to lie in this borderline area are Budget Secretary, Campaign Director, Campaign Division Secretary, Publicity Director, Research Director, and Financial Secretary.

In the fourth place, certain of these jobs clearly require knowledge of specialized functional fields as well as knowledge of and skill in community organization. Examples would be found in the jobs of the secretary of the health division of a community welfare council or executive or staff member of a national promotional agency for family service or mental hygiene.

In the fifth place, from the standpoint of job content and the skills involved, it would seem that we can distinguish nine major areas of job specialization:

1. Health and welfare planning. Carried on in councils and in certain state-wide and national agencies, and having many ramifications.
2. Community chest operation: joint financing.
3. Fund raising other than in community chests.
4. Social service exchange administration.
5. Promotion of programs in specialized fields.
6. Research.
7. Public relations.
8. Legislative analysis and promotion.
9. Teaching of community organization. . . .

The Role of the Community Organization Worker

At the last National Conference, Kenneth Pray eloquently maintained the thesis, which has been so widely discussed, that the community organization worker is essentially an "enabler" and not a manipulator.[3]

I think Kenneth Pray gave us insight here into a profound philosophical truth. I suggest that if we follow any community organization job back far enough into its ultimate nature and reason for being, we shall always find that the community organization worker is the agent of some group or aggregation of people—whether it is voters of the United States or the supporters of the local community chest—in carrying into effect some program which these people support either by contributions, or active assent, or at least by acquiescence. Certainly it is in harmony also with the fundamental ideas of democracy that the administrative agent or the practitioner enables the group to achieve its desires rather than commanding or manipulating the group.

Thus far I think we may go safely, but can we not go on from this point, and must we not also be on our guard against oversimplifying this matter of the role of the community organization worker? If you have a community or a constituency group that is substantially united in its thinking and knows what it wants to do, then you have perhaps a rather simple situation where the community organization worker acts as the agent of the constituency in helping it to attain its objectives. But is it not often true that the constituency group and even the governing board is not substantially united in its thinking and does not *know what it wants to do* except in very general terms? For example, a group of agencies and citizens in a community may form a community welfare council. They know that they want somehow to improve the well-being

[3] Kenneth L. M. Pray, "When Is Community Organization Social Work Practice?" *Proceedings, National Conference of Social Work,* San Francisco, 1947 (New York: Columbia University Press, 1948), pp. 197, 202.

of the community through better teamwork and joint planning and action. But as to how they should attain this result, or what should be their immediate objectives or program projects, they may have very little idea. Should they give priority or major emphasis to promoting a recreation survey, seeking a reorganization of the municipal department of public welfare, trying to raise standards among the child caring organizations, or interpreting social work to organized labor?

It seems to me the role of the community organization worker must often be that of *creative leadership*. Ordway Tead's well-known definition of leadership is "the activity of influencing people to co-operate toward some goal which they come to find desirable." [4] The community organization worker will usually give indirect, rather than direct, public or official leadership. But he must bring to the problems of his agency all the knowledge, imagination, resourcefulness, and creative craftsmanship that he can command. He must often interpret, suggest, and analyze alternatives, and enter fully as a dynamic partner into a creative group process by which goals will be chosen, decisions will be hammered into shape and translated into action. The final decision, the "last word," will be with a lay group; but I believe the community organization worker must be a creative partner and participant in the determination of objectives as well as the expert in the application of the process of community organization.

If one examines more closely specific roles which the community organization worker assumes in particular situations, I believe we shall find that frequently he must act in such a variety of roles as to be suggestive of the actor in the old-time theatrical "stock company." In an interesting article on "A Federal Agency's Relation to Community Planning," in *Social Forces* for December, 1946, Arthur Hillman pointed out that the Office of Community War Services at various times played the roles of the secretariat or clearinghouse; convener or mediator; attorney or advocate; and consultant or adviser. The roles of community organization workers on various jobs would probably run the whole gamut from fact finder, analyst, planner, catalyst, interpreter, educator, conferee, negotiator, mediator, and consultant to organizer, agent, executive aide, advocate, promoter, social actionist, and militant leader.

Moreover, Donald Howard and Hertha Kraus have recently challenged social workers in general and community organization workers in particular to produce leaders who can assume the roles of "social generalists" and social statesmen.[5] These are not flights of fancy; if we want examples of social statesmanship we can find two of them in the

---

[4] Ordway Tead, *Art of Leadership* (New York: McGraw-Hill Book Company, 1935), p. 20.

[5] Donald S. Howard, "New Horizons for Social Work," *Compass,* Vol. XXVIII, Nov., 1947. Hertha Kraus, "The Future of Social Work: Some Comments on Social Work Function," *Compass,* Vol. XXIX, Jan., 1948.

professional careers of those great civic servants of the last fifty years, Edward T. Devine and Homer Folks.

The Equipment of the Community Organization Worker

With all this variety of jobs and roles, is it possible to give any general answer to the question, What should be the equipment of the community organization worker? If we allow for numerous individual exceptions we can perhaps formulate at least a tentative and general answer.

Presumably the community organization worker will derive his equipment for the job from personal qualities and attributes, general education, graduate professional education, and experience.

Most of us would probably agree that a college education and two years of graduate professional education in an accredited school of social work, with some specialization in community organization, would normally give the best foundation for a social worker who wishes to become, sooner or later, a community organization practitioner.

There is not time to discuss here the problems that arise in the schools of social work in training for community organization. We shall do better, I think, to try to identify the specific kind of equipment which we want in the community organization worker in addition to the basic professional education that we may assume for any social worker. I suggest six elements in the equipment of the community organization worker:

1. *Firsthand experience in dealing with people,* preferably in a client-service agency. There is a difference of opinion on this point. I believe that the community organization worker should have had one or more years of previous staff experience (not merely field work) in a casework, group work, or other client-service agency; or perhaps a reasonable equivalent for such experience in a closely allied profession. Social work is concerned with serving people; its focus is on human needs and human relationships. I believe that the community organization worker should make his entrance into social work at the point of helping and working with people rather than at the point of committees, meetings, organization charts, plans, programs, surveys, or campaigns. I am convicted that social work cannot afford to have community organization leaders who have not worked directly with the consumers of social service, the clients—leaders who are remote from the experience of caseworkers and group workers, and who may tend to think of social welfare programs in abstract and impersonal terms.

2. *A sound working knowledge of the field of social welfare* and of types of social welfare resources on local, state, and national levels. In most community organization jobs, the worker must be a social work "generalist" rather than a specialist, in terms of his knowledge of functional fields.

3. *An understanding and working knowledge of community organi-*

zation—its objectives, the types of problems encountered, types and functions of agencies, methods and principles; and also at least an elementary understanding of the closely related subject of administration.

4. *Skill in the practice of community organization.* This is the element, above all others, that distinguishes the practitioner of community organization from one who merely "knows about" it. This skill is likely to be gained primarily from properly supervised field work and from experience.

5. *Personal qualities.* The community organization worker needs the personal qualities that are needed by any social worker,[6] and also many of the qualities that are needed by an executive.[7] Among the qualities that are important for the community organization worker we should certainly include integrity, courage, emotional balance and adjustment, objectivity, sound judgment, tact, sensitivity, adaptability, imagination, ability to work under pressure, an interest in and liking for people, and a deeply held respect for human personality. One can hardly insist, in addition, that a sense of humor be mandatory, but the worker will have a rugged life without it!

6. *A sound philosophy of community organization.* The community organization worker needs to have a philosophy and an over-all point of view about his job. To be sure, his community organization philosophy will be part of his philosophy of social work, his social philosophy, his philosophy of life. Authoritarianism, traditionalism, commercialism, lack of convictions, and a spineless opportunism are some of the antitheses of sound community organization. A sound philosophy of community organization would be rooted and grounded in democracy and oriented to its values of ultimate control by the whole people; the right of self-determination by the individual, the group, and the community; co-operation and mutual participation in the achievement of common goals.

How Shall We Develop Community Organization Workers?

We may work through many channels to develop the number and quality of workers that we need in community organization.

We must go on from our present encouraging but scattered beginnings in job analysis in community organization agencies. We must do a better job of recruiting for this area of social work, and we must put into our recruiting efforts some sense of the quality of social adventure which is inherent in community organization. We must greatly strengthen the programs of the schools of social work in training for

---

[6] *Social Work as a Profession* (New York: American Association of Schools of Social Work, 1947 ed.), pp. 10-12.

[7] Ordway Tead, *Art of Leadership* (New York: McGraw-Hill Book Company, 1935), pp. 82-114. See also Clarence King, *Social Agency Boards and How to Make Them Effective* (New York: Harper & Brothers, 1938), pp. 62-64.

community organization. I believe that even the best of these programs today are in a pioneer stage in respect to the number and nature of the courses offered and the kinds of field work training provided. We may need to supplement the regular curricula of the schools with more special summer institutes and opportunities for advanced study for those who have received their Master's degrees or who have had substantial job experience.

We must accelerate the production of one of our major tools, in the form of technical literature on community organization. Wayne McMillen has put us all in his debt by producing the most important and most valuable single book that has yet been written on *Community Organization for Social Welfare*. Other valuable additions to our literature are being made. But we are still a long way from an adequate working literature.

National agencies such as Community Chests and Councils, the National Publicity Council, the National Social Welfare Assembly, the Association for the Study of Community Organization, and others, may do much to raise the level of practice through research; publication; educational conferences, institutes, and meetings; field service, and other methods.

We can experiment with and gradually establish methods of recording that meet the needs of our jobs. Community organization workers are not likely to arrive at full professional status until they develop the self-discipline and the conscious direction of their use of community organization that will come with the development of adequate analytical operating records.

Finally, community organization workers in local communities, individually and collectively, can become the greatest single force for advancing the job and raising standards. The individual worker can advance through reading and study, through becoming more analytical about his own job, through experimenting and reporting the results of his experiments. In local community organization discussion groups, such as exist in at least eleven communities today, workers may strengthen and stimulate each other, exchange experiences and ideas, and get a sense of working together in a common professional service.

Community organization must never be seen as merely a job. We are working with the materials out of which a community is built, a cooperative society is fashioned. We are in the thick of the network of personal, group, and intergroup relationships that make up modern social life. The community organization worker needs a sense of vocation. He is performing an essential function. He is a producer and conserver of social values. He has a vital and crucial role to play in the social drama of our time—the role of a servant of democracy.

66

The Role of the Community Organization Practitioner [1]

By EDWARD D. LYNDE

Considerable interest was expressed at the National Conference of Social Work a few years ago when the author of the following paper introduced the label "COP" to designate the community organization practitioner. As executive secretary of one of the large independent welfare councils he has some very suggestive things to say about the professional community organization worker.

The latter's ability to meet a problem situation, he thinks, depends not so much on magical techniques or what he does at the moment of crisis, but rather on "what he has done months and years before—[and on] the leadership which he has helped to develop in his organization." The most significant characteristic of the successful COP, as this writer sees it, is a "deep and sympathetic understanding of the other fellow, his motives, and his impediments." Only on the basis of such knowledge can he hope to induce individuals and groups to work together toward the solution of common problems.

Edward D. Lynde was general secretary of the Grand Rapids, Michigan, Social Welfare Association from 1917 to 1922, and executive secretary of the Milwaukee Family Welfare Association during the following year, after which he became general secretary of the Cleveland Associated Charities. He was assistant general director of the Family Welfare Association of America (now Family Service Association of

[1] Excerpted from "The Role of the Community Organization Practitioner" (New York: Association for the Study of Community Organization, Community Organization Materials No. 4, May, 1953, 20 pp.). See also, *Selected Papers in Group Work and Community Organization*, Proceedings, National Conference of Social Work, Chicago, Ill., 1952 (Raleigh, N.C.: Health Publications Institute, Inc., Aug., 1953), pp. 118-128. By permission of National Conference on Social Welfare.

America) from 1933 to 1935 when he accepted his present position as executive secretary of the Welfare Federation of Cleveland. He is a member of Phi Beta Kappa and a graduate of the New York School of Social Work.

THE FRAMERS OF THIS PROGRAM have asked me to speak on how the COP can meet concrete problem situations. The first and most imperative step is to develop and hold influential lay leaders in our democratic movement. . . .

Some years ago in Cleveland an extremely powerful civic and business organization set out to oppose the passage of a tax levy which was necessary for the maintenance of county health and welfare services. The levy required a 65 per cent vote and their opposition would have defeated it. The president of the Welfare Federation, which is a Council of Social Agencies, asked that their board meet with our representatives. At this meeting, our president, a highly prominent business man, took one-half hour to tell them exactly what their opposition meant. Thereupon, they withdrew their opposition and the levy passed.

This was a problem situation involving our tax-supported member organizations, and it is illustrative of most problem situations in community planning. The COP's ability to meet them depends not so much on what he does on that occasion, but what he has done months and years before—the leadership which he has helped to develop in his organization. . . .

Another problem situation involved the merger of two agencies as proposed by the community planning organization. One agency board and staff was lukewarm, and the other was bitterly opposed to this merger at the outset. At one time, an able lay person saved the day by working out a compromise between two factions. Eventually, the merger took place as the result of public opinion, which had been developed in a series of many meetings involving many people, in which all points of view were heard and thoroughly debated. This was a vivid refutation of the idea that it requires a small elite group to effect difficult community action. On two different occasions, a small elite group had tried to accomplish this very merger and had both times failed. . . .

Analyzing those instances (and others), certain characteristics appear in all. On the average, it took seven years to bring about each of these achievements. Each of them was accomplished as the result of relationships which exist between the community planning organization and public officials or influential lay persons, or through the prestige of the board of the community planning organization. In one instance, a study and the documenting of the facts was an important influence. In another, an informal evening meeting at the home of one of our influential lay people helped iron out a difficult problem.

My paper was to include the role of the COP and the methods which he can use in problem situations. I firmly believe that it is altogether too late for techniques or methods to be of any great use by the time one is facing a critical problem situation. There is no magic wand which we can wave. As I stated before, the COP's ability to meet a crisis depends not so much on what he does on that occasion but what he has done months and years before—the leadership which he has helped to develop in his organization. As we review problem situations and substantial achievements that have occurred over a period of years, the four most influential factors in accomplishing satisfactory results have been (1) the securing and vivid presentation of facts and ideas (sometimes in personal interviews); (2) the quality of professional leadership in the agencies and in the central organizations; (3) the wholehearted co-operation of public officials; and (4) the deep concern and active participation of influential lay persons in the community planning organization.

Because of limited time, I shall devote myself here to the methods of securing the co-operation of public officials and securing and holding the participation of community leaders. Such co-operation and participation is cumulative. The more you have, the more you can get.

We have been told that in one city certain public officials declared that it was illegal for them to *participate* in the Council of Social Agencies because they would thus be abrogating their administrative responsibility. This is a good illustration of subjective thinking, as with the woman who entered a Nevada lawyer's office unannounced and demanded a divorce on the ground of her husband's infidelity. "And what makes you think that he isn't faithful?" asked the attorney. "Well," the lady replied, "I don't think he's the father of my child."

Success in securing the *co-operation* of public officials will depend largely on four factors: (1) The *kind* of public officials your community has. (2) Their participation in the community planning organization. The County Administrative Officer, one of the three County Commissioners, the City Director of Health and Welfare, the Juvenile Court Judge, and the Cleveland Superintendent of Schools are all extremely active in the Cleveland Welfare Federation and are members of our Board of Trustees and various committees. The regional head of the Federal Security Agency is chairman of an important committee. The feeling of complete partnership on the part of these and many other public officials throughout the Federation is due to some degree, we believe, to the fact that our budgeting is bound up with planning and that the planning function is separate from the money raising. (3) The degree of participation of influential lay leaders in your community organization. Public officials are naturally more interested in being part of a strong and influential organization. Our presidents and our lay leaders have been the type of people whose invitations to luncheon would be accepted by the Mayor or the Governor for a personal tête-à-tête on important issues. (4) The degree to which you can be of *assistance* to the public officials. In Cleveland, for example, we release our Director of Public Relations, free of charge, for a month nearly every year to conduct a campaign for a tax levy for the County and City governments and the School Board. We also help to finance the campaign. This might not be possible if we were responsible for the money raising, but it brings us much closer to the public organizations.

To carry on effective community planning, to hold the interest of public officials and to meet conflict situations effectually, the most important factor of all will be the strength and quality of the lay leadership. By influential lay leaders, we mean not only the largest contributors to a community fund, captains of industry and influential business leaders, though they are indispensable, but also labor union leaders, influential politicians, leading professional men, outstanding citizens, both men and women, newspaper editors, and religious, nationality, and racial leaders. . . .

The ability to secure and hold important lay leaders depends to a great degree upon the following factors:

1. The availability of such lay leaders in the community, and this, in turn, will depend mainly on the strength of agency boards and their recognition of the importance of central planning. The process of developing lay leadership is one in which the agencies must share. It starts at the agency level. It can also start at the fund-raising level. It will be helped tremendously by agency executives. Budgeting in the planning organization attracts lay leaders, and participating therein by agency board members broadens their interest beyond our agency.

2. Lay leaders must be made to feel the importance of the parts which they play in the community planning procedure. For example, I have seen meetings in which the professional workers were so vocal and so numerous that the lay people felt they had no acceptable contribution to make. In our Board of Trustees, I, myself, used to present the twenty-odd questions which the board was to consider at a meeting. Some years ago, I gave up this plan completely. For several years, practically all the items on our board docket have been presented by different board members, each with some knowledge or background for presenting the proposal. This has made a great difference in the interest in the meetings and the attendance. The COP has responsibility for imparting to each lay person a feeling of participation and 'achievement. If one lay person holds back in a meeting, a whisper from the COP may lead the chairman to draw that person out.

3. The lay leaders need to be fitted into important positions which suit their interests and capacities and with due regard to a broad and

balanced representation. The COP needs to be an expert on the personnel of committees.

4. Dockets must be carefully worked out by the COP to conserve
time, yet with each step visualized and alternatives clearly stated to
make progress and yet give a fair chance to all points of view. Meetings
should start on time and quit on time.

5. The COP needs to build up a personal acquaintance with large
numbers of lay people, but even more important, he or she needs to
have the personality, the ability, and the attitude which will win and
hold their support.

This is not possible if he erects barriers by religious, racial, or economic prejudice. The COP not only must be broad and sympathetic
with all religions, but he must be alert to every possibility of promoting
better mutual understanding among the adherents of different denomi-
nations. The COP must not be prejudiced by the color of a person's
skin.

He cannot be a bigot on economic questions. On the one hand, he
needs to recognize that liberal wages and salaries not only enhance the
health and happiness of the recipients, but also contribute to the general well-being through creating purchasing power in the community.
On the other hand, he must realize that adequate profits contribute to
the general well-being by inducing prospective investors to risk their
savings in hazardous but productive business enterprises and by enabling
business and industrial concerns to expand their plants and keep well
up-to-date in the introduction of labor-saving machinery, thus increasing the volume of products available to the general public and
improving the general standard of living.

Some of the greatest achievements in this world have been brought
about through fanaticism, but also, some of the greatest setbacks and
the greatest human misery and suffering. This job of community organization has no place for fanatics. Success in community organization is
based on understanding and respect for the other person's point of
view. The COP must be acceptable, personally, to a vast majority of
the people with whom he works.

If the COP is to do his part in holding lay people, he must understand and keep in touch with the thinking and interests of the average
person. A few professional social workers talk as though it would be
easy to secure long articles in the newspapers educating the public on
professional social work, or easy to raise money in a Community Fund
campaign through a purely high-brow scientific exposition of what the
social agencies are doing. They tend to criticize any emotional appeal.
Such a lofty attitude fails to take into account the psychology of the
average person.

The COP must not think of people as villains or heroes. He cannot
be too disillusioned or ready to condemn when some person fails to

measure up to his intellectual or moral standards and certainly not condemn because someone happens to disagree with him. One's success in holding lay people is often in inverse proportion to his tendency to become disgusted with people.

The COP, like the caseworker and the group worker, has learned not to assume the role of dictator. The COP must not have a compulsion for glory or to be expert on all health and welfare matters. He must err strongly on the side of letting other organizations and individuals get the credit and the publicity for his activities.

Sometimes he will need to express his own point of view and must not be pusillanimous (always use simple language like that!) when a real issue is involved, but he should be pretty sure of his facts in taking a position and he should never speak as though he were the organization. He must be the "enabler" not the "deciding person" and he must have a deep conviction that the responsibility for policy decisions is up to the various planning bodies; yet he must have the skill to transmit to them the techniques, the understanding, and the confidence needed for them to assume this responsibility.

The COP has a responsibility to see that the facts are adequately presented on all sides of a question and that all interested groups and organizations and points of view have representation from the initial articulation of a problem to its solution. He needs to see that there is fair play.

He must have a gift for knitting together apparently diverse points of view. Sometimes two groups seem to be in bitter disagreement because of fundamental principle when actually the difference may be one of semantics or personalities. The COP can sometimes present a clear statement on which both will agree or arrange a face-saving device.

Perhaps the most vital function of the COP is to stimulate and enable individuals, groups, and organizations to understand one another and to work together. To accomplish this, the COP must have a deep and sympathetic understanding of the other fellow, his motives, and his impediments.

Don't ever look for the living embodiment of all these qualifications, for "there ain't no such animal." But every one of these is requisite in high degree to hold influential persons and thus to meet problem situations. And they also represent my answer to my assignment of depicting the *philosophy* and the *role* of the COP.

We have spoken of the trends of the times; analyzed problem situations; described fundamental approaches in treating problem situations; and the philosophy of the COP and the manner in which he may fulfill his role. Now we come to the principles of community organization and our responsibility toward those principles.

These principles have been set forth as a policy statement by Community Chests and Councils in a brochure entitled *Community Planning for Social Welfare* [see Selection 50]. This set of principles should be every COP's bible. . . .

Note these principles well. Such principles are the foundation of our whole community planning structure. If the foundation crumbles, the structure will eventually disintegrate.

Every professional social worker, every COP, every person interested in the health and welfare field, and our own national organization, Community Chests and Councils, which published these principles, should be heart and soul devoted to them and whatever the personalities involved should persistently and courageously insist and continue to insist in every way possible on adherence to them in letter and in spirit.

The reported cleavages which are arising between agency and community planning representatives on the one hand, and money-raising groups on the other are quite unnecessary. There is no fundamental incompatibility between the interests of the money-raisers or the contributors and the interests of the agencies or the community planning body.

One cannot be critical of the fine concern which leads an agency board member or executive to defend and sponsor and promote his own agency. It bespeaks a sincerity and an earnestness which are definitely commendable. But if the persons connected with a national or a local social agency become so exclusively centered on their own activities that they fail to see the value of other services in proper perspective, their agency is likely to become self-centered and inflexible and if agencies show inflexibility in modifying their programs, such an attitude will naturally impress the contributors' and taxpayers' group with the feeling that they must step in to see that their money is properly used.

Similarly, the people who give generously of their time and effort to *raise* the *money* and those who *contribute* to social agencies have a logical and proper interest in seeing that their money is most effectively spent. But if the contributors or money raisers become so bigoted as to ignore or fail to give proper emphasis to the "know-how" of agency people, then those money raisers defeat the very purpose they are trying to accomplish, for if agency thinking is minimized, the money will be less effectively spent. Both contributor thinking and agency thinking need to be strongly represented in community planning and budgeting. Sometimes the largest contributors have been unable or unwilling to give time to the community planning activities or no serious effort has been made to enlist them and consequently they have acquired misconceptions as to the extravagance of agencies. Suddenly with a confidence in their ideas which comes from success in their own business they begin to interest themselves in radical action based on superficial knowledge of this field.

The value of the dollar must never be lost sight of, but, for the sake of everyone, community planning should not be submerged under money raising, nor should it be determined by a small group of persons.

In this country, we do not believe in autocracy in government and for very similar reasons we do not believe in autocracy in community planning. We are committed to a philosophy that places ultimate responsibility and authority with the people, that calls for the participation of the people in the solution of their problems and the delegation of authority to groups broadly and appropriately representative.

To sum up—in these troublous times, there are many and diverse trends. The growth and development of tax-supported agencies accents the importance of their having a wholehearted and genuine participation in the community planning organization and points to the desirability of a community planning organization separate from the money-raising organization.

Some trends indicate that the job of securing voluntary contributions may be increasingly difficult. At any rate, it is of transcendent importance that those responsible for raising funds for the voluntary agencies and those who are responsible for their expenditure and for community planning should work together harmoniously. It is of vital importance also to have, in the budgeting and the community planning, broad democratic participation involving large numbers of influential lay persons. Such harmony and such participation will depend greatly on the philosophy and the methods of agency executives and of community planning and money-raising executives. The principles set forth by Community Chests and Councils should be our guide and our bible and the violation of those principles should be of vital concern to every individual among us and should be the occasion for united and clarion protest from the entire body of lay and professional people concerned in the health and welfare program.

67

The Function of the Professional Worker [1]

By VIOLET M. SIEDER

An excerpt from this paper describing the evolution of the goals and methods of community organization is included in Part II (Selection 15). In the second section of the address the author develops her thesis "that community organization practice is identified with the generic concepts of social work, that it draws heavily on the processes of casework and group work, but that it also depends on specialized areas of knowledge and skill necessary for working with a community." The client in social work, she points out, "is always people"; individuals and families in casework, clubs and organizations in group work, and the community in community organization.

In the excerpt below Miss Sieder analyzes the role of the community organization worker and discusses the knowledge, skills, and tools he must possess and use. The balance of the paper is concerned with the nature of the community organization process and with its applications in new settings as well as in the traditional ones. She insists that community organization should be thought of as a direct service designed to strengthen the "basic fabric of the community through a practical involvement of people in identifying their problems, determining their own needs and shaping the services . . . they . . . use and support." Co-

[1] Excerpted from "What Is Community Organization Practice?", *The Social Welfare Forum,* Proceedings, National Conference of Social Work, St. Louis, 1956 (New York: Columbia University Press, 1956), pp. 167-174. By permission of National Conference on Social Welfare.

For a more complete analysis of the specific functions of the practitioner the reader is referred to a later paper by the same author, "The Tasks of the Community Organization Worker," *Planning Social Services for Urban Needs,* Proceedings, National Conference on Social Welfare, Philadelphia, 1957 (New York: Columbia University Press, 1957), pp. 3-16.

ordination of services, including welfare programs, becomes a means, community redevelopment, to the end.

Miss Sieder is a professor of social work at the New York School of Social Work, of Columbia University. Information concerning her background and experience will be found in the preface to Selection 15.

IN THE DIAGNOSIS of a community problem the worker first must know the environmental facts in the social situation including familiarity with the economic base of the community's life as reflected in its industrial, labor, and business patterns; sociocultural patterns such as class lines, minority groups, religious organization, ethnic groups, its customs and attitudes; its population characteristics as to age and sex distribution; the program and structure of its major social institutions, including differences and quality in services and approaches to problems, auspices and size of staff service. In this area, community organization needs to borrow heavily from the social sciences, not for the purpose of performing analytical studies of the community as an end in themselves, but as necessary tools for helping the community relate its strength to attainable goals on which diverse interest groups can find common concern. This also requires a basic knowledge of fact-gathering and research methods and development of work habits of applying research approach to the daily operation of planning as well as to special study projects.

A factual case picture of the community is sterile indeed unless it takes into account the psychodynamics of intergroup relations. The attitudes of groups toward each other will depend in large part upon their various value systems and goals, their historical development, the quality of leadership, the nature of membership, and social status factors. Facilitating purposeful group interaction involves professional knowledge and skill. In order to help the community to gather and assess facts for the purpose of defining and determining solutions to its problems, it is necessary to know which are the appropriate groups to involve in a given situation; how to time the planning steps from initiation of study to taking action on findings; when to draw what resources into the situation from within and outside the community; when to give positive or aggressive leadership and when to play a passive, supporting role; and ability to accept the well-considered decision of community leadership even at the risk of letting it make serious mistakes. Necessary to this process is the worker's ability to empathize with the community by feeling with various groups the meaning the problem has for them in terms of their own history, goals, and objectives; and at the same time being able to analyze the situation objectively so as to help the groups interact positively and move toward desirable goals.

Implicit in this professional skill is a knowledge of group process. Sensitivity to the interaction of members of a committee is doubly important when the committee itself is representative of other separate group interests. It is often said that the committee is the primary tool of community organization, just as is the interview for casework or group process for group work. In addition to the mechanics of getting the committee set up with an appropriate, clear-cut charge and with clear lines of responsibility within the organization, the skill of the worker rests in influencing the composition of the committee and his disciplined use of himself in its deliberations. It is necessary to understand and work with the differences and tensions that arise, to recognize subgroups, and direct and indirect leadership roles. Although this knowledge is based in group work, it is not used for the primary purpose of assisting individuals or the group to grow through group experience or achievement; rather the concern is with furthering movement in community process toward broader objectives.

And back of intergroup and group process is an understanding of the psychodynamics of individual behavior. The community organization practitioner must be able to relate to and accept all kinds of people regardless of his economic, social, political, religious, or other position. He must be able to recognize and interpret the meaning of aggression, defenses, and hostility; know how to ease tensions and create opportunity for healthy ego satisfaction. This knowledge and skill he uses toward his goal of expediting the achievement of community-selected objectives and not on an intensive basis of casework services to assist an individual to resolve personal problems. Much of the work of community organization goes on outside of, and between, group meetings in conference, consultation, and interview, where this knowledge and skill are of prime importance.

In the intergroup process the worker needs skill in stimulating participation and involvement not only of representatives but also of the groups they represent. This presumes clarity on the difference between the role of instructed delegate, the organization-selected representative, and an at-large representative of a point of view. Meaningful interaction between groups does not just happen when their representatives are physically at the same place. Facilitating methods must be applied skillfully and with professional self-discipline. The end result of this intergroup process is not just the reshaping of community services or the raising of standards, important as they are; there is also an intangible factor of a changing community morale or climate in which a spirit of mutuality makes for greater ease in reaching and extending future goals.

A community organization worker, no matter at which level of community he practices, must encourage interaction between planning organizations on the same horizontal plane and also vertically as between planes. For example, a community-wide council cannot hope to effect changes through the efforts alone of a top-level committee, no matter how expert and powerful the members may be. To achieve broad use and support of services, and indeed to assure that these services meet a genuinely felt need, it is important to involve participation in planning at district and neighborhood levels as well; and to provide channels for intercommunication and interaction between these district councils and between the district plane of activity and the city-wide plane.

Time does not permit a look at the tools necessary to the social worker's community organization kit. Suffice it to say that these must include research, public relations and interpretation, legislative and social action procedures, fund-raising and budgeting techniques, recording, and administration. The proper use of each of these tools necessitates community involvement and affects movement in process.

Just as in casework and group work, the community organization process is not an end in itself; it is problem-centered and is an effort to achieve movement toward solution of the problem. Although it starts at the point of readiness of the community to accept and understand some of the facets of the problem, it moves toward broader goals through the knowledge, understanding, and skill of the worker. His professional facilitating role will depend on the choice of methods he applies to the problem and his body of knowledge about sound organization, program content, administration, and social policy. Community organization is a dynamic concept in which change is brought about through helping people to reorient their attitudes toward themselves and others, toward programs and problems and to mobilize their forces to effect their chosen goals. This is the antithesis of a community association created and managed by experts to achieve preconceived goals.

Community organization becomes a direct service when the community, as a dynamic, living organism, becomes the client needing help with social integration and seeking service from the worker. The community organization worker, then, must be prepared to offer his professional skill in relation to the client's ability to use him and on problems which the community recognizes as important. The worker's effectiveness will grow with community understanding of his role, as he enables individuals and groups to make greater use of potential resources and to create a climate in which people and groups have significance and importance in their community.

This direct service, to be effective, must be offered on a community-wide basis and be so structured as to reach the several levels of administrative responsibility as well as to have broad geographical coverage. It must be flexible, and available on request of city-wide or local groups.

As in all fields of social work, helping with problems of human relationships is always difficult when the situation has reached a state of crisis. The community organization worker is learning this, too, as he is assigned to help resolve intergroup tension situations involving such difficult matters as racial, nationality, or class conflict. In such situations we find the worker moving in to help a subcommunity as it struggles to meet a crisis and serving to isolate or minimize the difficulty as a protection to the larger community. This aspect of community organization has overtones of what has become known as "aggressive" social work. As community organization workers are more readily available to assist the community, both as generalists and as consultants in specialized fields of service, they can serve an important role in prevention not only of crisis but of community deterioration.

Evidence of the "direct-service approach" at the community-wide level is found in the great ferment in community welfare councils over a project or problem-centered approach to planning to replace or supplement the cumbersome functional agency-centered divisions. It is argued that the various organized groups and citizen leaders of a community who must be involved in the planning process to achieve sound results can identify with a familiar problem but that they find little meaning or way to relate to interagency divisional structure; and even those councils which continue to have divisions are expanding membership to include citizen groups and are developing projects on community problems which cut across fields of service. The scope of council program is constantly broadened and begins to include such problems as housing, race relations, vice, and crime.

A growing number of councils in various-sized cities are offering not only the help of specialized consultants on a central staff but also the services of community organization generalists as consultants to work with areas, neighborhoods, and local groups which are struggling to find solutions to welfare problems.

A new and growing development is tax-supported community organization service under governmental auspices. This is found in the departments of welfare in Baltimore and Kansas City, in youth boards in New York City and in California; and in separate community organization service departments of the county in San Diego and Los Angeles.

Much attention has been given in recent years to the need for a closer working relationship between social welfare planning and city planning, housing authorities, schools, human relations, commissions. A natural and needed link has been found in those communities which offer to all central planning bodies channels of communication which go directly to people through a network of community councils staffed by community organization practitioners whether working under voluntary or public auspices.

The concept of community development as encouraged through the United Nations and as translated into program in many less developed areas of the world reflects the application of this same philosophy and approach.

Community organization practitioners, like those in other fields of social work, are finding an important place in nonsocial work settings. Housing associations and housing authorities have recognized community organization service as an integral part of their programs. In fact, community organization workers are needed to carry out Point 7 of the Workable Program for Urban Renewal under the Housing Act of 1954 which requires that any political entity which wishes to participate in federally aided programs for the renewal of blighted areas of a city must provide in its planning for "community-wide participation on the part of individuals and representative citizen organizations which will help to provide both in the community generally and in selected areas the understanding and support which is necessary to insure success." City planning commissions are also employing community organization consultants to advise them on the human relationship and social service aspects of their work.

These jobs, often operating at the neighborhood level and under supervision, open up new opportunities for community organization practice for people with limited experience in social work. This development offers a challenge to schools of social work in terms of criteria for selection of community organization students and in development of appropriate curriculum content and field work assignments. It is significant that city planners, housing authorities and associations, and city departments for community organization are turning to the schools of social work for people with a community organization major.

We also might well look to boards of education, courts, rehabilitation centers, and health departments as fields in which community organization is a recognized skill, and where there is need for closer collaboration with social work, both in training and as a member of the team of professional service workers.

For years, the community organization specialist has complained about the casework or group work practitioners' lack of community awareness, interest in broad social policy, and readiness to speak out and act on social issues. When councils have been weak, frequently the difficulty can be traced to the lethargy of their professional members.

Many caseworkers either fail to see their role as including help to the client in establishing satisfying relationships beyond the family, or they are reluctant to do so. Referral of a client with a housing problem to a community council or housing association through which he can contribute to the solution of his own and the community's problem is seldom considered.

The focus of recent years on the generic aspects of social work is putting a renewed emphasis on group and community process. Although community organization as a primary function of social work is still conceded to be an area of specialization, it is recognized that every social worker carries a secondary responsibility for community organization. To do so adequately will require a reorganization of class and field work. Some of us believe that we need a required course or sequence that would parallel that required of all students on the dynamics of human growth and development and which would examine the dynamics of community growth and development.

As we have noted, community organization as social work practice has a philosophy, methods, and skills. It serves a client—the community—with a direct service worthy of support in its own right, and not just as a hidden charge against family, child welfare, recreation, health, or other services. Community organization is not only professionally respectable as social work practice; it must make significant strides to keep abreast of the increasing demands being made upon it. It is therefore with deep gratification that we look to the newly organized Committee on Community Organization of the National Association of Social Workers and the interest expressed in the Council on Social Work Education in its curriculum study and its workshops as the means to hammering out the basic concepts and charting a future course as a guide to the continued development of community organization practice in social work.

68

Community Organization—Manipulation or Group Process? [1]

By DONALD VAN VALEN

This selection is typical of the objections raised against "manipulation" as a community organization procedure in contrast with "enabling," though the former may be simpler and more expeditious than the democratic approach in many cases.

In support of the latter procedure the author points out that the worker must understand the dynamics of the group process and be skillful in the employment of means by which it may be guided but not controlled.[2] The author then continues by a review of the four "basic convictions" which should be held by the community organization worker which constitutes the bulk of the paper. These include a belief in citizen participation, in democratic procedures, in the scientific method, in effective communication as basic to the understanding of the group process and essential to successful practice.

Van Valen throughout the paper argues against resorting to a "manipulative bag of tricks which may offer [a] temporary panacea, [but] which . . . does permanent harm to community organization." Instead, he visualizes two major roles that may properly be played by the worker: (1) helping committees to analyze information on problems confronting them and to understand the implications of such information as well as of the various alternatives open to them for some type

---

[1] Excerpted from article of same title, *Social Work in the Current Scene,* Proceedings, National Conference of Social Work, Cleveland, Ohio, 1949 (New York: Columbia University Press, 1950), pp. 325-342. By permission of National Conference on Social Welfare.

[2] In this connection the reader is referred also to other descriptions of the same process which appear in Part III under the section title of "Conferences and Committees: Achieving Integration."

of social action, and (2) helping them to overcome a natural resistance to any kind of change and insuring that they reach their own decisions.

Donald Van Valen, like many other community organization workers, began his career as a caseworker. Following his graduation from the School of Applied Social Sciences, of Western Reserve University, in 1932, he joined the staff of the Cleveland Associated Charities. Later he served as a county poor commissioner and Civil Works administrator in Kansas, as a case supervisor with the New York State Temporary Emergency Relief Administration, and as a caseworker in the New York State Department of Social Welfare.

In 1939 he became an area supervisor of social work in the New York State Department, a position that involved heavy community organization responsibilities. Four years later he moved to Cincinnati, first as a member of the staff of the Council of Social Agencies, and shortly thereafter as director. In December, 1949, he was appointed executive director of the Community Chest. He held this position until 1952 when he returned to New York as a regional representative of United Community Defense Services. During this period, which lasted until December 31, 1955, he enjoyed a rich and exacting experience in community organization on a regional level in Ohio and elsewhere. Following the contraction of the UCDS program he became associate secretary of the National Budget Committee until June, 1956, when he was named director of program planning, of the Pennsylvania State Welfare Department.

THE COMMUNITY ORGANIZATION worker is confronted with the continuing task of trying to understand the dynamics of human relations in the groups with which he is associated. To achieve this understanding, he must have some basic convictions which in turn must be reflected in his actions. One of these is that citizen participation to its maximum possible extent is essential to community organization programs. Another is that any community organization activity should be a shining example of the democratic process. Another is that in all community organization projects there should be application of the scientific method. Further, reaching through these and essential to lasting accomplishment in community organization is good communication.

Citizen participation as illustrated, for example, in a committee situation means that full opportunity shall be afforded committee members for genuine involvement in the problem faced. Such involvement precludes the concept of "using" volunteers. If the community organization worker is using volunteers, they are certainly not using themselves as members of the group, and the worker may well be guilty of personal manipulation of people to achieve an end decided upon by him, and thus reject before they are advanced the alternatives which the committee members may find. For if the vaunted concept of citizenship participation in community organization is accepted, the community organization worker is ethically bound to respect the participating citizen's right to a viewpoint, and to encourage that right to the end that his viewpoint can be reached on the basis of facts as commonly available to him as to the worker. Thus we must give very real study to method and to process in order that this basic right of the participating citizen may be upheld and advanced. Such study must contemplate recognition in depth of the dynamics of groups.

The worker's job is so to relate himself to a committee group that its members may develop the highest sense of responsibility toward accomplishment of the task with which they are identified. A worker should not believe that he may outline projects himself and then ask citizens on committees for their perfunctory approval. Nor should he believe that he may outline projects and then move upon agency executives or other individuals, and attempt to secure support without group discussion by all of those concerned. It is necessary that we continue to test and apply methods which will bring more and more people in the community into positions of responsibility for sharing decisions about social welfare services. We as community organization workers cannot presume that we have any responsibility for telling these groups what to do or what they should decide. But we must so handle our relationships with them that their combined thinking will result in joint constructive decision making.

Closely related, then, to the concept of citizen participation is the belief that a community organization worker must accept the democratic process; that the democratic process is essential and inherent in adequate community organization practice. The phrase "democratic process" is somewhat abstract and subject to many interpretations. But perhaps our key to a richer understanding and acceptance lies in a perception of the nature of democratic leadership as having little to do with content and subject matter, but very much with process. The community organization worker knows that on practically any committee there are people who as content-resource persons are far more knowledgeable than he. His job has to do with committee productivity. His professional role is one which includes fulfillment of a leadership position in such a way that he avoids first the pitfalls which arise if the committee situation has laissez-faire and anarchic characteristics, and second, the shallow victories incident to decisions reached by the autocratic pressures usually inherent in formalized group settings. The community organization worker has a far-reaching responsibility to estimate and evaluate group situations in order that he may discern to the best of his ability how he may assert genuine, dynamic, democratic leadership. Over and over we find that the community organization worker by the very nature of his job is in a leadership position, a circumstance which in itself requires study. A test of his ability in professional practice is whether or not he can through careful application of democratic leadership so handle his relationships with groups that they themselves will become leadership groups. Then the original position of the worker becomes less significant as the group grows in its own strength and in its own ability to make decisions. A worker may then become perhaps a resource person in the area of method and process.

A third basic element in community organization practice is that the application of the scientific method is essential. As implementation to the concepts of citizen participation and democratic process, the conscious application of the scientific method is most important. The members of a committee should be a part of the procedure in which facts are collected and developed, from the very outset. This does not deny the validity of having a specialist in social research as a resource person. But the committee itself should be involved in a determination of needed facts. The committee should with suitable discussion handle these facts and develop them into hypotheses which in some instances may be self-evident conclusions, or which may have to be tested in action in order to determine their validity. Information which develops as a part of the living experiences of committee members has far greater significance at the action end of the project than if the material were made available as a study by an expert not of the group.

This application of the scientific method might be described as consisting of a number of overlapping yet separately discernible processes which together form the whole. These are development of interest in the problem, determining what information is needed, collecting and organizing the information, hypothesizing from the information, examining and testing the hypotheses, moving into decisions about action, laying plans for action, taking action. So important are these, that elements of structure are, if we are to achieve community organization objectives, so secondary a consideration as to be not far from irrelevant. The important thing is relationships. For if these concepts of citizen participation, and use of the democratic process, and application of the scientific method in community organization are accepted, the worker is bound to respect the role which committee members play as they become related to the fulfillment of their objectives. The worker can, if he will, believe that his own individual viewpoints and opinions are, in the light of application of appropriate process and method, of vastly less significance than the shared group thinking and conclusions reached in committee; that all else must be subordinate in this view of the community organization job.

The accomplishment of such a task as has been suggested here is fraught with the greatest of difficulties. This is true chiefly because we have had little laboratory experience; this, in turn, may be so because of our failure to maintain or even to know how to maintain really adequate process records. . . .

Manipulation of people by a community organization worker is relatively easy in many instances. But upon what convictions can such manipulation be based? By what definition or description of the community organization worker's job can there be admitted any such personal manipulation, any autocratic handling of his responsibilities? Yet if the fear of having a laissez-faire committee situation besets him, or if he thinks he has too many jobs to do, he may make major decisions affecting the community practically alone and solely upon his own judgment.

In another type of problem there was conflict arising from competition among several people, each of whom was administratively responsible for one part of an over-all, community-wide operation in the health field. The problem was presented by one of these administrators to a group of about twenty people, all of whom had a genuine interest in how it was to be solved. The suggestion was accepted by the group that there might be advantage in having a visual demonstration. So three persons from the group sat together, somewhat as a small committee might, and in front of the people present they discussed the problem as though they had been by themselves. The rest of the group, observing what went on, discovered far more of what the problem entailed than they had realized heretofore. When this role playing was finished, the extensive and wholehearted discussion in the group, after groping for points of discussion previously, led to vistas of problem solving which certainly had not been contemplated.

Of real importance here was the insight achieved by the administrator who presented the problem originally, who let the group know that her own motivation had been at fault as she had failed to give sufficient recognition to the essential relationship of her own special problem to the whole community-wide program of which it was a part. Role playing was used in a simple, limited way. Members of the group perceived, however, through the discussion in the role-playing situation that the original statement of the problem was fairly superficial, for there was need for real analysis and discussion of certain elements which earlier had been accepted as simple facts, or had not been recognized at all.

Role playing is a difficult, and can be a dangerous, technique, but when used with skill it can isolate, and has isolated, problems which had not even been sensed but which were inherent in the situation. Its possibilities for enlisting discussion and eager participation when used appropriately can be very great. It is of importance to note too that role playing is of the democratic essence, for it does not lend itself readily to manipulation, if at all.

The community organization job can be construed as difficult and time consuming, and fraught with questions whose answers we are just beginning to ascertain. The task may be difficult because we have not yet had suitable, objective testing of our experiences. From such testing would emerge basic elements of method and process which would be complementary to our basic convictions. We have done little to relate theory to practice. We do not even have much of a language, the first tool of communication, by which we can readily describe for our common understanding the meaning and significance of our professional experiences. We can list our functions, but we stumble as we endeavor to relate not only how we do our work but also why we carry out a task in certain ways.

We are constantly in situations from which a change of some sort is expected to emerge. The community organization worker must somehow look at himself and understand his own motivations in relationship to the need for an indicated change. He must do this in such a way that he may be able to discover how he can help others who are working with him also to become aware of the need for change. He must know how to structure a situation so that there is the greatest likelihood of genuine collaboration among the individuals concerned. . . .

The advancement of citizen participation, the democratic process, the application of the scientific method, involve much more than the statement that they are desirable and necessary. To carry out convictions based upon these concepts the worker needs to understand something of group member roles and actually take time to study them. He needs to be aware of what is involved in group structure; of the nature of group cohesion; of the effects of premeeting and postmeeting communication; of measurement of group movement; and awareness of group sociometry. These and many other theoretical concepts can be related to actual situations if the worker will, instead of depending on what he thinks is his own good sense, really endeavor to assess each group situation with which he is identified. He needs to find its strengths and weaknesses so that he may be in a better position to help it to achieve ever higher levels of productivity.

In general, we have not yet developed in the community organization field the kind of disciplines for the worker's job which may, dynamically, influence him to consistent, constant practice in which there is orderly effort to implement his already accepted convictions. In the milieu of the community organization worker's daily life, amid the confusion of telephone calls, unexpected visits, suddenly developing problems, conferences, and all, we must, if we are to achieve perspective, realize that we ourselves should somehow plan to take time to create our own professional disciplines.

I have presented some very limited examples of efforts which have been made by workers to advance the quality of their perceptions in order that they might carry out their jobs more successfully in the light of their convictions. It is noteworthy that each has much to learn. It is also noteworthy that in each situation it would have been much simpler to have developed devices for manipulation, with the view that the job would have been accomplished more quickly. The workers learned much more than has been described; this was a somewhat intangible learning experience which perhaps can best be suggested as one in which there was increased insight about the forces which operate within groups. They learned too that such perceptional experiences are difficult to communicate to others. They learned of more effective ways of fulfilling their responsibilities as they took time to look ahead and look back upon the course of these projects. This was a looking based upon a vital sense of the obligations inherent in their roles as professional social workers.

As we shall achieve greater skill in isolating needs, so must we achieve greater skill in improving group process in community organization as our only way of solidly building the channels through which needs shall be effectively met. These channels are made of good communication. Our greatest hazard, as in most human relations matters, is lack of understanding. But as we use good process, good method, we improve communication in our committees and increase the likelihood of good communication to agencies, to organizations, and to others in the community.

We have two major roles as community organization workers. We must help our committees work through the data and information with which they are frequently confronted. Then they may as groups reach their own decisions as to the need for a particular, but not predetermined, change. We have then the added role of being helpers in overcoming the cultural and psychological resistances to changes whose need has been democratically and scientifically established through productive participation. We are social scientists who are somewhat unsure of ourselves in such roles. Yet we have a great possibility open to us in finding how we can be sure, simply by the study and evaluation of what we do in our jobs, the way we do it, and why we do it. Out of this will come our methodology, our disciplines. We must be willing to accept the possibility of some failures from which we can learn much; for we need to be willing to support our convictions at some possible cost as we move on, rather than revert to the manipulative bag of tricks which may offer [a] temporary panacea and which, because it does not carry participants along, does permanent harm to community organization and hence to the community which we strive to serve.

69

Volunteers in Social Welfare [1]

By MELVIN A. GLASSER

With so much emphasis today being placed on the need for professional education for social work in general and for community organization in particular, what becomes of the lay worker? In the 1890's there were no professional social workers and full responsibility for welfare programs was carried by laymen with the assistance of a few professionals from other fields such as law and medicine. By the 1920's a change had occurred, however, bringing with it new problems of relationship. "What happens," asked Eduard C. Lindeman in 1928, "when a discipline which arose from common-sense, humanistic, and empirical roots evolves into a technological profession?" [2]

Answering his own question, he replied that "professionalism" for one thing, "becomes a kind of cult . . . which isolates the layman." Lay and professional workers tend to misunderstand each other, and open conflict may even develop. Lindeman believed that volunteers had a valid role, not in imitating or competing with professionals, but in "performing tasks which can best be performed by laymen."

By 1952 the picture had changed, volunteers were more numerous, and Lindeman was asking, "What would happen if . . . volunteers . . . were to resign their posts?" It would be "difficult to imagine," he concluded, "what American life minus its volunteers would be like." Public welfare departments, he continues, "would take on . . . the coloration of bureaucracies. . . . Private agencies . . . would gradually wither and die. . . . Democracy will have committed suicide . . . [for]

[1] Excerpted from *What Makes a Volunteer?* (New York: Public Affairs Pamphlet No. 224, Aug., 1955), pp. 2-12. By permission of Public Affairs Committee, Inc.

[2] Robert Gessner, ed., *The Democratic Man: Selected Writings of Eduard C. Lindeman* (Boston: Beacon Press, 1956), p. 210.

494

they are to Democracy what circulation of the blood is to the organism." [3]

Eduard Lindeman, the beloved philosopher of social work and democracy, need not have feared for the future since, as Glasser, writing three years later, points out, volunteer service has become a part of our culture. In an article published the same year Clarence Hall estimates the total number of laymen active to some degree in "humane causes" of all kinds at 20 million and states that they "outnumber professionals about 250 to 1." [4]

Melvin Glasser holds an LL.D. degree from Adelphi College, Garden City, New York. He has had long experience with volunteer workers of many types in connection with the American Red Cross, as associate chief of the United States Children's Bureau, and as executive director of the Midcentury White House Conference on Children and Youth. Currently he is assistant to the president of the National Foundation for Infantile Paralysis and serves (1957) also as chairman of the United States Committee of the International Conference of Social Work.

VOLUNTEER SERVICE IS IMPORTANT in a multitude of groups and organizations—religious, educational, political, social, medical, professional, government, and many others. A host of volunteers is centered in the health and welfare agencies, and it is these agencies and their volunteers that are given particular attention here.

Volunteer service has become a part of our established social pattern, and the status of the volunteer has risen as more people have joined the ranks. During national emergencies of the past years, the volunteer has been the lifeblood of agencies, institutions, organizations, fund campaigns, and relief programs. The volunteer group, in many cases, has become an integral part of the agency.

We now find many more men as volunteers in jobs that were once thought suitable only for women. The main volunteer jobs of men used to be with the agency board and its committees, the financial drives, and the membership campaigns. Now men are active in the person-to-person volunteer jobs—in a hospital ward, for example, or on a playground.

The army of volunteers in the United States is larger than anywhere in the world—and stronger. As many as *464 national voluntary organizations with significant program emphasis on the young* were involved

---

[3] *Ibid.,* pp. 216-217.
[4] Clarence W. Hall, "America's Amazing Women," *Reader's Digest,* Vol. 67, No. 399 (July, 1955), p. 18.

in the Midcentury White House Conference on Children and Youth.

No one knows how many volunteers there are. They cannot be counted, because the number fluctuates constantly and because so many are volunteers in more than one agency. There are approximately ten million organized church women, three million volunteers in Community Chest and United Fund Campaigns, and another twelve million in the year-round activities of the Chests, Funds, and their member agencies. There are two million in the National Foundation for Infantile Paralysis, and a sizable army of volunteers for the American National Red Cross. This is just a part of the total volunteer army in this country. Millions more are ready to take on jobs that are of service to others in the community and the nation. They are of all degrees of competence. They are willing to do dramatic or humble jobs.

Why do men and women, who are already leading lives of responsibility and facing many problems of their own, give time and energy as volunteers? What are their satisfactions?

Why do agencies with professional staffs recruit volunteers and look upon them as essential to good agency functioning?

People Volunteer Because . . .

The tremendous growth of voluntary service in the United States is no accident, but a result of our background and our present way of life. There are many reasons why people volunteer their services to agencies. The ten most common reasons are considered here. *Your* reasons for being a volunteer are probably among them.

This is a strong tradition, springing from the need for help that faced all settlers in the American wilderness and on the frontiers. If illness struck, or crops had to be gathered in a hurry, or a shelter provided, a family had to look to its neighbors. Today, in case of disaster or need, help comes from many sources. The tradition of helping others persists, however, and finds its present-day expression in volunteer service, whereby the individual can help a neighbor, a stranger, or a group in another country.

The number of working hours in all fields of work has been reduced sharply in recent years. The majority of working people, no matter what their job, have a five-day week. Even the housewife, who puts in a far longer work-week, finds she has more leisure time because of techniques and inventions that ease her household tasks. More and more, people are devoting their leisure to volunteer work.

In this country women are not expected to devote themselves exclusively to family and church. Rather, it is assumed that they will give part of their time and energy to one or to several aspects of community life. Most families are smaller, allowing mothers more time for outside activities. Women are better educated than they were, and so they are better equipped to participate. They have found that they can make a place for themselves in a circle wider than the home. And though more women are working full-time outside their homes than ever before, many women who worked in their earlier years feel a great need for continuing outside activities in later years.

Family units in the United States today are almost 40 per cent smaller than in 1900. Then the average household had five and one-half members. Now it has three and one-half members. This decrease is due to fewer children and to the fact that there is no longer a place in the household for several relatives. Once the grandparents, widowed relatives, and maiden aunts lived with the family and helped with the work. The family produced much of what was consumed and found much of its social and recreational satisfaction in its own large circle. Today family members must seek some of this work and play satisfaction elsewhere. Many find the answer in volunteer services where they can share in group experiences.

Service to fellow man is a central idea of all major religions. Once, this idea could be expressed by taking food and clothing to the needy or by tending a sick neighbor. Society has become so complex that these direct acts of personal charity are not enough. Sporadic personal charity has given way to planned health and welfare services. Giving money to these agencies helps give practical expression to the will to serve one's fellow man. It is socially important, but for the giver it is at best a once-removed way of practicing the Golden Rule. Through volunteer service with health and welfare agencies a way is provided to put religious principles into action—to serve our fellow men more directly.

Volunteer service answers the need to belong that each of us has— the need to become associated with others in achieving some tangible goal. In so many jobs a man works on a "part" of something, or is a "specialist" in something. He may never see the whole job or the completed job. He feels the need to belong to a group of people with similar interests, to accomplish something he can see, to achieve satisfaction in a completed job. Volunteer service can be an answer to this need. For women, too, volunteer service helps to answer the need to belong to some group outside the family. Many women whose children are grown find volunteer work an antidote to feelings of emptiness and loneliness.

Many jobs call for little knowledge or skill. They are repetitious and routine. In volunteer service there is an opportunity to gain knowledge in a particular field: for example, what the educational needs of migrant children are, or how the Travelers Aid helps in emergencies. New knowledge and competency give the volunteer a feeling of self-esteem and confidence. He knows that he can speak about or demonstrate his subject and so interest and inform others.

Many people have organizational skills or creative talents that are used only for personal satisfaction, or even lie dormant. They are pleased when their skills are called into use by a campaign for Red

Cross disaster funds, a program to teach swimming to handicapped children, or a request to teach block printing in a settlement house. Volunteer service gives people the opportunity to *use* their particular talents in helping others.

Some people give volunteer service because it is easier to say "yes" than "no." Their friends and business associates *expect* them to do their part. Other people accept volunteer service because they *want* to meet the expectations of their friends and do as their neighbors do. Once engaged in a volunteer job, they find that their interests grow and their satisfactions are many.

For those who are moving up in their professions, volunteer activities provide ways to serve their community and opportunities to broaden social contacts. They become better known in their professional life because of their contributions as volunteers. Volunteer services may be a step to social success, to professional advancement, to public office. For those who do not achieve the business or professional success they seek, volunteer service offers another kind of success and recognition in the community.

What Can You Do for the Agency?

Volunteers are particularly essential in our private health and welfare agencies. Without them there would be no organization. There would be no funds. Few services would be performed. Research and experimental projects would be at a standstill. For example, the research on the relationship between smoking and lung cancer conducted by the American Cancer Society would have been impossible without the thousands of volunteers who agreed to participate as subjects or as collectors of statistics.

Volunteers help the agency to survive. They also help individuals to survive, to lift themselves from depression or destitution. Through a wise use of trained volunteers, the agency can spread its services over wide areas and reach great numbers of people. Think of the paraplegic and his Gray Lady. Think of the child from the slums and her Scout leader.

You can be one of the team of volunteers who help to spread the services of agencies. There are a thousand jobs to be done. Some of the main job areas are suggested here. Which one can *you* do best?

The patient in the hospital needs a doctor and nurse, and perhaps a social worker. He also needs companionship, recreation, someone to run errands. The serviceman at his base may need professional counseling, but he also appreciates the snack bar and reading room run by volunteers under some professional supervision. These services do not require professionals. They can best be performed by warm, interested, responsive volunteers.

It has been proved that volunteers, with good training and supervision, can perform many tasks formerly allotted to professionals, freeing the professional for the special job that requires his training. The widespread use of volunteer Nurse's Aides is an example. Men and women can be trained for work in diet kitchens, in nurseries, in clinics. Welfare agencies, too, are beginning to find that some tasks which the professional social worker has always done can be separated from his job and carried out by aides with less training and experience.

Another development is among the unions, where volunteers are being trained as counselors for fellow union members. Such volunteers are trained by staff workers from the local health and welfare agencies and provide liaison between agencies and union members.

Another type of volunteer service is needed by those agencies which provide group activities for adults, young people, and children. Such activities might include supervised play, athletic teams, teen recreation programs, discussion groups, and education or craft classes. Every agency with a group program can use volunteers who have the dependability, the ingenuity, and the sense of responsibility that make leaders.

There is always need for the man or woman who can act in a public relations or public information capacity. Education of the public is sometimes of crucial importance whether it is to spread information about the degree of effectiveness of a new polio vaccine or about the need for foster homes for dependent or neglected children. Agencies use the mass media of print, radio, and television to inform the public, but they need the volunteer, too, because he can help to change attitudes and opinions in his community. The five-minute speaker who goes from club to club speaking intelligently on the Mental Health Association campaign is as necessary as the professional who writes the five-minute radio plug. The woman who shows and discusses a parent-child relations film at a PTA meeting is helping to keep the public informed. The man who volunteers to write newspaper publicity for the Heart Association is giving a public relations service.

Volunteers are needed who can spend a few hours a week typing, sorting mail, answering the telephone, acting as receptionists, filing, interviewing volunteers. Volunteers with clerical skills can lighten the load of the professional staff, especially in a small, understaffed office. Trained volunteers can keep the office running in an emergency, too, when the whole attention of the staff must be focused on a situation outside the office.

Fund raising is considered a difficult job, but it is a job that just suits some volunteers. Participation in a well-organized campaign gives many people satisfaction because they can use their initiative and ingenuity in figuring out unique stunts, special events, and methods of organization to help achieve the campaign goal. When the satisfactions of creative achievement are combined with opportunities for the volunteer to have fun—to make an occasion of his fund raising—amateur talents can be wonderfully and usefully employed.

The development of large public health and welfare programs at the federal, state, and local levels is inevitable and essential to assure basic services to all people. It is estimated that $16,000,000,000 were spent in 1953 for social security and social welfare in the United States. Of this, only $1,000,000,000 were expended by programs under voluntary auspices. From this it is evident that the sphere of voluntary effort is relatively narrow. What voluntary agencies do, however, is crucial. They are in a position to take risks, to experiment, to demonstrate new and needed methods, techniques, and services. They can quickly mobilize resources around specific needs or situations. They are flexible *because* of their voluntary nature. For example, only a voluntary agency could, in a short period, mobilize so large an army of volunteers in peacetime as was needed for the polio vaccine field trial in 1954.

Voluntary agencies often lead the way. When they have demonstrated the value of a new project or procedure, the government sometimes takes over and includes the project in its health and welfare programs. To cite one instance: Following World War I, the American Red Cross pioneered in developing psychiatric social services for veterans. The government recognized the value of such services and now makes them available in veterans' hospitals.

The volunteer helps make the agency adaptable to the needs of the time and situation. His amateur standing often brings him closer to the recipient of services than the professional can be. He calls the agency's attention to needs. For example: In a number of communities organized groups of church women have stimulated the development of education and health services for children of migrant families.

The volunteer helps the agency to be creative, to try new approaches and new procedures. The professional is trained in the skills and techniques that work best in certain situations. The volunteer is without this training, and he frequently improvises. Sometimes he makes a mistake, but sometimes his improvisations are a new and better way of handling a specific situation. Eventually, these new methods may be incorporated into the agency's procedure. Music therapy for the disturbed in mental hospitals had its origin in the music provided by volunteers to cheer and soothe the patients. It was volunteers in the veterans' groups and other organizations who first saw the importance of furnishing equipment for recreation rooms in hospitals for veterans and service men.

PART SIX
COMMUNITY DEVELOPMENT
IN THE UNITED STATES
AND ELSEWHERE

Introduction

THE EMERGENCE OF "COMMUNITY DEVELOPMENT" in respect to newly developing or so-called technically less developed areas has been the most exciting trend in international social welfare, directly related to community organization, within the last decade.

Community development has been variously defined. Essentially it is organized efforts to improve conditions of living in a community, and involves (1) the application of technology or expert services, or both, from outside the community, and (2) the enlistment of self-help and co-operative participation on the part of the residents of the community. The term community development is usually applied primarily to villages or smaller communities.

The basic ideas behind community development are not new, and they are not unfamiliar in American experience. Rural sociologists, rural social workers, adult educators, and others have long been concerned with various forms of "community improvement" which differs little, if at all, from what we have described as community development. Illustrations of this may be found in the distinguished contributions of the Ogdens, of Sanderson and Polson, and such current programs as the one being carried out under the leadership of William W. Biddle.[1]

The first of the selections that follow, by Charles E. Hendry, serves to point up some of the basic elements in community development both in North America and in newly developing countries.

---

[1] Jean Ogden and Jess Ogden, *These Things We Tried* (New York: Harper & Brothers, 1946); Dwight Sanderson and Robert A. Polson, *Rural Community Organization* (New York: John Wiley & Sons, Inc., 1939); William W. Biddle, *The Cultivation of Community Leaders: Up from the Grass Roots* (New York: Harper & Brothers, 1953).

Although community development itself is not new, there are novel elements in the contemporary international manifestations of it. These newer elements include (1) the operation of international technical assistance programs, such as those of the United Nations and the United States; (2) the scope of the community development programs, including both economic and social aspects; (3) the emphasis on the total life of the community, as contrasted with its segmentation into areas of education, health, social welfare, agriculture, industry, and so on; (4) the organization and operation of national programs of community development; (5) the emphasis upon the integration of various specialities; and (6) the use of "multipurpose" village-level workers.

Lester B. Granger, in the second selection in Part VI, describes the place of the village-level worker in India, and raises some pertinent questions about the relation of the functions of the multipurpose worker to social work practice. The third selection, 72, portrays the beginnings of community development in a small village in the Middle East.

Some of the basic concepts underlying community development, or "rural reconstruction" are presented in Selection 73 by Mohamed M. Shalaby. Following this as Selection 74, is a statement of basic principles underlying community development, drawn from the United Nations monograph, *Social Progress Through Community Development* (1955)—a document which is one of the most basic and important publications at present available on this subject. Part VI closes in Selection 75 with a discussion of "Community Development Programs and Methods," written out of experience by Carl C. Taylor, and published by the U.S. International Co-operation Administration.

Community development is today one of the major frontiers of community organization and social welfare; and so the volume of readings appropriately ends on this note of the relation of community development and community organization to international concern for the millions of people who live in small countries and rural areas throughout the world.

*   *   *   *

The Leader

A leader is best
When people barely know that he exists,
Not so good when people obey and acclaim him,
Worst when they despise him.
Fail to honor people,
They fail to honor you;
But of a good leader who talks little
When his work is done, his aim fulfilled,
They will all say, "We did this ourselves."

Lao-Tse
(Circa 604–531 B.C.)

70

Community Organization—Teamwork in Rural Communities [1]

By CHARLES E. HENDRY

The following paper by Charles Hendry serves to bridge the gap between rural community organization in America and community development in underdeveloped countries by emphasizing the importance of promoting "community work" in rural areas and small towns in all parts of the world, as well as in cities. He proposes "four points of departure," illustrated by reference to his observations of the Rural Pilot Project, in India, for re-examining some of the basic assumptions of community organization; discusses the reasons that some community development efforts have failed; and suggests three steps that might be taken to avoid such outcomes in the future, including expansion of the role of universities, and of professional schools in particular, in developing a team approach to the problem.

Charles Eric Hendry is director of the School of Social Work, of the University of Toronto. He is well-known for his activities in group work, community organization, and research, as well as an educator and an author of half a dozen books. Although born in Canada he has spent most of his professional life in the United States, not returning to his native country until about ten years ago. Early interested in boys' work and the YMCA he taught sociology at George Williams College, the YMCA training school in Chicago, from 1930 to 1938, and while there in 1936, was instrumental in the founding of the National Asso-

---

[1] Excerpted from paper of same title, *The Social Welfare Forum,* Proceedings, National Conference of Social Work, Cleveland, 1953 (New York: Columbia University Press, 1953), pp. 266-278. By permission of National Conference on Social Welfare. Condensed from "The Contribution of Community Development to the Raising of Standards of Living in Underdeveloped Areas of the World," *Social Service and Standards of Living,* Proceedings International Conference of Social Work, Madras, 1952 (Bombay: The Conference, 1953), pp. 115-138.

ciation for the Study of Group Work (later the American Association of Group Workers). After leaving George Williams College he served as director of program and personnel for the Boys' Clubs of America for two years.

Becoming interested in the scientific study of group behavior and social relations Hendry spent the next six years in research work. From 1940 to 1944 he was director of research and statistics for the National Council of the Boy Scouts of America, and for the next two years he directed the research program of the (national) Commission on Community Interrelations. During the latter period he also served as research associate at the Research Center for Group Dynamics, at Cambridge, Massachusetts. Since returning to Canada he has been interested in international problems, and more recently, in research on group leadership.

I HAVE BEEN CONVINCED for a long time that the small city and the rural community have suffered appalling neglect from community organization workers. Social workers have tended to be preoccupied with welfare needs and services of large cities and metropolitan areas. Particularly has this been so in relation to community planning for social welfare.

Shortly after I returned to Canada after spending twenty years in the United States I began to realize that Canadians were guilty of this identical neglect and that it was true even in the University of Toronto School of Social Work. Consequently, I sought every appropriate opportunity to encourage intensive group field study, not alone in natural areas within Toronto itself, but in smaller cities and rural communities within reasonable motoring distance.

Our first field clinic involved a rural county. There was considerable advance study, planning, and briefing, and one key informant spent a session with the class before the trip. Through a steering committee the students were deployed to various fact-gathering field teams according to interest, each team being responsible for exploring the situation with reference to child welfare, health, education, economic organization, the co-operatives, recreation, organized religion, community organization, or other special aspects of county life.

We traveled by bus. Billets in private homes in small towns and on farms were generously provided, and private cars were made available to facilitate field observation. Considerable use was made of group interviews with professional workers, political leaders, and citizen representatives. At every possible point students sat in as participant observers on meetings of all sorts. The end purpose was to gain information and impressions from which an integrated picture might be developed of the county as a whole.

This was the forerunner of a series of field clinics, one of which was for the faculty members themselves. The reasons for thus closing down classes for three days in midterm were: (1) an acknowledgment of the fact that a majority of the faculty were from large cities and even from outside Canada; (2) if teaching, field work, and research were to be most useful to graduates, most of whom would be employed in smaller communities, the faculty, of necessity, was under obligation to become much more conscious of the social structure and dynamics of that type of community; and (3) before the faculty could be expected to sanction, let alone sponsor and support, a continuing program of field clinics, the faculty itself should have the experience of organizing and conducting such a field exercise.

It would be difficult to exaggerate the gains in sensitivity, in generic insight, and in group morale associated with this field clinic. Three special faculty meetings were required following the trip to Peterborough, a kind of Canadian "Middletown," to evaluate the experience and to draw out its many implications, not alone for field trip policy, but for the total policy and program of professional education of the school as a whole.

So convinced of the importance of the field clinic idea did the faculty become after its own pilot project, that a whole week was scheduled for joint faculty-student field trips the next spring. On the Saturday of field clinic week students and faculty met for a full day of reports and discussion.

It is not difficult to identify the influences that have sensitized me to the claim upon us of the small city and the rural community. My study of the Tennessee Valley Authority in the middle 1930's was a powerful influence. About the same time, I was associated in a study of the Tremont area in Cleveland, a physically, culturally, and psychologically isolated, natural area into which had come peasants from northern Slavic countries to work in the heavy industries of the "flats." This study sharpened my awareness of the impact of industrial technology on the personality, family, and communal structure of an essentially rural population. Still later, during the Second World War, I came to appreciate more fully the great need for a more adequate community organization approach to war-impact communities in relatively unserved areas. All of this was brought clearly to view through the work of the United Service Organizations (USO). Today we see much the same thing in the work of the United Community Defense Services (UCDS). However, the most powerful influences of all my experiences in the winter of 1952 were to be found in India, Pakistan, Israel, and Jordan; in my study in preparation for the trip; and in the writing of *The Role of*

Groups in World Reconstruction,[2] which was concerned essentially with group leadership in community development. In the process I developed a very healthy respect for what has been going on in many parts of the world, particularly through agricultural extension and public health programs.

One of the most valuable documents that has come to my attention is a modest pamphlet [3] containing the results of a Conference on Extension Experiences Around the World sponsored by the Co-operative Extension Service of the United States Department of Agriculture and the Office of Foreign Agricultural Relations in May, 1949. This small but significant publication has been a forerunner of several important documents, some of which are still in process or available only for restricted use. Douglas Ensminger, who has been the representative of the Ford Foundation in New Delhi, India, and who helped to write the pamphlet, has written a most excellent *Handbook for Village Extension Workers.* Dr. I. T. Sanders, of the University of Kentucky, has been at work on a somewhat more extensive handbook of the same type for the United Nations, with special reference to underdeveloped areas. The United Nations is also preparing a series of study kits for experimental use. These developments indicate that major attention is now being directed to the development of teamwork in providing services to small cities and rural communities, and that we have much to learn from so-called "underdeveloped" regions of the world.

In our part of the world the problem is not difficult to describe. Over 40 per cent of the population now lives in communities of 2,500 people or less; another 17 per cent live in communities between 2,500 and 25,000. On the other hand, our community chests and councils are concentrated in large communities and are now located in all but seven communities of 25,000 and over. This, however, is not the whole picture. The situation is greatly complicated by the fact of mobility and the rapid development of suburban and urban areas, especially acute in new defense communities.

Throughout the country as a whole, child and family welfare services are poorly distributed. Children's services, by and large, are on a state and county basis; family services are largely concentrated in two or three hundred of the larger cities. High-powered promotion continues in many quarters. Some personnel in some national agencies still operate as if they were in the hard-slugging, competitive period of the buccaneer in social welfare. Multiple pressures continue to harass local community leaders with the inevitable results—frustration, anxiety, guilt, and futility.

---

[2] Charles E. Hendry, *The Role of Groups in World Reconstruction* (New York: Woman's Press, 1952).

[3] *Experience with Human Factors in Agricultural Areas of the World,* Extension Service and Office of Foreign Agricultural Relations, U. S. Department of Agriculture 1018, pp. 11-49.

If values can possibly arise out of the tragedy of war, one of the notable outcomes of the Second World War and of the present so-called "cold war" is that we have been compelled by circumstance to re-think and retool our whole approach in providing services to communities, not just to select categories of people in certain kinds of communities. The USO and the UCDS represent social inventions of great significance. They represent imaginative capacity responding creatively to the imperative demands of a vast human emergency.

Not the least stimulating and significant result of this new mobility and this new mobilization of manpower is seen in communities directly related to the development of atomic energy. When we have such a concentration of scientists, technicians, and highly educated persons as is found in the Community of Chalk River, planned for employees of the Deep River Atomic Development Project, we are confronted with the necessity of dealing with problems of well-being among persons who reject the idea of "welfare" as such, or who think they do. What they are doing, of course, is rejecting some stereotyped, limited, and distorted conceptions that have been discarded even though welfare practices sometimes continue to be influenced by them. It may well be that one of the mighty by-products of atomic energy development will be a radical redefinition of conventional assumptions and arrangements relating to traditional welfare services in terms of a positive orientation to basic human needs and to the essential interdependence of the major human services.

I suggest four points of departure in attempting a re-examination of certain basic assumptions:

1. *Community organization is not a monopoly of social work.* Social workers as such do not have any monopoly on the knowledge, techniques, and skills in the community organization process. Community organization is something generic and universal having to do with the release of human resources and the relating of resources, both physical and human, to the needs of people.

2. *Community organization cannot be confined in its application to any one narrow, watertight area of human need.* Because the human situation is unitary in nature, so also is community organization essentially unitary and integrative. We must deal with total communities just as we must deal with total persons. We must recognize the essential interdependence of physical, economic, political, and social forces; in other words, we must deal with communities whole.

3. *Community organization cannot be limited by arbitrary or artificial political or geographical boundaries.* To be effective, community organization must identify, and identify with the natural social areas that combine vitality and validity in the experience of those who live and work there. Nor can community organization be limited to the natural social area. Problems are no respecters of geographical, economic, political, or social boundaries. Building solidly on the basis of

natural social units, the community organization process must enlarge and extend involvement to the degree necessary to command the resources necessary to tackle and solve the problems confronted. Some problems of small cities and rural communities can never and will never be dealt with effectively except on a district or on a regional basis.

4. *Community organization cannot rely chiefly on specialists who are only specialists.* "What village people need most today," writes Ensminger, "is a village worker who will come to them as a friend. The village worker does not work as a specialist in any one aspect of agriculture or village development. He is to be a friend and guide who helps the villagers weave a pattern of new life in all its angles."

I was greatly interested in the views put forth in Madras by the Australian delegation. They observed, rather cautiously but with real conviction, that

"past training [in social work] appears to have concentrated to some extent on certain forms of professional training such as casework and group work, but the needs of the moment would seem to demand experts in the total range of skills required by the wider approach to social welfare as a whole. Thus there would seem to be a need to develop a new type of 'multipurpose' and 'multiskilled' social worker."

Clearly, what is needed in small cities and rural communities, particularly in underserved areas, is a multipurpose approach; generalists in social work as in other professional fields; personnel fitted for multifunctional, multidisciplinary, and multicultural teamwork. But this partnership must go far and beyond collaboration between disciplines and professions. A genuine partnership must be established between the people and the experts. Without responsible citizen participation, that is to say, without the psychological involvement of those most directly affected, the specialized knowledge and recommendations of the expert are likely to remain his private possessions. People support what they have a share in creating, and people share when it is acknowledged that they have a stake in the situation involved.

Of all the community development programs I studied while I was in India, the one that impressed me most was the Rural Pilot Project undertaken at the initiative of Pandit Nehru and Pandit Paut, Premier of the United Provinces, under the technical direction of Albert Mayer, of New York City. Happily, this project now forms a part of India's new five-year plan.

This project began in a six-by-ten-mile area involving 64 villages in Etawah District in the region of the United Provinces. Some 87,600 of its 104,000 villages, containing nearly 50,000,000 people, lie in about 83,130 square miles of alluvial plain falling gently from the Punjab to Bihar. The area was chosen because it had agricultural and economic conditions that were fairly typical of twelve other districts of the province. The project has now been extended to embrace 600 villages. In the beginning the personnel included three Americans. After the second year, the only American connected with the project was Mr. Mayer himself, who spends a few months a year in India. All other personnel are Indian.[4]

A staggering inventory of physical activities might be recorded, ranging from improved wheat seed to the digging of sanitary soakage pits. But the important point is that the project selected and concentrated on only a few things at a time and then tried to do them thoroughly and completely. Selection, concentration, priorities, and timing were determined in relation to three criteria: what the village wants most; what is known best how to do; and what produces quickly visible results.

Impressive as the scope and success of the physical activities have been—productivity in some crops has been increased by 45 per cent or more; the two worst cattle diseases in the area have been wiped out; a number of schools have been built on the initiative of the villagers and paid for by them; many miles of roads have been built or restored— what holds greatest interest and meaning for social workers is the emphasis on human relations. Mayer has seen in the application of material improvements the opportunity, indeed the necessity, of village participation and the development of new levels of skills and new incentives to a higher standard of living.

The attention given to personnel selection at every level and in every functional area stands out as the most important single item of policy. In the first place, Mayer insists that "no work should be undertaken, however necessary, except in an emergency, unless effective personnel is available." "Effective personnel," requires technical qualifications and personality, and "of these two indispensables, personality," Mayer emphasizes, "is by far the more important." He elaborates on this: "Indispensable characteristics in personality are flexibility to new conditions, deep sympathy, receptivity without prejudice, personal resourcefulness in or out of one's own field." To re-enforce his view, Mayer further asserts:

"With such personalities, orientation courses in the particular country's history, philosophy, religion, social customs, are unimportant because the sympathetic person will grasp the spirit of the place he is working in, will find the need to study and learn as he goes along, and will do it. Without the personality, all the orientation in the world will do no good. The right man or woman will do equally well in India, in the Congo, or in Mexico."

Albert Mayer has important things to say also on teamwork and team understanding. He would not use individuals as such, but teams

---

[4] For a full account of the Etawah project, see Albert Mayer *et al.*, *Pilot Project, India* (Berkeley: University of California Press, 1958).

of individuals. What he is looking for is "an interlocking of personalities" and a "spill-over from one individual and field into the other."

In technical assistance programs we are accustomed to assume the
inclusion of such persons as the agricultural specialist, the public health
expert, the doctor, the industries expert, but we are not accustomed
to inclusion of the specialist in community life itself, the sociologist,
anthropologist, or social psychologist. Mayer is strongly of the opinion that "permanent, self-energizing and self-propagating progress cannot be made and solidly insured by the technical specialists alone."
This has two clear implications, each of which is illustrated in this
Indian Rural Pilot Project. The first has to do with what is termed
"village participation," something much more vital and pervasive than
"fundamental education," with which it is sometimes mistakenly identified. Each village development team maintains close and constant contact with the village residents through "village level development organizers," each of whom is responsible for eight villages. The objective
is to serve as a catalyst in stimulating villagers to self-help activities.
It is recognized, however, that this process is by no means automatic. It
is this fact that leads to the second implication, namely, the need for
what is called a "rural life analyst." He is a key member of the team.
His function is to interpret the culture and life of the villagers to the
technicians, and to guide the pace of technical innovations to meet
their evolving acceptance by villagers. In action-research terms this
has come to be known as the "feedback." It is intended to provide regular reporting and evaluation of results to enable adjustment of the
program to human reactions and to meet new needs created by change.
It is intended to serve as communication between highly skilled technicians and intelligent but unschooled village farmers and, over the
longer period, to encourage the development of genuine collaboration
and partnership.

The most critical problem now confronting this village development
project appears to be a growing tension between the older, established
administrators—a combination of tax collector and keeper of law and
order, enjoying the prestige of traditional authority—and the younger,
newly recruited development officers. The tension arises from what
may be perceived by the administrators to be a threat as the development project achieves greater success and recognition and as the initial
dedication becomes somewhat relaxed. The old system of "orders" is
beginning to reappear as the administrator seeks to reassert his authority. The success of the entire project seems now to hinge on an
effective resolution of this central conflict.

Why do some community development efforts fail or fall far short
of their objectives? Many years ago a farmer explained to me how he
handled the situation when the queen bee in one of his bee colonies
died. I believe the technique he used has applicability in relation to
man himself. A queen bee is placed in a small wooden container about

four inches in length and half an inch thick. A hole about an inch in diameter is bored through at the center. A passage filled with beeswax connects both ends. If the beekeeper pries off the wire netting of the container and frees the queen at the entrance of the hive, she will be pounced upon and exterminated in a matter of seconds; not having the same body odor as that of the bees in the hive, she will be rejected. But the experienced beekeeper placed the container by itself, queen bee and all, right in the hive. The queen continues to work at the beeswax, and the bees in the hive start to work on it also, from the outside. Together they work through the same passage, at the same problem, as it were, and when they finally meet there is complete acceptance and harmony. In the process of working together they have taken on a new odor.

When we analyze what actually takes place in community development projects of the type under consideration, particularly where the results leave much to be desired, it is not difficult to identify some of the principal causes. They may be grouped into three categories.

The first is simply failure to understand or to try to understand the people and their needs; in other words, failure to relate in a friendly and helpful way to others. Part of the difficulty arises from the incredible ignorance of urban workers concerning rural people and rural life. Too many workers in too many community development projects in underdeveloped areas have no liking for peasants. They do not want to go to the villages and they greatly dislike living in them. Many project workers are handicapped by never having plowed, cultivated, or harvested or never having worked in industry. Government officials frequently have little feeling for village people.

The second cause of difficulty, closely related, is the failure to relate responsibly to the needs of the people. Part of this is the result of personal limitation and inadequacy within the worker himself; part of it is the result of inadequacies in the institutional and administrative setting. Sometimes it is difficult to separate these two kinds of inadequacy. When a worker feels obligated to answer questions without being sure of the correctness of his answer both the worker and the community are the losers. When a worker tries to force or to scare people into following a recommended practice, failure has already occurred. When a worker tells people what their problems are instead of helping them to see and to understand their problems he has succeeded only in creating the absolute conditions for complete failure. These all add up to a reliance on pressure and manipulation rather than on participation and involvement. Often these limitations go hand in hand with not wanting to do or not knowing how to do the things that must ultimately be recommended. Pressures to show immediate results; primary dependence on promotion techniques; spreading oneself too thinly over too large a territory; unwillingness to recognize that village work requires intensive application—these reflect the larger institutional conditions.

"Failures," it was said at Madras, "are seldom failures to demonstrate but failures to motivate." When workers are responsive and responsibly related to the felt needs of the people, the needs of the institution or bureaucracy become relegated to their proper secondary place.

The third source of difficulty is failure on the part of many so-called "experts" and professional persons to become emancipated from their specialization. Too many professionals in too many professions simply do not realize that basic social change cannot be effected unless one is aware of the total situation. Preoccupation with professional status and rigorous adherence to jurisdictional refinements tend to create a kind of cult or professionalism. A common complaint is that most specialists move too rapidly and exhibit great impatience in imparting technical knowledge to illiterate people. This sort of professionalism has two great limitations: it makes interdisciplinary teamwork very difficult and it makes the discovery and development of community leadership among the people themselves well-nigh impossible. Of one thing I am certain, social workers cannot go on separating out the "professional self" and insinuating or insisting that such a "self" has any real functional validity apart from its harmonious integration with the social worker's "public self." Actually, these are simply roles that the self plays. If there is any basic discrepancy between these three roles, then to that extent is the self of the social worker deficient and self-defeating.

What about the future? In my opinion, one of the most promising developments is the creation by the National Social Welfare Assembly of its Committee on Basic Individualized Services to Small Communities. I am especially impressed with the inclusion on this committee of several outstanding specialists on rural life. The newly created Federal Department of Health, Education, and Welfare should prove of considerable value to the committee at certain stages in its work; its community organization potential is beyond calculation.

As I understand it, this committee is undertaking to get the facts on three closely related questions: What services are available? What agency structure has grown up? How are these agencies and services planned and financed? Obviously, this is just a beginning.

Three additional steps are clearly indicated, and they do not necessarily have to wait for completion of the fact finding. In a sense, the first is merely a refinement or an extension of this very fact finding itself. We very much need a careful examination and evaluation of certain, selected, major undertakings such as the UCDS. Any one of a number of rural areas might be selected, as, for example, the Savannah River area in Ohio. A combination of a socio-economic survey and a community organization process record is needed as documentation, an analysis of the social structure and dynamics of the total situation. The power structure of the small community and the rural community differs markedly from that of the large city. The school principal, the old resident, and church leaders frequently occupy positions of central, if not dominant, influence. In addition to systematic reconstruction of communities served by the UCDS, community organization records need also to be built up on state-wide projects where specific attention is focused upon small cities and rural communities. Some of the projects undertaken in connection with the Midcentury White House Conference on Children and Youth fall in this category. Other programs, initiated quite outside welfare circles, under agricultural extension, for example, but having a clear welfare component, are equally deserving of full documentation. Out of a series of such case studies of whole communities in action it should be possible to identify certain basic principles to guide the fuller development of teamwork in providing services in small cities and rural communities.

These principles will require testing, and this suggests the second step. The Committee should facilitate the design and development of one or more pilot projects, bearing in mind the interdependence of policy making (frequently at the national level), field supervision (frequently at the regional level), and the planning and provision of direct services (typically at the local level). All three levels will need to be included and involved.

The third step, intimately tied in with the second, relates to the role of the university and particularly the role of the professional schools in this whole approach. Schools of agriculture and schools of social work must be built into this team approach, and also schools of medicine and public health, schools of education and theological seminaries. Block placements, work-study plans, interdisciplinary field clinics, and other arrangements yet to be invented will be required. Throughout the entire operation whether it be formal classroom study, field work, or research, great emphasis must be placed on helping the professional worker cultivate the spirit and acquire the skills needed to stimulate citizen participation on a scale far beyond anything yet achieved or imagined possible. Happily, some schools of social work are beginning to move boldly in this direction. The essential mobility and flexibility required of professional schools and of agencies alike must await a conviction so compelling that patterns of service will respond to patterns of need as readily, as creatively, and as daringly as industrial technology responds to the rapidly changing pressures of production and of market.

71

Social Work and the Social Problems of India [1]

By LESTER B. GRANGER

Lester B. Granger, executive secretary of the National Urban League since 1941, and president of the National Conference of Social Work in 1952, wrote this article against the background of attendance at the International Conference of Social Work, at Madras, India, in December, 1952.

This is one of the earliest statements in the literature of American community organization to raise explicitly the question as to the kinds of contributions which social work can make to the almost overwhelming problems of health and welfare in a so-called "underdeveloped" country such as India.

Mr. Granger stresses the need for "the multipurpose community worker"—a new concept to most American social workers—and he urges "a closer acquaintanceship with social welfare methods abroad" and a new look at the task of social work in the world of today.

SOCIAL WORK HAS A CLOSE relationship to these technical assistance programs because social work methods can greatly stimulate determination on the part of individuals and groups to help themselves as a first step toward making technical assistance effective.

There can be no flat-footed dogmatic assumption as to which social

[1] Excerpted from "Passage to India," *Community* (New York: Community Chests and Councils of America), Vol. 28, April, 1953, pp. 152, 157. By permission of United Community Funds and Councils of America, Inc.

needs in any given country must receive first priority at any given time, because conditions and, therefore, problems vary so greatly in a geographical, as well as a time sense.

Professional training for social work and technical assistance in solving social problems must be adapted to the ways of life in the country under consideration. No consultant service can possible be effective unless it is geared to the needs as well as the social attitudes of that country.

On Staying Alive in India

Aside from these broad agreements many American delegates came back with a sobered consciousness of the tremendous need that exists in the less-favored areas of the world, and with the unarguable fact that whether we like it or not, human suffering on a vast scale will continue for a number of years, regardless of how rapidly and devotedly the better-favored nations organize humanitarian services to relieve that suffering.

The conference sessions made it clear again and again that in great stretches of world territory inhabited by hundreds of millions of people, there is simply not enough food produced to keep all the people alive— and that the governments are too poor to purchase food from outside sources.

Frequently the people are too illiterate to be taught in a hurry how to produce more food through better agricultural methods. Even when they know how to produce more they often cannot; scanty rainfall and lack of irrigation keep their lands parched and infertile.

India itself is a dramatic case in point. Eighty per cent of India's 360-million population live in rural districts or are scattered throughout the country in a half-million villages. When the rains fail, the land ceases to produce. When crops fail, the people die. It is precisely that simple.

With 80 per cent of the population illiterate, it is almost impossible to conduct a program of mass community instruction by the professional methods depended upon in the United States. With 100 million people suffering from malaria and a million each year dying of it, health problems attain a formidable importance in Indian life. The average life expectancy is less than 30 years compared to the American 66 years. It is easy to see how a phlegmatic spirit of resignation can be interpreted as indifference to human suffering and even human death.

The Multipurpose Social Worker

The Americans who attended the Madras Conference came away with a new and sober appreciation of the importance of the community welfare worker in the underprivileged community and the underdeveloped area.

Many of us saw the need for a re-evaluation of our own social work techniques if professional schools in the United States are to be expected to train workers for social service abroad.

Our emphasis in recent years has been placed more and more upon specialization, with casework as the solid base upon which all training is founded. In Asia, Africa, and most countries of Latin America the principal need is not for the caseworker, nor even for the casework approach. The need is for the multipurpose community worker—not the community organization specialist, but the social worker who is able to work in the community on a jack-of-all-trades basis.

There should be no difference in the basic philosophies held by social workers, whether in underdeveloped or highly developed areas. In one sense there is no difference in their basic skills, for those skills are fundamentally the ability to analyze social conditions, understand psychology, work with people, and get people to work with each other.

The professional techniques superimposed upon those basic skills, however, do vary widely between, for instance, Asia and the United States. As the free world moves forward with the process of exchanging professional experience and pooling professional resources, of sharing consultative services, and training an adequate supply of professional workers, it may be necessary for American social work leadership to take a fresh look at the international aspects of professional training. That is one big lesson brought home from Madras.

A second lesson is this: social work in the United States can profit from a closer acquaintanceship with social welfare methods abroad. I say social welfare methods rather than social work, because many of the operations described in the Madras sessions would, in this country, more properly belong to the related fields of education, health, and general public services.

Many of us left those meetings with a feeling that by figuratively watching our colleagues at work on basic human needs in a primitive social setting, we had been able to see more clearly the basic outlines of the task which we are carrying on in this country on infinitely higher professional levels.

It is possible that we at home have become so deeply—and necessarily—involved with definition of agency functions, improvement of agency administration, specialization in professional techniques, and the intermeshing of public with voluntary services, as to get out of touch with the fundamental job of keeping human beings alive, healthy, and aspiring. . . .

72

Community Development in an Egyptian Village[1]

By U. S. INTERDEPARTMENTAL COMMITTEE ON INTERNATIONAL SOCIAL WELFARE POLICY

The nature of "community development" in an economically underdeveloped country is vividly portrayed in this case story, entitled, "From a Swampland in Egypt." This is a part of a brief bulletin "prepared by the United States Interdepartmental Committee on International Social Welfare Policy in connection with its consideration of the problem of community welfare centers." These "community welfare centers" are one aspect of broader programs of community development. In this instance there is no "center," in the sense of a building: rather, the emphasis is on the relationships and interplay between the community development worker and the villagers, and particularly on the theme of "self-help" in community improvement.

From a Swampland in Egypt

MOHAMED S—— was different from any other government official the fellaheen had ever known. He didn't collect taxes. He was not interested in catching criminals. He just walked around the village,

---

[1] Excerpted from *An Approach to Community Development* (Washington: for Interdepartmental Committee on International Social Welfare Policy, by International Unit, Social Security Administration, Federal Security Agency, now Department of Health, Education, and Welfare, SOC D-24, 1952), pp. 5-6.

talking to people and helping them with whatever task they happened to be doing.

At first, the fellaheen were suspicious, but as time went on, they began to take him for granted and no longer fell silent when he joined a group of them.

One day, he came upon three fellaheen angrily discussing their school fines. It was bad enough that the children must go to school in another village three miles away, but it was worse that the fathers must pay when the children failed to arrive. The fines were large. It would take three days' work to pay them off.

"Why don't you build a school here?" asked Mohamed. "Then you could see that the children arrived."

The fellaheen shook their heads. They had thought of that, but every inch of ground was under cultivation and could not be spared.

"Build it over there," said Mohamed, pointing to a strip of useless swampland.

Everyone laughed, but Mohamed persisted. The land could be filled with rubbish and dirt from the streets. Level off the hills and the bumps in the roads and there would be plenty of earth to add to it. The government might loan them a truck.

The men shook their heads, but they began talking about it and soon everyone in the village was talking. Some old men, no longer able to go to the fields, began collecting the rubbish into heaps. Soon almost everyone was picking up rubbish as he walked along and the rubbish heaps grew bigger and bigger, the streets cleaner and cleaner. The truck came. The swamp disappeared.

By the time the school was built, the village was almost convinced that the government really had sent Mohamed there for no other reason than to help them. They talked to him about many other problems.

"Is the rich water of the Nile unhealthy as some have tried to claim?"

When Mohamed showed them what the water looked like under a microscope, the fellaheen began to talk about a well. But, again, there was the problem of finding land on which to place the central tank, and again, it was the old swampland that held the answer. Deep underground water, entirely suitable for drinking, was found beneath the filled-in land.

This true episode illustrates how rural development projects are helping the people of Egypt to attain a better life for themselves. With the program direction centered in the Ministry of Social Affairs, rural social centers have been established to serve more than 150 Egyptian villages. Over-all co-ordination and planning is provided through a co-ordinating committee of ministries in the field of social affairs, public health, agriculture, and education. Developed on democratic plans of local initiative and active local participation, the centers are a first step in village planning for essential community programs.

Centers already established include such services as agricultural cooperatives, recreation rooms, small libraries, training classes for boys and girls in crafts, adult education, public assistance offices, badly needed clinics, dispensaries, and emergency hospital facilities.

73

A Plan for Community Development [1]

By MOHAMED M. SHALABY

This excerpt from Mohamed M. Shalaby's *Rural Reconstruction in Egypt* highlights the common ground between "community welfare organization," as it has been known in the United States, and "community development" as it is being applied today in rural villages in economically "underdeveloped regions." Clearly, the two approaches have common roots and spring from the same philosophical ground.

Mohamed Shalaby is one of the pioneers of the modern community development movement. From 1939 to 1944 he was the resident social worker in El-Manayel, "a primitive village of 1600 inhabitants near Cairo." Later he received his Master of Social Work degree from the New York School of Social Work and served on the staff of the United Nations Secretariat, in the unit concerned with community development. In 1956 he was awarded the Ph.D. degree by Teachers College, Columbia University, and returned to Egypt to become social affairs advisor, Bureau of Research and Projects, in the Ministry of Education.

Eduard C. Lindeman wrote in the introduction to Mr. Shalaby's monograph: "He has written about the rural people of one section of Egypt but what he has to say is applicable in most regions of the world."

The editors of these readings are indebted to Walter W. Pettit for directing their attention to Mr. Shalaby's monograph.

---

[1] Excerpted from *Rural Reconstruction in Egypt,* Egyptian Association for Social Studies (Cairo: Social Art Graphique, 1950), pp. 40-44.

THE BASIC ELEMENTS for successful rural reconstruction in Egypt could be evolved only through a well-planned and efficiently executed educational program.

The reason for this plan of approach may be found in the background and attitudes of the people. They are uneducated people, culturally, socially, and emotionally bound to the traditions and practices of their great-grandfathers, ignorant of what lies within their reach, and with no knowledge of how to reach for it. Compelled to live in the world in which they found themselves, they have learned to accept their lot with an attitude closely akin to fatalism. More than 5000 years of cultural stagnation has closed their eyes to the vision of a better future, and their experience contains nothing that would cause them to anticipate a better way of life. They are people without a leader, in need of being awakened to a realization of their needs and fired with a desire for progress.

To provide an educational program that would develop leadership and awaken the people to a realization of their ability to solve their problems independently is the greatest need in our rural community. A tension between the existing and the ideal situation should be brought to awareness; out of such tension between social organization and cultural ideals are drawn the forces of social dynamics. We must believe that things don't just happen. Things are brought to pass. The interest of the people must be the first concern as any attempt to reconstruct the countryside will fail if it does not take into account the circumstances of their lives.

In preparing a plan to meet the needs of the people in the light of the sources available, we must begin where we are. A program, to qualify, must afford opportunity for participation in planning as well as in execution by those whose lives are affected. This not only assumes better planning in the sense of better adaptation to local needs but it will also eliminate many of the administrative frictions which develop around programs which are handed down from above.

The program to be effective must begin with the interests of the people. It must meet those interests, and use them as a springboard for developing further interests. Many times the interests of the rural people are not the interests of the professional worker. Even though he sees the needs of the people better than they do themselves, he must begin with the interests and needs as they see them. Once he has their confidence he can branch out and develop their interests into broader channels. His success in teaching will be through the reconstruction of the experience of the people. Beginning with them, with their experiences and their customs, he can help them to change their ways and progress in desirable directions.

Growth results from participation in the solution of problems. A good program is directed toward assisting rural people to work out their own problems rather than giving them ready-made answers. People who

521

study their own problems and work out solutions are more likely to assume responsibility for their own programs and develop leadership in the work. Experience in these things creates self-confidence. They learn to do by doing.

It takes patience and time in getting people unaccustomed to participating in group work, to reach the point where they assume initiative and responsibility. They learn through encouragement and by doing. Education is often a slow process.

People differ from one another. Groups differ from other groups. Conditions differ. No one teaching method is effective under all conditions. Reading materials are for those who can read, radio programs for those who have radios, meetings for those who can attend, demonstrations of recommended practices for those to see who can come to the demonstration place. Farm and home visits, by far the most valuable method, take considerable time. New methods must be devised to meet new situations and changing conditions. The use of teaching methods must have flexibility.

The professional leader has the serious obligation to find and develop the local leadership and to strengthen the participation of the people through all the resources at his command. Successful group action cannot occur without a wholehearted belief in its desirability by a good majority of the group, and to achieve this will require a considerable period of educational discussion.

In our opinion, certain lines of action should be taken as a possible way to solve the rural problems:

1. Recognition should be given to representation of all rural communities in a planning program.

2. Representation in program planning of different economic groups would be desirable. Both lay and professional workers should participate in the process and should interpret their ideas to each other in this way.

3. Youth should be made acquainted with the nature and purpose of the planning as fully as practicable.

4. More widespread participation in a planning program by the general population of the communities is needed before the objectives of planning can be fully attained. Such participation should ignore class distinctions.

5. Greater emphasis needs to be placed on the importance of social factors in a planning program in communities. The social resources are fully as important in community organization as are the economic resources.

6. Attention should be given to the problems of health, education, agriculture, and the general conditions of living in the village.

7. Greater co-ordination between the schools and the community and more emphasis on educational values merit consideration in order that existing educational facilities may be fully utilized.

8. Decentralization of government should be our trend. Local governmental bodies should be based on the participation of the local people and given some local legislative powers.

9. The system of tax on property should be changed. Certain minimum income should be executed [*sic,* established] and a limited maximum income must be fixed. The general tax system of the country should be revised.

10. Leadership developing out of local community situations should be stimulated. Continuous training of old leaders and discovery of new ones and of new leadership groups should be brought as problems, and crises are faced by all concerned.

11. The program should be considered as part of a fundamental educational movement. It should be realistic and immediate and at the same time it should be thought of as part of a long-term continuous procedure.

12. The development of greater emphasis on personnel standards and policies as a part of social planning process.

As a first step in planning we should define the objectives we wish to achieve. Our objectives are to improve village life by the gradual betterment of moral, social, and living conditions; to bring about a better and more adequate knowledge of the needs of the people; and to foster good will and co-operation among the various groups within each village and to secure the social resources necessary to normal healthy life for its residents.

These objectives lead to the following two questions:

1. The kind and amount of facilities and services that the village needs.

2. The money needed to support the program.

As planning will deal with resources, needs, and income of local population, it might be the first step to begin with local studies. In planning, research is considered the most important step. It is not easy to find out the social problems and to discover the needs without a real scientific study.

Community planning is concerned with getting the facts in regard to the total community situation, organizing and evaluating this data with all those concerned, doing something about it, and providing for continuous study, evaluation, and synthesizing, as new facts and new conditions emerge.

A village must know its needs, understand available resources, and draw upon them rather than accept more or less blindly what might be offered by any governmental department or a private institution interested in doing good.

74

Principles of Community Development [1]

By UNITED NATIONS

"Community development," especially as applied to economically "less developed" societies, is one of the most important facts in the
world today. Community development is closely related to community
organization, although it transcends "community welfare organization"
as usually conceived of in Western nations.

The United Nations report on *Social Progress Through Community
Development,* issued in November, 1955, is the most definitive and most
important single statement yet published on this contemporary movement, containing as it does untold potentialities for the enrichment of
the lives of millions of men, women, and children in twenty or thirty
nations and territories. This excerpt begins with the UN definition of
"community development," and a footnote distinguishing it from "community organization." The excerpt continues with a summary of one of
the most valuable sections of the report: a statement of ten "basic elements of community development." In the report itself, each of these
elements or principles is followed by a brief discussion.

[1] Excerpted from *Social Progress Through Community Development* (New
York: United Nations, 1955. E/CN. 5/303/Rev.1.—ST/SOA/26), pp. 5-13. By
permission of Publication Service, United Nations.

THE POLICIES OF SECURING social progress through local action, the methods used, and procedures applied are usually termed "community development." [2] . . .

Community development can be tentatively defined as a process designed to create conditions of economic and social progress for the whole community with its active participation and the fullest possible reliance upon the community's initiative.[3] "Community development" implies the integration of two sets of forces making for human welfare, neither of which can do the job alone: (1) the opportunity and capacity for co-operation, self-help, ability to assimilate and adopt new ways of living that is at least latent in every human group; and (2) the fund of techniques and tools in every social and economic field, drawn from world-wide experience and now in use or available to national governments and agencies. . . .

Basic Elements of Community Development

The principles underlying community development are not new but have evolved simultaneously through practical experience in the various substantive fields such as public health, agricultural extension, co-operatives, home economics, fundamental education, social work. Each of these fields has contributed to a common fund of knowledge of working with people in local communities. In general, experience in each field has demonstrated that the solution of village problems requires concerted action at the local, district, and national level. . . .

On the basis of experience up to the present, it appears that successful community development programs stress the following basic elements:

1. Activities undertaken must correspond to the basic needs of the community; the first projects should be initiated in response to the expressed needs of people.

2. Local improvements may be achieved through unrelated efforts in

---

[2] The term "community development" is currently used mainly in relation to the rural areas of less-developed countries, where major emphasis is placed upon activities for the improvement of the basic living conditions of the community, including the satisfaction of some of its nonmaterial needs. The complementary term "community organization" is more often used in areas in which levels of living are relatively high and social services relatively well developed, but in which a greater degree of integration and community initiative is recognized as desirable. Both terms, as well as the combined form "community organization and development," refer to similar concepts of progress through local action.

[3] Used in a generic sense this term includes (1) physical improvements such as roads, housing, irrigation, drainage, and better farming practices, (2) functional activities such as health, education, and recreation, and (3) community action involving group discussion, community analyses of local needs, the setting up of committees, the seeking of needed technical assistance, and the selection and training of personnel.

each substantive field; however, full and balanced community development requires concerted action and the establishment of multipurpose programs.

3. Changed attitudes in people are as important as the material achievements of community projects during the initial stages of development.

4. Community development aims at increased and better participation of the people in community affairs, revitalization of existing forms of local government and transition toward effective local administration where it is not yet functioning.

5. The identification, encouragement, and training of local leadership should be a basic objective in any program.

6. Greater reliance on the participation of women and youth in community projects invigorates development programs, establishes them on a wide basis and secures long-range expansion.

7. To be fully effective, communities' self-help projects require both intensive and extensive assistance from the government.

8. Implementation of a community development program on a national scale requires adoption of consistent policies, specific administrative arrangements, recruitment and training of personnel, mobilization of local and national resources and organization of research, experimentation, and evaluation.

9. The resources of voluntary nongovernmental organizations should be fully utilized in community development programs at the local, national, and international level.

10. Economic and social progress at the local level necessitates parallel development on a wider national scale.

75

Community Development Programs and Methods[1]

By CARL C. TAYLOR

The following statement, which is reproduced in full, was prepared by Dr. Taylor in 1954 when he was serving as Regional Community Development Adviser in the Foreign Operations Administration.

THE LOOSE WAY IN WHICH the now popular term "community development" is used has created a great deal of confusion. Many types of undertaking can contribute to the improvement of the productive capacities and living conditions of the hundreds of millions of people who live in the hundreds of thousands of local villages in underdeveloped countries. It is doubtful, however, whether it is either conceptually or administratively helpful to call all of these types of undertaking "community development." Needless to say, "community development" cannot be administratively promoted or practically implemented unless it is used to mean something less than everything that contributes to economic and social welfare and something more than a pious slogan.

The seventy-five per cent or more of all the people in underdeveloped countries who live in local village communities are so poverty stricken, so much in need of more food, of better housing, health, and sanitation, that any and all programs designed to meet these needs [are] likely to be called "community development." Because most of these people live in

---

[1] Community Development Review (Washington, D.C.: International Co-operation Administration), No. 3, Dec., 1956, pp. 34-42.

a relatively high degree of physical and cultural isolation, any and all programs designed to better their means of transportation and communication or to improve their capacity to read are likely to be called "community development." In some countries, most of them are landless farmers. Land reform is a necessary condition to their economic and social advancement and therefore land reform gets included in so-called "community development" programs. All of these things need to be done, but most of them are either the products of community development, plus other kinds of development, or they are conditioning factors in community development. They are not, in and of themselves, community development.

Community development, in this statement, is used only to describe the methods by which the people who live in local villages or communities become involved in helping to improve their own economic and social conditions and thereby become effective working groups in programs of national development. The term community development programs is used to describe only those administrative plans and operational procedures which implement community development objectives.

It is impossible for economically underdeveloped, or any other, countries to provide enough financial or technical assistance to make all the economic and social improvements which are needed and desired in their thousands of local communities. Many, if not most, such improvements must depend on self-help local community efforts. If and when such efforts are aided, not only the manpower, but the ingenuity and enthusiasm of these thousands of local communities, are mobilized for all kinds of needed improvements. Furthermore any aid provided to such self-help groups is much more effective and goes much further because each local community usually supplies all needed manual labor, in the majority of cases the foremanship, nearly always part of the materials, and quite often part of the cash cost. More important is the fact that once self-help activities are initiated the self-help group tends to perpetuate itself by seeking out and doing additional worth-while improvement undertakings. Unless and until such self-perpetuating groups are developed, communities as such have not developed no matter how many things have been done for them.

There are enough programs now in operation in enough underdeveloped countries to make analysis of their practical operation feasible and profitable. Differences in these programs and the diversity of the cultural conditions in which they operate, instead of obscuring, help to reveal their common denominators of success or failure. Their failures, or lack of success, and their violation of sound community methods reveal equally as much as do their successes and their use of sound methods and procedures.

These experiences reveal that violations of sound community development methods and procedures are most often due to one or more of the following: (1) A belief that providing, no matter how, such things as water and sewer systems and community facility buildings, specifying types of community organization, operating pilot plants or demonstrations, and so on, are the best methods of inducing local communities to undertake, or widely participate in economic and social improvement programs. (2) A belief on the part of many outsiders that because they can more objectively, and probably more scientifically, analyze the agricultural, health, educational, and other needs of people than can local villages, therefore they can induce local communities to undertake, or enthusiastically participate in programs of improvement which they prescribe. (3) A failure to understand that they, and no one else, can do things for local communities and hand responsibility for them down from above; that such responsibility has to be developed within local community groups by doing things for themselves.

Experiences have also shown that the use of sound community development methods and procedures most often, if not always, are due to the three following: (1) A belief, or knowledge, that the manpower, ingenuity, and enthusiastic participation of the millions of people who live in thousands of local villages, or communities, is imperative to national, economic, social, and political development. (2) A knowledge that even isolated and illiterate villagers can be mobilized to help in national improvement programs only if they are permitted to be at least partially responsible for improvements in their own villages. (3) The establishment and operation of programs to train persons who will live and work among villagers to (a) stimulate and assist them to organize self-help undertakings, and (b) act as a bridge or channel between villagers and the agencies of government, which stand ready to aid them in these undertakings.

The basic prerequisite to the use of community development as one of the methods of economic and social development is a knowledge that illiterate villagers, no matter how isolated physically and culturally they are, have self-recognized needs and have desires to satisfy these needs. It needs also to be understood that if these villagers are seemingly lethargic and not interested in change, it is chiefly, if not solely, because they have never been permitted to participate, much less to lead, in programs for improving their own lot in life. They have been told by others what their needs were. Overhead government, colonial or feudal, has provided for the minimum of these needs through a hierarchy of officials who as often as not were also inspectors and tax collectors. As a national director of general health, in a country which has started a nation-wide community development program, said recently, "We are completely reversing the direction of things. We have always tried to develop local communities from the top down. Now we are going to develop the nation from the bottom up. That is what community development is."

Because local villages and communities, in economically underdeveloped countries, are so physically and culturally isolated from the stream of state and national events, their chief concerns are about local needs. It is therefore easier to enlist their interest in local community improvement than in national development programs. If helped to understand that any organized self-help efforts on their part will be aided by technical, and even some material, assistance, they become ready and eager candidates for community development. They put not only their manpower but their ingenuity and enthusiasm into all kinds of improvement when they know their felt needs are going to be met and they are going to have a leading part in deciding what shall be done.

The validity of these statements [has] now been attested by experience in a number of underdeveloped countries where sound practical methods of community development are being used. Because of these experiences it is possible to specify the steps in the methods of local community development. This is not to say that these steps can be blueprinted and precisely followed like the steps in building a house or that the members of a local community can, like an army platoon, be commanded to take them. They are, however, steps which any group of people, if permitted and assisted, will themselves take to meet needs which are common to all of them.

Methods of Community Development

The first step in community development is systematic discussion of common felt needs by members of the community. Unsystematic discussions of various kinds and on various topics are continuously going on among persons and families who literally live, as they do in rural villages, all the time in each other's presence. Such discussions are, however, either mere gossip or concerned with complaints. It is only when discussions are systematic, even though among a relatively few representative persons or families, that analysis of important commonly felt need is accomplished. Such discussion is readily induced when local villagers have cause to believe that any organized self-help efforts on their part will be encouraged and assisted by their government or some other dependable agency. This simple but necessary first step is not taken when community councils or other village bodies are created by law or overhead administrative directives, as has been done in some underdeveloped countries which are trying to initiate community development programs. It is not taken when some technical agency or welfare organization decides to initiate some improvement just because it has the consent, or even the invitation, of the headman of the village to do so. It is not taken by finding one willing innovator who will try out one improved practice.

Sound community development programs, now in operation in a number of underdeveloped countries, provide both personnel to stimulate systematic discussions among villagers and technical, sometimes material, assistance to organize community self-help undertakings.

The second step in community development is systematic planning to carry out the first self-help undertaking that has been selected by the community. The most important thing learned by the community in taking this step is that nothing by way of community development occurs if a project is nominated the carrying out of which is totally beyond its local community's self-help capacity. The community may think its greatest need is canal water for irrigation, which water can be provided only by constructing a great dam a hundred or more miles distant from the village. This it cannot do or even help to do. Or it may think that its greatest need is for more commercial fertilizers which would require the construction of a factory and the development of a market distribution system. The first of these is an undertaking for national or state governments, and the other an undertaking for government or some business entrepreneur.

Systematic planning for aided self-help community undertakings leads to the selection of the type of first project which, because it is practically feasible, will mobilize the local manpower and ingenuity of those living in the community. It leads to the actual task of enlisting persons who will contribute their labor and talents, and often materials and money, to carry out the project. It accomplishes realistic and responsible thinking about what should be and what can be done. It is a step that starts to mobilize the community to do something for itself.

All kinds of experiences have been had and are being had in the task of mobilizing local communities for effective action in those underdeveloped countries which are promoting programs of community development. In some countries, however, the government jumps in and does the job which the headman or some small local group specifies as the first basic need. It may employ local laborers and pay them wages, thus using the community's manpower but developing no local community-group responsibility. It may pour in so much material assistance and so many outside technical experts that the undertaking is in no sense even a demonstration of what local communities themselves can do. There are other countries which are encouraging local communities themselves to take this second step. It is always, by necessity, taken by doing relatively small community improvement projects. With a small amount of technical assistance and the very minimum of material assistance, local communities are building hundreds of miles of village feeder roads, building hundreds of schools, digging hundreds of wells to supply both domestic and irrigation water, improving sewer systems, and so on. Equally or more important with these accomplishments is the development of the responsibility, initiative and self-confidence of village community-groups.

The third step in community development is the almost complete mobilization and harnessing of the physical, economic, and social potentialities of local community-groups. Once a goodly sized organized local group starts working on a project which if completed will yield obvious and early benefits to the whole community, members of the community who have thus far been only mildly interested or even skeptical start contributing to its successful completion. There are so many examples of this that what happens time after time no longer constitutes feature stories in the newspapers in some of the countries where community development programs are in successful operation.

Unfortunately some state and national leaders who have witnessed one or more local communities mobilize in this way jump to the conclusion that a whirlwind nation-wide propaganda campaign, offering of community improvement prizes, or some other mass stimulation and mobilization technique can be used to start a rash of community development activities. Many experiences in this type of undertaking have also been [seen]. They teach almost as much as do sound programs of community development. What they teach is that there is no substitute for what have been described here as the *first and second steps* in community development. Even more important they teach that the next and most important step is seldom taken as the result of furious campaigns of propaganda and competition.

The fourth step in community development is the creation of aspiration and the determination to undertake additional community improvement projects. Until this step is taken the universal problem of how to get local villages and villagers to desire and initiate improvements is not solved. Many community organizations promoted by outsiders never take this step. But there are both good physical and sociological reasons why the majority of community-groups, which have come into existence and progressed by taking the three previous steps described here, do take this fourth step. The physical reason is, there are other improvements which need to be undertaken which are within the now developed competence of the group. The sociological reason is that every human group that has successfully accomplished worth-while undertakings is proud of itself and tends to seek out and do other things to justify and feed its group pride. It has developed team spirit, *esprit de corps,* patriotism, or, in simpler terms, group sentiments. Even Charles Darwin asserted that sentiment is the cement of groups. This cement, because it is sentiment, not only holds groups together but makes them seek to perpetuate themselves. When they have developed it they seek things to do the undertaking of which will effectively perpetuate them as functioning, aspiring groups.

There are plenty of examples of community groups which never have taken this fourth step, and there are plenty of examples of groups which have. Two specific examples will serve to show why some so-called *community projects* have not led to the taking of the final step in *community development.* One is the experience of a country where the central government urged local communities to build community halls. In order to induce them to do so, it paid one half the costs. A number of communities organized campaigns which involved a large per cent of all members of the community in one or another type of participation. In most cases these campaigns were sponsored by the most prominent citizens in the community. In most of the communities where halls were built the community has done nothing more in an organized way and has even been unable to stimulate any great community use of the halls.

In another experience, in a different country, an enterprising and altruistic government official tried to convert a dilapidated village of very low-income families into a model community. By providing all types of technical advisers and a great deal of financial aid, he stimulated the villagers to clean up their streets, change their methods of sewage disposal, and even build new homes. The official now testifies that in less than ten years the village was just as dilapidated as when he started to change it. In this example, as in the other, the whole community helped in the project and some community improvement was accomplished. In neither case did the community seek out and accomplish other community improvement projects.

But there are examples in underdeveloped countries where the final step in community development has been and is being taken. A community which started by building a small but badly needed footbridge across a stream, built a half mile of feeder road out to a highway, constructed a school with crude poles, straw and mud, cleaned out a spring to provide a clean domestic water supply, or made some other simple improvement which met a commonly felt need, has gone on to more and larger undertakings. These communities went on from the first project to another, and another because out of self-motivated, self-help experiences they developed not only self-confidence and competence but group pride and aspirations. It is out of such accumulated and cumulating experiences, successful and unsuccessful, both quite numerous, that sound methods and procedures of community development can be analyzed and fairly precisely stated.

Before those methods and procedures are restated in something like a prescription for organizing and operating a community development program, two important facts should be stated, an understanding of which helps to guard against probable disappointment. This understanding also derives from the experiences of agencies which promote community development programs and attempt to use community development methods. The first is that to expect all members of a local community to mobilize, to promote and undertake the community's first self-help improvement undertaking will lead to disillusionment and disappointment. Such an expectation often leads to all sorts of frantic efforts to mobilize everybody and a failure to go ahead when some smaller group in the community is ready and anxious for constructive action. The second is that it should not be assumed that just any local group in a community that wants to do something can be the nucleus of a community development program. Some groups are, and do not intend to be, anything other than selfish special interest groups. They may even be only a faction or a narrow clique in the community. There are numerous instances of agencies helping them and thereby dividing rather than mobilizing the community. The nucleus of a community development group must be composed of a goodly number of local citizens who are accepted as representative by the members of the community and whose proposed undertakings are for the benefit of the whole community. It is because of the necessity of starting community development through the instrumentality of such groups, that personnel working at the village level are a necessity in any nation-wide community development program.

Community Development Programs

Some countries may not be basically interested in the results which local community development secures but some of them honestly are. If and where they are, they should be helped to know the experiences in community development of the countries whose successful experiences have furnished the validity of the methods which have been all too briefly analyzed here. Those experiences can be summarized in something approaching a prescription which a country needs to follow if it desires to promote and implement a community development program.

A country wanting to promote and implement a community development program will need to recruit a large number of workers from local villages, or communities, as grass roots village workers. The reason it will have to do this is that it does not now have enough technical personnel to help all, or even a small portion, of its local communities to develop and mobilize their potential capacities. Because of the existent class structure in some countries, many of the technically trained persons they do have are not skilled in working with simple villagers. Only persons born and reared in local villages, who are socially, economically, and intellectually not too far in advance of simple village people have been found to be effective channels between them and the technical knowledge which they need, and the technical agencies whose assistance they must have.

It will need to set up training institutions especially designed to train village level workers and those who supervise them. It will need to do this because very few of even the best villagers selected for village work are sufficiently competent to assist village people either in technical improvements or community development. They must therefore be given enough training in agriculture, health, sanitation, literacy education, and so on, as will prepare them to render first aid assistance to village groups which want to improve both their production and use of goods and services in these fields. Village workers will also need to be trained in the methods of mobilizing and organizing village groups for effective action in any and all of these fields. They will need to be taught where to seek and how to secure technical assistance which is far superior to that which they themselves can render to village groups. They will need to learn what kinds and amounts of material or financial assistance are available to villagers, and from what sources.

National and state governments will need to develop competent technical institutions and agencies to supply dependable technical assistance to village level workers. This is absolutely imperative and emphasis should be placed on the fact that this assistance needs to be dependable. Village workers who by necessity are qualified to render only first aid assistance in technical fields must be backstopped by persons professionally more competent than themselves. These persons must be supplied by the technical agencies of government and these agencies must therefore be adequately staffed with a corps of competent technical personnel and must be dependable in rendering technical assistance to village workers and the local villagers they serve.

Unless the two fundamental services of local village workers and well-trained technical personnel are combined, a village development program is inadequate, in fact ineffective at either the top or the bottom and if it is ineffective at either it is ineffective at the other. Local communities cannot raise themselves solely by their own boot straps. They can do a lot by well-organized self-help undertakings. They can be stimulated to and helped in such undertakings by local village workers. But they must have the assistance from all technical ministries of government if they are to go very far in agricultural, health, sanitary, and educational progress. One of the chief services of village level workers is to encourage villagers to request technical assistance. If these requests are not answered by competent technical persons from National or State Ministries, self-help village groups are frustrated and sometimes defeated in their self-help undertakings.

A prescription for an effective community development program stated with the finality of the three underlined statements above is not based on examples of a few countries which have perfectly operating programs of community development. Rather [it is] based on observations of a fairly large number of countries which have programs called "Community Education," "Social Programs," "Cultural Missions," "Welfare Commissions," "Rural Centers," "Rural Social Centers" or "Village Aids," and only a few called "Community Development." They are based on observations of countries which have attempted to promote such programs with no adequate corps of grass roots village workers, of some countries which tried either to use untrained village workers or expected local communities to carry out improvement projects under the "remote control" of the totally inadequate corps of technicians which various national ministries could provide. They are based also on the observation of some quite successful nation-wide community development programs and on the observation of some elements in other programs which provide proof of their validity. Above all, they are based on the judgment of a goodly number of persons who have had practical experience in directing and trying to administer these types of programs. They are stated with a degree of finality because the evidence is that they are fundamental procedures in the implementation of a nation-wide community development program.

Index